ANGER MANAGEMENT IN SPORT

Understanding and Controlling Violence in Athletes

Mitch Abrams, PsyD
Learned Excellence for Athletes
Fords, NJ

Human Kinetics

Library of Congress Cataloging-in-Publication Data

Abrams, Mitch, 1972-
  Anger management in sport : understanding and controlling violence in athletes / Mitch Abrams.
    p. ; cm.
  Includes bibliographical references and index.
  ISBN-13: 978-0-7360-6168-1 (hard cover)
  ISBN-10: 0-7360-6168-1 (hard cover)
  1. Athletes--Mental health. 2. Anger. I. Title.
  [DNLM: 1. Anger. 2. Adaptation, Psychological. 3. Competitive Behavior. 4. Sports--psychology. 5. Violence--prevention & control. 6. Violence--psychology. BF 575.A5 A161a 2010]
  RC451.4.A83A27 2010
  616.85'82--dc22

                                                                    2009019487

ISBN-10: 0-7360-6168-1 (print)
ISBN-13: 978-0-7360-6168-1 (print)

The Web addresses cited in this text were current as of February 2009, unless otherwise noted.

Acquisitions Editor: Myles Schrag; **Developmental Editor:** Kathleen Bernard; **Managing Editor:** Melissa J. Zavala; **Assistant Editor:** Casey A. Gentis; **Copyeditor:** Robert Replinger; **Indexer:** Craig Brown; **Permission Manager:** Dalene Reeder; **Graphic Designer:** Joe Buck; **Graphic Artist:** Angela K. Snyder; **Cover Designer:** Keith Blomberg; **Photographer (cover):** Debora Robinson/NHLI via Getty Images; **Photographer (interior):** © Human Kinetics, unless otherwise noted; **Photo Asset Manager:** Jason Allen; **Art Manager:** Kelly Hendren; **Associate Art Manager:** Alan L. Wilborn; **Illustrator:** Alan L. Wilborn; **Printer:** Sheridan Books

Printed in the United States of America

10 9 8 7 6 5 4 3 2 1

The paper in this book is certified under a sustainable forestry program.

Human Kinetics

Web site: www.HumanKinetics.com

United States: Human Kinetics
P.O. Box 5076
Champaign, IL 61825-5076
800-747-4457
e-mail: humank@hkusa.com

Canada: Human Kinetics
475 Devonshire Road Unit 100
Windsor, ON N8Y 2L5
800-465-7301 (in Canada only)
e-mail: info@hkcanada.com

Europe: Human Kinetics
107 Bradford Road
Stanningley
Leeds LS28 6AT, United Kingdom
+44 (0) 113 255 5665
e-mail: hk@hkeurope.com

Australia: Human Kinetics
57A Price Avenue
Lower Mitcham, South Australia 5062
08 8372 0999
e-mail: info@hkaustralia.com

New Zealand: Human Kinetics
P.O. Box 80
Torrens Park, South Australia 5062
0800 222 062
e-mail: info@hknewzealand.com

E3563

Contents

Preface

This book is the product of a 12-year journey of formally studying the relationship between anger and sports. This journey was originally fueled by what I observed growing up. As a child, I lived in Starrett City, a federally subsidized housing development in the southeast corner of Brooklyn, New York. Initially, there were housing quotas to insure a racially diverse neighborhood in a rent-controlled environment. Starrett City is surrounded by three very different neighborhoods. To the east and to the west respectively were Howard Beach and Canarsie which, at that time, were two decidedly Italian/Jewish American neighborhoods with a strong thread of racism pervading them. Starrett City, however, was bordered on both sides by water and wasteland making those two neighborhoods seem much farther away. Immediately to the north were East New York and Brownsville—two of the most crime infested sections of New York and they had a much greater influence on Starrett City than their other neighbors.

Crime, and ultimately gangs, made attempts to infiltrate our neighborhood. Strangely, segregation amongst us was based more along the lines of whether or not you were an athlete than the color of your skin. There was a sense of community that didn't tolerate the intrusion of "outsiders." Like many neighborhoods, the power of quick money and local fame led some to change their paths. Many of the people from that neighborhood are now dead or in jail. The one thing that always troubled me was: With so many great athletes (I can tell you from seeing high school to professional athletes competing up close, there were some from our midst that "coulda been a contender"), why were none of them getting to the next level? Why were some able to keep their heads on straight and others turn to the world of violence? In Brooklyn, many of the best athletes never played a day of school-organized sports. Whether it was because of the limited resources of the PSAL (Public School Athletic League—New York City's High School Sports Authority), the lack of contacts that the coaches had in getting them into impressive college sports programs, or because they didn't care to go to school long enough to participate. Many of the best athletes played "street ball" and never got out of the 'hood. Why not?

This question led to my formal pursuit of the answer. In graduate school, I was mentored by Dr. Eva Feindler who is one of the nation's experts in child and adolescent anger management. I immediately wanted to both learn about the treatment of anger and understand what role it plays in sports. As an unknown in sport psychology, a pesky graduate student, I was fortunate enough to meet Dr. Shane Murphy at a conference

eBook
available at
HumanKinetics.com

in Long Island and after only a couple of conversations, I was fueled with the motivation to go develop a niche in the sport psychology field – developing anger management programs for athletes.

Like all overzealous graduate students I developed a hypothesis, combed the research, pretended to ignore the influence of the media, and set out to cure the world of violent athletes. The research (as will be reviewed later) pointed to athletes being angrier, more delinquent and more violent than non-athletes. The numerous books, chapters, and texts that argued the point leaned towards similar conclusions…if they addressed anger and violence in sports at all. A lot of "experts" were talking about anger and violence in sports, but no one was really talking about what to do about it…or if anything should be done about it. I bought the opinion glorified by the media (and only partially supported by the research) hook, line and sinker.

I developed a program that taught anger management skills to athletes, and it worked. It took some time however to realize that I was operating on basic assumptions that turned out, in my opinion, to be a complete falsehood. The idea that athletes are more violent than non-athletes is a myth.

Anger, violence, and impulse control problems are reaching epidemic proportions in the United States and believing that somehow being an athlete completely insulates them is ludicrous. I believe that there is some insulative value to sport participation and many athletes that come from violent backgrounds appear to show lower incidence of violence than would be expected based upon their peer-group—and we will discuss why.

The major theme of this book takes the position that although athletes are not convincingly more violent than non-athletes, they represent an at-risk population for three major reasons:

1. The belief that athletes are healthy and immune from "normal" problems.
2. There are added stressors that athletes face that they may have difficulty coping with.
3. Athletes will be scrutinized due to their popularity and as such they need to be even more cautious to manage their emotions.

There are glaring problems with the study of violence in sport and the bulk of the "research" is, in fact, opinion. In the absence of good research (and the study of this topic does not lend itself to such research), opinion becomes the benchmark that people in the field look to. Therefore, much of what will be presented in this book, though fueled by theory in many areas of study, will not be directly supported by research. My opinions come from working with hundreds of athletes at varying levels of competition, in different sports and sport contexts, as individuals, as teams and as groups. My observations come from solid training in the clinical assessment and treatment of violent people and from my experience working with some of the most dangerous people in society—inmates in State Prison. I have studied anger and violence from the relatively harmless high school athlete struggling for playing time while not passing his classes to the hardened psychopath (with an athletic history) who would have no problem harming himself, you, or anyone else in the quest for his goals. I have come to these conclusions from thinking about the topic, implementing programs, and learning and consulting with colleagues, students, athletes, coaches, parents, members of my audience, and anyone else who can help me understand this paradigm better. The position is psychologically sound, useful, and, most importantly, makes sense. It will open the discussion about this topic and light the path that research should go.

We will start by examining the major theories that help explain anger and aggression in sport, but this can only be meaningful after new definitions are introduced that are much more pragmatic than previous models.

Then, we will provide a review of the history of violence in sport without spending an exorbitant amount of time on it because this is one of the few areas that has been well-covered by other authors.

This will segue into how anger management skills are performance enhancing in sport and in life. They are life skills that everyone would benefit from, but assuming that athletes have been taught these skills when so many people in our society have not, would be a mistake. We will also focus on the role of coaches. Perhaps no group of people can do more to help with this problem. For many years (and for some, up until this very moment) coaches believed being angry helps their athletes become successful. As will be outlined, it can...up until a point, and then it becomes a powerful detractor from success.

Presented to you will be a comprehensive anger management program that includes many of the "how-to" specifics. Assessment tools will be reviewed as well as other evaluative techniques that are used in this work. When athletes need to be referred to clinical personnel for treatment of more severe anger problems will also be highlighted, as well as the pluses and minuses of individual vs. group interventions.

As previously mentioned, athletes may be vulnerable to the same problems as are other people in society (the critical period for presentation of signs of mental illness is between the ages of 16 and 35). This age group also represents the largest percentage of athletes that participate in organized sport. Therefore, an examination of clinical issues that athletes may present with related to anger and violence is prudent. This focus needs to include different aspects of depression since an athlete that is depressed may act out on their emotional pain in the form of hostility towards others. Further, biologically based impulse control disorders, whether part of a psychotic presentation, severe mood disorder, or even a seizure disorder, merit discussion regarding how this may present itself in athletes and what the appropriate course of action would be. Because of the many restrictions placed on medications by Anti-Doping agencies, ethical issues will be discussed when athletes would benefit from medications to treat their emotional problems. Similarly, we must explore the relationship between substance abuse and violence and athletes. This includes the use of anabolic steroids, and I will present the somewhat controversial opinion that steroids don't cause violence.

Related to this view is the exposure to violence that many athletes have while growing up. Some of them will develop a view of the world that legitimizes violence as a way to solve problems. This view, further compounded by an anti-authority perspective, will make it very difficult for them to consider other ways of solving problems. It also presents obstacles regarding their coachability. In the worst case scenario, some may in fact turn out to become psychopaths. Psychopaths have no conscience nor regard for the rules of society. Short of incarceration, there is little that can be done stop their behavior. Do I believe that there are proportionally more sociopaths in the NFL, for example, than in society at large? No, but statistically, there are some and they will continue to break team rules, societal morals and state and federal law until they are arrested, because that is what they do.

There are some individuals that are of the belief that athletes are more likely to be accused of sexual assault, rape, domestic violence and even murder because they are famous and targeted for a big legal payday. Issues related to criminality will be explored as well as the experience of victims of such crimes who come forward. There is no evidence that rape is false-reported more than any other crime; in fact, it is under-reported. However, when there is fame and fortune involved, might it slightly increase the likelihood of false reports? Yes. But, if you expect to exonerate all athletes as if they *never* engage in such behavior, then you are misleading yourself.

This topic bears greater attention; from the unlikely responsibility of young millionaires, to groupies, to aspects of the athletic culture that may propagate the belief that athletes are above the law, these ideas need to be discussed in the context of violence if plans can be made to eradicate their incidence. We will discuss plans that organizations, including professional sports organizations, may consider to address this problem as well new and creative ideas like entourage training. The idea in this concept would be that any professional athlete could send one person from their entourage to get training on how to keep them out of trouble. If one takes the stance that the athletes, at times, are the victims, then it makes sense to train one of their associates to learn conflict resolution, identification of pending problems, anger management, etc., to help the athlete avoid such quandaries where the wrong decision could result in them losing their opportunities. Therefore critical issues related to Dating Violence will be discussed with an educational plan provided to give athletes the information they need to know to stay out of trouble, if that was there inclination or trajectory, for any of a number of reasons. The legalities will be introduced as well, as it has become clear from my experiences that male athletes are shocked when they learn the laws regarding dating violence and rape.

To close out the book, I hope to set the course for future navigation in these understudied waters. I challenge my colleagues, athletes, coaches, students and anyone else invested in sports to think about the relationship between anger and sports. I hope that future examination answers more questions and this problem, which is truly not unsolvable, gets reeled in. In its current trajectory, this problem can only put a black eye on sports. And that, given all of the positives that people get from sports, would be a damn shame.

Acknowledgments

This book has been the product of seemingly endless conversations, consultations, observations, arguments, self-reflection, research, and stubbornness. It has gone through several iterations, reviews, updates, and restarts. A great number of people have made this book possible. I knew as I generated this list that it would not be exhaustive, but I will try to mention everyone who helped me understand this complex issue of anger in sport.

First, I want to thank Myles Schrag, Kathleen Bernard, Melissa Zavala, and all the folks at Human Kinetics who stayed with me and tolerated me through the production of this book. I know that I was not always easy to work with, but I am proud of our collective product.

Drs. Eva Feindler and Stephen Ruffins stood out as those who taught me the most early in my career. Eva was my mentor in graduate school and paved the road for me by honing my skills as a psychologist and showing me what an expert in anger management looks like, acts like, and presents like. Stephen, more than any other professor I had, taught me how to think, to consider the less common possibilities that may explain a person's experience, and to avoid falling into the perilous world of pathological certainty: When you think you have it all figured out, you don't. I would also like to thank Dr. Norman Weissberg, who mentored me in Brooklyn College years ago and showed me what a "real clinical psychologist" does as well as the path to become one.

Some of my early coaches—Joel Wayne, Sal LoBello, Bobby Donahue, and Doreen Rallo—helped me learn that having fun, learning skills, and wanting to win can all go hand in hand without anyone walking away sad or angry.

I need to thank some fellow professionals who never read the sign that said, "We're too old to play football." A motley crew of doctors, lawyers, engineers, personal trainers, writers, and executives: Vinny Matthews, Michael Drehwing, Robert "Sid" Sidbury, Randy Williams, Russell Ford, Ed Schlenoff, Andre Best, Rich Chang, Danny Dutton, George Kolbe, Richie Coronato, Brian Coughlin, Mike Freeman, Ralph Vacchiano, Jay Glazer, and our brother we lost on September 11, John Schroeder. Thanks for always making it fun, especially when we took ourselves too seriously.

My colleagues in the sport psychology world who have put up with me for the past 10 years complaining about what we "should" be focusing on. Most specifically, Drs. Shane Murphy, Chris Carr, and Jim Bauman, who have modeled for us what sport psychologists do. Dr. Burt Giges, whom you cannot walk away from without feeling as if you just got smarter, the depth of your thinking is endless. I just try to keep up. Dr. Sharon Chirban, the best sport psychologist who gets the least press: It is only a matter of time before everyone starts to learn how to understand the world the way that you do.

Throughout my career I have spent more time with the students than with the professionals, primarily because the students were hungrier, more curious, and more energetic, and because they represented the future that I wanted to be a part of. Some of those students are now successful professionals. Some stayed in sport psychology, and some pursued other endeavors. Thank you to the "partners in crime" whom I came up with: Glenn Pfenninger, Brad Jurica, Tim "Sully" Sullivan, and Drs. Rob Fazio, Josh Avondoglio, Wally Bzdell, and Latisha Forster Scott.

I learned a great deal about anger management and violence while working in the prison system, and I need to acknowledge a couple of people that I met there. Psychiatrist Dr. Peter Martindale is the smartest person I have ever met and is uniquely able to assess a person in crisis in a moment's time and then write a chart note that reads like a novel, providing the exact phenomenology of the person he evaluated. You can almost see the person in front of you. Watching your mastery has taught us all more than you know, but your courage to make difficult decisions is inspiring. I can only hope that it has been contagious. LaWana Darden is the best therapist I have had the privilege of working with. She has the unique ability to tow the line, hold someone accountable, communicate when their behavior is inappropriate and won't be tolerated, and then forgive them and give them a fresh slate the next day. She carries herself with balance, grace, and compassion. She is the epitome of what a strong woman is, and I can only hope that I raise my daughters to carry themselves so evenly. Learning from her has been a blessing. Drs. Dennis Sandrock and Harold Goldstein are two excellent psychologists whom I would trust with any client at any time. I refer to and consult with them more than any others. You would never know by looking at them that Dennis rides motocross and that Harold is a rock-climbing, mountain-biking, poison-ivy-wearing injury waiting to happen, but nothing slows either of them down. Thank you for helping me ferment my thinking about athletes over time.

I would like to thank Richie and Donna Standowski for treating me and mine as yours from day one. I can never thank you enough for your generosity. Jason and Kerri Standowski, I am very thankful for how close we have become.

If there is one person in the world I want on my side when things are tough, it is my best friend, my brother, Adam Foresta. No one has stood by me, no questions asked, like you have. I will always be available to return the favor. You are my family and your family is my family.

I would like to thank my parents, Lloyd and Barbara Abrams, who are both gone from my physical presence but reside with me always—in my humor, in my head, and in my heart. I owe all that I am to you. Both of you always told me to let the world know what was on my mind. I hope that people are thankful for your advice. You have inspired this book. I miss you both terribly. To my sister, Alicia, you were gone too soon, but I see you pop up in my daughters' faces, and it makes me smile.

Three girls are responsible for increasing my gray hairs and taking me on never-ending adventures: Lea Nicole, Melissa Brianne, and Aviva Elle. Lea, you have grown into a beautiful, well-mannered, intelligent young lady. I am proud of you and you will always be in my heart! Melissa, you are forever smiling and making everyone around you happy. I hope that you are always able to let things roll off your back and really enjoy life. Thank you for making my reflection look good. And then there is Aviva, our diva—you bring out the best in everyone around you. You follow your own rules yet are so easygoing. You make me smile every day, even on the hard ones. I am thankful for each of you individually and together. You inspire me to find new ways to make you laugh, show me time and again the value of play, and have even helped me learn better ways to control my own anger. You will have the best, I promise you that.

And last but not least, I would need another 200 pages to thank my beautiful wife, Christy. But in the simplest words, I could not have gotten here, and I would not have wanted to, without you. You have given me strength when I thought I had run out, you believed in me when I did not believe in myself, and you have stood beside me through difficult times. You have been a sounding board, a confidante, a teacher, and my inspiration. Thank you for understanding during all the times when I was working on this book instead of being with you, and for showing patience when you did not have to. Before anyone, this book would not have been possible without your support.

A NEW UNDERSTANDING OF ANGER AND VIOLENCE IN SPORT

For every athlete associated with off-the-field violence, you can find 10 who have never been accused of anything as severe as stealing a pack of gum. For every athlete accused of violence, there is one who has never faced such allegations: For every Ray Lewis there is a Bruce Smith; for every Kobe Bryant there is a Michael Jordan; for every O.J. Simpson there is a Walter Payton; for every Ty Cobb there is a Cal Ripken; for every Marty McSorley there is a Wayne Gretzky. Yet despite the overwhelming number of innocent athletes, the perception is growing that athletes are more violent than nonathletes. Although some athletes engage in appalling behavior, you will be reminded throughout this book that sport is a microcosm of our society—that the violence that we see athletes engage in is a reflection of the overall hostility that pervades our culture. To clear the reputation of sport, intervention is needed. We must look at the issue objectively and realistically. This book does not espouse political correctness at the expense of accuracy. Instead, it challenges you to think about anger and sport in a new, more meaningful way.

When first examining the relationship between anger and sport, we may be tempted to subscribe to the media's portrayal of athletes as a particularly boisterous bunch. Accepting this as true, the idea of developing anger management programs could spring from the fantasy of preventing athletes from being arrested and winding up in jail. A more realistic appraisal, however, would lead us to realize that our prisons are not overrun with athletes. Not until after I completed my dissertation and left the academic world did I start to realize the value of anger management as a performance enhancement tool for athletes. In fact, the coaches and athletics directors who initially turned me away caused me to think about the topic further.

Anger, a normal emotion, can help an athlete's performance. This tennis player can use his anger as motivation and determination to improve his score and win the match.

© Sport the Library/C Harris

They were afraid that I would turn their male athletes into a bunch of sissies. These athletes, they believed, needed their anger to be successful. Given the often-accepted analogy of sport and warfare, I had to stop and reconsider (a) why anyone would want to think about anger management for athletes and (b) what I was really trying to do by teaching athletes these skills.

The reasons to do this work are simple. First, anger is an emotion that, at high levels, interferes with peak performance in much the same way that anxiety does, yet only a fraction of the attention paid to anxiety has been directed to anger. Second, anger and violence are confusing constructs in sport. Differences of opinion have been further complicated by terminology problems. For this reason, discussion about the language used to describe this phenomenon is needed. Third, there is no reason to believe that all athletes have learned to manage their emotions when many people in our society have not. Finally, I wanted to understand (and then teach) why some athletes can harness their anger whereas others trip on it and self-destruct—either in their sport arena or outside it.

I believe that the idea that athletes are more violent than nonathletes is a myth. Whether you come to the same conclusion or not by the end of this book, I will help you understand how to manage any violence, including violence that comes up in sport. First, we must come to some agreement on language and terminology.

A NEW VERNACULAR

I believe that the definitions used in the sport psychology field regarding anger and violence require streamlining. As we go through relevant terminology and definitions that I think should be standardized (if for no other reason than to have pragmatic language that people can agree on), I will explain why I have made refinements to previously used terms.

Anger

Anger is a normal emotion. Anger is neither good nor bad, and no judgment need be attached to it. Some people believe that a problem arises if a person becomes angry. This idea is not true. To pass judgment on anger and condemn those who admit to becoming angry is the equivalent of robbing people of their humanness. Disallowing oneself from any part of the human experience weakens the experience in its totality. Sadness gives a reference point that makes happiness more appreciated. Tension can be better understood when compared with relaxation. It is about time we stopped making value judgments about anger. No one has ever gotten in trouble for becoming angry. You could be furious right now, but no one would know it unless you demonstrated some behavior associated with the anger. The belief that anger is bad is so strongly engrained that people will sometimes deny its existence even when it is spilling out all over the place. We have all heard someone with a red face expel incendiary words accompanied by saliva and then follow up by saying, "I am *not angry!*" The bad rap that anger has received has made it even more resistant to examination.

Truth be told, anger can be harnessed and used as fuel to assist in performance. Can it interfere with performance? You bet! Does it have to? Absolutely not. I have helped athletes compete harder with greater intensity for longer periods, motivated by their anger. The issue is not a matter of eliminating anger; it is a matter of keeping it at a level where it assists, not detracts from, performance.

Studies have shown that as anger increases, cognitive processing speed goes down, fine motor coordination and sensitivity to pain decrease, and muscle strength often increases. So for some athletes doing some tasks, anger can be helpful. For example, the defensive lineman who must make his way past a blocker to make a tackle might benefit from having some level of anger. For other tasks, anger would be a hindrance. The quarterback who needs to read the defense before deciding which receiver to throw to would likely perform better if he was not angry. In fact, some research supports this thesis. Players at football positions that require a lot of decision making tend to demonstrate lower levels of anger than players at positions that do not.

Therefore, when we talk about anger management for peak performance in sport, we are not always talking about making athletes polite and calm. Rather, we are referring to their ability to self-regulate their emotions to what their tasks require.

Aggression

What does it mean to be aggressive? Definitions that have permeated sport psychology for decades have stated that aggression has harm to another as a goal. It is no wonder that people frown on aggression in sport; it means that someone has to get hurt. This statement is not true. The adverb *aggressively* describes the method by which people go after their goals. It refers to the tenacity, the hunger, and the determination that people embody when striving for accomplishments.

I checked: The women who succeeded on Wall Street climbed the corporate ladder aggressively. Success in life is not just handed to people. They have to want it. They have to go get it themselves. At the heart of Nike's "Just Do It" campaign is the idea of not waiting for it to come to you. Instead, you go from being passive to active and doing it yourself. Aggression is a necessary requirement for success in sport and in life in general.

Aggressive behavior can be broken down into various categories. The delineation that makes the most sense is that between instrumental aggression and reactive aggression.

Instrumental aggression is goal-directed aggression in which harm to another is not the primary goal, although it can be a secondary result of the action. In sport, an example would be the basketball player who slashes to the basket, leaps over a defender, and accidentally catches another defender with an elbow on the way up to scoring two points with a resounding dunk. The goal was to put the ball in the hole, not to harm an opponent. People who participate in sport know that injury is always a possibility. Accidental injuries happen. No blame should be assigned, and nothing in the rules of the game bans these incidents. Instrumental aggression is the hallmark for success in life and in sport and should be encouraged.

Some authors have described instrumental aggression as assertiveness. I believe that in making this distinction, psychologists are trying to soften things up in defense of the position that aggression is bad. Let us examine this for a moment. To be assertive is to stand up for one's rights. In fact, in the psychotherapy world, assertiveness training is used for people who have self-esteem problems. We teach them communication skills (we will revisit this topic later in the book) that will help them effectively and appropriately have their needs met.

To illustrate how assertiveness is not the same as instrumental aggression, consider the following: The tailback is 10 yards out from the goal line. Three defenders block the path between him and six points. Will he assertively communicate to his opponents, "Excuse me, gentlemen, would it be OK if you just acquiesced and allowed me to run past you? After all, it is my right to score this touchdown, you know"? Of course not! The tailback has no entitlement to score. He has no right to win. He succeeds only by aggressively going after his goal. So when you see the tailback launch his body through the air like a missile trying to bowl over the last defender after skillfully dancing his way between the other two, do not think assertive; think Walter Payton—aggressive.

But that is not the whole story on aggression. Another type of aggression is called reactive aggression, sometimes referred to as hostile aggression. Reactive aggression is behavior that has as its primary and sometimes solitary goal to do harm to someone. Usually, this action is in response to a perceived injustice, insult, or wrongdoing. This form of aggression is related to anger and is the behavior that gets athletes in trouble, both on and off the field. An example of reactive aggression may be the pitcher who is furious that the last time a certain batter came to the plate, he hit a 450-foot (140-meter) homer that cleared the bleachers. Still fuming, the pitcher aims his 95 mile-per-hour (150-kilometer-per-hour) fastball between the hitter's shoulder blades.

Violence

Reactive aggression, in its most extreme forms, is violence, but the definition is not reflexive. Not all violence comes from anger and reactive aggression. Violence has, at its root, harm to another as its planned result.

Predatory violence, for example, is behavior in which the hunter seeks the hunted. In the animal world, the stealthy lion waits patiently in the brush for its prey to wander close enough to be ambushed. In the world of serial killers who hunt their victims, predators often do not have an increase in heart rate or sympathetic nervous system activity that usually accompanies anger. Anger is not related to this activity and in fact would interfere with the ability to hunt.

Terry and Jackson (1985) clarified sport violence as harm-inducing behavior outside the rules of sport, bearing no direct relationship to the competitive goals of sport. This definition nicely carved out a type of violence different from society's violence.

In an attempt to explain sport violence, I developed the Abrams model of sports violence (figure 1.1) that reflects the seeming overlap between aggression and violence. Understanding that injury can be part of the game, we can differentiate violence in the same way that we differentiate aggression. Incidental violence is violence that does not have harming another as its sole goal; it is directed toward sport goals. In contrast, reactive or hostile violence has the specific goal of causing harm to someone else.

Both represent behaviors that may go beyond the rules of the sport, but incidental violence is an extension of acceptable behavior. Checking in hockey provides a useful example. The line that differentiates checking from cross-checking or boarding, both of which are penalties, is often blurry. Overzealous players can certainly have their behavior spill over

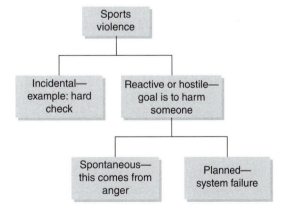

Figure 1.1 The Abrams model of sport violence.

to being illegal. This behavior is different from reactive violence, in which the behavior is retaliatory. This kind of behavior can also be broken down into two categories. The first is the spontaneous response. There are some players who pride themselves on their ability to get inside their opponents' heads and will deliberately provoke them to take them off their game. New York Rangers forward Sean Avery, often described as an agitator, is particularly proficient at this. So, the player provokes the other repeatedly, perhaps by checking them with their stick. Finally, the provoking player checks the first player one too many times, and the player turns and swings the stick at the opponent's head. The response, although extreme, was not planned. This is spontaneous reactive aggression and is directly related to anger. Anger management programs specifically target reducing this type of behavior. More immediately though, the league or organization must penalize, fine, or suspend players engaging in such behavior as it can very easily cause serious injury.

Finally, the worst category of sport violence is planned violence, where a coach or players agree and plan to hurt another player. This behavior is premeditated and criminal. When this type of behavior is condoned, it represents a complete system failure and is the worst behavior that can occur in sport. Besides criminal prosecution of such behavior, leagues must have mechanisms to police themselves when such behavior permeates their midst.

When a coach plans to have his or her athletes deliberately injure an opponent, a failure of the system has occurred. All the goodness of sport goes right out the window. Is this circumstance connected with anger? Not necessarily. That is what is most disturbing about it. When no impulsivity is involved, when a deliberate decision has been made to harm another person, the behavior is unacceptable. Sport organizations need to remove coaches who condone such behavior.

On February 22, 2005, Temple University's men's basketball coach John Chaney inserted seldom-used 6-foot-8-inch (203-centimeter), 250-pound (113-kilogram) Nehemiah Ingram into the lineup. Ingram proceeded to deliver five fouls in less than six minutes—including a crushing foul on St. Joe's senior forward John Bryant, which resulted in a broken arm. Before the game, Chaney, angered by what he thought were illegal screens by Saint Joseph's, stated that he would bring out his "goon" to deliver hard fouls and send a message. Chaney was suspended for three games. Bryant's season was over. The surprisingly short period of public outrage and the swiftness with which concerned parties moved on (a month later, on March 22, Temple announced that Chaney would be returning for the 2005–2006 season, and on April 8 Coach Chaney was inducted into the Philadelphia Sports Hall of Fame) speak to our society's tolerance of such behavior. If we do not reverse course by not tolerating such blatant disregard for the value of sportsmanship, why should we expect our athletes to behave appropriately?

Before moving on, let us think about some sport examples to illustrate various types of aggression or violence and determine whether they are problematic.

• Bob Gibson was known for pitching high and tight. Many pitchers today try to employ this strategy. When is pitching high and tight considered "trying to establish the inside part of the plate," and when is it "throwing at the batter"? Perhaps the more pertinent question is why the pitcher is throwing to the particular location. If Mike Piazza drilled a home run the last time he batted, "chin music," a ball thrown near his face, is the likely retribution. Does this mean that after a batter hits a home run, the pitcher cannot throw inside? If the pitcher cannot throw inside, he may as well step off the rubber. To be successful, a pitcher needs to be able to keep the batter off balance. So if the pitch comes up and in after a home run or a batter's showboating, it will likely be perceived as deliberate, regardless of the true intention. Therefore, from a strategy standpoint, pitchers should seek to establish the inside part of the plate early. Retribution is planned, hostile violence that has no place in sport.

• Jacksonville safety Donovan Darius almost decapitated Packers wide receiver Robert Ferguson during a contest in 2005 at Lambeau Field. He received a fine, and many people believe that the punishment was too lenient.

• Eric Barton, linebacker of the New York Jets, received an unnecessary roughness penalty after finishing a hit on Chargers quarterback Drew Brees with an enthusiastic elbow to the head. His play almost cost the Jets the game. Barton admitted, "It was a stupid play and I was wrong. If we hadn't won, I would have taken full responsibility." But Jets quarterback Chad Pennington never blamed his teammate. Pennington was quoted as saying, "I don't fault Eric Barton. We voted him the most inspirational player on this team. Every down and every game he plays like it's his last. That was one play where his aggressiveness backfired."

• In 2002 Warren Sapp, then of the Tampa Bay Buccaneers, blindsided Green Bay offensive tackle Chad Clifton far from the play after an interception. The injury was so severe that initially it was not clear whether Clifton would walk again. The hit was unnecessary.

So, in collision sports, when is it OK to unleash such fury?

In Super Bowl XXIII, Ickey Woods of the Bengals ran for 27 yards on his first four carries. On his fifth carry, the big tailback from UNLV was knocked backward by a devastating hit from 49ers safety Ronnie Lott. The shot shifted the momentum of the game, and Woods became a non-factor for the reminder of the contest. He gained only 460 more yards in his career. Obviously, a big hit can change the momentum in sport. Prohibiting these hits would likely leave many athletes and fans feeling somewhat empty. The issue is not whether people can be aggressive in sport. They *must* be aggressive to be successful. The key is for players to be aggressive with measured emotion. As we will see later, uncontrolled aggression can cause devastating results.

Hostility

Different from anger, which tends to be short lived, hostility is a long-lasting emotional state characterized and manifested by a desire to harm others (in one way or another). Hostility might be thought of as chronic anger. Everyone seems to know at least one person who fits this description—the person who gets up on the wrong side of the bed everyday. People who are frequently hostile, psychologists have learned, tend to have a different way of looking at the world than other people do. This distorted cognitive set is called a hostility bias. People with a hostility bias tend to have the characteristics outlined in table 1.1.

Cognitive restructuring to address such cognitive distortions must be central to any effective anger management program. These thought patterns did not arrive overnight and likely will not dissipate quickly, although the younger the athlete is, the easier it is to change the person's worldview.

THEORIES

Now that we have gone over the characterizations of some important terms, we can review the several theories that have been proposed over time to

Table 1.1 Problematic Cognitions Associated With Hostility Bias

Cognition problem	Example
Tendency to perceive neutral stimuli as provocative.	While walking down the hallway and talking to a friend, Susan did not see Michelle and accidentally bumped into her. Michelle is positive that Susan did it on purpose to challenge her. Michelle will not be disrespected, and she is ready to fight.
Difficulties identifying nonhostile explanations for an event.	When asked whether she could come up with another explanation for why Susan bumped into her, Michelle replies, "Nope, she just did it on purpose."
Difficulties generating alternative non-violent responses to handle a situation.	If you ask Michelle to generate a list of other ways that she could handle the situation without getting into a fistfight, you would see a confused look. Violence is the only way she knows to handle problems. She has difficulty brainstorming any other solution.
Legitimization of violence. It is not that Michelle cannot come up with other ways to handle her problem, she just does not choose to. Might is right.	Often, because of the environments that people grow up in, violence is modeled as the preferred response strategy. This method is so engrained that issues of power, respect, and authority become confused. "It is OK to demonstrate your authority by physical means. You should not allow anyone to disrespect you because it makes you look powerless." The issue of personal power is critical. When threatened, people often become afraid or angry. The natural response is to run away or fight. People do not have to think about the response. It is almost automatic. If the response is automatic, would not a person demonstrate a great deal of power by not responding in that way? True power lies in self-control, in not allowing others to cause a response that is not consciously chosen.

explain aggression in sport. Note that professionals have inappropriately used the terms *aggression* and *anger* interchangeably over time, although this is less common today than it was 10 years ago. The first theory that will be examined, the frustration–aggression hypothesis, was originally presented in 1939. Aggression is an extremely general term that has been correctly used for a wide variety of acts that involve attack (Reber, 1985).

Frustration–Aggression Theory

In 1939 Dollard, Doob, Miller, Mowrer, and Sears, at Yale, first presented the frustration–aggression (F–A) hypothesis in their book *Frustration and Aggression*. They began by explaining that "aggression is always a consequence of frustration." Frustration was defined as an interference with the occurrence of an instigated goal-response at its proper time in the behavior sequence. Hence, frustration, to those authors, meant the inability to achieve a goal because of some type of impediment. In particular, an impediment to a goal is not a frustration unless the person is striving, implicitly or explicitly, to reach the objective. The greater the satisfaction anticipated on attaining the objective, the more aggressive people will become when they are kept from reaching their goal. Furthermore, the magnitude of the expressed aggression depends on the intensity of the frustration, the person's threshold for frustration (people can tolerate different amounts and types of frustration), the frequency of the frustrating incidents, and the severity of the consequences for acting aggressively.

This theory translates to sport easily because athletes are continually trying to reach their goals and are usually competing against each other to reach a single goal. When one person or one team reaches that goal first, the other will be frustrated, and thus more likely to lash out.

Completion Hypothesis

Thirty years later, in 1969, Leonard Berkowitz began reviewing the classic F–A theory and later updated it. Berkowitz noted that all organisms react aggressively when they experience aversive stimulation. He recognized that a person does not always experience frustration as aversive, so a one-to-one relationship does not exist. People do not always become aggressive when frustrated. Whenever people experience an aversive stimulus, which could be heat, noise, or feeling tired, they are more likely to experience negative emotions. These emotions, modulated by associated thoughts, can lead to the instigation of aggressive behavior.

This theory also lines up well with sport. Because athletes play under many different conditions, numerous environmental factors can cause changes in internal emotional and physical experiences. Although one athlete may experience the sound of cheering fans as invigorating, a competitor may experience the same sound as an obnoxious roar that interferes with the ability to concentrate.

It follows then, when thinking about mental toughness, that athletes who are able to control their response to aversive stimuli will be in the best position to succeed. We might think of such athletes as being covered with Teflon. The pressure just does not penetrate them.

Catharsis

Drive theory states that people have certain instinctive drives. Sigmund Freud, the father of psychoanalysis, proposed two basic drives: eros and thanatos. Eros is the productive, creative, and positive form of mental energy, whereas thanatos is the destructive, death-seeking force. Freud believed that these drives were biologically based and required expression. If the drives were denied expression, they would build up pressure like steam in a boiler (Tedeschi & Felson, 1994).

Before Freud developed the concept of thanatos, he explained that blockage of a person's eros (positive energy) was frustrating and led to attacks against the source of the frustration. This idea was the springboard from which the frustration–aggression hypothesis was generated.

In any case, whether we call the aggressive drive thanatos or not, the release of pent-up emotions from these drives is called catharsis. Some authors have disputed the cathartic aspect of sport. Bennett (1991) noted that "football breeds aggression and then supposedly catharts it" and that "since aggression is an integral part of continuing victory, its catharsis is not conducive to a winning season." The argument is that catharsis, this release of energy, would predict a lack of success in the future. This result does not occur because athletes are able to motivate themselves between competitions. Furthermore, even when drained of mental and physical energy toward the end of a competition, many athletes can find reserves that they did not know they had.

The debate continues about whether or not sport can be cathartic. Perhaps the more pertinent question is whether catharsis is helpful or harmful.

You will often hear people say that when you are angry you can punch a pillow or scream at the top of your lungs. You will then feel better. You may recall the scene in *Analyze This* when Robert DeNiro's character Don Vitti is instructed by Billy Crystal, playing psychiatrist Dr. Ben Sobel, that he will feel better if he takes his anger out on a pillow. So when he becomes angry, he fills a pillow with bullets. Does he feel better? Surprised, he says, "Actually, yeah."

You do feel better when you release that pent-up energy. For an athlete, however, what happens when that pillow is not available but Bobby is? Bobby winds up being hit. Although catharsis is helpful in stress reduction, the subsequent "better feeling" is a reinforcer that could increase the likelihood of acts of aggression like those seen in sport. And to make matters even more complicated, people reinforced for being aggressive in one arena may have difficulty knowing where it is OK to act that way and where it is not. Violence, therefore, begets violence. For this reason, aggression can be a double-edged sword. If sports that condone and reinforce aggression leave their athletes unchecked, a reasonable deduction is that some athletes will act aggressively outside the sport arena. This circumstance presents a stimulus differentiation problem that future research may need to address.

Reciprocal Inhibition

Another psychological concept associated with aggression in sport is reciprocal inhibition. Counterconditioning, as Joseph Wolpe explained it in the 1950s, refers to the substitution of an emotional response that is appropriate or adaptive to a given situation for one that is maladaptive. Simply stated, two opposite experiences cannot occupy the same space. A person cannot be both physically exhausted and full of rage at the same time. As you will read in the following chapters, when a person becomes angry, the nervous system kicks in and prepares the person to fight. This process requires energy. The person may have violent thoughts or inclinations, but if the gas tank is empty, she or he cannot act on them.

If a person can substitute angry impulses with an incompatible emotion, the anger cannot lead to violence.

BEHAVIOR MODIFICATION

Although many people have already learned about these topics, they are worth reviewing briefly because cognitive–behavioral interventions are at the heart of anger management. The behavioral component relies heavily on learning theory.

Reinforcement and Punishment

Reinforcement is any consequence that will increase the probability that a behavior will happen again. Reinforcement can occur in two ways: positive and negative. Positive and negative do not translate to good and bad. Instead, think of positive and negative as adding something or removing something, respectively.

Positive reinforcement is adding a pleasant consequence to a behavior to bring about its reoccurrence. A sport example would be a softball pitcher who is substituted in at the last minute to start a game. She shows good command of her pitches and throws a shutout. The coach rewards her with another start.

Negative reinforcement is causing a behavior to reoccur by removing an unpleasant factor. Let us say that a basketball coach ends every practice with suicide line drills. The team had practiced hard the previous week to reduce mental errors, and they executed flawlessly in their last game, soundly beating their cross-town rival for the first time in three years. The coach decides to give the team a break from the suicides on Monday as a reward for their hard work.

Punishment comes in both positive and negative varieties as well. As you are probably aware, punishment is any consequence that decreases the likelihood that a behavior will happen again.

An example of positive punishment, in the form of the introduction of an undesirable stimulus, would be making the team run sprints at the end of practice for poor attention to details and fundamental errors during drills. Coaches should be mindful of using this approach because punishing bad behavior in sport with exercise is not good practice. This method has the potential of changing athletes' view of exercise from good to bad. Moreover, coaches would always prefer to reinforce positive behavior rather than punish negative behavior.

A coach can also use differential reinforcement. After six players on his baseball team did not run out fly balls during a game, the coach demanded that each of them take extra batting practice. When asked why he chose that activity as punishment, he stated, "They don't do the basics, so they have to do more work." But if the players want to improve, extra batting practice would be reinforcing. Instead, the coach could choose to reinforce the other members of the team with extra batting practice. That approach would be a creative way to kill two birds with one stone. He reinforces the behavior that he was looking for (running out fly balls) while simultaneously decreasing the likelihood of a repeat performance by removing a positive stimulus (the opportunity to take extra batting practice). This method is known as negative punishment.

Understanding aggressiveness in this type of paradigm is important. Aggressive behavior is most often reinforced. The bully in school who steals a classmate's lunch money is rewarded for his behavior by having more money. Why should he stop? This type of behavior will continue until it becomes more of a negative experience than a positive one.

In sport several examples of this come to mind. A blitzing linebacker has a clear shot at the quarterback from his blindside. He knows that the quarterback can sense him coming and honestly he is not sure whether he will be able to get to the quarterback before he releases the ball. But hey, this is a contract year. If he goes in hard, maybe even at the quarterback's head, he may be able to knock him out of the game. His team would have a much better shot at winning if this All-Pro signal caller is not on the field. Why shouldn't the linebacker take him out? Well, hurting someone is morally wrong, and it violates the rules of the game.

Hitting in football is not outside the rules of the game. Hitting someone after the whistle is, but if the reward (removing the opponent from the game) outweighs the potential penalty (15 yards for unnecessary roughness), not all athletes will make the same decision.

Do not misinterpret what I am saying here. Engaging in these behaviors is not OK, but if the punishment does not outweigh the reward in a particular case, the behavior is likely to continue. And to change the behavior, the rewards and punishments have to mean something to the athlete. Punishment will not work just because the person deciding the punishment thinks it will matter.

Although we will further explore this issue later in the book, fining multimillionaires $25,000 for a blow to the head does not work. Suspensions work, however, for three reasons: First, a suspension is negative punishment when it takes away what players love to do—participate in sport. Second, when players do not play, they do not collect a paycheck. They do not receive their reinforcement. Third, a suspension sends a message to the team that an athlete who may be needed to win will not be available if he engages in this behavior. This generates social pressure to create norms of acceptable behavior. That 15-yard penalty is only the start of the consequences that the linebacker will face, but if that penalty puts the opponent within field goal range with 30 seconds left in a tie game, the team may not celebrate such violence.

Extinction

In a behavioral framework, people do not just continue to engage in behaviors randomly. They do so because circumstances continue to reinforce the behavior. It can be as simple as the joy that they get from doing what they do. But behavioral theory also adds that when a behavior is not reinforced, it will become extinct.

Parents and teachers use this premise when they give a child a time-out. If you have been either, you may be a member of the large group of people who believe that time-outs do not work. They absolutely do, but you must be consistent and precise and you need to know the secret.

Extinction is an intervention of choice in dealing with trash talking. An athlete who can effectively get in another athlete's head by talking smack during competition will have an advantage. If your opponent recognizes that he or she can get you off your game, you are reinforcing the person to continue the harassment. If you want to get the other person to stop, you cannot do it by engaging in the same banter. That approach will only escalate the situation, which may even become physical. The way to stop the behavior is to stop reinforcing it. It will then become extinct, correct?

Well, there is a catch. A part of this that most people do not talk about is the same reason that time-outs often do not work. People expect that as soon as they stop reinforcing a behavior, it will just disappear. The process does not work that way because of a phenomenon known as the extinction burst.

When a behavior has been reinforced for a while, the person expects that the reinforcement will continue. When it is not reinforced, the behavior will initially increase in intensity and frequency before it subsides. We might consider it a "just to make sure" response. This progression is depicted in the figure 1.2.

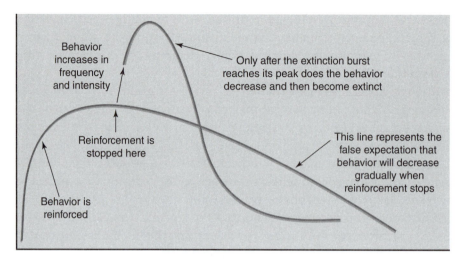

Figure 1.2 Illustration of an extinction burst.

Consider the following example: An eight-year-old student has been disruptive in class. After the teacher realizes that the behavior will not stop because his classmates are all laughing at the faces that he is making, she decides to give him a time-out. She sits him in the back corner of the classroom, away from his peers. Would you expect him to stop his behavior immediately? No, he has to see whether he can still gain the cheers of his audience. So he increases the disruption. Only after the other children do not acknowledge him for a time does he begin to become quiet.

Those who are not aware of the extinction burst will become even more frustrated when the trash talking increases. Athletes who know that they can get under an opponent's skin can use this psychological weapon to advantage. To short-circuit it, the opponent has to ignore it and be prepared to weather the storm for a while before it dissipates.

Modeling

Through modeling—observing the behavior of a model and then repeating the behavior—people can acquire responses never before performed or displayed and strengthen or weaken responses that already exist in their repertoire of behavior (Bandura, Ross, & Ross, 1963). Modeling, also known as observational learning, really refers to a process of how we learn by watching. Albert Bandura, the theorist who studied modeling most extensively, noted that learning would be "exceedingly laborious, not to mention hazardous" (1973) if people had to figure out everything by themselves.

Four processes underlie observational learning (Kearsley, 1994c):

1. Attention
2. Retention
3. Motor reproduction
4. Motivation

The first subprocess, attention, refers to the fact that learners must focus on the model in order to view the target behavior. They must watch and pay attention to the model. By doing so, they can begin the second subprocess, retention.

Retention concerns the subject's ability to create an internal representation of the target behavior. Such a representation is necessary if the person is to reproduce the behavior in the absence of the model. Simply stated, learners must remember what they saw.

The third subprocess, motor reproduction, includes the use of internal representations to perform the target behavior. This component refers to the ability of the subject to replicate behaviors; the subject cannot perform the behavior if he or she lacks the physical or mental abilities. Learners must practice to shape their behavior to match the behavior of their model.

The final subprocess, motivation, suggests that the subject will translate learning into performance only if a favorable incentive is present. If positive consequences are absent, the person has no reason to acquire these new behaviors.

Youngsters who watch athletes want to be as skilled as their models, or as popular. They do not necessarily stop to think about whether the behavior they are replicating is in their best interest. In their minds, if they are like the athlete, they will emulate every aspect of the athlete's life. This is true for the young baseball player who copies Albert Pujols' batting stance with the hope of having his success or the adolescent who joins a gang and wears the identifying colors. Young people believe that "if I watch them and do what they do, I can be like them."

Nike made millions of dollars on the "I Wanna Be Like Mike" campaign. Not long afterward, however, Charles Barkley was smeared by the media for saying that he was not a role model. Many people thought that he was wrong, but Barkley was not completely off the mark. Where he was mistaken was in believing that, despite his popularity and fame, he could turn off the adoration of others and prevent children from looking up to him. Not a chance. Where he was right, however, was his statement that parents should do a better job of being role models that their children can look up to. But parents are not the only ones who need to be conscious of their effect on young people. Coaches, teammates, older kids in the neighborhood, and others need to understand that children are like sponges. They soak up what they see. In a scene in *A Bronx Tale* starring Robert DeNiro and Chazz Palmintieri, the child star watched the neighborhood mafia wise guy, who held complete power over the community. The child watched his idol's mannerisms and impersonated them to the last detail, right down to the way he leaned over to talk to someone with his middle and ring fingers down while he pointed at the listener.

People are more likely to adopt a modeled behavior if the model is similar to the observer, the model has admired status, and the behavior has functional value. For this reason, coaches should be mindful that although their players may want to mirror the mannerisms of pro athletes, better models are those who are similar in age and slightly better in ability. This sort of modeling leads to easier acquisition of new skills and less frustration because the learner can more readily replicate the model's behaviors.

Albert Bandura spent a good deal of time studying aggressive behavior and found that the parents of aggressive children were aggressive and that the parents of inhibited children were inhibited. The study that Bandura is most famous for is the Bobo doll experiment. In this experiment, he had children witness a model who aggressively attacked a plastic clown called the Bobo doll. Children watched a video in which a model would aggressively hit a doll— beating it with a hammer, throwing it down, and throwing balls at it. After the video, the children were placed in a room with attractive toys, but they could not touch them. The children became angry and frustrated. Then the children were led to another room that contained toys identical to those used in the Bobo video. Bandura found that 88 percent of the children imitated the aggressive behavior. Eight months later, 40 percent of the same children reproduced the violent behavior that they observed in the Bobo doll experiment.

So, if you want your athletes to manage their anger and not be violent, you had better practice what you preach. All too often, athletes, parents, and coaches wind up in arguments and fights with each other, with officials, or with fans. Modeling appropriate behavior is important when working with all athletes, but the younger the athletes are, the more impressionable they are. All leagues need to have a code of conduct that is strictly enforced. All participants—athletes, coaches, parents, and others—must follow it.

In numerous incidents, which I will discuss in detail later, violence has been severe enough to be considered criminal. Some leagues have implemented codes of conduct or have had speakers come in to do anger management presentations just to avoid legal vulnerability. The belief is that if the organization provides this service and someone acts out, the league is not liable. Although codes of conduct or presentations may or may not insulate a league from legal proceedings, if the problem is left unaddressed, the frequency and severity of the incidents are likely to continue to spiral upward.

A study completed by Mugno and Feltz (1984) supported the effects of modeling. It noted that youth league and high school male football players claimed on self-report inventories that they learned aggressive sport acts by observing college and professional football players (Mugno & Feltz, 1984). Besides the military, sport is the only legal organized activity in the United States that condones and reinforces aggression.

Deindividuation and Disinhibition

Have you ever seen someone do something completely out of character? You might see a behavior that leaves you thinking, "Wow, I never thought Shane would do something like that!"

Bandura and Walters (1963) used lynch mobs and protest demonstrations as examples of how a person in a crowd can perform or act in ways that he or she would never have acted if alone. In large groups, people sometimes lose their individuality and follow the group's direction. This process is called deindividuation.

Disinhibition refers to a weakening of an inhibition of behavior. Although some people may be able to control their behaviors, circumstances may weaken that inhibition, leading to behaviors that the person may not have done under normal conditions.

> *The disinhibitory power of modeling is enhanced when observers are angered or otherwise emotionally aroused, when they have developed aggressive styles of conduct, when the exemplified aggression goes unpunished or produces good results, when the aggression is socially justified, when the victim invites attack through actions that facilitate attribution of blame, and when the injuries suffered by the victim are minimized or sanitized (Bandura, 1986).*

In several cases in which young men participated in gang rapes, everyone who knew them swore that it was not in their character to engage in such behaviors. Fraternities and athletic teams are two groups on a college campus that are ripe for such deindividuation processes to occur. Fraternities and teams represent groups of people who are tightly knit, and individuals within the groups want to maintain their membership. Furthermore, on many occasions alcohol flows freely. Alcohol has been shown to contribute to both deindividuation and disinhibition. Finally, in some cases, a misogynist belief system is present. Group members may believe that it is OK to use women to meet their needs. When these conditions coincide, a powder keg is waiting to be lit.

Following a presentation given on dating violence and the effects of alcohol on that act, one female college student stated, "You know, you hit it right on the head. You can have a guy that's cool, but get him with a bunch of his jock friends and add alcohol . . . and you get instant idiot!"

Yerkes Dodson Law, aka the Inverted U Hypothesis

In sport, mental states have a significant effect on performance. Taylor (1996) summarized the connection:

> *The most critical factor prior to competition is intensity because no matter how confident, motivated, or technically or physically prepared athletes are to perform, they will simply not be able to perform their best if their bodies are not at an optimal level of intensity, accompanied by the requisite physiological and psychological changes.*

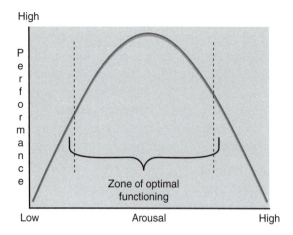

High

P
e
r
f
o
r
m
a
n
c
e

Zone of optimal
functioning

Low   Arousal   High

Figure 1.3 The Yerkes–Dodson law (also known as the inverted U hypothesis) represents the curvilinear relationship between arousal and performance. Performance is highest at moderate levels of arousal and lowest at the low and high ends of arousal. Variations of this theme have been established depending on the task and the person involved. Hanin noted that the zone of optimal functioning shifts according to these factors.

Intensity was defined by Zaichkowsky and Takenaka (1993) as a multidimensional construct that performs the energizing function of the mind and body. Intensity may be experienced positively as increased confidence, motivation, strength, and heightened sensory acuity, or negatively as loss of concentration, fear, or dread (Taylor, 1996).

Yerkes and Dodson (1908) suggested a curvilinear relationship (the inverted U theory) between intensity and performance. They posited that increases in intensity produce proportional increases in performance up to a certain point. After that point, intensity interferes with performance. Studies in the sports of baseball (Lowe, 1971), basketball (Sonstroem & Bernardo, 1982), and swimming (Burton, 1988) have produced evidence that confirms the Yerkes–Dodson law. For that reason, in the sport arena athletes need to find their zone of optimal functioning, which is the level of intensity "that enables a particular athlete to perform his/her personal best" (Hanin, 1989; see figure 1.3).

Overintensity, which is counterproductive to athletic success, is recognized by physical symptoms such as extreme muscle tension, shaking muscles, breathing difficulty, increased heart rate, and excessive perspiration (Landers & Boutcher, 1986). Affect states most often associated with this sympathetic nervous system response are anxiety and anger. The reduction of anxiety to elicit peak performance has been a focus for sport psychologists for more than 15 years (Nideffer, 1981; DeWitt, 1980; Rotella, 1985).

Further research over time has expanded our knowledge about the relationship between arousal and performance. For one thing, although the relationship is called the Yerkes–Dodson law, a more appropriate title may be the inverted U hypothesis because the word *law* implies that the relationship holds without exception. We have learned that the Yerkes–Dodson law is more like a theme that is affected by various factors. To clarify, it is true that at extremely low levels of arousal—when sleeping, for example—performance on most tasks is correspondingly poor. Likewise, it is also uniformly true that at extremely high levels of arousal—when in a rage, for example—performance is also poor. Even if the goal is violence, being successful when in a rage is difficult because fine motor coordination, decision making, and cognitive processing speed all deteriorate.

The areas where further clarification is needed are the issue of individual differences and the variations in the curve as related to the task at hand.

People respond to situations in different ways, and some people are more comfortable than others in certain emotional states. When I first started working in prison, one of my colleagues from outside the prison setting noted that I seemed comfortable working in chaotic environments that most people would avoid. Before I worked in prison, I worked in a city hospital that was more dangerous than prison because it lacked the same level of security and control. Earlier, I trained in a state hospital. Certainly, some people can tolerate particular emotions better than others can.

When I thought about this more, I realized that even when I became angry in confrontational and potentially dangerous situations, I did not have the intense physiological response that would normally correspond to the emotion. That is not to say that I did not get there; I just did not get there as readily as the people around me did. What I came to realize was that for many reasons, certainly related to my personal history, I was comfortable when angry—it was egosyntonic for me. As a result, I was able to stay calm and make decisions without much interference until I reached higher anger levels.

Although I came to this conclusion myself from my own anecdotal information, some people in sport obviously have similar characteristics. Some of them are unflappable.

Think about Michael Jordan. People often said that the last thing you wanted to do was piss him off because he performed better when he was angry. That explanation may not be the only one. Perhaps, he did not get better but that as he became more competitive, transforming the contest from a team affair into a one-on-one confrontation, his performance did not deteriorate while his opponents made mental mistakes or lost their coordination. In truth, the many who tried to trash-talk at Jordan found that the strategy backfired. Or perhaps Jordan became moderately angry and was able to use his anger as a cue to focus himself, concentrate more, and center himself in "the zone." His opponents would become increasingly frustrated that they could not knock him off his game, and they, in effect, wound up knocking themselves off their own game.

Likewise, when Roger Clemens and Bob Gibson took the mound, they had a nasty irritability to them. Either could be pretty intense. Neither had a second thought about throwing a ball at 98 miles per hour (158 kilometers per hour) right below the batter's chin if he was crowding the plate a little bit. Think about how much control it takes to be able to throw high heat with such precision and not hurt anyone (Clemens' plunking of Mike Piazza aside). Athletes like Clemens and Gibson could use their anger for fuel and be comfortable with it, even at high levels where few could go without imploding.

So one variable in the inverted U hypothesis is the person involved. You should not assume that everyone will respond in the same way, nor should you assume that because a given circumstance would produce a certain emotional response in you, everyone would experience it the same way.

The other variable is related to the task in question. Some sport-related tasks are less negatively affected by intense emotion. Tasks that do not require many decisions to be made, involve intense speed or strength, and do not require much fine motor coordination can better afford emotional intensity. A good example is the play of a defensive lineman.

Before I have Michael Strahan chasing me, I am in no way making any implications about the intelligence of defensive linemen. I am simply pointing out that some positions in sport require more decision making than others do. Except when a zone blitz is called and a lineman must drop into coverage, defensive linemen generally do not have to make many decisions. Although the following is an oversimplification, the general job description for a defensive lineman is to remove, run over, run past, or hurdle the man trying to block him and go get the man with the ball—either the quarterback during a pass rush or the tailback on a running play.

A reasonable conclusion is that as we progress toward the defensive backfield, football players can less afford to be overintense. A study that pointed toward this finding was the research by Nation and LeUnes (1983), who compared college football players by position and by redshirt status using the Profile of Mood States (POMS), a questionnaire that rates the subject on six mood states: vigor, anger, depression, fatigue, confusion, and tension. This instrument will be discussed further in chapter 3. In the study, the authors found that defensive backs had lower anger scores than either linebackers or defensive linemen. Continuing that trend, quarterbacks, running backs, and wide receivers all had lower average anger scores than defensive linemen and linebackers. Linebackers had the highest anger scores across the board.

In 1991 Newby and Simpson published a similar study using the same premise and the same tools, but they analyzed nonscholarship athletes at a smaller school. They found the same themes. Linebackers again had the highest average anger scores.

This fascinating line of research should be expanded to include all sports. The findings raise the question of whether certain positions require higher levels of anger for success. Figure 1.4 depicts the shift in performance that occurs when athletes engage in high-intensity activities that require less cognitive activity.

Conversely, some tasks require fine motor coordination that involves automatized behaviors. Arousal would be likely to interfere with performance of such tasks. Golf is a perfect example. Whether the task is a swing for a drive or the sensitive stroke of a putt, intense, tight muscles interfere with optimal performance.

Along those lines, activities that require focus and aim such as archery, biathlon, and even pitching are subject to the deleterious effects of overintensity. Many pitchers, when they become too amped, lose control over their mechanics. They lose their release point or overthrow and lose their feel for the ball. Just keeping the hands steady is difficult when adrenaline is pumping through the body. So, for sports that have those types of requirements, the zone of optimal functioning is at lower levels of arousal, as seen in figure 1.5.

SUMMARY

Over the preceding pages, several theories that frame the study of anger and sport have been reviewed. Further, a vocabulary that challenges and replaces some of the previously used definitions was offered. This book is intended to be a challenge. I have devoted a great deal of time to thinking about, studying, and working with athletes who are dealing with anger. Although I know the subject well, my standing as an "expert"

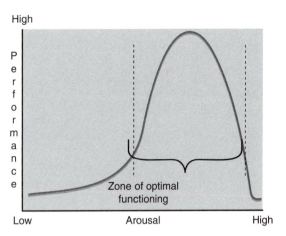

Figure 1.4 Shift of the zone of optimal functioning for tasks that require high intensity and fewer decisions. An example could be a defensive lineman rushing the quarterback which does not require complex cognitive functioning.

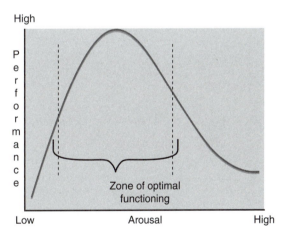

Figure 1.5 Shift of the zone of optimal functioning towards lower levels of arousal predicting higher performance. This is necessary for tasks that require fine motor coordination.

on this topic is partly the result of the fact that not many people talk about or study this issue. I challenge you to think about this issue and not take the views expressed as gospel, as the only way to look at these issues. This book is an attempt to be comprehensive, but you should recognize that it is not exhaustive. See this book as a springboard. Together, let us fill in the holes of knowledge that prevent us from fully understanding this complex topic.

THE SCOPE OF VIOLENCE AND AGGRESSION IN SPORT

As will be a theme throughout this book, the amount of attention that violence in sports gets is both impressive and dramatically amplified. Considering the frequency with which athlete transgressions hit the popular press, it should not be surprising that people become conditioned to the idea that athletes and violence go hand in hand. What further compounds this, however, is that there is history that accompanies this theme. It is not as if there was a short period of time that people were talking about sports propagating violence. The connection was made long ago. We will begin this chapter by reviewing the historical antecedents that have paved the way to society's current view of violence in sports.

This will lead into a review of publications where the author used his thesis (that athletes represent a criminal population) as a filter through which data was analyzed. That same data will be reviewed, offering alternative hypotheses as well as the challenges of studying violence in sports. Lastly, we will review some of the higher profile incidents where athletes were involved in aggression or violence. This will provide a springboard from which we can study the phenomenon and offer strategies to curb both the transgressions and the misperception that those transgressions occur more frequently amongst athletes.

HISTORICAL CONTEXT

Chapter 1 laid the theoretical groundwork to the topic of anger in sport. In this chapter we begin to set the context of the theme. One way to achieve this is to provide a historical perspective on the relationship between violence and sport.

The relationship between violence and sport is not new. From boxing, to chariot racing, to gladiators fighting to the death in the Roman Coliseum, violence and sport have long been intertwined. This chapter spans many domains and facets of violence in sport with the goal of establishing why this book is overdue. The hope is that a review of some of the big stories will serve as a springboard to the what, why, and how of anger management in sport.

A good place to start thinking about violence in sport is with Ty Cobb. In the infancy of America's pastime, baseball, Ty Cobb was the game's biggest star. He became the first player voted into the Hall of Fame, finished with a career .367 batting average, and once stole 96 bases in a season. But the fire in his belly that drove him to succeed also drove him to see other players as his enemies in a war. Irritable and belligerent, Cobb fought with fans and players on the opposing team several times during his career. He believed that violence was often justified, as some of his quotations show:

> *The base paths belonged to me, the runner. The rules gave me the right. I always went into a bag full of speed, feet first. I had sharp spikes on my shoes. If the baseman stood where he had no business to be and got hurt, that was his own fault.*

> *The great American game should be an unrelenting war of nerves.*

> *When I began playing the game, baseball was about as gentlemanly as a kick in the crotch.*

> *[Boston Red Sox pitcher Hub Leonard] would aim bullets at your head, left-handed to boot. . . . I dragged a bunt . . . which the first baseman was forced to field. Leonard sprinted for first to take the throw and saw that I was after him. He wouldn't have been safe that day if he'd scrambled into the top bleachers. I ignored the bag—since I was already out—and dove feet first right through the coaching box. He managed to duck, but . . . the escape was close enough medicine for him. He never threw another beanball at me.*

> *I had to fight all my life to survive. They were all against me . . . but I beat them and left them in the ditch.*

Ty Cobb was not concerned with sportsmanship. He was worried about performing his best and winning, sometimes at any cost. He was said to have practiced sliding until his legs were raw. But this drive led to success. Do we not want athletes to be driven? In fact we do, but we also need to teach them where to draw the line. This may be the single most confusing thing for young athletes. They are taught to be hungry and driven—almost to the point of "kill, kill, kill," but we do not spend enough time teaching them how to slow down and focus on the task at hand.

Incidentally, not all of Ty Cobb's behavior was rooted in anger. Some of it was deliberate and psychologically grounded. He was one of the first athletes to talk about how he mastered the mental side of the game. He would deliberately torment his opponents to gain the upper hand, as evidenced by this statement:

> *Most of all I was saddling that team with a psychological burden so that they would be muttering, Cobb is crazy. He'll run anytime and in any situation. It would help give them the jitters and they'd concentrate so much on me they were not paying any attention to the business at hand. My failures rarely were complete failures. They were more like future investments.*

To this day, bench-clearing brawls occur in baseball at least once a year. Whether they stem from "chin music," a ball close to a batter's head, or an attempt to injure another player with a hard slide, violence springs up on the diamond with alarming regularity. When you think about intimidating athletes, you would probably include the likes of Roger Clemens and Bob Gibson, who could throw up and in at nearly 100 miles per hour (160 kilometers per hour) to remind the batter who owned the inside part of the plate.

Football—better described as a collision sport than a contact sport—features bone-crushing hits with great regularity. The number of injuries that football players incur is startling, yet players still love the game. And many of them love to hit. Whether they like the feeling of intimidating the opposing team and gaining the upper hand or simply enjoy the feeling of supremacy when they physically dominate their opponent, hitting is a part of the game that they enjoy. Likewise, many fans appreciate the sound of one player being demolished by another.

Here too it can get out of control. We ask football players to destroy their opponents, but they may not realize that turning it off is not easy. When a linebacker is reinforced for flattening a tailback coming around the corner, why should we assume that he would be able to stop himself in his tracks after the quarterback releases the ball so as avoid hitting him? Players face a stimulus differentiation problem. In a matter of seconds, the player is asked to go from full steam ahead to pulling up or avoiding the target at the last second. I am not implying that football players are intellectually slow, but to assume that all football players have the processing speed to make the correct decision in a small amount of time might be unrealistic. The inability to do so could cause the player thousands of dollars. Making the correct decision quickly is not easy, but it is necessary. It is in the rules, but it is not easy. Moreover, it would not be a difficult stretch to realize that for some athletes, being reinforced for aggression in one arena may make it more difficult to curb themselves in another. It could lead one to hypothesize whether athletes may be at greater risk for involvement in abusive relationships as a result.

Football has a very rich history of considering the impact of violence on sport. At the turn of the century, violent play in football grew to such proportions that President Theodore Roosevelt took an interest. In 1905, 18 deaths and 159 serious injuries occurred in college football. The president called representatives from Harvard, Princeton, and Yale together to discuss the issue. This meeting led to the formation of the Intercollegiate Athletic Association of the United States (IAAUS) to regulate the rules of football. Football was almost abolished. In 1910 this organization changed its name to the NCAA (Fleisher, Goff, & Tollison, 1986). So the very organization that governs collegiate sport was originally instituted to curb violence in football. Here we are in 2010, and the NCAA does not have a plan in place to keep violence on and off the field to a minimum.

Hockey—how do we even discuss hockey in the context of violence? In the pro game, fighting, although it is outside the rules, is a predictable and accepted part of the game. Not always based on angry, reactive aggression, fights are often deliberately provoked to intimidate the opponent or provide a spark to teammates.

Despite studies that have shown that the number of penalties that a team gets (both violent and nonviolent penalties) is inversely proportional to hockey success, you can bet that fighting will remain part of the game.

Fighting, especially in hockey and baseball, may be purposely used to intimidate opponents. As a planned part of the game, coaches may be willing to sacrifice certain players or penalties in order to gain the mental upper hand.
©Gary Rothstein/Icon SMI

Fighting occurs because the "goons" must protect the skilled players, and some coaches are willing to sacrifice one of their less-talented players by having him attempt to take out an opposing star, even if it costs the team a penalty or even a game misconduct.

Fighting increased steadily until the 1980s, when Wayne Gretzky arrived and changed the NHL. At that time, on average more than one fight per game occurred. The "Great One" was extremely quick and skillful, but he was only 6 feet (183 centimeters) tall and weighed about 185 pounds (84 kilograms). If not for the protection of Mark Messier and Marty McSorley, Gretzky's numbers might not have been so gaudy.

The NHL started instituting rules such as the third-man-in rule in 1977, which gave an automatic ejection to the first player to join a fight already in process. The instigator rule added an additional two-minute penalty to any player who started a fight, and two violations in a game became grounds for ejection. Although some alarming incidents have occurred in hockey (Marty McSorley, Todd Bertuzzi), the number of fights has fallen to just over 0.61 per game, the lowest total since the 1976–77 season.

Former New York Rangers head coach Colin Campbell, currently the NHL's executive vice president and director of hockey operation, has been identified as the league's discipline czar. His task is to mete out appropriate sanctions for transgressions that go beyond the NHL's limits. Even with Campbell in place, the number of fights increased from 2007 to 2008. According to hockey-fights.com, a Web site that keeps track of fights (the NHL does not release fight-related statistics), 351 fights had occurred during the 2008–09 season as of December 28, 2008, up from 308 over the same period the previous year. Colin Campbell, commenting in the *New York Times* article that reported the findings of the Web site, said that stick fouls such as cross-checking and slashing were down substantially but admitted that fighting had increased. Fighting "is considered a safety valve," he said. So even those charged with curbing violence must sometimes admit that reversing the upward trend is difficult.

With that historical context and the theoretical underpinnings laid out in chapter 1, the stage is set for the discussion of the perception that people have about athletes and violence. Although discussion of the media's reactions to athletes' transgressions appears throughout the book, we will initiate the examination by reviewing the writing of Jeffrey Benedict.

Most of you will not recognize this name. He is not an athlete, and he has not been arrested for attacking an athlete. He is, in fact, a lawyer, an author, and the former research director at Northeastern University's Center for the Study of Sport in Society. He conducted the nation's first study on student–athletes' violence against women on college campuses, developed a database for tracking athletes accused of crimes against women, and has proposed policy changes related to athletes' violence against women.

He has written four books about the topic:

1. *Athletes and Acquaintance Rape* (Sage Publications, 1998)
2. *Public Heroes, Private Felons: Athletes and Crimes Against Women* (Northeastern University Press, 1997)
3. *Pros and Cons: The Criminals Who Play in the NFL* (coauthored with Don Yaeger, Warner Books, 1998)
4. *Out of Bounds: Inside the NBA's Culture of Rape, Violence, and Crime* (Harper Collins Publishers, 2004)

When I first read Benedict's work, I had mixed feelings. On the one hand, it was apparent to me that he had an agenda. His position was that athletes are involved with violence and crime at a rate disproportionate to that of nonathletes, and that they get away with it. Furthermore, the athlete culture supports this misconduct. Although I did not agree with the conclusion, I was impressed with the amount of energy that he put into the research for these books. He accumulated a great deal of data and offered compelling evidence to prove his case; after all, he is a lawyer.

He described the sundry ways in which the NFL tried to interfere with his research and the publication of *Pros and Cons*, and discussed the obstacles that he encountered when investigating cases. He demonstrated courage in completing the project. One wonders why both sides would invest so much if his position did not contain a central truth.

Nonetheless, I took umbrage with his conclusions and sought to challenge or clarify some of them. What follows is my analysis of the data provided in *Pros and Cons* and my commentary on the related issues. I do not believe that Benedict was entirely wrong. To the contrary, on some issues he was right on the money. Athletes are arrested for doing bad things, and many of them get off. My contention is that their escaping prosecution is related more to the reality that the judicial system is overwhelmed and that plea bargains are accepted with regularity to avoid going to trial. As entertainers, athletes often can afford high-powered attorneys. And, of course, most athletes never become involved with the law.

The actual statistics on the number of athletes who commit acts of violence are limited. In their 1998 book *Pros and Cons: The Criminals Who Play*, Benedict and coauthor Don Yaeger estimated that approximately 21 percent of the players in the NFL had been charged with a serious crime. They defined serious crimes as offenses ranging from driving under the influence to murder. Of those, 53 percent were for traditionally violent crimes: assault, sex crimes, domestic violence, and murder. Only 16 percent of those charged were convicted. The remainder either plea-bargained, were acquitted, or had their charges dropped.

Further examination showed that of the 1,590 NFL players who played in the 1996–97 season, only 509 were researched regarding criminal history. Of those, 109 were found to have been charged with a serious crime. Thus, the 21 percent figure reported was based on analysis of only one-third of the total NFL population. If you look at the total population, only 7 percent were charged with a serious crime. This distinction is salient because statistics presented in different ways can provide different pictures. Do you extrapolate the 21 percent figure to the athletes for whom no data are available, or do you consider the 109 found and compare that number to the entire population of 1,590 players? Your viewpoint will likely determine which way you present the data.

In reviewing Benedict's data, I found some interesting points that athletes, coaches, owners, and agents should be aware of, not to damn the players, but to educate them about the realities of the legal process, even among "protected" members of society. Table 2.1 breaks down the 265 charges that Benedict's research team found. Of the 109 players found to have criminal records, almost all of them had multiple charges, which explains the discrepancy between the numbers. Note as well that when a person is arrested for a crime that transcends numerous laws, the suspect often receives multiple charges. Those charges may be tried individually or combined, or some of them may be thrown out for redundancy. This procedure varies by state, by the amount of evidence that the prosecutors have to support each charge, or by other variables. In addition, if found guilty for multiple charges and incarcerated, a criminal may serve a sentence concurrently (three counts of assault, each receiving 5-year a sentence, can be served at one time) or consecutively (each charge must be served individually, resulting in a 15-year sentence in the same situation).

Table 2.1 Crimes and Results of the Judicial Process

	Sex crimes	Assault	Domestic violence	Theft	Drug related	Homicide or murder	Trespass	Other	Total
Convicted	1	9	3	3	15	0	2	9	42
Plea bargained	11	29	10	4	18	0	5	8	85
Acquitted	4	10	2	1	3	1	2	2	25
Dismissed or dropped	7	19	10	7	6	3	3	9	64
Other	1	15	6	4	14	0	1	8	49
Totals	24	82	31	19	56	4	13	36	265

I grouped the crimes into categories based on a review of the authors' analysis. The last category, "other," represents crimes that do not easily fit into the other categories. These crimes may or may not be violent. Some charges that went into the "other" category included gun charges, eluding, fraud, threatening a witness, perjury, and vandalism.

A couple of trends jump out right away. First, if you group sex crimes, assault, domestic violence, and homicide or murder into a category of violent crimes, together they represent 53 percent of the charges. Thus, more than half of athletes' arrests are related to violence.

Second, with regard to those violent offenses, the conviction rate was only 9 percent. Technically, one could conclude that 91 percent of those arrested were innocent. But that conclusion rests on faulty logic. In our legal system, a person is innocent until proved guilty, and the person is proved guilty only when convicted. A person who plea-bargains is not exactly admitting guilt to the crime but is willing to plead guilty to a lesser charge for any of a number of reasons:

1. The person may in fact be guilty of the higher offense and is willing to accept a lesser sentence in exchange for the poor press and resultant expenses (e.g., legal fees and lost revenues in abandoned sponsorship monies) that go into a long, drawn-out, public trial.
2. The person may be concerned that as more information (including research, time, and stress) goes into the process, the stakes may become higher.
3. The defendant's lawyers may recommend making a deal because the person could be found guilty and the result could be harsh.

If we include plea bargains with convictions, the proportion of those considered guilty reaches 47 percent. Conclusion: A person arrested for a violent crime will be found guilty of something, even a lesser crime that the person pleas to, almost half the time. Further, the charges are dropped or dismissed only 28 percent of the time, and acquittal occurs about 9 percent of the time. What this tells athletes is that if there is sufficient reason to be arrested and charged, they should not count on the charges disappearing. This conclusion challenges the idea that good legal representation causes legal problems to vanish. A good attorney may prevent conviction or heavy jail time, but is risking an arrest really worth the gamble? The only way to win this game is not to play; a lesson that someone like Michael Vick might have preferred to know prior to his legal troubles.

Examining all the charges together does not produce different results. With all charges, a conviction or plea bargain is the result in 49 percent of the cases and charges are dropped in only 24 percent of the cases.

Another interesting finding is related to the common perception of people in the sport world that sex crimes are falsely reported. Many studies have analyzed whether rape is falsely reported. The number most often sited by the FBI's studies is 8 percent.

Often, the statistics used depend on the theoretical position of the author. Some authors who take a strongly feminist stance, such as Susan Brownmiller in her book *Against Our Will*, report that the number of false accusations of rape is as low as 2 percent. Responding "men's groups," who include cases in which the charges are "unfounded" (which means that the evidence to proceed with a case is insufficient, which is not the same as a false report), argue that the rate of false reports is as high as 50 percent; which is no doubt overinflated.

Jim Hines, formerly the male outreach coordinator at Michigan State University's Safe Place, a program to provide safety and support for victims of domestic violence, summarized the data concerning the variability of such estimates. He noted that about 1 in 10 rape reports is false, when all the various studies are considered. He also noted that only 1 in 3 rapes is reported. Thus, for every false report, about 29 rapes occur.

Hines' data is also an estimate, though an important one. Even if we consider some inflation of false reports because of the fame and money of professional athletes, we are still talking about a great many legitimate victims. Based on Benedict and Yaeger's information, the charges are dropped or dismissed in about 30 percent of the cases and acquittal is the result in 17 percent of the cases. A conviction or a plea bargain is the result 50 percent of the time. See figures 2.1, 2.2, 2.3, 2.4, and 2.5 for more information.

The conclusions made in *Pros and Cons* have limited generalizability. We do not know whether the same dynamics are at work in other sports and at other levels. Although Benedict explores these issues in *Out of Bounds*, focused on

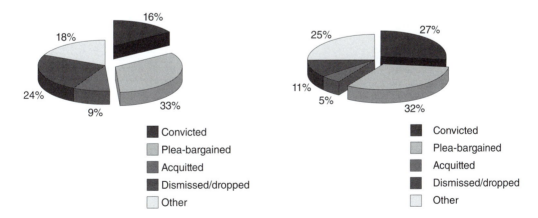

Figure 2.1 Outcome of all charges filed against NFL athletes.

Data from J. Benedict and D. Yaeger, 1998, *Pros and cons: The criminals who play in the NFL* (New York: Warner Books, Inc).

Figure 2.2 Drug-related crimes broken down by outcome.

Data from J. Benedict and D. Yaeger, 1998, *Pros and cons: The criminals who play in the NFL* (New York: Warner Books, Inc).

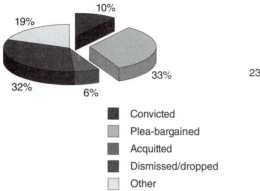

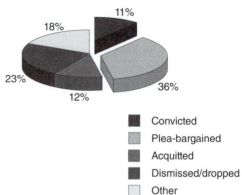

Figure 2.3 Domestic violence broken down by outcome.

Data from J. Benedict and D. Yaeger, 1998, *Pros and cons: The criminals who play in the NFL* (New York: Warner Books, Inc).

Figure 2.4 Assault broken down by outcome.

Data from J. Benedict and D. Yaeger, 1998, *Pros and cons: The criminals who play in the NFL* (New York: Warner Books, Inc).

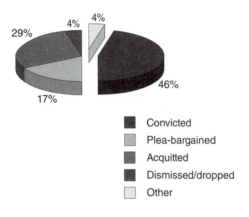

Figure 2.5 Sex crimes broken down by outcome.

Data from J. Benedict and D. Yaeger, 1998, *Pros and cons: The criminals who play in the NFL* (New York: Warner Books, Inc).

basketball, and *Public Heroes, Private Felons*, which predates *Pros and Cons* and examines other sports as well, in both books the examination is more anecdotal than statistical.

Benedict did report that he received considerable resistance when trying to complete his research, specifically from NFL personnel. He and Yaeger reported that a private investigator hired by the NFL visited one of their graduate students at his fraternity house when he was not there to explore the student's intentions in working on *Pros and Cons*. Benedict and Yaeger also expected that the NFL would criticize the book as perpetuating racial stereotypes because most athletes in professional sport (at least football and basketball) are black.

Concerned about that criticism, they asked several experts on race to weigh in, among them Reverend Jesse Jackson and Minnesota Supreme Court Justice Alan Page, former Viking and a member of the NFL's Hall of Fame. The experts all stated the obvious—that the relationship between race and criminality is, and has been for a long time, inappropriately raised to justify differences in treatment.

Jesse Jackson was quoted as saying, "Crime is not a function of race; crime is the function of sociology and psychology, your environment, and your mind-set. While race does not cause people to commit crime, the absence of any real consequences does" (Benedict & Yaeger, 1998, p. 169). Jackson proceeds to explain how minorities are exploited in sport:

> *Men being used who come out of very desperate straits, having extraordinary, exploitable, commercial talent. They are put on a pedestal in high school . . . are recruited for top colleges. Students who score 1,200 on the SATs and make straight As can't get in, yet some of the athletes get in with lower scores and study less difficult subject matter. These guys have been exploited from the time it was obvious they could jump higher and run faster. . . . Once their use is gone, they are no longer protected.*

Jackson's statement reminds me of what a black (specifically not wanting to be identified as African American because his parents were proudly from St. Thomas) two-sport star player (football and basketball) told me. When I asked about his consideration of colleges in middle America like Nebraska or Oklahoma, he retorted, "Are you kidding me? If I tear up my knee or something, I will just be another n----- (racial epithet) they'll be looking to lynch. A city kid like me has no business being out there." Although he may have been developing reasons not to pursue those schools for fear of being rejected, he was certainly aware of athletes of color being exploited while they could score touchdowns and hit winning shots but having their value questioned should those abilities dissipate for any reason.

Jackson also noted that those athletes who "are the most commercially exploitable are [also] taught to live with the least amount of social responsibility." He expands this idea to explain that "when they are no longer playing, these players often crash. There is a 75 percent divorce rate. Guys who made all kinds of money can't get a job. Drugs and liquor become anesthesia for their pain, and some get caught selling it."

From my experience, I have seen sport be a wonderful equalizer of racial divides. Although a few bigots out there will always find a reason to hate any given person, sport celebrity transcends color, age, and belief. Athletes like Michael Jordan (African American), Carlos Delgado (Hispanic), Yao Ming (Chinese), Sandy Koufax (Jewish), and Tiger Woods (Cablinasian, a term that he made up reflecting his Caucasian, black, American Indian, and Asian heritage—his father is of black, Chinese, and Native American ancestry, and his mother is of Thai, Chinese, and Dutch lineage), have been adored worldwide. They have become the heroes of our generation and certainly do not project images of violence.

Given the way in which Benedict depicted athletes and the organizations that employ them, it should be no surprise that others have come to the same conclusion—that athletes are a privileged bunch and that they are protected when they do something bad. By reviewing some of the incidents that have been covered by the media, you will see that the transgressions of some athletes have been alarming. The thesis of this book is that athletes have problems with their anger, as do most people, but that athletes are no more violent than the general population. The problem arises from the fact that the media often do not report on nonathletes who engage in criminal behavior but are ready to report the news when athletes transgress. The following section provides reported athlete behavior. You have probably heard about some of the incidents; others you may not know about. Athletes should be aware that these highly publicized cases have caused considerable concern. Because athletes are unlikely to get the benefit of the doubt, they need to do a better job of not winding up in a headline in the first place.

ATHLETES AND VIOLENCE MAKE GREAT NEWS

In the following pages, I will review some of the most notable cases of violence in sport over the past years. The list is not exhaustive, but it should provide some perspective on these behaviors. For the record, let me state that I did not directly interview any of the parties involved. My opinions are based on viewing the footage, reading the reports, or hearing the description of the events. My goal is not to be judgmental. Any conclusions that I make should be seen as preliminary and made without all the data. I hope to shed some light on the athletes' experiences, the seriousness of the problem, and the need for the interventions discussed later in this book. Similarly, I invite anyone who has more knowledge about the event to correct me and share with me his or her views because I believe that we need to talk a great deal more about these situations, not for the sake of sensationalism but for the sake of understanding and preventing serious injury. Finally, pay attention to the details. These incidents vary widely in type and intent; in many cases we can only hypothesize about the intent of the participants. As you are reading the stories, ask yourself how these situations could have been prevented. What you will likely conclude is that for some of the people, impulsivity was involved. Those who had difficulty controlling themselves may be excellent candidates for anger management. Others may believe that the criminal behavior they were involved in was OK and that they are above the law. Those individuals are poor candidates for treatment because the violent behavior is egosyntonic for them. They are comfortable with it, believe it is justified, and are exceedingly unlikely to be willing to change their ways. We want to be able to identify the athletes who may benefit from treatment so that we can focus our resources on them and, even more important, identify those who may be at risk and provide proactive programming before an episode occurs.

Youth Sport Gone Wrong

An incident in April 2005 demonstrated how youth sport could go tragically wrong. A 13-year-old boy killed another teen with a baseball bat after a Pony League game in southern California. The victim, 15-year-old Jeremy Rourke, was struck in the knee and head as he and the assailant waited in line at the concession stand after the game. It was reported that Rourke was a known bully who intimidated other youngsters. On this day he picked on a scared young man who fought back. That young man will be in prison until he is 25 years old. Was this murder about baseball? Not directly, apparently. Baseball was just part of the scenery in this particular case of youth violence backfiring on a bully. Nonetheless, I am convinced that it would not have received as much press if it had not happened at a baseball game.

In July 2000 a horrific circumstance unfolded in front of children's watching eyes as two hockey fathers fought and one died. Thomas Junta went to pick up his son and two of his friends from a local hockey rink in Reading, Massachusetts. When he got there, he did not like what he saw. He reported that Michael Costin was refereeing a pickup game and allowing too much roughhousing. A confrontation between the two eventually ensued, which culminated in the 275-pound (125-kilogram) Junta pinning Costin to the floor and punching him, all as children were watching. Costin never got up and died two days later. It was reported that both Junta and Costin had histories of violence including allegations of domestic violence and restraining orders aplenty. The victim seemingly had the worse history. The result was that Costin's four children, whom he was raising alone, were orphaned.

Was this incident about hockey? Who cares? It occurred around kids who were playing a sport. We must protect our kids from seeing these types of things. When parents attend sport events, they must remember that children are watching. I have seen many sport psychologists struggle with recommendations for leagues and coaches about parent involvement. On the one hand, we want parents to be involved and share in the experience with their children. On the other hand, some become intrusive and interfere with what the coach is doing. In still other cases, parents are all too quick to drop off their children at practice, in the responsible hands of another adult, so that they can go do what they want with some free time. The issue is complex, but it does not take a psychologist to know that parents who cannot check their behavior at levels far below the hostility displayed in the preceding case should not be anywhere near a sport event.

High School and College—Training Grounds

As the level of competition goes up, the pressure increases and, I hypothesize, so does the likelihood of violent acting out. What is interesting, though, is that violence seems to be a predictable proving ground for young bodies who are getting to know their new friend, testosterone (I am referring to puberty here, not steroids). We see violence not only in the heat of battle but also in social settings and in hazing.

Before we discuss hazing on sport teams, let me remind you that sport was not the lens that focused hazing on our collective consciousness. Although it has been defined in many ways, a simple and accurate definition of hazing is "intentionally or recklessly engaging in an act that endangers the health or safety of a student for the purpose of initiation into an organization."

Fraternities and sororities have been widely known for their hazing practices. Although much of the hazing that occurs in Greek life has been driven underground, hazing is prevalent in sport as well, where it has greater visibility.

When considering how to decrease hazing, one might wonder who should be held accountable. I believe that the people who engage in the act need to get the brunt of the consequences. At the same time, the adults involved in any organization are responsible for creating a culture that has no tolerance for such behavior.

In March 2005 a hazing incident in Florida led to the resignation of a baseball coach. Apparently, members of the Big Walnut High School (Columbus, Ohio) baseball team were in Florida for a preseason training camp (one of the more likely settings for these events). Although it may not have demonstrated any premeditation, the older players used a paddle that they had made in shop class to spank other players. This incident led to the suspension of eight players. The coach, who believed that the school blew the situation out of proportion, resigned, stating that he wanted to take responsibility so as to avoid damaging the program. Exemplifying a common theme, many parents responded with hostility to the sanctioning, stating that the paddling incident was just harmless fun.

The granddaddy of hazing incidents in sport occurred in August 2003 when Mepham High School (Bellmore, New York) football players attended training camp in rural Pennsylvania. More than 20 felony charges resulted from events that took place over several nights at camp. In attacks reminiscent of the Abner Louima case, at least three members of the team aged 15 to 17 rubbed mineral ice on broomsticks, pinecones, and golf balls and used those items to penetrate freshman players anally while the rest of the boys in the cabin bore witness.

Rumor had it that Mepham High School was steeped in a tradition of such hazing and that the head coach was tolerant of the practice. When the football season was cancelled, members of the community were incensed because the team was interwoven into its fabric. Instead of being concerned for the victims, people subjected them to a second round of abuse. They were taunted as "fags" and "broomstick boys." Some of them may have enjoyed it, one student offered. They were the guilty parties, the reason why the season was canceled. The three young men who would never be able to forget what happened to them, one of whom required surgery to repair the damage, were seen as the provocateurs. "I will never trust anyone again. They did not come to help me," said one of the victims.

Parents who stood up to show support for the victims and their families received profanity-laced letters that threatened the same brutality that the victims received if they did not keep quiet.

What was the response of the school? Coach McElroy responded, "We as coaches do not see this incident as hazing . . . but as a criminal act." The kids were responsible, not the school and not the coaches. Considering that the Abner Louima case eventually settled for $8.75 million, if the school district had been held accountable, the financial penalty would have been devastating.

Both sides have supporters. Some state that Coach McElroy was like a father figure who was a mentor to his players; others state that he had allowed this type of hazing for years.

Could they both be right? Assuming that the former is true and that Coach Mac (as he was called by everyone) was caught up in the bad behavior of a couple of out-of-control players, the episode should be a lesson to all coaches. Whether they believe that low-level hazing has a team-building aspect (this is not my position, though I do believe that the threshold of what is considered hazing is a moving target that sometimes lassoes benign acts that I would not consider hazing) or are adamantly opposed to it, coaches must be mindful that their livelihood could rest on the shoulders (and actions) of their players. For this reason, coaches must be proactive about hazing, not just as a risk management tool to prevent legal liability but because hazing activity may change the lives of everyone involved for the worse.

Criminal Behavior of the Stars

College athletes have been involved in plenty of criminal incidents, although they do not always receive the publicity that their richer, more famous professional counterparts do. Some college stars have never reached the next level because of their behavior, and some have crashed and burned as a result.

Hakim Hill, a star high school running back in Iowa who for one year led Arizona State in rushing, was suspended in his freshman year in 2005 for trouble that he ran into in high school. He was convicted of driving while intoxicated and stealing paint ball equipment. Hill also faced third-degree sexual assault charges, a case that was later settled as serious misdemeanor assault causing injury as part of a plea agreement, although Hill did not admit guilt. Hill was eventually booted from ASU after violating team rules. Northern Iowa was willing to look past the events and give Hill a second chance, being a local product and all. Hill did not even make it to spring practice after he was arrested at a Sheraton Hotel in downtown Iowa City for fighting with police officers and threatening to kill their families. Apparently inebriated at the time, he resisted arrest by refusing to be handcuffed and kicking the officers trying to subdue him. That this young man would act this way was not surprising. He had been in trouble before. Some can be saved by football; others cannot. Coaches and administrators may ignore a criminal history and use a young person's athletic prowess to improve their records. If sport truly involves character, it cannot be a selective, convenient proposition.

One of the most bizarre stories seen in sport was the Mike Danton murder-for-hire case. Although much speculation has occurred, probably only the participants understand the whole story.

On April 16, 2004, St. Louis Blues forward Mike Danton was arrested for planning the murder of his agent David Frost. Danton had reportedly contacted a friend of his, Katie Wolfmeyer, 19, whom the FBI said had signed a confession and cooperated with them to provide details about the plot. The plan was for the victim to be killed in what would look like a botched burglary. At the time of the contact, Danton was in San Jose with his team, Wolfmeyer was in Missouri, and the hit man was in Illinois. Supposedly the hit man was to be paid $10,000 for the murder.

The whirlwind of speculation surrounding the crime included commentary about Danton's upbringing, his friends, and the people who were running his hockey career. Rumors touched on homosexuality, promiscuity, substance abuse, and child neglect. Most of the story remains a mystery, or at the very least is not completely substantiated. Police reported that on at least three occasions over the six months before his arrest, Danton tried to hire a hit man to murder Frost.

Some believed that Danton was paranoid because of drugs that he was abusing. Frost said that the hit man was a product of Danton's deluded mind, adding that Danton was not thinking straight because he was depressed and on pain medication and sleeping pills. Frost described Danton as a good kid who needed psychiatric help. Others thought that Danton's plan was a rebellion against the mind control that Frost seemed to exhibit over many of his players. Danton's parents accused Frost of being a monster and manipulator who turned young hockey players away from their families to establish their careers in minor hockey. Mike and his parents, who had the surname Jefferson, had problems of their own. Mike had reportedly changed his name to distance himself from his parents, who were supposedly abusive themselves.

Danton's story caused such controversy that it may hasten adoption of rule changes for a Canadian junior hockey system that sends 15-year-old players away from home and parental guidance. The NHL Players Association was also criticized for certifying Frost as an agent despite their knowing that he was an outcast in the junior league after pleading guilty to slugging a player during a game. Sorting out what was what in this case is difficult. Danton seemed troubled. According to the FBI, Danton said that he set up the plot because he feared for his life.

Frost seemed almost maniacal in his control of his players and denied that Danton wanted him killed, but the result was a conviction. On November 8, Danton was sentenced to seven and a half years in prison.

An excellent book on the topic of sexual assault and abuse in Canadian hockey is Laura Robinson's *Crossing the Line: Violence and Sexual Assault in Canada's National Sport*. For more on the topic of coaches' sexual harassment not specific to hockey, please review the work of Dr. Celia Brackenridge and an up-and-comer in the field, Dr. Joy Bringer.

Murder in Waco

In one of the scariest scenarios in recent memory, Patrick Dennehy, who played for Baylor University's basketball team, was murdered by teammate Carlton Dotson. Amidst the scandal, some people failed to appreciate the tragedy of a young athlete's death. Baylor basketball coach Dave Bliss and athletics director Tom Stanton resigned after school investigators reportedly discovered that Bliss was involved in helping two players receive improper financial aid and that staff members did not properly report failed drug tests. One of the players who received the improper financial aid, which apparently was payment of part of his tuition by boosters, was Patrick Dennehy. Baylor's religious orientation only made things more complicated.

NCAA president Myles Brand felt the need to address the situation and described the season as a "crime wave" and "the worst situation I've ever heard of in college sports." He insisted, however, that the vast majority of schools, coaches, and student–athletes abided by the rules.

"I find the current situation abhorrent," Brand told the *Daily News*. "But let's not automatically assume college sports is filled with bad actors. We can't let the bad apples tarnish our view of college sports."

At Baylor, in the weeks after Dennehy's body was discovered, a university panel found that coach Dave Bliss violated the NCAA limit on scholarships by paying tuition bills and other expenses for the slain player and a teammate. Failed drug tests were not reported, and Baylor investigators learned that Bliss secretly videotaped visiting teams' workouts at the university arena, a violation of Big 12 rules. The coach was later taped trying to persuade others to portray Dennehy as a drug dealer rather than the recipient of under-the-table payments from the coaching staff.

"I thought I'd seen it all," said Indiana University professor Murray Sperber, the author of *Beer and Circuses* and several other books about college sports, "but what Bliss did is a new low" (T.J. Quinn, *New York Daily News*, August 3, 2003).

Baylor University became the recipient of appropriate criticism, but the timing of the discovery of the scandal could not have been worse, especially because it had nothing to do with Dennehy's death. Many people were distracted from the heinous crime that took place that only Dotson knows the true reasons for.

His defense attorney stated that Dotson was paranoid and believed that people were trying to kill him. He thought that Dennehy was going to kill him, so he had to act preemptively. It was reported that Dotson told the FBI that he was Jesus, the son of God, and that he confessed because a higher power told him to do so.

People who are truly paranoid may indeed act in response to beliefs that are not based in reality, but Dotson's mental status came under scrutiny when the medical examiner's report showed that the victim's wounds were likely not caused by Dotson's having to act in self-defense. The victim was shot twice: once near his right ear and the other in the back of his head. Dotson was initially found incompetent to stand trial and was sent to a mental hospital. His competency was restored, but he was advised to keep taking antipsychotic medication. If the violence was in fact caused by psychotic process, staying on medications to prevent further violence would be prudent. A forensic psychologist, however, reported that Dotson's claims of auditory and visual hallucinations were suspect, implying that Dotson likely fabricated them to escape culpability. His attorneys later decided not to use an insanity defense, and Dotson pled guilty, resulting in a 35-year sentence.

Dotson's mother, Gilreatha Stoltzfus, who shook hands with Dennehy's relatives in the court room and urged her son to plead guilty, said that Baylor should be held responsible for not supervising the athletes more closely.

A Myriad of Offenses

Any attempt to read the sports pages or surf the Internet without coming across incidents of athletes' transgressions is increasingly futile. Every time I sat down to write a chapter of this book, another story broke and I had to decide whether it was severe enough or significant enough to include in the book.

Maurice Clarett, the Ohio State tailback who sat out the 2003 season after he was charged with filing a false police report claiming that more than $10,000 in property was stolen from a car he had borrowed from a car dealership, reported that coach Jim Tressel arranged for players to receive free cars, improper academic assistance, and cash (which the NCAA could not corroborate). Clarett dropped out of Ohio State and then challenged the NFL's requirement that players wait three years after high school before turning pro. The case went all the way to the Supreme Court before Clarett lost. He was eventually drafted in the third round by the Denver Broncos in 2005 but was cut in August. Clarett was arrested in December 2005, accused of brandishing a gun while attempting to rob a man and a woman in Columbus, Ohio. Acquiring other charges along the way, Clarett accepted a plea agreement and was sentenced to seven and a half years in prison in September 2006.

Marcus Vick, the younger brother of Atlanta Falcons quarterback Michael Vick, and a talented quarterback in his own right for Virginia Tech, was given one more chance to compete after a litany of criminal allegations. These included a conviction of contributing to the delinquency of a minor stemming from a drinking party with underage girls (which originally included a sexual offense charge), suspension of his license after he pleaded guilty to reckless driving and no contest to marijuana possession, and a misdemeanor charge for driving with a suspended license. Vick was allowed to return to play if he steered clear of trouble. After being greeted with "Rapist" chants at a 2005 game, he reciprocated with an obscene finger gesture. Vick was later caught on film during a replay of the Gator Bowl against Louisville, where he was seen to be deliberately stomping on the leg of defensive end Elvis Dumervil.

When accused, Vick claimed that he apologized. Dumervil told reporters that he never received an apology and described Vick as "a no-character individual." Because he violated the university's trust, Vick was permanently dismissed from the Hokies. Almost immediately, he declared that he intended to enter the NFL draft. Less than a week later, he was arrested and charged with pulling a gun on three teenagers during an altercation in a restaurant parking lot. He was charged with three misdemeanor counts of brandishing a firearm and was released on $10,000 bond.

What Is a Little Saliva Among Friends?

Few actions show more disrespect to a person than spitting on him or her. Accident, you say? Not likely.

Back in 1996, what may have been the inaugural event of an athlete's spitting occurred when second baseman Roberto Alomar, then playing for the Baltimore Orioles, spat in umpire John Hirschbeck's face while arguing a called third strike. His punishment was a five-game suspension that was not enforced until the following year.

In December 1997, linebacker Bill Romanowski, then of the Denver Broncos, spat on 49ers wide receiver J.J. Stokes. His punishment was a $7,500 fine.

In December 2000, Raiders defensive lineman Regan Upshaw spat in the face of Steelers punter Josh Miller. His punishment was a $29,000 fine.

In January 2006, during a playoff game between the Redskins and the Tampa Bay Buccaneers, then Skins safety Sean Taylor was ejected and penalized for unsportsmanlike conduct for spitting in the face of Tampa Bay running back Michael Pittman (who himself had been arrested for domestic violence). The punishment was a $17,000 fine. The offense was not Taylor's first; he had been investigated the previous year for allegedly spitting at Cincinnati wide receiver T.J. Houshmandzadeh.

An angry response is almost guaranteed when someone is spit on. In the incident just described, Joe Theismann, the ESPN analyst for the game, berated Pittman for swinging at Taylor. Earlier in the broadcast, Theismann had informed the audience that Joe Gibbs wanted only high-character guys on his team. When the replay showed Pittman slapping Taylor, Theismann and the other commentators, Paul Maguire and Mike Patrick, went on a tirade; it was a disgrace, they said. They swore that the officials got it all wrong and even demanded a change in NFL rules to allow the replay booth to overrule the call on the field. Disregarding the fact that referee Mike Carey was right there in the middle of the whole exchange and had ejected Taylor for the sharing of bodily fluids, they implied that Taylor was the victim, probably because of his past. "Sean Taylor has had his problems, but if he's being ejected for this, it's wrong!" Patrick said.

Moments later, the ESPN commentators were informed of what had actually taken place, that Taylor's flag and ejection were due to his spitting on Pittman. Not a word was heard from the team of commentators. No apology for getting it wrong, nothing.

Now that is not to say that it was OK for Pittman to raise his hands to another player. He probably should have received a flag too (two wrongs do not make a right), but the ref, in the heat of the moment, believed that Taylor's behavior was so egregious that Pittman's response was understandable. Grown men, professional athletes, spitting on each other—that is a problem.

The Big Cases

The big cases involve big crimes. Probably the four biggest criminal cases involving athletes were the murder trials of O.J. Simpson, Rae Carruth, and Ray Lewis, and the rape trial of Kobe Bryant.

Regardless of his propensity for always being in the right place at the right time on the football field, on January 31, 2000, following a Super Bowl party in Atlanta, Ray Lewis found himself in the wrong place at the wrong time. He was arrested along with two of his friends, Reginald Oakley and Joseph Sweeting, for the murders of Jacinth Baker and Richard Lollar. Baker and Lollar were stabbed to death outside a nightclub during a fight. To avoid prosecution, Lewis agreed to testify against his friends in exchange for his guilty plea to a lesser misdemeanor charge of obstruction of justice. He received a one-year probation for this plea.

It was reported that the Atlanta Police Department and district attorney's office believed that Lewis' associates were guilty, but because of inconsistencies in the reports of witnesses, conviction was difficult. Note that one witness who a friend of the two victims stated that the fight was initiated when Baker hit Oakley in the head with a champagne bottle. Some reports also stated that the Ravens linebacker funded Baker and Lollar's high-priced legal representation. They were found not guilty in June 2000.

Four years later Lewis reached a financial settlement of at least $1 million to settle the pending civil case with the four-year-old daughter of Richard Lollar, India, who was born shortly after her father's death. A suit filed by Baker's family had been settled previously, although the terms were not disclosed.

The lessons of the story are that (a) any involvement in a violent incident can cost a lot of money, even if a person is innocent, and (b) professional athletes, because they are celebrities, should surround themselves with people who will keep them out of trouble, not escalate situations.

I believe that the most significant factor in athletes and other celebrities being found not guilty of crimes (whether they are guilty or not) is not the color of their skin, not which sport they play, or, for that matter, not the facts of the case. The key element is the quality of the legal representation that the person can afford. Ray Lewis, O.J. Simpson, Robert Blake—the theme is the same.

Some have the courage to come out from the athletic midst and make a statement about how deplorable certain behavior is. A piece posted by *Sporting News* senior writer Paul Attner (Attner, 2005, *Sporting News* Web site) related what former San Francisco 49ers center and current football analyst Randy Cross had to say about domestic violence:

> *Memo to any man out there who resorts to hitting, grabbing or shoving a woman. You are the lowest form of the male species and your cowardly acts should be severely punished not only by the law in your local municipalities but in the case of a professional athlete in your respective leagues. This is a subject not spoken of often enough, and violence against women has been on the rise in all corners of our society for years. This is not a disease, calling it one only enables and legitimizes these cowards and it has absolutely no excuse. It is a basic character flaw and, more often than not, the individuals who commit these acts will repeat them time after time.*

Attner wondered how beneficial it would be if other athletes came out with the same message.

Even if an athlete does not recognize the inherent wrongness of raising his hand to a woman, we would think that he would at least be concerned about suspension, arrest, or his career, right?

At about 1 a.m. on Sunday, January 15, 2006, only hours after he had started at right tackle for the Seattle Seahawks, who beat the Redskins 20-10 in the first round of the playoffs, Sean Locklear was arrested and held without bail after witnesses said that they saw him grab the woman he was with by the neck, "putting both hands around her neck." Officers reported visible redness on her neck and chest, although the woman reportedly began to cry and refused to provide any more information. Locklear, it was reported, admitted that they argued but said that he grabbed the front of her shirt, not her neck. Seattle coach Mike Holmgren's initial response, when asked whether he thought the incident would be a distraction to the team's focus on the playoffs, said, "What I know about it so far—and I don't know everything—it should not be" (CBSSportsline.com, January 16, 2006, "Seahawks' Locklear jailed after domestic violence complaint").

Seattle's defensive back. Ken Hamlin, was lost for the season when he incurred a fractured skull and brain clot during a fight at a Seattle club. Tight end Jerramy Stevens had several brushes with the law since his days at the University of Washington. From an organizational point of view, even if these are isolated incidents, how can the numerous distractions not have an effect on reaching collective goals? Note that you rarely see these types of behaviors on a Bill Belichick or Bill Parcells team.

Athletes themselves can be the victims of angry outbursts and crime. Some evidence suggests that athletes are specifically targeted for crime because of their wealth or fame, or because others are jealous. Athletes increasingly feel the need to protect themselves. Given some of the incidents described here, it is easy to see why.

When well-traveled Venezuelan relief pitcher Ugueth Urbina was arrested for attempted murder in his country, the incident received almost as much press as his mother's being kidnapped and held for ransom. Urbina was mandated by a Venezuelan tribunal to remain in jail until his trial for charges of attempted murder, conspiring with others to commit a crime, illegal deprivation of liberty, and violating a prohibition against taking justice into his own hands. If found guilty, he would face up to 20 years in jail. It was reported that Urbina returned home to his cattle ranch to find several new workers sitting in a swimming pool drinking alcohol. Later in the evening, an altercation apparently occurred, which led to machete wounds and burns inflicted by Urbina, according to the victims. They also stated that Urbina told them that if they reported anything, he would kill their families as well, not to mention the possibility that they would be buried under the ranch. Urbina repeatedly denied involvement with the violence, saying that he was asleep at the time of the attack and that the incident was a continuation of a trend. He stated that he loved his country but was concerned that he was a target for extortion there. Whether this is all factual is for the courts to decide, but this incident received no less press than the kidnapping of his mother.

Urbina's mother, Maura Villareal, 54, was rescued by police after more than five months in captivity. She had been kidnapped by abductors posing as policemen. The abductors detained her in a dense jungle and reportedly surrounded the area with explosives to keep her from fleeing. During the raid, which lasted about eight hours, one of the captors was killed, two were captured, and at least seven escaped. Villareal was reportedly not harmed. The kidnappers had taunted her by saying that her son did not love her because he would not pay the $6 million ransom that they demanded.

The Urbina family had been a victim of crime before. His father was murdered in a robbery attempt 10 years before these incidents, even before he made his riches.

Remarkably, when Urbina and his family were the victims, the incident received less press than his arrest for attempted murder.

When competition produced too much pressure, Tonya Harding thought that she could level the playing field by hiring someone to break the knees of Nancy Kerrigan. On January 6, 1994, Kerrigan was clubbed in the knee by Shane Stant, who was hired to harm her by Harding's ex-husband Jeff Gillooly and friend Shawn Eckhardt. Despite being an innocent victim, Kerrigan was mocked by the media. Just a month after the attack, Kerrigan went on to win the silver medal in the 1994 Lillehammer Winter Olympics.

Former top baseball prospect Dernell Stenson, 25 years old at the time (November 2003), was murdered in Arizona by two men who kidnapped him outside a Scottsdale nightclub, stole his SUV, and drove to Chandler. According to court documents, Stenson put up a fight as one of the defendants turned the vehicle around in a Chandler neighborhood. Although he had been shot several times, Stenson tried to escape but became entangled in the seatbelt and was dragged for 1,100 feet (340 meters). After the results of a psychological exam on one of the suspects became available, prosecutors reconsidered seeking the death penalty. Not surprisingly, as a result, the defense attorneys are now working on a plea deal to prevent a capital sentence.

Recently recaptured in the 2006 Steven Spielberg film *Munich*, the Munich massacre was a terrorist attack during the 1972 Olympic Games. These Olympics were the first to take place in Germany since the Nazis hosted the 1936 games in which Hitler was humiliated when Jesse Owens almost single-handedly eradicated the idea of Aryan supremacy. So tensions were high in 1972, especially because many Israeli athletes had family members who had been murdered during the Holocaust or were themselves Holocaust survivors.

At about 4 a.m. on September 5, eight Palestinian terrorists jumped the fence around the Olympic Village and went straight for the Israelis' quarters. They killed two members of the Israeli Olympic team who put up a fight and took nine others hostage. They wanted 234 prisoners released from Israeli prisons and 2 from German prisons. The situation escalated when their demands were not met. Numerous plans to storm the terrorists were foiled by their being aware of the attacks before they occurred, some of which they found out by watching television! The situation eventually ended in a huge gunfight that left five of the terrorists and all nine of the hostages dead.

Celtics Forward Paul Pierce was nearly murdered at a Boston area club in 2000. Not knowing that he was walking into the territory of a notoriously violent gangster-rap group, Pierce's fame was apparently perceived as a challenge by his assailants. A small conflict with one former criminal quickly escalated. Pierce, who was at the Buzz Club with teammate Tony Battie and his brother Derrick, was hacked into with a knife, pummeled, and kicked by about 10 men. His expensive leather jacket and shirt was ripped off him before security could intervene. Three men were arrested and two were convicted and sent to jail, but Pierce was happy to be alive and was not particularly helpful in the investigation.

NFL players have been the victims in some of the most severe episodes of violence against athletes.

Fred Lane was an undrafted free agent signed by the Carolina Panthers for the 1997 season. Despite early success, he started having personal problems two years later and was suspended by the Panthers for off-field issues, namely a domestic violence complaint filed by his wife Deidra. In July 2000, despite an indictment in Tennessee for drug charges, he was traded to the Colts to back up Edgerrin James. Lane hoped to get a new start but never got the chance. On July 6, as he entered his house, he was the recipient of a shotgun blast fired by his wife. Initially, she claimed that she acted in self-defense, but her argument lost credibility when the prosecutor reported that she initially shot him in the chest and then walked through his blood and shot him again in the back of the head. Prosecutors portrayed her as a cold-blooded opportunist who murdered her husband with hopes of collecting on a $5 million life insurance policy.

This version clearly was not the whole story, any more than the defense team's report that she was a battered wife who killed in self-defense. Fred Lane's previous arrest for domestic violence may have had an effect on their troubled relationship, but with his packed bags still by the door (he had just returned from visiting his family in Tennessee) and the keys still in the door, the attack was determined to be premeditated. Deidra Lane was charged with murder in August 2000 and was free on $100,000 bond until she was arrested a month later for a 1998 bank larceny charge, which further damaged her credibility.

She pleaded guilty to voluntary manslaughter and received the maximum sentence because the judge ruled that the slaying was deliberate and premeditated and that she acted with malice when she shot him a second time after the first shot rendered him helpless. She was sentenced to nearly eight years in prison.

Washington Redskins free safety Sean Taylor was murdered on November 27, 2007, at the age of 24, dying from critical gunshot injuries inflicted by intruders at his Miami-area home. Observers believed that the thieves were aware of his property and wealth and targeted the house as a result, but did not expect him to be home at the time of the burglary.

In September 2008, Jacksonville Jaguars offensive tackle Richard Collier was shot 14 times as he and a former teammate were waiting to pick up two women whom they had met at a nightclub. The shooting left Collier paralyzed from the waist down and required his left leg to be amputated above the knee. Tyrone Romaro Hartsfield, 32, was arrested but pled not guilty to charges of attempted murder and possession of a firearm by a convicted felon. Police believe that he was retaliating against Collier for an earlier altercation at a nightclub.

What I have been trying to demonstrate is both sides of the story. Are some athletes violent? Yes. Are some athletes victims of violence? Yes. Unfortunately, the world that we live in is violent. Athletes, unless they are sectioned off from the rest of society, will be exposed to violence as well, either as perpetrators or victims.

And Then Sometimes, They Do It to Themselves

New York Giant Super Bowl hero Plaxico Burress accidentally shot himself in the right thigh in November 2008 while he and teammate Antonio Pierce were enjoying a night on the town at the Latin Quarter, a restaurant and nightclub in New York City. It was reported that Burress shot himself with a handgun that he did not have a license to carry in New York. Burress was charged with this crime and subsequently suspended for the remaining four games of the regular season.

Have you ever been so angry that you just wanted to hit something? If so, you are not alone. We have all seen the slapstick comedy in which someone gets angry, punches a wall, and then bulges out his or her eyes with pain from the self-inflicted injury. Fiction, you say? Not so! Several athletes have made themselves unavailable to play because of such injuries. And I am not talking about the incident a couple of years back when the Jaguars' punter, Chris Hanson, accidentally gashed his leg with an ax in the locker room. Coach Del Rio had brought the ax and wood in as a metaphor for "chopping away at it." The player required minor surgery to repair his injury.

In September 2004, the New York Yankees were coming down the stretch for a playoff run when starting pitcher Kevin Brown, ironically frustrated about dealing with minor injuries and struggles all season, punched a wall with his left hand, breaking it, requiring surgeries and pins, and missing about a month. That injury probably did not help the Yankees' cause. Manager Joe Torre and GM Brian Cashman were clearly disappointed that the player's action could have hurt the whole team. But that player was not the innovator of this behavior in baseball. Cardinals closer Jason Isringhausen broke his right wrist by punching a garbage can while on a minor league rehab assignment with the Mets in 1997, and former St. Louis reliever Mike Matthews dislocated a bone in his pitching hand in 2000 when he punched the dugout bench in frustration.

Predictably, the trend continues. Then of the Pittsburgh Pirates, left-handed ace Oliver Perez had a fit of temper land him on the disabled list in June 2005 when he broke his left big toe by kicking a laundry cart in the clubhouse. The injury sidelined him for almost two months.

Not to be outdone, Texas pitcher Kenny Rogers was enjoying a good season in 2005 when in June he broke a bone in his nonpitching hand by hitting a water cooler in frustration after being pulled from a game against the Nationals. It was reported that Rogers was visibly upset when umpires ruled that the final Nationals hitter he faced had checked his swing on a full-count pitch. Rogers spiked the ball to the ground when Texas manager Buck Showalter came out to remove him from the game, and he found the cooler soon after that. Rogers had been catching heat from the media all year, which he was pretty much boycotting, because it was reported that he was threatening to retire if he was not given a contract extension.

Shortly thereafter, he was back in the news after an outburst that sent a TV camera operator to the hospital. Rogers was not feeling particularly media friendly, and the media compounded the problem by aggressively approaching him as he walked out onto the field for a pregame warm-up. Rogers shoved the two camera operators, knocking a camera to the ground. When the other reporter resumed filming, Rogers shoved him again and this time kicked the camera when it fell again to the ground. Teammates restrained him, and management sent him home. One of the camera operators filed assault charges from the hospital.

Commissioner Selig was appalled. He suspended Rogers for 20 games and fined him $50,000. The penalty sent a powerful message. On Rogers' appeal, an arbitrator ruled that the penalty was excessive and trimmed the suspension to 13 games.

Although Rogers' behavior cannot be excused, fans and media personnel need to remember that having a camera or a mike shoved in one's face can become tiresome. The privacy of athletes is often challenged. They are bombarded with questions in many situations, not only during press conferences or while sitting on a stool in front of their lockers. So although Rogers really needed to do a better job of controlling his emotions, people should be sensitive to the fact that athletes are human. Frustrations come along with their jobs, and they will not always be at the top of their game. By giving athletes some space, the media are more likely to receive the time that they need to do their jobs. Invading their space only creates a barrier between athlete and reporter.

In a league that has tolerated violence for years, the NHL saw one of the most horrific displays of violence seen in a sporting event when Vancouver Canucks power forward Todd Bertuzzi assaulted the Colorado Avalanche's Steve Moore during a March 2004 game.

Losing 9-2 to Colorado, Bertuzzi and the Canucks were understandably frustrated. Their foul mood was compounded by the Avs' Steve Moore February 16 hit on Canucks captain Markus Naslund, who suffered a concussion and missed three games. Bertuzzi punched Moore in the back of the head from behind and drove him headfirst into the ice. Moore incurred deep cuts on his face, a concussion, and two broken vertebra. The punch received a great deal of media attention, including a headline in the *Toronto Star* that read, "Does someone have to die?"

Bertuzzi was suspended indefinitely, which turned out to be for the remainder of the season. Because of the lockout, however, his actual time away was only 13 games, a period that some people believed was too short. He ended up losing approximately $800,000 between salary and endorsements and was tearful when discussing the issue on television.

Although the league thought that the punishment was appropriate, Moore wanted to explore further legal avenues because there was a certain injustice to Bertuzzi's return to the ice while Moore was dealing with a possible career-ending injury.

Upon Bertuzzi's return, NHL Commissioner Gary Bettman stated that Bertuzzi had paid an emotional price (uncertainty, anxiety, stress, and emotional pain) and had hurt his team because the Canucks would likely have had more playoff success with him than without him. Bettman warned Bertuzzi that he was "on probation" for the 2005–06 season. "Mr. Bertuzzi is on notice that he will be held strictly accountable to a higher standard than other NHL players for his on-ice conduct during the 2005–06 season," he said. In actuality, I am not sure, considering NHLPA's collective bargaining agreement with the league, that any player can ever have a different set of standards than their class peers.

Moore's lawyer argued that he should have received at least the 82-game penalty that McSorley received for his assault on Brashear.

Wayne Gretzky, Team Canada's executive director, spoke about the incident in an interview:

> "I'm glad the NHL has finally stepped in and put him back in the game and reinstated him. Nobody condones what Todd did. I'm sure he'd be the first one to tell you it was a mistake. But you know it's time to move forward. We will invite him to our training camp. He's an elite player and I expect him to have a great year and be part of Team Canada come February in Italy.

In December Bertuzzi pleaded guilty to assault causing bodily harm and received a conditional discharge. He was sentenced to a year of probation and 80 hours of community service. Somehow, I do not think that an ordinary citizen would have received such a light sentence with thousands of witnesses to a crime.

Remarkably, over time many of the perpetrators in these incidents are portrayed as victims. The poor guy served his time. Can he just go back to earning millions and entertaining us all, please?

A fair and salient question, however, concerns what has been done for Todd Bertuzzi or other athletes to help them be less likely to act out in a moment of rage, vengeance, or anger. Punishment. That's it. Without training about how to manage anger, punishment is unlikely to change everything. More events are certain to follow.

On December 9, 1977, early in the second half of a game between the Houston Rockets and the Los Angeles Lakers, Rockets center Kevin Kunnert and Lakers star center Kareem Abdul-Jabbar fought for a rebound. Kunnert won the battle and kicked the ball ahead to a teammate. Lakers power forward Kermit Washington, whom some in the league identified as the NBA's strongest man, served as a protector of the Lakers' stars, playing a role similar to that of enforcers in hockey.

After Abdul-Jabbar and Kunnert got free of each other, Washington grabbed Kunnert's shorts to stop him from getting up the court for offense. Kunnert swung his elbow at Washington, hitting him in the arm. What happened next is unclear. Washington insisted that Kunnert threw another elbow, Abdul-Jabbar said that Kunnert threw a punch, and Kunnert claimed that he threw only the first elbow. In any case, Abdul-Jabbar returned to the tussle and grabbed Kunnert from behind to pull him and Washington apart. Abdul-Jabbar's action only made Kunnert more vulnerable when Washington's first punch hit Kunnert in the head, knocking him to one knee.

Kunnert's teammates, All-Star Rudy Tomjanovich and Calvin Murphy, saw their teammate being attacked by two opposing players and rushed down the court to help. Out of the corner of his eye, Kermit Washington stated that he saw a "blur of red" (the Rockets' jerseys are red) and believed that he was about to be attacked. He turned and hit Rudy T. right under the nose, breaking his nose, causing multiple facial fractures, and rupturing his brain capsule, which caused cerebrospinal fluid to leak into his mouth from his brain.

In his book *The Punch: One Night, Two Lives, and the Fight That Changed Basketball Forever*, John Feinstein described the event in great detail, including how it affected the two players and the NBA after the event. Feinstein reported that Tomjanovich's first question was "What happened? Did the scoreboard fall on me?" Feinstein's excellent book discusses the many ways in which such incidents affect the athletes, besides what the public sees.

In the end, Tomjanovich required five surgeries to repair and reconstruct his face. Months later, he returned to the court. Washington was fined $10,000 and suspended for 25 games.

On November 19, 2004, fans witnessed one of the most chaotic displays of athletes' losing control in the brawl that took place between the Indiana Pacers and the Detroit Pistons in Detroit's Palace of Auburn Hills. Later given sensational names such as the Malice at the Palace and the Throwdown in Motown, the incident was heavily covered by the media, who missed no opportunity to hype the event as they would the lead-up to a heavyweight championship boxing match. This hype, of course, is part of the problem.

The incident took place with about 45 seconds left in the game and Indiana coasting to a 97-82 victory. No love was lost between the two teams. During the previous year, they had fought (metaphorically here) intensely in the Eastern Conference Finals, which the Pistons had won on their way to the NBA Championship. This game was their first rematch.

When Detroit forward–center Ben Wallace received a hard foul from Ron Artest, Wallace became irate, figuring that the game was basically over and that he could have been seriously hurt (foreshadowing some of the reasons why people become angry). Wallace shoved Artest. Players from both benches joined the fracas, but Artest removed himself from the situation. He first sat at the scorer's table and then got up and laid down on it. Artest seemed to enjoy his ability to provoke Wallace, and Wallace threw a towel at him. Artest did not want much to do with Wallace. Who could blame him? Ben Wallace was one of the most physically imposing men in the NBA.

The towel that Wallace threw could have been put to use when a fan threw a cup of beer at Artest. Without delay or consideration, into the stands he charged to confront the man who he thought threw the beer. Artest had the wrong guy, and in such situations, it often is the wrong guy. In any case, teammates Stephen Jackson and David Harrison followed Artest into the stands. A steady exchange of punches ensued, thrown by both players and fans. Lots of beer was tossed around as well, a not-to-be-ignored detail that often contributes to (note that I do not say that it causes) such ugly events.

Two spectators made their way onto the court, and one of them confronted Artest, who punched him, thus beginning round 2 of the match. This time teammate Jermaine O'Neal became involved and was seen on video punching the second fan. The game was called at that point. Two days later, the NBA announced the following suspensions:

- Ron Artest: remainder of the season, which amounted to 86 games—73 regular season games and 13 playoff games
- Stephen Jackson: 30 games
- Jermaine O'Neal: 25 games (reduced to 15 games in the only successful appeal)
- Ben Wallace: 6 games
- Anthony Johnson: 5 games
- A game each to Reggie Miller, Chauncey Billups, Elden Campbell, and Derrick Coleman for leaving their bench during an altercation

What are the take-home messages to this incident?

First, do not blame Artest's entering the stands as a result of impulsive anger that he could not control. Ben Wallace had just directly confronted and challenged him physically, and Artest chose not to engage him. Artest deserves kudos for that, but unless you want to argue that the fan was more wrong or more challenging, or that Artest was displacing his anger toward Wallace to the fan (possibly displacing his anger to an easier opponent), he has no excuse for going into the stands and swinging at fans.

But I do understand that the provocation of the thrown beer is an explanation. The difference between an explanation and an excuse is huge. Palace security was not able to contain the fans' behavior, alcohol consumption contributed to the fans' unruliness, and access to the stands was problematic, as it is generally in sport.

To understand more clearly the difference between an excuse and an explanation, consider the situation in January 2006 when Knicks forward Antonio Davis entered the stands because he believed that a fan was harassing and threatening his wife. Most people understood his position, including his coach, Larry Brown. Davis was wrong to enter the stands, but the explanation for why he did it, to protect his family from a perceived danger, makes sense. He received a suspension, but it was nowhere near as severe as the penalties that resulted from the Detroit incident.

Second, athletes and fans should not be able to mix as they did at the Palace. From a business point of view, how could an owner not be furious if a fan were to cause a serious injury to a player and render the athlete unavailable to compete? An incident of that sort could become expensive.

The availability of alcohol at sport venues contributes significantly to conflicts between fans and athletes. As a result, management at many stadiums have changed their distribution policies. This book does not focus on fan violence, so I will not spend an exorbitant amount of time on this topic (refer to chapter 6 for a discussion about alcohol and violence for athletes), but suffice it to say that one way to diminish the occurrence of incidents is to decrease the number of drunk fans doing stupid thingsSummary

In this chapter we explored the historical relationship between violence and sport. This connection is not a recent development. Fierce completion and extreme tension can lead to violence in sport, and our society pays an enormous amount of attention to the relationship.

Jeffrey Benedict, whose books have been the product of a great deal of research, demonstrates various ways that data can be presented and how tricky the perception of violence can be because of presentation style. Benedict is not alone in his belief that athletes (especially professional athletes) are more violent than nonathletes and are less likely to be held accountable for their actions. The way in which writers formulate, conceptualize, and shape this notion has a large and confusing influence on the reputation of sport. I do not believe that writers intend to tarnish sport, and I do not deny that the behavior of some athletes paints sport in a negative light. At the same time, I believe that the behavior of a few should not be used to tarnish the character of the many athletes who do not engage in such behavior.

Nonetheless, to give a context of the severity of some of the situations that athletes have been in, a review of some of the lowlights is warranted, so we spent time on that in this chapter.

But this review is only the beginning of our examination of the issue of violence among athletes. From here, we must examine why this phenomena is so easily misunderstood. In the next chapter we will tease apart the nuances of the study of anger and violence, especially with regard to how anger plays out in the world of sport.

CHAPTER 3

ASSESSING ANGER IN SPORT

Although on the surface anger and sport would seem to be a simple topic to study, it is surprisingly elusive. The reasons are complex and plentiful. In this chapter, we will review some of the common problems encountered in this sort of research, look at what the sport psychology field has done so far, and conclude by examining what happens when someone studies this phenomenon with a preconceived agenda.

EXPERIMENTER BIAS

OK, sports fans, I want you to do an experiment. I want you to think about the team that you watch more than any other—the team whose box score you check first thing in the morning or the team that causes you to be chronically sleep deprived because you have to stay up for ESPN's SportCenter review of their games. For most fans, one team stands out. It does not have to be a pro team, or even a high-revenue, high-exposure sport. Nonetheless, many of us have a team that we affectionately identify as ours.

Now I would like you to think of the many times that you have watched highlights of past games, as well as drafts or signing-day events that show what your team will look like in the future. Do you care? You bet!

Keeping your team in your mind, now I want you to think about the sport that your team plays. Do you consider yourself a fan of that sport? If so, do you identify yourself as a football fan, or as a baseball fan? More likely, you consider yourself a Duke fan or a Flyers fan first and then secondarily a fan of the sport. Most fans identify with players or the team's colors more than they do the specific sport.

We are going to extend this a bit further. Have you ever had a conversation with a New York Yankees fan and thought, *Man, they think every player on the team is the best ever?* Bernie Williams could be considered a Hall of Fame Yankee, but even past his prime, some Yankees fans were still rating him as a great player.

For evidence of this, you need look no further than baseball's All-Star Game. The starters for the Midsummer Classic are determined by fan ballots. Every year, fan favorites commonly receive more votes than those whose production would merit their selection as All-Stars.

In the 2005 All-Star Game, the fans voted Scott Rolen to be the starter. Behind him in votes were Aramis Ramirez of the Chicago Cubs and Morgan Ensberg of the Houston Astros. Both Ramirez and Ensberg had significantly better statistics going into the Midsummer Classic. In an injury-riddled year, Rolen was struggling at the plate. He was surely a phenomenal ballplayer, but that year he was voted in based on his history, not his current production.

Similarly, Carlos Beltran of the New York Mets beat out Miguel Cabrera of the Florida Marlins when Cabrera was far superior in batting average, home runs, and RBIs.

This phenomenon is common in sport. Fans' expectations about athletes' performance, not to mention their popularity, lead to misperceptions about how well they are really performing.

To demonstrate how this plays out in the world of research, we need to understand the basics of the scientific method. Five basic steps are carried out in scientific research:

1. Identify the problem and form a hypothesis.
2. Design the experiment.
3. Conduct the experiment.
4. Test the hypothesis by analyzing the data.
5. Communicate the research results.

People tend to study a topic that interests them, and they usually form a hypothesis that makes sense to them. From the very beginning of the research, they have a vested interest that severely hampers their ability to be objective. Therefore, from the time that the researcher identifies the problem and forms a hypothesis (step 1 in the scientific method), she or he is at risk of being biased and thus corrupting the objectivity of the study. Without careful controls in place, experimenter bias can compromise the research.

Experimenter bias occurs when the investigator has certain expectations about the outcome of the experiment. These expectations can contaminate the entire process. The experimenter can subtly alter his or her behavior in carrying out the experiment in any of a number of ways and thus produce biased results (Reber, 1985). Arguments in the field have occurred for many years about whether or not this is a conscious process. Unconscious or not, the results are the same. Research is susceptible to being biased by the motivations of those doing the research.

When pharmaceutical companies fund research for drug trials, can the research be truly unbiased? Obtaining unbiased results would seem to be nearly impossible.

Note that psychologists tend to pay more attention to the scientific model than some other researchers do. Even so, safeguards must be in place to prevent infiltration of experimenter bias. Briefly, I will describe some safeguards that can be used to preserve the sterility and objectivity of research.

SAMPLING

In an experiment, the best way to determine whether an intervention has an effect is to select a sample of subjects randomly from a population. Random selection means that any member of the population has an equal probability of being selected. As an example, if a researcher is trying to study the effects of laser vision surgery on batters who wear contact lenses, the population would be batters who wear contact lenses. The investigator would break them down into two groups: those who have the laser surgery and those who do not. Each subject would be randomly assigned to one of the two groups; each would have an equal probability of being in either group. This method controls for any variability in a group. Simply stated, even if the groups are not exactly the same, each has the same likelihood of including any subject.

One group, called the experimental group, receives the procedure. The other group is called the control group. Those subjects do not receive the intervention but instead receive a placebo. The placebo is neutral and should yield no change. Of course, even this approach does not work smoothly

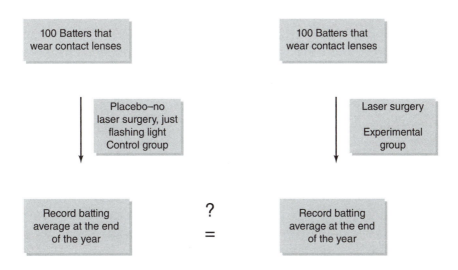

Figure 3.1 Illustration of how an experiment could be devised to measure the effects of placebo (i.e., the belief that the subject is receiving treatment when what they are receiving has no effect) versus a known treatment.

because research has found a powerful phenomenon known as the placebo effect. The placebo effect is any observed effect that is "caused" by a placebo, despite the fact that the placebo has no power to cause change. The subject's belief that what they are receiving can cause a change is what leads to the change. Do you see how complicated this becomes?

After the two groups receive the intervention (control or experimental), they are compared statistically along some resultant factor to see whether they are different. The assumption is that because they were the same before the experiment, any change would be attributable to the intervention.

Scientific research is done in this basic manner to determine whether an intervention works. Even in descriptive research, which is used to describe how often something happens, the basic principles of sampling should be used if the conclusions are to be valuable.

How many sport psychology studies of anger and violence do you think use random sampling? Not many. Furthermore, the number of participants in those studies tends to be small. The researcher therefore needs to find extremely robust statistical differences to reflect a significant difference. Also, with small Ns (N is the research term for the number of participants in a study), generalization to other athletes becomes more suspect.

DOUBLE BLIND

Another way to protect against experimenter bias is to use what is called the double blind model. The double blind model keeps both the experimenter and the subject unaware of whether the subject is in the experimental group or the control group. Thus, the researcher is unable to sway the results one way or the other.

In the previous example, subjects who received laser vision correction would be likely to know that they had received the procedure. That problem could be controlled for as well by requiring all applicants to be within three lines of 20/20 vision without their contact lenses to participate.

By not letting the participants know which group they are in, the differences would show the effects of the surgery without experimenter bias. However, the problem of the placebo effect remains. Some batters may do better because they think that they can see better and thus have more confidence. Better performance is the result.

To solve the problem, a third group could be added. Those subjects would be placed on the waiting list. The researcher then compares all three groups. The analysis becomes more statistically complicated, but the researcher could then determine how much improvement occurs with no intervention (waiting list) versus placebo (flashing light) versus the experiment (laser surgery).

To summarize, studies can be designed to be less subject to experimenter bias. The two methods mentioned here are not the only ways to maintain objectivity. In any case, those who study anger and violence in sport generally do not use these methods.

WHAT GETS PUBLISHED AND PRESENTED

Often, when doing research, people are passionate about what they are studying. I was no different in this regard. Researchers invest a great deal of time and energy into their work, and when it is completed, this product, their product, is part of their identity. The sport psychologist who works in a specific area tends to be associated with it. People in the field know this, and people in the public tend to find out as well.

If I want to know something about the psychological factors related to rehabilitation from sport injury, I know to start with the work of Britton Brewer at Springfield College. Eating disorders? Karen Cogan. Drugs and alcohol? Chris Carr.

So who in the sport psychology field is the expert on anger and violence in athletes? Because surprisingly few people have been working on this topic, the answer is less clear.

With the many incidents of violence frequenting our sports pages and highlight reels, one would expect to see great demand for discussion of this topic. Surprisingly, this has not been the case. The American Psychological Association's division 47 is the Division of Exercise and Sport Psychology. Neither at its annual convention nor at the convention of the Association for the Advancement of Applied Sport Psychology (AAASP) has anger and violence been an area that has received a lot of attention. Why not?

As is usually the case, the answer is not simple. One could conclude that sport psychology has avoided being associated with anything pathological because talking about athletes and violence might lead to the assumption that they belong together. So much stigma is attached to the word *psychologist* that many sport psychologists change their titles to avoid the negative, "crazy" connotations. While our children are watching their role models on Court TV standing trial for rape, the field pretends that violence in sport is not a sport psychology issue. One goal of this book is to raise consciousness about this problem and confront it openly and honestly.

How do presentations and publications make their way to a public forum anyway? In the ideal scientific world, submissions are reviewed blind. A blind review removes the author or presenter's name and affiliation and considers the value of the work based solely on its content. As with the experimenter bias problem, rarely is a review truly blind. When humans being are involved, opinions and desires infiltrate. What occurs, then, is that a great deal of information never makes its way to publication or presentation.

Moreover, let us not forget about studies that find no significant results. They somehow do not fill journals and books, but you know that they occur.

If I am interested in studying anger and athletes and my intervention does not yield significant results, do I submit it for publication? No. I route it to the circular file (the trash can). Journals tend to be filled with what has been found to work, not what was tried and did not work. The latter can be of greater value in some cases.

ANGER AND VIOLENCE SPECIFICALLY

To study any topic, the researcher must have a way to measure it. How does a researcher measure anger, and what exactly does that measurement mean? To simplify matters and to avoid going into the exhaustive research and inventories on anger and violence, I will clarify the basic themes regarding assessment of anger and then introduce the instruments with the greatest utility.

On a basic level, anger is a normal experience. Anger has cognitive components in the form of thoughts related to the emotion. It also has physiological components.

These physiological components are tied to the sympathetic nervous system and have similarities with any emotion associated with arousal. Although anger is not identical to anxiety and fear, strong similarities (increased heart rate, breathing rate, and so on) exist. Measurement of the electrical conductivity of subjects' skin has been found to indicate changes in emotion state. Nevertheless, using physiological measures presents clear problems.

First, although we can stimulate a subject into an angry state in an experimental session, the circumstance is not the same when the person is angry in vivo (in real life). Furthermore, measuring a person's physiological response does not necessarily translate into quantifiable levels of anger that can be compared from person to person. Complicating matters even more is the issue of differences in individuals' baseline emotionality in the first place. Similar to the sociopath who engages in predatory violence, some people are physiologically underaroused. A stimulus that might yield a tremendous bodily response in one athlete may not cause a twitch in another. Finally, if the goal is to help athletes learn how to identify and measure their own anger, extra devices are not user friendly (that is not to say that biofeedback systems do not help athletes learn how to relax themselves). Because anger has complex physiological, cognitive, and motivational factors that overlap and interact, a physiological system may be a valuable component to an assessment system, but it is not a comprehensive, exhaustive tool that grabs the totality of the experience of anger.

One may claim that arrest records may give some information about anger. Jeffrey Benedict, for his books *Out of Bounds: Inside the NBA's Culture of Rape, Violence, and Crime* and *Pros and Cons: The Criminals Who Play in the NFL*, invested a great deal of time and energy researching the criminal records of athletes who play in professional sports. Although the methodological problems with his approach were outlined and its conclusions were challenged in the last chapter, it will briefly be explained here why arrest records do not tell us much about anger, or even violence.

In America, being arrested means only that enough data surrounded an event that a police agent concluded that a law was broken. "Being taken down to the station" does not constitute an arrest. Furthermore, even if charged for a crime, a person is presumed innocent until proved guilty.

A person can be found not guilty for many reasons. If the police investigation does not produce enough evidence that the prosecutors, in a criminal case, can prove guilt beyond a reasonable doubt, the case will be dismissed or the charges will be dropped. As in the O.J. Simpson murder case, if the police do not acquire, collect, and manage the evidence in a case appropriately or if they do not obtain their evidence through appropriate practice of legal search, probable cause, and so on, evidence necessary for a conviction may become inadmissible in court. If the victim refuses to press charges, the accused will not be found guilty. Another important reason that an arrest may not lead to a conviction is that the accused person is not guilty. We cannot presume that someone who is arrested is guilty. Similarly, we cannot necessarily assume that someone who is found not guilty is innocent. Legal matters are complicated. Many people who are in prison might not have been found guilty had they received better representation than what they received from a public defender. Often, an accurate predictor of being found not guilty or of being able to plea-bargain down to a lesser charge with a much lesser sentence is the cost of the attorney.

Many people believe that professional athletes receive favoritism from the courts and that their sentences are lighter than those meted out to less-celebrated peers. The truth is that if the media reported how often criminals with extremely serious offenses are released to the street or receive shockingly short sentences for heinous crimes, the public would be appalled. One could certainly argue that the single greatest contributor to athletes' getting off has nothing to do with their popularity as athletes, but rather to their celebrity status as entertainers, which directly correlates to the size of their bank accounts and the quality of the defense that they can present. This argument transcends race. John Doe, a minority male charged with a crime, is more likely to go to jail than Ray Lewis or Michael Jackson not because he is a minority, but because he cannot afford first-rate representation.

If arrest records are untenable in analyzing athletes' propensity to be angry, why not consider convictions? Does anyone truly believe that our prisons are filled with athletes? No evidence supports that proposition. If you study conviction rates, the numbers are small and inconclusive. Worse still, for what crimes do conviction rates matter? Assault? Murder? Harassment? Burglary? Many criminal activities have nothing to do with anger. This line of study is a dead end.

USING PSYCHOLOGICAL INVENTORIES

The hallmark of psychology research is the self-report inventory. Many inventories were developed with the hope of capturing an emotion in a questionnaire. These too present problems.

The first problem with anger inventories is that they tend to be high in what researchers call face validity. The validity of a test is the extent to which it measures what it is supposed to measure. Face validity is the extent to which a test, on the face of it, measures what it is supposed to. Subjects who take tests that are high in face validity can easily tell what the researcher is measuring. For an emotional state like anger, which many people recognize has a negative connotation; subjects can provide answers that depict themselves in a favorable light. The test is easily faked. For that matter, if a subject wants the researcher to draw a particular conclusion, he or she can make the test show those results. Subjects respond in the ways that they do on such tests for many reasons. Those with an acquiescence bias will give the answer that they believe the researcher wants. Some want to paint themselves in a positive light. Some really do not pay attention to how they feel, and their self-report may not be based on reality. Some people lie. This may surprise you, but some people who lie do not have a specific reason to do so. A common false assumption is that people lie only if they have a good reason to do so, if they have something to gain. But, people lie for the fun of it, for the excitement of it, because they enjoy deceiving people, or for no reason at all. And the problem is that on these tests, it is hard to tell when someone is lying if the person lies consistently throughout the answers.

The second problem with anger scales is that a one-to-one correlation does not exist between measures on self-report inventories and behavior. Does every person who scores high on anger scales get in fights? No. One might even hypothesize that athletes who scores high on a self-report measure are less likely to act out because they have some awareness of their anger. Moreover, many of these scales were originally developed to measure pathology. Suppose that a student scored higher than everyone else in the class but her or his score did not reach the threshold of where anger is considered a problem. Can we say that this student is angrier than the other students? Maybe, but what does it mean? Not much.

The last problem with self-report measures is that even the ones that measure anger in state (being in an angry state right now) and trait (pervasive pattern of anger) dimensions, if not given when respondents are angry, may not reflect the true intensity of their emotions.

Nonetheless, self-report questionnaires are probably the best standardized tools that we have. Although several are available, I am going to focus on two that seem to be the most commonly used in the sport and clinical psychology literatures.

Profile of Moods States (POMS)

Originally developed in 1971 by McNair, Lorr, and Droppleman, the Profile of Mood States (POMS) has been cited in approximately 300 articles in the sport and exercise psychology literature. The test is a self-report measure in which subjects report on a Likert scale to what degree they experience the word describing an emotional state. The 65 words or phrases load into six mood states: tension, depression, anger, vigor, fatigue, and confusion. These six states can then be charted and their relative elevations noted.

Early research by William Morgan in the 1970s yielded the "iceberg profile" of elite athletes. While consulting with the United States Olympic Committee, Morgan found that successful elite athletes could be differentiated from unsuccessful candidates by this profile. Successful athletes had an elevation in vigor but much lower values for all the other mood states. This model has come under greater scrutiny over time, most notably in a meta-analysis of the articles that studied the iceberg profile (Rowley et al., 1995). Although that study found the iceberg profile to be a weak predictor of athletic success, the Profile of Mood States is still widely used and is currently found in approximately 1,500 published articles when you include studies outside of sport psychology as well.

The ease of administration paired with its established place in the sport psychology world makes the POMS one of the two instruments of choice in measuring anger in sport.

State-Trait Anger Expression Inventory-2 (STAXI-2)

The State-Trait Anger Expression Inventory-2 (STAXI-2), developed by psychologist Charles Spielberger, is the gold standard for anger assessment. STAXI-2 is a self-report inventory that measures anger in multiple dimensions. By responding to 57 items on a four-point scale (with 1 equating to "not at all" or "almost never" and 4 equating to "very much so" or "almost always") assessment of the subjects' anger includes "either the intensity of their angry feelings at a particular time or how frequently anger is experienced, expressed, suppressed or controlled." (Spielberger, *STAXI-2 Manual*, p. 4) The inventory is simple to administer, requiring only about 15 minutes, is normed for adolescents and adults, and is written at a sixth-grade reading level. Although it has not been normed specifically on athletes, its utility makes it ripe for such an extension. Finally, the inventory can be administered individually or in group settings.

The STAXI-2 measures anger along seven major scales and five subscales:

1. State Anger (S-Ang)—the intensity of and extent to which a person feels like expressing anger at a particular time.
   a. Feeling Angry (S-Ang/F)—the intensity of the anger that the person is currently experiencing.

  b. Feel Like Expressing Anger Verbally (S-Ang/V)—the intensity of the current feelings to express the anger verbally.

  c. Feel Like Expressing Physically (S-Ang/P)—the intensity of the current feelings to express the anger physically.

2. Trait Anger (T-Ang)—how often angry feelings are experienced over time.

  a. Angry Temperament (T-Ang/T)—measures the disposition to experience anger without specific provocation.

  b. Angry Reaction (T-Ang/R)—the frequency that angry feelings are experienced in situations that involved frustration or negative evaluations.

3. Anger Expression-Out (AX-O)—how often anger is expressed in verbally or physically aggressive behavior.

4. Anger Expression-In (AX-I)—how often anger is experienced but not expressed.

5. Anger Control-Out (AC-O)—how often the person controls the outward expression of anger.

6. Anger Control-In (AC-I)—how often a person attempts to calm down to control angry feelings.

7. Anger Expression Index (AX Index)—a general index of anger expression.

As can be seen, the STAXI-2 does not just measure anger along different dimensions; it also taps the different methods that subjects report using to manage their anger. In my opinion, it is the most useful anger assessment tool available because it not only describes the person's anger but also gives the sport psychologist the starting point of knowing how the person assesses his or her own anger management tendencies.

Considering the lack of study that anger, aggression, and violence have received in sport psychology as a whole, it is not surprising that few sport-specific anger measures are available. The Bredemeier Athletic Aggression Inventory (BAAGI) (Bredemeier, 1975) deserves some attention because it measures instrumental aggression as well as reactive aggression. Following the theme that instrumental aggression is what we want to reinforce and reactive aggression is related to anger and needs to be curbed, this instrument may prove to have significant utility in future anger management studies of athletes.

One of the newer instruments to be introduced is the Competitive Aggressiveness and Anger Scale (CAAS; Maxwell & Moores, 2007) developed by Jon Maxwell and his colleagues in Hong Kong. Initial findings suggest that the CAAS is a valid scale for the measurement of aggressive tendencies (aggressiveness) and anger in sport. Because it attempts to overcome the shortcomings of other instruments, it has promise.

Other Methods of Assessment

Methods of assessment that do not have the psychometric integrity of the instruments described earlier can nonetheless be valuable in assessing anger problems before determining how to proceed in managing said concerns.

Keep in mind that most referrals for athletes who have problems with anger are not self-referrals. In my practice, more than three-quarters of those referrals come from parents and coaches rather than from the athletes themselves. Often, the athletes do not even identify anger as a problem, and in some cases, they are correct. To evaluate convergent validity (is everyone seeing the same thing?), information should be obtained from as many different sources as the client will allow. Having a preconceived understanding of the problem before even meeting the athlete is a slippery slope, primed for self-fulfilling prophecies, including one in which the athlete refuses to work with the sport psychologist. Therefore, the best approach is to allow athletes to say as much as they can about themselves, especially with regard to how they handle their emotions.

Verbal report is an important place to start, because it both familiarizes the athlete with talking about his or her anger (something not often encouraged) and leads to the person paying more attention to it. In this way, verbal report can easily lead to self-monitoring. Athletes are accustomed to their performance being monitored and studied in many ways by many people. These people can provide useful information about their experience with the athlete in regard to her or his management of anger (consent must be obtained first), but no one knows the athlete's experience better than the athlete. Athletes need to get in the habit of paying attention to how they handle their emotions and what skills they use.

One such tool is the hassle log (see "Hassle Log"). The log is printed on an index card so that it is easy to carry

Sport psychologists rely on athletes to fill out hassle logs, which detail how the athletes handle themselves during anger-provoking situations. The athlete and sport psychologist can use this tool to monitor anger management progress.

HASSLE LOG

Name: _____

Date: _____

Mor. _____ Aft. _____ Eve. _____

WHERE WERE YOU?

Class_____ Gym _____

Locker room _____ Outside on-campus _____

Home _____ Dining _____

Off-campus _____ Home _____

Other _____

WHAT HAPPENED?

Somebody teased me. _____
_____

Somebody took something of mine. _____
_____

Somebody told me to do something. _____
_____

Somebody was doing something that I didn't like. _____
_____

Somebody started fighting with me. _____
_____

I did something wrong. _____

Other: _____

WHO WAS THAT SOMEBODY?

Teammate_____ Teacher _____

Coach_____ Parent _____

Sibling_____ Other adult _____

Other_____

WHAT DID YOU DO?

Hit back_____ Told supervising adult _____

Ran away_____ Walked away calmly_____

Yelled_____ Talked it out_____

Cried_____ Told a peer_____

Ignored_____ Broke something _____

Was restrained _____

Other_____

HOW DID YOU HANDLE YOURSELF?

1	2	3	4	5
Poorly	Not so well	OK	Good	Great

HOW ANGRY WERE YOU?

1	2	3	4	5
Burning mad	Really angry	Moderately angry	Mildly angry	Not angry at all

around and requires little time to complete. People use the log to track how they are doing in anger-evoking situations. Anyone can use the log as a self-awareness tool, but people who are targeting their anger problems (athletes, coaches, parents) and are working with a sport psychologist on these issues will find that the log readily provides data for discussion in the next session about what skills they used and how effectively they used them.

Any method that can be used to gain information about the athlete's experience of anger will be useful in planning interventions. By communicating the normalcy of anger as a common human emotion that requires no judgment, the sport psychologist allows the athletes to become more comfortable talking about it. That step is critical to achieving any progress.

SUMMARY

What should be clear at this time is that anger and violence, especially for athletes, are difficult to measure and study. Psychological tests or inventories have severe limitations because subscribing to certain attitudes or self-reporting anger does not translate predictively to violent behaviors. Nonetheless, development of such tools has promise when it comes to assessing anger, both for establishing norms for athletes and for assessing the effectiveness of intervention programs. Furthermore, because people have reasons to admit to or to deny violent behavior, arrest and conviction records may provide some insight into athletes' behavior. This approach proves difficult as well because examination of the criminal justice system shows that an arrest is not the same as a conviction. In addition, guilt is not the only factor that determines a conviction. As the study of anger and violence in sport expands, the methods of assessment must be in the forefront.

CHAPTER 4

UNDERSTANDING THE ATHLETE CULTURE

Sport is a central part of American society. For many of us, a day does not go by without a check of the Internet for the scores, a few minutes of SportsCenter before sleep, a snippet from the local sports talk radio station, or a glimpse of the back of the newspaper. Nevertheless, we all have slightly different views of the culture of athletes. We will consider our own perspectives before we spend some time examining the athlete culture.

Although many perspectives can provide insight into the athlete culture, obtaining a complete view of the experience is difficult for those who are not really immersed in the culture. Current and former athletes, coaches, sport administrators, and some parents have the purest view of it because they live it. The athlete culture is the backdrop, the scenery that their life plays out in front of. Being a fan is not the same. Fans have their own culture, and it is intimately related to the game (read Dr. Dan Wann's interesting work on fandom), but it is not the same as the athlete culture. To be objective about the culture, or to be as unbiased as we can be, we need to understand what shades our view of "the game."

Differences are present among the various levels of competition. Division I sports draw a bigger following, but Division III teams can undoubtedly have high levels of team cohesion and identity. They share many aspects of the athlete culture, as do high school teams, depending on the sport, the athletes involved, and the community's investment in the local athletics programs.

Now, this is not to say that there are different points of view to being an athlete. After all, what is the definition of an athlete? One definition is "a person who actively participates in physical sports and is highly skilled in sports." Does this definition include recreational walkers? What about traditional games like bowling and billiards? Sports networks are covering these games, as well as poker. Furthermore, each sport may have its own culture.

What stands out to me, however, is how the culture changes when the level of competition increases.

Unfortunately, this change sometimes appears much earlier than is developmentally appropriate. Parents and coaches act as if the Pop Warner championship is at the same level as the Super Bowl. I will address this in the "Parents" section because the topic deserves more attention.

As we proceed through this chapter, I will direct most of the discussion to the higher levels of competition in revenue-producing sports because I believe that the bulk of our collective experience of the athlete culture comes from that part of sport.

COACHES

Coaches, like other people, are vulnerable to anger, but they have the added pressures of being models for their athletes and of being in the public eye (so that no transgression escapes media attention). They are often expected to be responsible for ensuring that all their athletes are well behaved. Perhaps the most vulnerable feeling in sport is knowing what needs to be done in a given situation, having the right strategy, having the right personnel, and then still having to depend on someone (or some people) to execute it. Furthermore, depending on the level of athletics, the coach's job security may absolutely depend on the team's win–loss record. This pressure can cause even the most even-tempered people to lose their cool at times.

Joe Torre managed the Yankees through a period during which the team dominated like few others had in baseball history. From 1996 through 2007,

When Winning Goes Too Far

In June 2005 in a suburb of Pittsburgh, a 27-year-old T-ball coach was arrested and charged with criminal solicitation to commit aggravated assault and corruption of minors. What did he do? He paid one of his players $25 to hurt an 8-year-old mentally disabled teammate so that he would not have to put the boy in the game, specifically offering money to hit the boy in the head. T-ball! Do you think that the coach was taking things a little too seriously? Some people take winning to scary extremes.

The father of a hockey player was charged in March 2005 with felonious assault after he allegedly broke the leg of the opposing team's assistant coach. It was reported that Jeffrey Church, 39, was irate about a check that his son had received in the game. He took matters into his own hands and assaulted the coach, Michael Balzarini, and the assistant coach, Joseph Pacella, whose leg was broken. This all occurred in the context of 13- and 14-year-old travel youth hockey.

he led the Yankees to six World Series. The Yankees won four of them, made the playoffs every year, and averaged more than 97 wins per season during that stretch.

Despite this, when the Yankees and their 200 million dollar payroll struggled in early 2005, there was talk that Joe Torre would be fired by George Steinbrenner. This possibility occurred despite many obvious reasons for the team's struggle: First baseman Jason Giambi, preoccupied with a pending steroids investigation, underachieved mightily (compared with his previous performance) for half of the season. Huge contracts given to Jaret Wright and Carl Pavano turned out to be bad investments. The players produced disappointing results when they were healthy enough to take the field. Veterans Bernie Williams' declining skills were a natural result of aging. Despite his managerial success, the Yankees were losing and Joe Torre was in the crosshairs. He was not alone. General manager Brian Cashman seemed to have a bull's-eye fastened to the back of his suit as well. But Cashman and Torre survived that season and made the playoffs yet again. At the end of 2007, the Yankees offered Joe Torre a $5 million dollar, one-year contract that represented a cut in salary. It was Torre's time to move on, and he did. Quickly, the Los Angeles Dodgers hired him to be their manager; and he in turn took the Dodgers to the playoffs while the Yankees for the first time in years were on the outside looking in during October playoff baseball. The point is that coaches, no matter how successful, are vulnerable because ultimately they are only as good as the performers on the field.

This circumstance is not unique to professional and college coaches. As seen in H.G. Bissinger's book *Friday Night Lights*, which spawned the movie and TV series, high school coaches can face harsh scrutiny as well. After a difficult loss, Bissinger came back to his house to find "For Sale" signs on the front lawn. A community that takes ownership of a team can be like parents who live vicariously through their children. A loss reflects poorly on the town. This phenomenon is not restricted to high school or to football. Coaches at all levels can be the unwilling recipients of pressure from the expectations of the community. And the climate can change quickly. A coach can go from a hero to a target in a short time. Florida State football coach Bobby Bowden summed it up this way, "Winning coaches always remember that there is only a one-foot difference between a halo and a noose."

Of course, good coaches can improve their athletes' performance through structure, discipline, technique, strategy, and so forth. But from the perspective of the coach's chair, take a moment to think about what this means. Whether you boast a .750 winning percentage or have not had a winning season in years, you have likely spent a great deal of time trying to help your athletes improve but then have seen little of that effort translated into results. How do you manage the resulting frustration? Do you manage the corresponding anger in a way that you want your athletes to emulate? For many young athletes, the coach is the most influential adult in their lives. Many athletes whom I work with respect their coaches more than they do their parents, and adhere to their guidance more closely. In that role, however, coaches rarely get a day off, when they can say to their athletes, "Do as I say, not as I do," and expect their guidance to be effective. If athletes are role models and they complain about the burden, what must coaches think? They have an even greater burden and often do not enjoy the accolades that come with success. Legendary UCLA basketball coach John Wooden said, "Young people need models, not critics." Although this maxim is certainly true, observing it consistently is arduous. Wooden did not mention how difficult it can be to take on that role as a coach.

In lower levels of competition, coaching is easier, at least in theory. The younger the children are, the greater the emphasis should be on the process of learning sport skills. We want youngsters to have fun and become more proficient. The people who teach coaches how to coach say that, especially with younger athletes, worrying about winning is putting the emphasis in the wrong place. Coaches should teach skills, ensure that the activity is fun, and provide guidance and instruction. Winning will come. The seven-year-old who is absorbed with batting .500 by the end of the year but has not yet mastered any level of the game is misguided. This ill-advised focus is often fueled by, and in some cases caused by, the coaches and adults involved in the game. Ultimately, being a coach is demanding, and many parents who coach in Little League, police athletics leagues, local soccer leagues, and so on have no training about how to coach the sport. So in addition to having a massive responsibility, many adults who coach youngsters are inadequately trained. Even worse, many either do not know it or will not admit it.

The many factors and experiences that coaches go through give them a perspective that is related to the athletes' perspective, although it is still different. Certainly, coaches influence the athlete culture on their teams, but they should examine these contributions from not just their viewpoint, but from the perspective of the athletes.

PARENTS

Parents' involvement in violent outbursts has become embarrassingly commonplace, and the age of the participating children does not appear to deter the behavior. Parents have a role in preventing violence among their children, but this job must start with practicing what they preach. Some parents experience their children as extensions of themselves. Their children's successes and failures become theirs. This ego involvement makes such parents ripe for the emotional overflow that has led to criminal behaviors. Parents need to ask themselves a few simple questions.

What do you truly want out of your child's athletics experience? To what degree is playing on three traveling teams and spending countless hours in private lessons your decision? Does your son or daughter want to be the best athlete that he or she can be? Or is that your desire?

I strongly recommend three books to parents of athletes. Reading these books will help them understand the athlete culture and decrease the likelihood that they will engage in angry outbursts on the field that will hurt their children.

The first book that I recommend for parents and coaches is Dr. Jack Llewellyn's *Let 'Em Play*. Although the book focuses on youth baseball, the take-home lessons apply to most sports. Dr. Llewellyn notes that although many children play baseball, 75 percent drop out by the time they are 13. This decline in participation occurs for a reason.

That is not to say that parents are the root of all evil in Little League America. In fact, the author estimates that about 95 percent of parents do a great job. The remaining 5 percent can wind up in the local newspaper after engaging in all types of bizarre behavior.

In *Let 'Em Play*, the author repeats the mantra, Fun is the goal of youth baseball. As former Pittsburgh Pirates first baseman Willie Stargell said, "Nobody ever says 'work ball.' They always say 'play ball.' To me that means having fun."

Llewellyn explains, "Two factors help your child reach that goal: first, learning how to play; and, second, knowing you are going to be there to support him and to assure him that he has a 'winning' experience." Llewellyn argues that parents lose this focus at times. Finding the right program for their children and shopping for qualified coaches with the right temperament are places where parents can profitably invest their energy to help their children. Good coaches understand the game, but more important, they understand kids. They need to know something about where children are developmentally and how they best learn new skills.

Of further value is Llewellyn's succinct note that what parents can give in their brief time at the park can be expressed in two words: support and encouragement. The value of parents' involvement in sports cannot be understated, but they must understand the difference between their perspective and the perspective of the athlete.

Llewellyn's advice is about all youth sports, not just baseball. Youth hockey in Massachusetts was the scene when two fathers fought in July 2000. In one of the most horrific circumstances to arise in a sport arena, children watched a fight that left one father dead. Thomas Junta had gone to pick up his son and two of his friends from a local hockey rink in Reading, Massachusetts. When Junta got there, he did not like what he saw. He reported that Michael Costin was refereeing a pickup game and allowing too much roughhousing. A confrontation between the two ensued, which culminated in the 275-pound (125-kilogram) Junta pinning Costin to the floor and punching him, all as children watched. Costin never got up and died two days later. Junta and

Costin, it was reported, both had histories of violence, including allegations of domestic violence and restraining orders aplenty. The victim apparently had the worse history. The result was that Costin's four children, whom he was raising alone, were orphaned. One of them was extremely distraught and reportedly tried to climb into the coffin at the funeral. Junta was sentenced to 6 to 10 years in prison, although parole eligibility was expected after approximately 5 years.

Was this tragic incident about hockey? Who cares? It occurred around kids who were playing a sport. We must protect our kids from seeing these types of things. When parents attend sport events, they must remember that children are watching. I have seen many sport psychologists struggle with recommendations for leagues and coaches about parent involvement. On one hand, we want the parents to be involved and share in the experience with their children. On the other hand, some parents become intrusive and interfere with what the coach is doing. In other cases, parents are all too quick to drop off their children at practice in the responsible hands of another adult, so that they can go do what they want with some free time. The issue is complex, but it does not take a psychologist to know that parents who cannot check their behavior levels far below the hostility displayed in the preceding case should not be anywhere near a sport event.

One might think that with the Massachusetts incident receiving such widespread media attention, parents would be more mindful of their behavior. Not necessarily. A couple of years later, in March 2005, the father of a hockey player was charged with felonious assault after he allegedly broke the leg of the opposing team's assistant coach. It was reported that Jeffrey Church, 39, was irate about a check that his son had received in the game. He took matters into his own hands by assaulting coach Michael Balzarini and assistant coach Joseph Pacella, resulting in Pacella's leg being broken. This all occurred in the context of 13- and 14-year-old travel youth hockey.

The second book is Dr. Joel Fish's *101 Ways to be a Terrific Sports Parent*, probably the most comprehensive book I have read about the topic. It covers everything from kids specializing in sports to sibling rivalry to injuries to dealing with coaches. Well-grounded in both theory and experience, Dr. Fish provides great technical information in an easy-to-read, self-help format.

Fish also covers issues that are relevant to the development of young athletes but do not always make their way into this type of book. He talks about educating young athletes about performance-enhancing drugs and supplements. He identifies puberty as a time when more tolerance is needed. Demonstrating that the book is for parents of both males and females who play various sports, he includes valuable information about nutrition and eating disorders. The book offers one-stop shopping for parents.

The only criticism is that the book focuses a little too much on the positives. Directions are more geared toward what to do rather than what not to do. Reinforcing the positives is always better than punishing the negatives, but ugly realities occasionally arise in sport. To see that side of the issues in greater depth, I recommend that parents turn to Dr. Shane Murphy.

In his book *The Cheers and the Tears: A Healthy Alternative to the Dark Side of Youth Sports Today*, Murphy outlines what he describes as the "crisis in youth sports" by illustrating the de-evolution of sports that sometimes undoes the beneficial gains achieved by sport participation. Courageously, he delves into the murky waters that others have cautiously avoided. But he does so in a balanced way, not just identifying the problems such as parent overidentification, overvaluing of competition at an early age, and taking the fun out of sports for kids but also providing solutions. Dr. Murphy even demonstrates how the good aspects of parental involvement in their children's sports world can easily slip over to the "dark side."

Probably of greatest value is the honest debate that he engages in about whether or not competition is healthy for children. Murphy cites Alfie Kohn, author of *No Contest: The Case Against Competition*, who strongly argues that competition produces inferior performance, produces losers with low self-esteem, and creates an inherently unpleasant experience. Murphy responds point by point. He notes that people tend to perform better when competing than when performing alone and that competition offers the opportunity for excellence to emerge. Responding to the idea that competition leads to low self-esteem, he gives examples of athletes who lose and do not necessarily have low self-esteem. Note that some of the best athletes of all time never played for a champion. Finally, Murphy points to the fact that people continue to compete because they enjoy competition. Kohn's points are not without merit. Competition can indeed lead to negative consequences, but it does not have to produce such results. To reduce the likelihood of harmful outcomes from participation in sport, parents of young athletes should read Murphy's book.

As their children grow and the competition level increases, parents become increasingly less influential in the actual events of the sport participation. College coaches and professional coaches do not receive the same "play my kid" demands that coaches of youth sports do. This transition of letting go, one could argue, should occur much earlier. Some sport psychologists have advocated keeping parents as far from their children as possible in youth sports because of the interference that they can have. Jay Goldstein, a doctoral student at the University of Maryland, has been studying the topic of sideline rage, analogizing parents' difficulty in managing their tempers to road rage. Increased attention to this problem may lead to more proactive programming that will minimize parental transgressions at sporting events.

Children's growth into adolescence and then young adulthood presents other factors that parents need to be aware of. Parents' belief that their children's involvement in sport and their subsequent need to take good care of their bodies will preclude experimentation with (and possibly abuse of) drugs and alcohol is unrealistic. This topic will be discussed in detail in chapter 5, but the important point here is that parents need to know that drugs and alcohol can be part of the athlete culture. Proactively educating their children about these issues is advised. The same goes for deviant behavior. Parents cannot place on coaches the impossible burden of keeping their kids out of trouble. Parents are responsible for safeguarding their kids.

Despite the many transgressions committed by athletes and parents, quite a few parents these days seem to understand the problem. Over the past five years, my colleagues and I have seen an increase in referrals by parents looking for sport psychology services geared to helping their children prepare mentally and emotionally for the changes that they will experience as they progress to new situations, new coaches, more temptations, and greater pressure. Prophylactically working with young student–athletes is much easier than trying to undo problems in reaction to poor behavior.

REFEREES AND OFFICIALS

Few people realize the value and importance of these often-striped folks who devote a great deal of time and energy to the actual operation of athletic contests. Officials must perform the trifecta—curb athlete violence, punish transgressions, and manage their own emotions, even when they may be the target of hostility by athletes and fans.

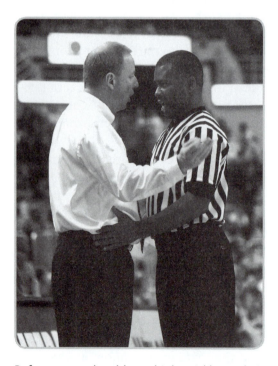

Bestowed with great authority, officials must make split-second decisions. They must trust their eyes, even when they later realize that their eyes at times deceive (betray) them. Acting as the judges (in the sense of judicially enforcing the rules, not judging a scorecard) of sport, their perspective of the athlete culture is interesting as well. And with the ever-present instant replays and QWESTEC (a system put in place to measure the fidelity of umpires to the strike zone), errors in judgment are made obvious. This added pressure can make the officials' job even more difficult.

Referees must be able to think quickly on their feet, not only when making split-second judgments, but when explaining their decisions while keeping their cool.

Some people have argued that veteran players get the benefit of the doubt with calls, that Michael Jordan got the benefit of liberal officiating, that Patrick Ewing's drop-step was an uncalled travel. What about the strike zone? Is it OK that different umpires have different versions? Most players simply hope for internal consistency. An umpire who calls low strikes all game for both sides usually does not catch much flack.

Nevertheless, officials are human, and they have to deal with many competing issues to preserve the integrity of the game. When NBA referee Tim Donaghy was arrested for his involvement in a gambling ring, the sports world trembled. Could Donaghy have fixed games and determined their outcomes?

The point is that officials are also affected by the athlete culture. Referees may know as much as anyone about anger in sport; they often catch hell from both sides. They are a target for verbal abuse and sometimes even physical attacks. All the while, they are responsible for ensuring a safe environment, without violence, for the participants at play.

Those who wear "the stripes" may be able to use the anger management techniques discussed later in the book. Their patience is tested regularly.

ATHLETES

Let us start by stating that the athlete culture varies along many dimensions. The culture can vary by the age of the athletes, the sport in which they participate, the type of sport (individual versus team sports), the competition level, and the revenue generated by the sport. Differences also occur based on the neighborhood in which the athletes grew up, the socioeconomic status of those around them, the athletes' exposure to good role models, and, to a varying degree, the athletes' ethnicity. From a research point of view, understanding the true relationship and interaction effects of all these variables is a statistical nightmare, and that problem would surface only if the investigator could qualify or quantify those factors in a meaningful way in the first place.

One of the beauties of sport is that when people are actually participating, immersed in the competition and the thrill of the game, the environment can transcend the factors that separate people in other arenas. As I mentioned in the preface, I grew up in a neighborhood that had little concern about skin color. The predominating segregation, at least for the boys, fell along the lines of sport participation. I have seen people with strong prejudices practically forget that they exist when they are playing on a team with a member of an "other" ethnic group. I am willing to bet that many of you have seen that as well. Stereotypes are broken and forgotten when people come together for a common goal. Sport is part of our world culture because we all love to play.

Racism exists in sport. This statement should come as no surprise because sport is a microcosm of society. Just as we live in a violent society, we should expect some violence to occur in sport. My point is that prejudice occurs in different ways in sport. As mentioned earlier, sometimes it becomes a nonissue. At other times, it is more overt.

For example, many African American collegiate athletes who are on full scholarships to play high-revenue sports are the stars of their schools. They are worshiped and privileged. They receive opportunities that their non-athlete peers do not get. But when a serious injury occurs and the "athlete" title disappears, the situation may change. I once worked with an African American football player at a competitive Division I school who tore his ACL. He described going from being part of the team to being "out of place" by the time he reached the sideline.

Whatever biases people may have, they are willing to let them go when they can get something from someone. But when that someone is no longer of use, the hate resurfaces. Many inner-city minority athletes have serious culture shock when they find themselves playing big-time college sports. They are not sure what to do with their racial identities. Should they conform to the society that they are now a part of or hold on to their individuality but hope not to rock the boat too much? Counseling centers need to pay particular attention to this issue. Athletes are at risk because their vulnerability is hidden under a perfectly sculpted athletic body. Nothing about being an athlete makes a person impervious to all the struggles that his or her peers face. In some ways, athletes are at greater risk.

Let me offer a different explanation for the origin of racism. Perhaps racism is not based on the fear of differences, as many people suspect, but on the fear of sameness. Its origin might then make more sense. From the time we were very young, way before we picked up our first golf club, we were trained to believe that we were special. Our mothers or fathers looked down on us, smiled at us, and catered to us. This is when we first understood our specialness in the world—when our caregivers doted over us. Well-adapted people have a core feeling of specialness, and who would not want to feel special? But how special can I be if I am exactly like you? Not very. So to preserve specialness, people start to pay attention to the differences between each other. This process can develop into racism, but it does not have to. We can pay attention to the differences among people and appreciate the uniqueness of each person. The special qualities of someone else need not diminish your value, but if we are all the same, holding on to our specialness will be more of a challenge.

As evidence for this explanation, consider that for any ethnicity, religious background, neighborhood, or other characteristic, people can find a way to divide the group further. For those of Jewish descent, it is the Ashkenazi versus the Sephardic versus the Orthodox versus the Conservatives. For the Hispanics, it is the Dominicans versus the Puerto Ricans versus the Spaniards. Italians judge one another by the relative status of their town of origin. For some immigrants, the first to arrive in the new country hold greater prestige among the group. New Yorkers bond together, but if you tell someone from Brooklyn that you are from Queens, she or he may be offended. Even street gangs turn on themselves. Bloods from one area of the country may compete with Bloods from another.

We humans find new ways to subdivide and marginalize ourselves all the time. Even so, I think of the heartening image of several children of different races, of different cultures, from different neighborhoods, getting together for a pickup game of soccer or whatever sport they play. Sport can achieve this in a way that occurs in few other areas of society.

But sport presents many challenges, and as the level of competition increases, so does the pressure that athletes face. That pressure has some predictable, though not always beneficial, effect on athletes' personalities.

ATHLETES AND EXTREME CONFIDENCE

Athletes that do not believe in themselves and do not have confidence are at-risk for being consumed by their self-doubt. Conversely, too much confidence can be a problem as well. We will now examine the origin of extreme confidence in athletes and how it impacts the athletic culture.

How Did They Get So Cocky?

In examining athletes along the developmental timeline, we might wonder both when and why athletes become cocky. Although we often think of professional athletes having this brash arrogance, the personality change probably occurred well before the signing of that first multimillion-dollar contract. In fact, the top draft choices in every sport usually experience a significant number of bumps (both physical and emotional) during their first year in the pros. They developed their cockiness long before they reached that level. The various aspects of personality and even psychopathology related to violence will be discussed later in the book, but there is reason to believe that this narcissism is a natural side effect of progressing up the ladder of success, a consequence of chronic winning.

At the core of competition is the idea that one person is better than the other. Therefore, successful athletes often develop features of overconfidence and arrogance.

By winning, especially in individual competition, the young athlete often naturally starts to build confidence. We often believe that this level of confidence results from the entitlements that they get, the gifts and praise that they receive from their parents, coaches, and society in general. But it is more than that. At the heart of competition, one person wins and one person loses. Even when you are competing against yourself, you are constantly trying to better yourself. Wins can be experienced without a competitor. When you continue to improve, when you continue to master, when you continue to dominate, when you win more than you lose, of course you become accustomed to winning. Of course, you start feeling superior. So we need to understand that this progression is normal, an expected part of the process. Humility is not something that we can take for granted. But we need not take confidence from athletes to make them humble. The two traits are not mutually exclusive. A person can be both humble and confident. The confident athlete does not have to let everyone know. Confident athletes have faith in their ability, and they do not worry about trying to prove it to anyone.

Because arrogance can easily develop along with a successful athletics career, parents, coaches, and sports officials should take active steps to prevent this seed from growing. Several approaches are effective, but awareness is the first step. Young athletes should be taught the importance of sportsmanship, of not gloating, of respecting the game and thus themselves. Good coaching and adult guidance can go a long way toward preventing the development of the athlete egomaniac.

Not long ago, I gave a presentation to the football team at Dunbar High School in Washington, D.C., on emotion management for peak performance in sport. We were talking about how athletes can manage their emotions and specifically about being resilient when behind in the game. One of the players, not realizing how profound and mature he was for saying this, calmly said,

> *I don't even pay attention to the score of the game. If I play my game, I know we will win. I don't even have to worry about it, so it doesn't matter if we are behind. I always play my best and I know what kind of results that leads to.*

Later, I asked head coach Craig Jefferies, whose teams have won several championships, with a bit of awe, "Who was that kid?" He smiled and said, "Yeah, he's something special isn't he?" The player could not have been more than 16 years old, but he had the confidence and humility of a seasoned pro. He did not have a hint of arrogance. Considering how good his coach said he was, some cockiness would have been justified, but this balanced, well-coached young man knew his strengths and let them speak for themselves. The coexistence of his confidence and humility was the antithesis of pathological narcissism, a vital formula to personal growth that would lead to success on and off the football field.

We should understand that narcissism, rather than being pathology or the cause of athletes' problems, is a common side effect of chronic winning. As such, we need to work with athletes to keep them grounded so that they can win, succeed, improve, feel good about themselves, and, in fact, dominate, without developing the belief that they are above the rules, above the law, and above other people. We want them to have an aggressive fire inside them so that they compete to win, but not at the cost of sacrificing their morals or the rules of the game. We want them to be able to relish their victories, done in the right way.

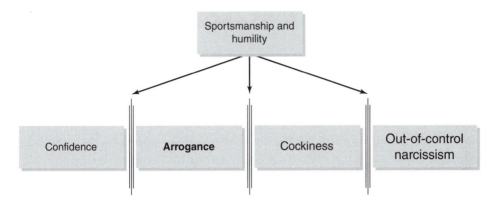

Figure 4.1   Illustration of the natural progression that develops from chronic winning. Confidence can grow to arrogance, cockiness, and ultimately narcissism. Good coaching that highlights the importance of sportsmanship and humility can prevent this evolution.

One could argue that this process of building overconfidence can be, and should be, limited by stressing the importance of sportsmanship. Teaching respect for the game and all parts of it, including the opponent, can balance this budding confidence and provide important lessons in humility. We would all be pleased if children always came off the playing surface smiling—win or lose. Although people place different values on winning, at the age when sport becomes important, losing hurts. Some children equate losing with being a failure. But as long as they keep trying, they can never be failures. NHL Hall of Famer Wayne Gretzky tells people that they cannot succeed any other way: "You miss 100 percent of the shots that you don't take."

Another beauty of sport is that children learn many life lessons without even trying. If humility is the antidote to narcissism, sport provides a great arena to be humbled. In baseball, failing at a 70 percent rate (batting .300) can get a player to the Hall of Fame. Sport requires the performance of many difficult tasks. If we put the tasks in perspective, we realize that not achieving our goals is not something to avoid; it is something to accept. We try to minimize the frequency of failure, but it is part of the game. If it were easy, there would be no challenge to it. If we knew who would win all the time, why would we play the game? We play the game because no matter what anyone says, on any given day, the outcome can be different. Sometimes we need to put things in perspective, especially difficult sports tasks.

During my 18 years I came to bat about 10,000 times. I struck out about 1,700 times and walked maybe 1,800 times. If you figure a player will average about 500 at-bats a season, that means I played seven years in the major leagues without hitting the ball.

—Mickey Mantle

SPORT ADMINISTRATORS AND MANAGERS

Administrators and managers get little credit for running smooth, safe, competitive, noncriminal sports organizations. What do they need to know about the athlete culture? Where do they fit in, especially with regard to violence?

Obviously, administrators and managers are a heterogeneous group of people. For simplicity, I will break the group down into two categories: youth sports and recreation and higher-level competitive sports, which includes organized sports from the high school through professional levels.

Youth Sports and Recreation

The administrators who run sports leagues, academies, and so on have already read much of what they need to know. They likely have seen the dynamics in their athletes, coaches, parents, and officials. What has not been covered is their responsibility to keep the peace.

We know that neighborhoods do not always wait until kids are in high school to identify with a team and become rabid with enthusiasm, so one daunting task is to be able to roll with the punches (figuratively, I hope) while holding firm to guidelines needed to provide safety. Although I will later discuss the details of what should be included in such guidelines, a crucial first step is to meet with the board of directors, higher administration, or anyone who manages legal affairs to discuss the liability that the organization may have if a violent incident takes place at one of its venues.

Although the perpetrator is held responsible when behavior reaches criminal proportion, those who provide the venue are also expected to provide safety. A useful step may be to have a meeting with a local representative of the police department to discuss ahead of time their expectations regarding sports events. I know of one town in which so much conflict occurred that the police department asked for a schedule of the games to aid in planning their patrols. In these situations, proaction is always preferable to reaction.

Let us not assume that conflict happens only with youngsters and their parents. Recreational leagues are a common setting for former competitive athletes to continue to play and get their exercise. Competitive fires continue to burn, and sometimes they get too hot. The codes of conduct that are prepared and distributed to kids and their parents should be amended and given to every person who joins a gym or league so that all participants know what will be tolerated and what will not be tolerated.

Administrators have a responsibility to provide an environment that is considerate to all patrons. Some places have gone as far as developing rules that prohibit dropping weights and grunting. Planet Fitness, a company that boasts 120 gyms across the country, received some attention after having police escort a patron out of one of their New York facilities because he grunted while lifting weights. Promising to provide an unintimidating environment for all their members, Planet Fitness has an alarm that sounds when someone violates the rules. This policy may seem extreme, but the company was sufficiently concerned with providing a certain type of environment that they made enforceable rules to create it.

Administrators can do other things as well. The staff can be trained in conflict resolution and anger management techniques. Whether the organization is a fitness club (though when dealing with the paying public, many other concerns may be present) or a youth sports league, if more people are familiar with resolving these problems, the likelihood of a quick de-escalation of a conflict increases.

In any case, keeping excellent records is crucial. Whatever the code of conduct, each member, athlete, parent, and so on must receive it. Mandatory seasonal workshops on topics such as sportsmanship, conflict resolution, and expectations of behavior are useful. I recommend charging a small fee for these workshops (which might pay for the speaker as well as contribute to funds for equipment and other needs) because people often perceive free events as not having much value. Putting together a schedule of presentations provides an organization with the opportunity to be proactive by making sure that all participants are appropriately educated ahead of time. Furthermore, this type of educational program may provide some legal protection should people transgress because it demonstrate the value that the organization places on preventing these incidents.

Higher Competition

The higher the level of competition, the more the sport administrators' job is connected to budgets. Whether it is a matter of selling memberships, selling tickets, negotiating salaries of coaches, or balancing budgets (which somehow seem to shrink more often than they grow), money becomes increasingly entangled in the operation. Knowing the staff and the people who are participating in sports is not just an operational issue now; it is a fiscal one as well. Nasty arguments and violent incidents can drive money away. As an example, when a university's reputation is tarnished by the repeated arrest of its athletes, enrollment of new students normally decreases. Athletes and sport organizations are hiring public relations firms to help them with their public perception and their handling of news of negative behaviors. Some organizations have their own media relations departments to focus specifically on these issues.

So, as a sport administrator, how do you know who is playing for you? And, what do you know about them? For high schools, the athletes are the kids from the local neighborhood. You need to know about gang involvement and propensity toward violence. Gangs do not exist only in lower-income, minority communities. Gangs are showing their colors everywhere these days.

What is your coach's view of violence? Does the coach strive to maintain a disciplined team with a code of conduct, or does she or he care about what the athletes do only when they are involved in team functions? Knowing this information is important because coaches can have a powerful influence on their athletes, especially because adolescents are progressively less interested in listening to the rules of parents and other adults. Coaches who are concerned about teaching the right lessons as well as winning should be given as many opportunities as possible to learn about anger management. The information is for them as well as their athletes. Being able to manage anger will improve their performance and help them navigate difficult players, coaches, administrators, and officials. They will also be better able to model appropriate behavior for the kids who are watching them. Coaches are human, and they make mistakes. If we sometimes excuse athletes for being unable to keep their tempers in check and believe that they need to learn how to do that, then why do we not do more to teach their teachers about the same subject?

In the progression from high school to college athletics, and from NAIA up to NCAA Division I, a proportional increase occurs in intensity, fandom, and the celebrity status of those associated with athletics programs. This greater scrutiny leads to greater visibility. People in the athletics department may quickly find themselves frequent flyers on media circuits. People do not get the benefit of the doubt. The court of public opinion is always open. The arrest of a person associated with an athletics program is newsworthy, although other people arrested on the same day for the same offense do not even make the police blotter section of the newspaper.

Whether you are a sport administrator, coach, athlete, or parent of an athlete, do not feel bad about the fact that people do not talk about these issues. Sport psychologists do not talk about these issues as much as they should. So do not waste your time questioning what you should have already done or put in place. Just do it.

SPORT PSYCHOLOGISTS

Surprisingly, sport psychologists talk little about anger and violence. Many of those who do seem to have limited experience in dealing with serious levels of anger and violence. Talk about these emotions and behavior as an academic exercise does little to translate into action and intervention.

I believe that this shortcoming is the result of two factors. First, many of the sport psychologists out there are not psychologists by training. Their education comes from the sport sciences, and they have had little exposure to dealing with problematic behavior. The other reason is that angry outbursts by athletes that reach the threshold of requiring a serious intervention do not occur frequently. Simply stated, managing anger can be a problem for athletes because it can be a problem for everyone, but anger is not a problem that frequently yields a referral to a sport psychologist.

The problem of sport psychologists not dealing with anger and violence has not gone completely unnoticed. Gershon Tenenbaum, Bob Singer, Evan Stewart, and Joan Duda published "Aggression and Violence in Sport: An ISSP (International Society of Sport Psychology) Position Stand" in 1997. Since then, they have debated back and forth with John Kerr about their position. Feel free to read the papers mentioned above for the specifics, but what is salient for this debate is the fact that many of the recommendations made by both sides never came to fruition. The recommendations were not acted on for various reasons, but probably the main reason was that the recommendations were not practical and meaningful to the people in the sports world who actually read the statement in the first place. Banning alcohol, of course, was a recommended action that would certainly reduce violence among fans, but that proposal was unlikely to be implemented because of the large sums of money made by selling such beverages.

In any case, I believe strongly that sport psychologists need to move from academic conversations to meaningful interventions. The first step for you as a sport psychologist is to understand your limitations in dealing with these problems. Anger problems are not simple to cope with. You cannot just read a manual and then know how to deal with them. Anger problems can easily escalate out of control, and they may result from serious clinical issues. So the first step is to recognize what you do not know and then go learn about it. The consequences and likelihood of these problems suddenly becoming more than you can handle is, I believe, higher than any other problem you will face.

Next, you must be comfortable with your own anger and how you deal with it. If you cannot model the ability to do this, you are done. Of course, you do not have to be perfect. In fact, demonstrating an ability to cope may enhance your credibility. As with athletes, anger at high levels will interfere with your ability to think straight. To be your best, you have to keep your cool.

If you believe that you never become angry you are lying to yourself (everyone becomes angry, but you may just deal with it differently) and you will be in a poor position to relate to athletes who do, overtly or covertly, become angry.

Sport can be frustrating. Athletes do not always meet their goals, and someone (either the athlete him- or herself, when competing individually, or others) is always trying to impede them from achieving success. Athletics is a ripe environment for anger. If you think that becoming angry is abnormal or a problem (remember that people get in trouble for their behaviors, not their emotions) and you cannot normalize the experience, you will lose the athlete and she or he will not want to talk to you about it. When talking with athletes, ask them, "Does becoming angry lead you to the athletics success that you want?" Expect them to say yes, because at times it does, just as the bully is reinforced for taking your lunch money.

Although you can point to the inverted U hypothesis to explain to them why intense anger interferes with success, the simplest answer is right in front of you: "Why are you here talking to me?"

When trying to understand the athlete culture, keep in mind that your place is usually outside it. Sport psychology still has a lot of stigma attached to it. Coaches and athletes refer to visiting my office as "going to the shrink." The athlete culture, the microcosm of society where sport lives, has a wonderfully homeostatic, protective nature. Members of the culture circle the wagons to keep out any perceived threat. Although at times they may seem to be sticking their heads in the sand and pretending that a problem does not exist, athletes know how much they and those around them are scrutinized. You cannot barge in like an expert ready to tell them everything. You must offer information. Ask to be invited in. Explain how you can help them and their athletes better themselves.

I learned this the hard way. When I started studying anger and sport and wanted to work with athletes, I was armed with all the media clippings and articles that pointed to higher levels of anger in athletes. I started making calls. Even when a local incident precipitated my call, athletics departments often went into damage control mode.

I was fortunate. I met a high school basketball coach who was a real character guy. He was interested in more than just teaching his kids the Xs and Os. He was concerned about their overall development. He did not let the boys practice until they had completed their homework. He kept himself aware of what was going on in their social lives. When he heard what I was trying to do, he realized before I did that the goal was not to keep his boys out of jail. His was an upper-middle-class high school that had no real problem children. He knew that the program could help his players come together as a team, improve communication, learn how to calm themselves and each other down, and develop self-discipline. So I worked with them for 10 weeks. We met as a group and worked through the manual that I developed with my mentor, Dr. Eva Feindler. At the end of it, I realized that many gains could not be grasped with statistics. I saw the athletes using the skills during games, before games, and when struggling with how to communicate with their coach about something. The program seemed to improve their performance and not because it kept the kids out of jail.

I completely changed how I packaged the program, including the stated goals. The objective was not to fix the "bad kids." Certainly, those with serious anger problems could benefit, but the main goal was to help athletes improve their performance by mastering the mental side of the game, by being able to modulate their emotions.

I realized that some of the defensiveness that I faced earlier when I approached coaches and sport organizations was completely justified. I was going to help them fix a problem that was just not a problem. Sure, some athletes need targeted intervention because they are violent and cannot control their anger, but most of them do not. Athletes need these skills because people assume that they can handle every situation perfectly. So, if we are going to help athletes, we must give them a chance to learn new life skills.

SUMMARY

In this chapter we reviewed many aspects of the athlete culture. We started by acknowledging that the term *athlete* can be defined in various ways. At the extreme, millions of people can be considered athletes. Breaking the culture down into subdivisions allowed us to recognize some of the unique struggles that coaches, parents, referees, and sport administrators face in managing their anger. The role of sport psychologists in this endeavor was explored as well.

Ultimately, however, the perspective of the athlete is paramount. The confusion that athletes face in dealing with their emotions, as well as how people treat them when they are chronically successful, provides an understanding of how athletes can become arrogant and entitled. The escalating pressure that occurs at higher levels of competition can affect how they manage their emotions. This topic was juxtaposed with a recipe of how to prevent problems, stressing the importance of good coaching, sportsmanship, and humility. These elements can help develop athletes of high character.

This chapter leads into the next, which discusses how the interface of mental illness and sport can lead to difficulties with anger management, even in the best of circumstances.

CHAPTER 5

MENTAL ILLNESS AND VIOLENCE IN SPORT

Many athletes would consider consulting with a sport psychologist if the word *psychologist* was not part of the professional's title. To avoid the stigma associated with mental illness, many sport psychologists advertise themselves as sport consultants or other titles that do not include the word *psychology*. This omnipresent stigma is an important place to start the discussion of the relationship between mental illness and violence, especially as it applies to sport because there is a basic assumption that athletes are healthy people. An extension of this thinking is that if an athlete goes to see a sport psychologist, "a shrink," he or she must be crazy.

Propagating this myth offers no benefit, so let us dispense with the suspense and just put it on the table. What does it mean to be crazy? Do athletes go crazy? Are crazy athletes violent? And if athletes are violent, does that mean they are crazy?

To begin, people have different ideas about what constitutes being crazy. The same holds true for what is considered normal. Location, culture, and experience all shape what someone may consider to be within the loosely defined parameters of normalcy. This holds true at the lower end of craziness as well as at the higher end. A couple of examples should illustrate the variability in this idea of normalcy.

Although the consensus in American culture is that marriage and monogamy are supposed to go hand and hand, certain groups accept polygamy as a way of life. In other cultures, polygamy is not only accepted but expected.

What about something more bizarre, further down the craziness scale? Coprophagia is the act of eating one's own feces. Most people are disgusted by the thought of this behavior and would assert that no sane person would engage in it. In fact, in psychiatric hospitals, it is generally believed that this or related behaviors, such as smearing feces, is a sign of either severe psychosis or profound mental retardation.

In prison, however, coprophagia is not so abnormal and not as rare as an outsider might suspect. Although some who are severely ill engage in the behavior, many inmates who do not have a severe mental illness engage in it as well. For them, it is more an expression of their anger or self-hate. Smearing feces or throwing it on staff is a literal metaphor of their "shitting on you." Prisoners learn to manipulate their environment by engaging in behavior that is traditionally considered crazy. So, if a person eats and smears feces in prison, does it mean that he or she is crazy? Maybe or maybe not.

Of greater value is understanding the functionality of the behavior. Why people do something is often more important than what they do. Often, they have a goal. People who engage in self-injurious behavior like cutting themselves (sometimes called cutters) may gain many utilities by their behavior. For some, physical pain is preferable to emotional pain. Some may relish the attention that they receive or feel empowered that they can control their usually out-of-control lives. Others may get a rush from the endorphins that accompany the injury; similarly, bulimics may enjoy the rush associated with the temporary loss of oxygen to the brain when they induce their own vomiting. Although people have many emotional responses when they hear of such behavior, a common opinion is "You must be crazy to do that." In practice, when working with cutters, people must not emotionally overreact to the behavior and demand that they immediately stop it lest they end up dead. A counselor can get great mileage from validating the person, not judging her or him, and acknowledging that the cutting obviously worked—it achieved something. What was the person trying to achieve, and how can she or he do it in a less self-destructive manner? With that approach the person can learn to self-soothe in a positive way without the negative consequences that can accompany behavior like cutting, including accidental death.

Some inmates who engage in bizarre behavior are not in the slightest bit psychotic. One such inmate was trying to gain access to a forensic hospital that was co-ed. He was not crazy; he was goal directed, and more dedicated to reaching his goals than most people are.

The things that I observed while working in a prison system could fill a book, but even the most hardened prison psychiatrists and psychologists concede that certain behaviors in prisons must be the work of mental illness. In a particularly tragic case a schizophrenic male amputated his own penis. In any context, that behavior reaches the threshold of insanity.

The point is that we need to consider behavior in its context and recognize our biases when assessing behavior. In addition, a dichotomy of crazy versus normal is not a fair depiction. Behavior occurs along a continuum, and people may have different ideas about where to place a behavior along that scale.

This point is important because as we discuss mental illness, examples will be provided of how psychopathology presents to avoid overwhelming you by the description. This approach can help you better comprehend the relationship of psychopathology (or lack thereof) with violence.

PSYCHOSIS

Note that the term *crazy* is not well received in the world of political correctness. *Crazy* is a colloquial word that has many meanings, but it will be included in this conversation because its use is commonplace. We may have difficulty wading through a statement such as "The person was experiencing an acute psychotic episode manifesting itself through somatic delusions, labile mood, and disorganized thought processes." The goal is not to burden the reader with an entirely new vocabulary of psycho-jargon but rather to explain things in both common language and technical terms to promote greater interchange between the layman and the professional.

Most commonly, when someone is identified as being crazy, what the observer is describing is the person being psychotic. The most pronounced aspect of psychosis is the gross impairment of reality testing. That is, the person is unable to determine whether what he or she is thinking is consistent with reality.

Psychosis generally presents in one of three ways: hallucinations, delusions, or thought disorders. Hallucinations are sensory experiences created by the mind and are not connected to any real event. For instance, those who state that they are seeing people who are not really there are experiencing visual hallucinations. Similarly, people who report hearing voices talking to them when no one is around are having auditory hallucinations. Tactile hallucinations occur when people feel something touching them but no corresponding stimuli are present.

People who experience hallucinations are not necessarily psychotic. If they know that the voices they hear are part of their mental illness or that their minds are playing tricks on them, they are able to test reality and therefore are not psychotic.

Delusions are belief systems that are not consistent with society's general understanding of reality. Examples include paranoid delusions in which people believe that everyone is out to get them. Delusions can be quite elaborate and incorporate all kinds of conspiracy theories. Somatic delusions are the belief that things are going on inside the body that are not true. For example, people may believe that snakes are crawling around in their intestines. Those with delusions of grandeur believe that they are the greatest, most special person in the world. In extreme cases, they may believe that they are God or some equally powerful entity.

Thought disorders are symptoms in which the person is unable to think clearly and thus has difficulty communicating. The person may stop in the middle of a sentence, interrupted by what she or he may be hearing internally (hallucinations). Sometimes, the person's mind is racing through different thoughts in a disorganized matter such that concentration is impossible. These three symptom constellations, when they co-occur with poor reality testing, represent psychotic symptoms.

As we move on to mood disorders, you will see that people can have psychotic episodes while in a depressed or manic state and not be schizophrenic.

Schizophrenia

Schizophrenia is a brain disease of physiological origin, meaning that it is caused by neurochemical abnormalities. Specifically, it was originally believed that the symptoms of schizophrenia were caused by elevated levels of dopamine (a neurotransmitter) transmission. The more common belief now is that other neurotransmitters and brain structures are involved. Schizophrenia is a progressive disease. Age of onset is usually in young adulthood, although slight variations are noted between men and women.

Peak ages of onset are 10 to 25 years of age for men and 25 to 35 for women. Approximately 2.2 million Americans, or about 1 percent of our national population, are diagnosed with schizophrenia. As mentioned earlier, it is a progressive, degenerative disease for which there is no known cure. Medications are the primary treatment of choice. With supportive psychotherapy, medications can reduce the symptoms and slow the degenerative process. People diagnosed with schizophrenia have significantly shorter life spans, most prominently because of poor self-care resulting in acceleration of medical problems and a higher rate of suicide.

People who suffer from schizophrenia can present with hallucinations, delusions, or pronounced thought disorders, which are called positive symptoms. Alternatively, they may present primarily with negative symptoms, which include social withdrawal, poverty of speech (alogia), flat emotions, poor grooming, and lack of motivation. This severe and debilitating illness has a poor prognosis.

Hallucinations and thought disorders tend to respond better to medications than delusions and negative symptoms do. My hypothesis about why this is the case goes this way: Even before their first hallucinatory episode, children who are predisposed to schizophrenia realize that they are different in some way, that they have difficulty fitting in. When we are young we all have the fantasy that we are the most special person in the world. How do you deal with the feeling that you are different? One way is to make your difference mean that you are special. Rather than developing low self-esteem, your mind (and not consciously) creates a belief system that makes you special. All delusions have, at their core, an element of the person's being special. Think about it. If you are paranoid, you must believe that you are special because you have to be special for everyone to want to get you. These delusions are a defense mechanism that helps people deal with the world. Perhaps this is why those with delusions are impervious to intervention.

Some schizophrenics do not want to take their medication because they believe that it is poison. One hypothesis is that medication poisons them by weakening their defenses, by removing their symptoms, which, in a distorted way, protect them from the world.

By now you may be saying, "OK, fine. What does this have to do with athletes and sport?" The answer is, not much. The point is that seriously debilitating mental illnesses, such as the various forms of schizophrenia, are so compromising that athletes with this type of illness would be exceedingly unlikely to reach a highly competitive level before the disease affected their functioning. Nonetheless, it is conceivable that the onset of schizophrenia could coincide with the timing of an athlete's making it big.

> *While schizophrenic illnesses occasionally have been reported in elite athletes, the process of selection probably operates most mercilessly on the individual suffering acutely from these disorders. The developmental time core for the onset of these illnesses has individuals becoming most symptomatic at the very time that the pressures to perform as an athlete are the greatest. . . . It is nonetheless conceivable that a highly talented athlete with either mild positive symptoms or a late onset of a schizophrenic illness could reach an elite level of competition before being diagnosed and, hopefully, treated. (Burton, 2000, chapter 4 in Sport Psychiatry: Theory and Practice)*

How often do athletes have psychotic episodes? Rarely, it would seem, both because the incidence rate of psychosis is low to begin with and because many athletes with these types of problems wind up having to leave sport because the severity of their symptoms requires treatment. But in some documented cases, athletes have experienced psychotic episodes that have affected the image of athletes and violence.

In September 2004 former Oakland Raiders kicker Cole Ford was arrested for shooting at the Las Vegas home of illusionists Siegfried and Roy because he believed that "what was wrong with the world was linked to the illusionists' treatment, dominance, and unhealthy intimacy with their animals." He went on to state that he believed that Siegfried and Roy threatened the world and he was trying to figure out how to stop them. He was arrested and found incompetent to stand trial because of his mental illness. In fact, his illness was severe enough for a judge to order him to be medicated over his objection.

The treatment of choice for psychotic disorders is unequivocally medications. Some common medications used for these problems are Risperdal, Geodon, Zyprexa, Haldol, Prolixin, Seroquel, Abilify, Mellaril, Trilafon, Thorazine, and Clozaril. People who are well managed on medications can function in society without anyone detecting their mental illness. Schizophrenia, like other illnesses, is most manageable when treated aggressively, consistently, and early in its presentation. It is unlikely, although possible, that someone would be able to play at a high level when diagnosed and on medications to treat the illness.

As previously mentioned, psychotic episodes can occur in people who are not suffering from schizophrenia. Much more prevalent are mood disorders such as depression and mania. In extreme cases, those disorders can lead to psychotic episodes. The next section will explore this topic further.

Mood Disorders

Mood disorders encompass a large group of disorders identified by extremes highs or lows in mood, commonly referred to as mania and depression respectively. Moods should not be thought of as good or bad, or black or white. Like most dimensions of the human condition, they occur on a continuum. At the lower end of severity, times of sadness are commonplace and normal. When sadness pervades for a long period and impedes functioning, it is considered pathological. Although mood disorders are more common and generally more treatable than psychotic disorders, at the extremes they significantly affect functioning as well.

Depression

Depression encompasses much more than just being sad. Depression can manifest itself in multiple ways. Frequently, it can be seen by a loss of energy and interest in activities that the person usually enjoys (such as sexual behavior), difficulty concentrating, loss of appetite, changes in sleep habits, and suicidal thoughts. These symptoms, which resemble those of someone who is deteriorating from poor self-care (poor hygiene, looking disheveled, not eating to the point of malnutrition—symptoms similar to those seen in eating disorders, although different factors are at work) are called vegetative symptoms. In these states, people are at risk of passive suicide, of dying from lack of self-care. In extreme cases these people have to be hospitalized and fed through a tube. Occasionally, they receive electroconvulsive therapy (ECT), which induces a seizure by applying electricity to the brain. This therapy is remarkably effective for some patients. Incidence rates are much higher than the rates of psychotic disorders. Approximately 10 to 25 percent of women and 5 to 12 percent of men have a major depressive episode over the course of their lives. The average age of onset for major depression is about 40 years, and more than half of all patients have onset between the ages of 20 and 50. Recent evidence points toward an increase in depression among people younger than 20 years of age. These findings may be related to the increased use of alcohol and drugs of abuse in this age group.

Moreover, several factors contribute to changes in a person's mood. Depression is not believed to be driven solely by biological causes. Events in a person's life and environmental factors can affect mood. Correspondingly, the treatment for depression does not always reside in a prescription bottle. Psychotherapy can be extremely helpful, and research evidence is increasingly showing that exercise has its own antidepressant effects.

As Dr. Lynette Craft of Northwestern University's Feinberg School of Medicine noted, findings from meta-analytic studies indicate that exercise is effective for both men and women of all ages, including those who are initially severely depressed. When exercise was compared with other traditional treatments for depression, exercise was found to be just as beneficial and not significantly different from psychotherapy, pharmacological therapy, and other behavioral interventions. Comparison of exercise program characteristics across studies indicates that aerobic and nonaerobic exercise are both effective in reducing symptoms of depression. Furthermore, exercise need not be lengthy or intense or promote fitness gains for patients to experience positive benefits.

Craft also reminds us that many symptoms of overtraining are similar to those of clinical depression. Therefore, if an athlete seeks help for a depressed mood, changes in sleep patterns and appetite, or feelings of agitation, a careful evaluation is recommended to determine whether a mental health issue or overtraining syndrome is occurring. For athletes suffering from overtraining, exercise for the purpose of mood elevation may be contraindicated because it could exacerbate the overtraining syndrome rather than alleviate the mood disturbance.

Depression is not generally considered a precursor of violence, although some have hypothesized that depression is anger turned inward. The converse—that anger is depression turned outward—may have some validity as well. Some people experience what is called agitated depression. People suffering from this form of depression do not present with vegetative symptoms but instead are active and easily irritated. At times, they act out physically. Those with an agitated depression are more likely to become violent than those with more traditional vegetative symptoms.

Returning to Berkowitz' completion hypothesis (chapter 1), remember that any negative affect state can be a precursor to aggressive behavior. Additionally, emotions are not mutually exclusive. Someone can be both sad and angry. Symptom clusters that do not traditionally occur together can at times happen simultaneously.

But as I mentioned earlier, depression is not solely a biochemical disorder. Life stressors can certainly bring about depressive episodes. Recently, we have heard more about athletes who have struggled with depression.

WNBA All-Star forward Chamique Holdsclaw was playing for the Washington Mystics when a depressive episode ended her season in July 2004. She considered retirement because of the blanket of darkness that she fell under. It was reported that she traced the root of her depression to the death of her grandmother a year before the crisis. Her grandmother had raised Holdsclaw and her younger brother in Astoria, Queens, and she was Holdsclaw's primary emotional support throughout her life. When she died of a stroke, Chamique suppressed her grief and returned to play only days after the funeral. Her grief proved to be too much, and Holdsclaw isolated herself and slept a great deal. She returned in 2005 to play for the Los Angeles Sparks. Holdsclaw was open about her hesitance to discuss her struggles with depression publicly. It may not have been a coincidence that she came to the Sparks, who also

WNBA All-Star forward Chamique Holdsclaw suffered from depression after her grandmother died. While depression didn't lead to anger and violence for Holdsclaw, it was a hurdle she had to overcome to continue playing well.

©Darrell Walker/UTHM/Icon SMI

had point guard Nikki Teasley on their roster, another WNBA star who had struggled with depression.

For some athletes, depression carries hardly any risk of resultant violence. Conversely, for some, depression can increase the risk, as Hall of Fame Quarterback and Sunday afternoon analyst for Fox NFL Sunday Terry Bradshaw noted when describing his depression:

With any bad situations I'd experienced before—a bad game or my two previous divorces—I got over them. This time I just could not get out of the hole. The anxiety attacks were frequent and extensive. I had weight loss, which I'd never had before. I couldn't stop crying. And if I wasn't crying, I was angry, bitter, hateful and mean spirited. I couldn't sleep, couldn't concentrate. It just got crazy." (Morgan & Shoop, 2004)

Depression has the potential to lead to violence toward others as well as toward oneself. In the worst-case scenario, athletes have committed suicide, self-directed violence at its most extreme. For example, University of Pennsylvania senior running back Kyle Ambrogi ended his life two days after he had one of the best games of his football career. He had scored two touchdowns as Penn soundly beat Bucknell, 53-7. Despite his struggles with depression, most observers were shocked, considering all that he had going for him. An excellent student, he already had job offers already coming in. His life was seemingly about to take off, but by Monday October 10, 2005, he was dead.

When people are so despondent that they no longer care about their future, they can be extremely dangerous. The following example depicts how depression can devolve into a murder–suicide attempt.

Donnie Moore was a pitcher for the California Angels who unfortunately is most remembered for the home run that he gave up to Dave Henderson during game 5 of the 1986 American League Championship Series. Moore, pitching in relief, had brought the Angels to within one strike of clinching their first pennant. But Henderson's home run started the Red Sox on a comeback from a 3-1 series deficit. Boston went on to win that game and the series, and they moved on to play in the World Series. Many fans never forgot the game or forgave Moore for his role in it. The stress related to this incident paired with his long battle with depression and substance abuse culminated with his attempt to murder his wife and his suicide by gunshot.

Depression and violence do not necessarily go hand in hand, but when reviewing mental illness in athletes, we should not assume that depressed athletes cannot be dangerous.

A factor that may compound this is the stress faced by athletes in the public eye. Privacy is limited, and any struggle or scandal will undoubtedly be all over the headlines. The Mitchell Report on steroids in Major League Baseball is an excellent example. Players were named as potential users of steroids without any evidence other than the testimony of Brian McNamee. People who are sensitive about their public image could have severe emotional reactions. When a person is in front of the cameras day in and day out, it is simply a matter of time before the person has an overemotional reaction.

Furthermore, in analyzing the outcome of a game, the media often devote as much time to the players who failed as they do to the heroes. A certain degree of mental strength is required to shake off this criticism. Not all athletes have this toughness, especially young ones. Hearing some of the harsh criticism that parents throw at Little Leaguers (including their own children) is enough to make an observer cringe. At any age and any level, losses, failures, poor performances, and criticism can trigger an emotional response. In extreme circumstances, depression, anger, and even violence can result. Criticism from teammates or coaches, especially publicly, can lead to a downward spiral. Identifying when athletes need greater support, and possibly even counseling, is helpful in preventing tragic outcomes.

Injuries

When athletes are injured, especially with severe injuries, a wide array of emotions often comes as part of the package. I remember that when I tore up my knee (ACL, MCL, and meniscus), I had a whirlwind of feelings. I remember being angry at my body for failing me, upset with myself for not being able to prevent the injury (my own fantasies of invincibility), frustrated that healing and recovery would take a long time, afraid that I would never play sports the same way again, and depressed, for many of the same reasons. All that, and I did not even mention the pain that followed reconstructive surgery. I was not a happy camper. Those emotions, among others, would be found on most athletes' list when they have to deal with serious injuries.

Some sport psychologists have offered the hypothesis that athletes go through the stages of mourning that were outlined by Elizabeth Kubler-Ross in her book *On Death and Dying*. These stages of grief—denial, anger, bargaining, depression, and acceptance—are hypothesized to occur for athletes, especially when they experience a career-threatening injury. If this model applies, then it would follow that both depression and anger would be present in athletes as they struggle with injury.

World-class skier Picabo Street openly discussed the depression that she coped with following a seemingly catastrophic knee injury that kept her off the slopes for a considerable time. The point here is that nothing about being an athlete makes a person immune to emotional problems, including depression. In fact, because people assume that mental health coexists with physical health, athletes may be at greater risk because symptoms are not identified early. For that reason, treatment may be significantly delayed.

Treatment for depression most commonly includes both psychotherapy and medications. The medications are usually well tolerated and rarely interfere with sport participation.

Manic Episodes and Bipolar Disorder

The "polar" opposite to a depressive episode is a manic episode; bipolar disorder refers to the opposite poles of depression and mania. Manic episodes are denoted by an elevated, expansive mood that may take the form of euphoria or irritability. Manic episodes may include pronounced grandiosity, decreased need for sleep (possibly staying up for days on end unaided by substance abuse), being more talkative than usual or using a pressured speech delivery, having racing thoughts that jump from one topic to another with little logical transition (called flight of ideas), distractibility, psychomotor agitation (unable to sit still), and an increase in participation in pleasurable activities, often without concern for the consequences. Such activities may include hypersexuality, increased shopping and spending (at times running up thousands of dollars of credit card debt), and risk-taking behaviors such as reckless, high-speed driving and gambling. People in a manic episode may have a feeling of invincibility and believe that rules do not apply to them because they are special. Not surprisingly, in extreme cases a manic episode can leads to or coexist with a psychotic episode. A person's emotions may spin so far out of control that his or her thinking becomes derailed, causing logic to fall by the wayside.

Women in a manic episode can sometimes be picked out of the crowd by the extremely bright colors or excessive amounts of makeup that they wear. Regardless of gender, people in a manic episode may be preoccupied with religious, political, sexual, or persecutory ideas that reach delusional proportions. That is not to imply that women in a manic state engage in benign though bizarre wardrobe choices whereas men engage in violent behavior. Those prone toward violence, whether male or female, are more likely to act as such when in a manic state. Furthermore, because people in a manic state feel as if they are on top of the world, why would they want to come down from it? Like a cocaine high, a manic state is a powerful feeling. People often do not even realize that they are out of control. Hospitalization or the intervention of an outsider is often required to get the person help.

The age of onset for bipolar disorder ranges from childhood to 50 years of age or even older, but the average age of onset is approximately 30 years of age. People with bipolar disorder go through cycles of mania and depression, sometimes with long periods between episodes and sometimes with episodes in close proximity. They may also experience what is called a mixed episode, in which energized emotion, racing thoughts, and bizarre behavior coincide with suicidal ideation, self-destructiveness, and poor self-care.

Athletes, of course, are not immune from bipolar disorder. Although it is not a common illness, bipolar disorder, when untreated, can destroy a person's life and the lives of those nearby. In an article written by Mark Kram of the *Philadelphia Daily News* about former NFL defensive lineman Alonzo Spellman's battle with bipolar disorder, Spellman is depicted during a manic episode on a plane.

The article was titled "The Brutal Trip Down: A Tale About Alonzo Spellman, His Illness, and a Terrifying Flight That Landed Him in Jail." The author described the experience of a Philadelphia family returning home from a vacation in Michigan in July 2002, when they found themselves sitting in front of 6-foot-4-inch (193-centimeter), 330-pound (150-kilogram) Spellman in the midst of a manic episode. He rambled loudly about terrorism and began hurling profanities and threats toward the scared parents with their two small sons. It was reported that the agitated Spellman threatened to tear the emergency door off and to assault the captain of the plane.

Through the course of the article, Kram described previous episodes in which Spellman's illness got the better of him, beginning with conflicts with coaches early in his career and progressing to an incident in which he barricaded himself inside the home of his publicist while paranoid. The 10-hour standoff ended only when former Chicago Bears teammate Mike Singletary talked him down and got him to agree to undergo a 72-hour observation in a nearby hospital. The following day he was found dressed only in his hospital pants walking barefoot along a highway.

Spellman told the media that he did not like the emotional numbness that he experienced with medications, and court documents indicated that he self-medicated with illicit drugs. Even his sister conceded that Spellman had little insight into his illness.

Ultimately, Spellman was charged and convicted for the events on the plane and spent 16 months of an 18-month sentence in federal prison. He would later attempt a comeback and played football for Las Vegas' Arena League football team, but the effect that his mental illness had on the people around him and his career was irreversible.

As scary as Alonzo Spellman's episode was, it was upstaged by an incident involving Barrett Robbins, who formerly played center for the Oakland Raiders. His bipolar illness came to public attention when he went AWOL from his hotel before the Super Bowl. It was later discovered that he went on a drinking binge in Tijuana, Mexico, while in what sounded like a mixed episode (when a person is both manic and depressed at the same time). This episode was not his first, but it occurred at the most inopportune time. His life was spiraling out of control. Instead of playing in the Super Bowl, he was hospitalized for treatment of his bipolar disorder and was on suicide watch.

After a stay in the Betty Ford Clinic, which was reported to be shorter than doctors advised, he stopped drinking and was taking his medications—Depakote, a mood stabilizer; Risperdal, an antipsychotic; and Wellbutrin, an antidepressant, for a while. Often, people who suffer from bipolar disorder either (a) enjoy being in the manic state, full of energy and life, and have no insight into their pending self-destruction or (b) try to self-medicate their condition with alcohol or drugs, or stop their medications, precipitating a decompensation. The logic goes this way: If you feel as if you are on top of the world, why would you take advice from anyone about doing something so that you would be OK? So they convince themselves that they are fine. They stop taking their medications and fall apart. What makes this situation even more complicated is that when some people stop their medications, they become sick after missing a single dose. Others can go weeks before any symptoms return. This stable period without medications only convinces them that they do not need the meds.

As often happens with this disorder, Robbins began skipping his medications and slowly started to unravel. His wife filed for divorce in November and eventually got a restraining order. It was reported that Robbins began sharing suicidal thoughts with his wife. She hoped that his contemplation of suicide would be a wake-up call for him to take better care of himself and return to treatment.

The situation culminated on January 15, 2005, when police responded to a burglary call in an office building that had a nightclub in it. They found Barrett Robbins in a women's restroom. When an officer told him to put his hands on the wall, Robbins became agitated and wrestled with three officers. It is reported that he threw at least two of them around and tried to reach for their guns. An officer fired five shots, and two hit Robbins—one in the heart and one in the lung. Robbins survived the near-fatal wounds and later faced three felony attempted-murder charges, punishable by as much as life in prison. Under a plea agreement, Robbins pled guilty to five charges, including the felony attempted-murder charges, and was sentenced to five years of probation, ordered to receive treatment for his bipolar disorder, and directed to avoid alcohol. In 2007 a warrant was issued for his arrest when he violated parole related to the charges.

As demonstrated in the Spellman and Robbins episodes, bipolar disorder has a significant biochemical component. Without medications, maintaining stability is difficult. The medications commonly used to treat bipolar disorder, called mood stabilizers, are Lithium and antiseizure medications such as Depakote and Tegretol. Newer medications that are being used include Lamictal, Topamax, Zyprexa, and Geodon. The goal of these medications is to decrease the intensity of the peaks and valleys as shown in figure 5.1.

In manic or depressive episodes, the patient may become psychotic. In those circumstances, an antipsychotic medication may be necessary as well.

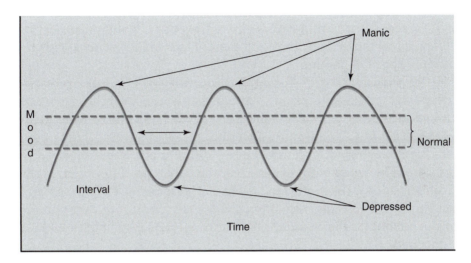

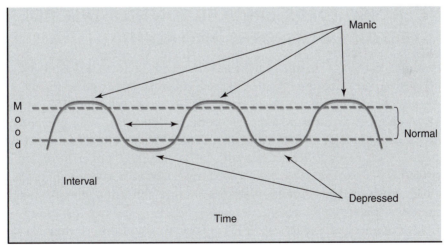

Figure 5.1 Fluctuations in mood seen in bipolar disorder. In bipolar disorder, the person experiences extreme manic highs, sometimes called peaks, and extreme depressive lows, sometimes called valleys. The goal of medications known as mood stabilizers is to decrease the extremes of those peaks and valleys so that the fluctuations of mood are within normal limits, to increase the interval between mood episodes, and, ideally, to prevent mood episodes altogether. Many people require an antidepressant medication in addition to a mood stabilizer to prevent recurrence of symptoms.

Mood disorders, both depressive disorder and bipolar disorder (which are sometimes referred to as affective disorders), often co-occur with substance abuse. A common hypothesis is that some people with mood disorders try to self-medicate by using their drug of choice to alleviate their symptoms and make themselves feel better. Rarely does this work. Most often, the substance abuse will exacerbate the already existing symptoms. Because research suggests that athletes are at risk for substance abuse, those who might be quietly predisposed toward unipolar depression or bipolar disorder may, by taking drugs, introduce the catalyst that crystallizes those symptoms. For those individuals, taking drugs is the equivalent of lighting a fuse that leads to an emotional keg of dynamite.

The long and short of it is that athletes are not beyond the reach of severe mental illness. Although exercise and physical well-being in general can act as an insulator to protect some who may be susceptible from depression, athletes are not immune to such illnesses. The onset of these illnesses often occurs during adolescence and early adulthood. Those involved with sport should be aware of these illnesses, whether related to violence or not, and obtain appropriate referrals to clinical psychologists or psychiatrists when needed. These illnesses do not magically remit, but early intervention and adequate adherence to the prescribed treatment greatly improves the prognosis.

ANGER DISORDERS, IMPULSE CONTROL DISORDERS, AND SEIZURE DISORDERS AND ADHD

Although many experts in the field have argued for formal diagnostic categories for anger disorders, the *Diagnostic Statistical Manual of Mental Disorders* (*DSM-IV*; American Psychiatric Association, 1994, 2000), the bible of psychological diagnoses, does not contain them, nor does the *International Classifications of Diseases* (*ICD-10*; World Health Organization, 1999). "Instead," according to Kassinove and Tafrate (2002), "anger is treated as a peripheral part of other diagnostic categories such as borderline personality disorder, antisocial personality disorder . . . intermittent explosive disorder . . . conduct disorder . . . etc."

Eckhardt and Deffenbacher (1995) argued this point more than 10 years ago when they proposed five anger diagnoses:

1. Adjustment disorder with angry mood
2. Situational anger disorder without aggression
3. Situational anger disorder with aggression
4. General anger disorder without aggression
5. General anger disorder with aggression

Nonetheless, no change has been instituted thus far, so those of us who work with people with anger disorders either have to work without a diagnosis that exists in the *DSM-IV* or determine whether a person's experience could be explained by another diagnostic category. Often it cannot be. The tragedy of this is that diagnosis is supposed to direct the practitioner toward treatment. In those cases, the practitioner proceeds with the appropriate treatment despite not have having an appropriate diagnosis.

Often, people who are angry also wear the title *impulsive*. Loosely defined, an impulsive person is someone who cannot control her or his impulses, whether those impulses are sexual, violent, larcenous, gambling related, or anything else. People who are truly impulsive are unable to control their impulses. They can be differentiated from those who choose not to control their impulses.

I do a great deal of work in dating violence prevention (as discussed in chapter 9). I often encounter young men who promulgate the myth that once they get going, they cannot stop. I counter by asking, "If the young lady's father was walking up the stairs, would you be able to stop then?" Undeniably, they would not only be able to stop but also be able to get their clothes on and jump out a window in record time. Many people who say that their behavior was impulsive are not being truthful.

In prison, inmates use the phrase *blacking out*. It is also used in the inner city and as a slang phrase. Blacking out in this context should not be confused with the blackouts that alcoholics have when they have blocks of amnesia during a drunken binge, nor should it be confused with dissociative episodes that survivors of trauma experience. An example may best describe the phrase.

Juan Rivera (not his real name) was a 24-year-old man incarcerated in a New Jersey prison. He was serving a 5-year sentence for aggravated assault. Juan was in an anger management group that I was running when he chose to disclose the events that led to his incarceration. Juan stated that another young man from his neighborhood, for reasons irrelevant to the purpose of this example, punched Juan's pregnant girlfriend in the abdomen, causing her to bleed vaginally. The story was immediately incredible because Juan did not appear to have the social skills necessary to have a relationship with a young lady, let alone gain the opportunity to impregnate her. Nonetheless, Juan stated that when he saw the assault he just "blacked out."

The term was not new to me, but I was going to use his example to disprove to the group the logic that he used to absolve himself of responsibility. I asked him to describe what happened when he blacked out. He said, "Well, I got pissed so I picked up a pipe off of the ground and I hit him over the head with it until he was on the floor bleeding."

"OK, why did you pick up the pipe?" I queried.

"Because I wanted to kill him . . . I wanted to make him pay for what he did," he replied.

"Why didn't you just attack him with your hands?"

"Because I wanted to hurt him bad, and I knew that a weapon would make that easier."

"So during this period of 'blacking out' when you don't remember anything and shouldn't be held accountable, you made a conscious decision to pick up the weapon rather than just going after him with your hands?" I asked.

"Yeah," he replied.

"Alright, then exactly when were you not thinking clearly and unable to make decisions and therefore shouldn't be held accountable for your behaviors if you made a decision to pick up a weapon with the intention of inflicting more damage? Or are you trying to say that you weren't considering the consequences of your actions?" I asked.

"I wasn't thinking about what would happen afterwards," he admitted.

"Exactly, so that was a huge mistake. You were caught up in the moment and didn't think about the consequences, but that isn't the same as 'blacking out' and therefore not being responsible for your behavior, is it?" I asked him as he realized that he just walked into a blind alley of reasoning.

"Shit, you put it that way, you might as well be the prosecutor."

I responded, "If you engage in that behavior you should expect to have to answer questions from the prosecutor and your answers have to be better than that. Because you didn't care about the consequences doesn't mean that you don't have to face them."

That was the last time anyone on that unit used the phrase "I just blacked out."

Two disorders directly associated with impulsivity are intermittent explosive disorder and attention deficit hyperactivity disorder (ADHD), especially the hyperactive types.

Intermittent explosive disorder is rare and has been has been referred to as epileptoid personality (see Kaplan and Saddock, p. 783) because of behavioral outbursts that appear seizurelike and inconsistent with the individual's usual behavior. The assumption is that intermittent explosive disorder is caused by damage to the brain. The person tends to have several features normally associated with epilepsy, such as experiencing auras before the seizure, experiencing smells and tastes without any explainable cause, having partial amnesia after the event, and being hypersensitive to light and noise. Immediately after the episode the person is often apologetic for his or her behavior. These disorders tend to be treated with antiseizure medications like those listed earlier. Although an athlete could conceivably have a seizure disorder and have times of impulsivity associated with seizures, this person would be different from those who justify violence as an acceptable way to solve problems. Furthermore, many people with seizure disorders show no increase in the likelihood of violence. Therefore, seizure disorders are a red flag to look for, but the presence of a seizure disorder should not unilaterally be considered the explanation and excuse for violent behavior. Each incident should be examined individually to understand the behavior in its context.

With ADHD on the other hand, we may be opening Pandora's box. Sport psychiatrist Dr. Robert Burton (in Begel and Burton, *Sport Psychiatry*) wrote that athletes may be overrepresented when compared with the general population. He noted that young people with ADHD are more inclined towards physical activities and hypothesized that they may use them as a way of managing emotions or that they may perceive that their physical skills are more proficient than their mental or verbal skills, thus being even more drawn to sport.

ADHD, in and of itself, does not necessarily equate to violence, although they often co-occur. What makes ADHD a challenging problem for athletes, whether violent or not, is that the treatment of choice is stimulant medications. The most common medications used are Adderall, a form of amphetamine, and methylphenidate (most common brand names: Ritalin, Concerta, and Metadate). Adderall and the different formulations of methylphenidate are all central nervous system stimulants. These medications have been shown to be by far the best medications for treating ADHD. Paired with cognitive behavioral psychotherapy (at times parent training is important), this combination has been shown to be the most effective treatment for ADHD.

Giving someone who is already hyperactive a stimulant medication may seem a little odd. But the medications appear to work by activating the parts of the brain that are responsible for slowing down thinking, allowing the person to focus and attend better. We might best understand the medications as helping the person's brakes work more effectively.

Many people are concerned that children and teenagers will become addicted to or abuse these medications. First, the dosages that have been shown to be effective are not high doses. Second, children and adolescents who have ADHD and do not take medications may be more likely to abuse drugs as a way to self-medicate. Think about caffeine and nicotine—stimulants that people use to self-medicate. And third, many of the people who abuse these medications would often be abusing other drugs that they could get their hands on anyway.

A particular problem for athletes is that treatment options are often limited, which is important at the higher levels where governing bodies prohibit the use of stimulants. Athletes may have some hope, however, because the NCAA has opened the door for medical exceptions for positive stimulant drug screens on athletes with documented medical need provided before being tested positive (Hosick, 2004, NCAA article online). The World Anti-Doping Agency and the U.S. Anti-Doping Agency do not offer the same flexibility, but the NCAA action is a start.

Sports agencies are appropriately scrutinizing ADHD diagnoses and the use of stimulants because they can be performance enhancing. Interestingly, the problem lies on how many professionals diagnose ADHD.

Though the name would imply that assessment originates in assessing the subjects' ability to pay attention, most often ADHD is diagnosed behaviorally. The *Diagnostic and Statistical Manual of Mental Disorders, Fourth Edition (DSM-IV TR)* list behaviors that are supposed to be diagnostic, such as often having difficulty organizing tasks and activities or being forgetful in daily activities as indicators of inattention and fidgeting and often interrupting or having difficulty waiting their turn as signs of hyperactivity or impulsivity. Further, there are requirements of the number of symptoms present for a diagnosis of inattentive, hyperactive or iImpulsive, or combined types, and the frequency, intensity and severity of symptoms are taken into account, but at the core of any diagnosis, it must impair functioning. There are several questionnaires available that assist with tallying the symptoms from multiple sources (e.g., the student, the parent, the teachers, the coaches, etc) and the most popular are the Conners 3, developed by Dr. C. Keith Conners and the Brown Attention Deficit Disorder Scales developed by Dr. Thomas E. Brown.

A major shortcoming of this diagnostic method is that it implies that those behaviors are the result of attention problems but the dynamics of the behavior are not often explored for alternative etiologies. For example, someone who has a history of trauma and dissociates could easily look like someone inattentive. Similarly, someone carrying an Oppositional Defiant Disorder (ODD) or Conduct Disorder (CD) (described below) who is very aggressive may be seen as impulsive or hyperactive. Though there is a high incidence of co-morbidity between ADHD, ODD, and CD, it is important to understand that why someone acts a certain way matters. If you want to assess attention, assess attention.

An increasingly popular and effective method of assessing attention is by employing Continuous Performance Tests (CPTs). The most common CPTs available are the Conners Continuous Performance Test (CPT) and the Test of Variables of Attention (TOVA). Basically, they are deliberately boring video games (though some come with options to test auditory, in addition to or instead of, visual cueing) that measure one's ability to stay focused on a task that lasts approximately 30 minutes. One of two stimulus targets is presented on the screen. The subject is to press the trigger as quickly and accurately as possible when it is the stimulus identified as a "hit" and not when the target is not a "hit." They measure inattention during a phase where the ratio of hits to targets is low and impulsivity when the ratio is high (many hits of the targets presented). Errors of Omission, where the subject does not press the trigger for a presented "hit" are also signs of inattentiveness while Errors of Commission, pressing the trigger for a "hit" when it was not the cue to do so, are indicative of impulsivity. These tests were designed to measure attention.

These tests are not foolproof. If so inclined, one can fake results and look like they have attentional problems when they don't, but this problem prevails for many psychological tests. Motivation has a huge impact on performance, a point never lost on sport psychologists.

The take-home message is that if sport psychologists are involved with assessment of ADHD in athletes and this may lead to a physician prescribing medications to treat the disorder, it is imperative to give the assessment its due diligence. That includes using standardized measures of attention, such as the CPTs, in conjunction with a good clinical interview and obtaining data from across sources; using established questionnaires is part of the current standard of practice. When doing so, the sport psychologist puts himself in the best position to identify problems that the athlete may legitimately require treatment for to assist in all-around-performance and sort out those who are looking for a ticket to "speed."

Other medications that are prescribed to treat ADHD, although not with the same reported success, are Strattera, Wellbutrin, and Effexor, none of which are stimulants. Governing bodies in sport are not as concerned with these medications because they are not stimulants, but this judgment may be misguided because Wellbutrin and Effexor both have stimulating properties.

Hyperactivity often leads to acting out, and at times the method used is violence. Comorbidity rates between ADHD oppositional defiant disorder and conduct disorder are predictably high. Oppositional defiant disorder and conduct disorder are both childhood disorders significant for disruptive behaviors. Oppositional defiant disorder is identified by a pattern of negativistic hostile and defiant behavior such as

- losing one's temper,
- arguing with adults,
- defying or refusing to comply with rules,
- deliberately annoying people,
- blaming others for one's own misbehavior or mistakes,
- being touchy or easily annoyed,
- being angry and resentful, and
- being spiteful and vindictive (*DSM-IV*).

Conduct disorder, the more severe of the two, is highlighted by a repetitive and persistent pattern in which the rights of others are violated. It manifests itself in one of four basic domains:

- Is aggressive to people and animals
  - Often bullies, threatens, or intimidates others
  - Often initiates physical fights
  - Has used a weapon that can cause serious physical harm
  - Has been physically cruel to people
  - Has been physically cruel to animals
  - Has stolen while confronting a victim
  - Has forced someone into sexual activity

- Destruction of property
  - Has deliberately engaged in fire setting with the intention of causing serious damage
  - Has deliberately destroyed others' property
- Deceitfulness or theft
  - Has broken into someone else's house, building, or car
  - Often lies to obtain goods or favors or to avoid obligations
  - Has stolen items of nontrivial value without confronting a victim
- Serious violations of rules
  - Often stays out at night despite parental prohibitions, beginning before 13 years of age
  - Has run away from home overnight at least twice while living in parental or parental surrogate home
  - Is often truant from school, beginning before age 13 (*DSM-IV*)

These childhood and adolescent onset disruptive disorders result from many causes. They are multiply determined and do not appear to be purely physiological. Many biopsychosocial factors appear to contribute to their development. These include harsh, punitive parenting characterized by severe physical, verbal, and emotional abuse. Parental beliefs that legitimize the use of violence as a means to solve problems or contribute to a chaotic world in which the young person lives can increase the risk. Socioeconomically deprived children with poor social support and limited access to medical and mental health care are at higher risk. Many believe that sport can be a salvation for inner-city kids who are prone to such conditions by giving them a place to focus their energy more positively.

These disorders are often assumed to be natural developmental precursors to antisocial personality disorders (described later) and potential sociopathy. In fact, estimates are that less than 50 percent of children with conduct disorder will meet the criteria for antisocial personality disorder when they grow up. This finding supports optimism for the use of therapy and should encourage us to do all that we can to help these children live up to their potential.

On the other hand, we would be making a mistake to assume that children who grow up in a crime-infested area where criminal behavior is the norm will automatically forget those circumstances when they progress to higher levels of sport competition. A basketball player who grew up in Camden, New Jersey, one of the most crime-ridden cities in the country, who had gang-bangers as friends, who saw his father beat up his mother, who was a victim of racism, is unlikely to see the world through different eyes just because he is playing for a number 1 seeded team in the NCAA College Basketball Championship. Can it happen? Absolutely, with the right support, discipline, coaching, and influences, but we should not assume that this will happen. We should be making a more concerted effort to get all athletes, especially those at the college level and higher where big money is invested, the support that they need so that they can succeed as well-rounded people, and these services should be sensitive to the specific circumstances from which they came.

Additionally, we should remember the risks that come with sport participation. We talk about the powerful, positive influence that coaches can have on their athletes, and I believe that this effect cannot be understated. But some coaches out there advocate violence in sport, believe that retaliation is an appropriate strategy, and in general are poor role models for those whom they coach. Therefore, we should listen to organizations like the Positive Alliance for Youth Sports that pay close attention to the importance of continued coaching education. The athlete's character derives from many sources: biology, upbringing, friends and social network, and, undeniably, coaches and the environment that they create. Good coaches can often turn at-risk athletes into great people.

PERSONALITY DISORDERS

When you think about someone's personality, you are thinking about general themes that persist over time. You think about how the person sees the world and responds to situations, how much his or her emotions vacillate, and what types of behavior are predictable or consistent with the person's personality.

DSM-IV lists the following personality disorders in three clusters:

- Cluster A
  - Paranoid
  - Schizoid
  - Schizotypal
- Cluster B
  - Antisocial
  - Borderline
  - Histrionic
  - Narcissistic
- Cluster C
  - Avoidant
  - Dependent
  - Obsessive-compulsive
  - Personality disorder not otherwise specified (NOS)

Of the various clusters, the cluster B personality disorders are most often associated with violent behavior. In reading the following brief summary of the clusters, be aware that symptoms overlap in the disorders.

Starting from the bottom of the list, people who meet the criteria for narcissistic personality disorder believe that the world is centered on them. They have a grandiose sense of self-importance and think that their achievements are more significant than those of anyone around them. They are preoccupied with their beliefs of unlimited success, power, beauty, and overall greatness. They need the attention that is associated with greatness and sometimes engage in exaggerated and dramatic behaviors to achieve that end. They exploit others for their own gain and do not often care what their "victims" feel about it.

I have not met Terrell Owens, so my use of him as an example is extracted only from what has appeared in the media. This example may be a misrepresentation of who he truly is. But think about his behavior over the past few years. He scored a touchdown, ran to the center of the field, and dramatically placed the ball in the middle of the star during a Dallas Cowboys game. After scoring a touchdown on another occasion, he pulled a Sharpie from his sock to sign the ball. He has demanded ever-growing contracts and trades. He has criticized his teammates, coaches, and organizations. Only after the Philadelphia Eagles suspended him for four games and notified him that he was done for the 2005 season because of "conduct detrimental to the organization" did Owens publicly apologize for his behavior, which included blatant criticism of the team's quarterback, Donovan McNabb. Seen more as a malcontent that hurts his team more than helps them despite his unquestionable athletic talents, Owens has had trouble staying in one place. At the end of the 2008 season, he was released by the Dallas Cowboys. He was quickly swept up by the Buffalo Bills, but it is hard to predict a different outcome in a different location considering his history.

Whether Owens stages this behavior primarily to further his status as an entertainer, which professional athletes are, only he truly knows. These behaviors are consistent with someone who has a narcissistic personality disorder, although Owens may not have truly reached that level. An interesting thing about narcissism is that at higher levels of competition it is almost a prerequisite to success (and its genesis was explained in the previous chapter). If you do not think that you can win, you are defeated before you set foot in the arena. The question is how this supreme confidence translates to behavior in the sport. Again, this topic was examined in chapter 3. Although athletes may have a fair representation in this diagnostic category, NPD is not a predictive precursor to violence.

Those with histrionic personality disorder also need to be the center of attention and often use their physical appearance to draw people to them. They are theatrical, often show exaggerated emotive presentation, and can be quite seductive and provocative. These people cannot miss the opportunity to be the center of attention. Their mannerisms have an almost syrupy feeling. This disorder is diagnosed more frequently in men than in women. Although one may argue that the theatrics that hockey or soccer players engage in to sway officials are histrionic, I can think of few athletes who would meet the criteria for this disorder, if for no other reason than that the energy, training, and hard work that go into training as an athlete are incompatible with being constantly worried about outward appearance.

Antisocial personality disorder is diagnosed in men twice as often as it is in women. Many men diagnosed with antisocial personality disorder may actually have borderline personality disorder (BPD). Those with BPD often seem to be in a state of pending crisis. They have mood swings and great difficulty managing their emotions. They can fly into a rage and be severely self-destructive or dangerous to others. They make frantic efforts to avoid real or imagined abandonment and may reach the point of self-mutilation or suicidality. They tend to be impulsive and link their identity to their relationships. For this reason, when they fear that a relationship (romantic or otherwise) may end, they experience this possibility as the end of themselves, sometimes threatening, "If you leave me, I will kill myself." Often those with BPD engage in an approach-avoidance dance by seducing someone in to be close to them and then rejecting the person before they themselves can be rejected.

A growing literature shows that a percentage of men who engage in domestic violence do so because of borderline dynamics. These men may truly love the women they are with, but they love them so much that the thought of losing them is terrifying, the ultimate assault on their manhood and identity. To prevent this from happening, they attempt to control "their" woman through social isolation, financial dependency, emotional belittling, spoiling them with gifts, and at times physical domination.

Professional athletes have been involved in domestic violence. For some of them, this is the dynamic that takes place. Remember that the symptoms overlap and that nothing will set someone off like a narcissistic injury—an injury to pride.

Professional Athletes and Domestic Violence

O.J. Simpson had a history of domestic violence toward his wife that preceded her murder. Even after their divorce it was believed that the thought of her being with anyone else burned him up. Although he was acquitted of the criminal murder charges, which have a higher burden of proof, he was found guilty in the civil wrongful death suit, which awarded millions of dollars. One hypothesis was that he lived his life by constantly feeding his ego, doing whatever he wanted, including having affairs and engaging in domestic violence several times for various reasons. One could argue that this was a narcissistic, borderline dynamic. The fear of abandonment and the humiliation of knowing that his wife (because she would always be his wife even if divorced) was with someone else led to such pain that he exploded in rage. Domestic violence, given its high incidence, does not commonly lead

(continued)

to murder, but when people have the feeling that their life as they know it will end, they may become desperate.

Orenthal James Simpson, former USC standout and Hall of Fame NFL running back, was accused of violently murdering his ex-wife Nicole Brown Simpson and a male acquaintance, Ronald Goldman. It was believed that the murderer attacked with great force with a sharp knife that nearly severed Nicole Simpson's head from her body. In the criminal case, O.J. was found not guilty. But in the civil case (which requires a lower burden of proof), he was found responsible for their wrongful deaths and was ordered to pay $33,500,000 in damages.

Again involved with the law, O.J. Simpson was indicted following a 2007 arrest in which he and confederates allegedly robbed memorabilia dealers at gunpoint in a Las Vegas hotel. He was found guilty on October 3, 2008, of numerous felonies, including robbery with a deadly weapon, burglary with a firearm, assault with a deadly weapon, first-degree kidnapping with use of a deadly weapon, coercion with use of a deadly weapon, conspiracy to commit robbery, conspiracy to commit kidnapping, and conspiracy to commit a crime. On December 5, 2008, he was sentenced to 33 years (with a minimum of 9 years) in a Nevada state prison.

Rae Carruth was a promising wide receiver for the Carolina Panthers. Named to the all-rookie team in 1997, he started 14 games and caught 44 passes for 545 yards. He signed a four-year $3.7 million deal out of college and appeared to have a bright future. In 1998 he was slowed by a broken right foot incurred in the first game of the season and went on injured reserve.

Carruth played in the first six games of the 1999 season before his football career and life took an about face. His girlfriend, Cherica Adams, seven months pregnant with their son, was murdered when she was shot four times in a drive-by shooting in Charlotte, North Carolina. She died a month after the shooting. The baby, who was delivered by emergency Caesarean section premature and in distress, has cerebral palsy.

Carruth turned himself in and posted bond. After she died, he became a fugitive. He eventually was caught and stood trial. He was found guilty of conspiracy to commit murder, shooting into an occupied vehicle, and using an instrument to destroy an unborn child. He was sentenced to 18 to 24 years in prison with an 18 year, 11 month minimum.

Although he never stood trial or provided any details of his motive, it was strongly suspected that his motive was related to his not being able to afford the lifestyle that he had become accustomed to. In 1997 he lost a paternity suit and was mandated to pay $3,500 per month in child support. With poor investments and injuries making his financial future uncertain, having to support another child apparently seemed untenable. It was reported that he asked Adams, a former exotic dancer, to abort the baby, but she refused. An ex-girlfriend of Carruth's testified in the trial that Carruth admitted to being involved in the murder but did not pull the trigger. Now, three lives have been lost or permanently damaged. Adams is dead. Their son, Chancellor, now lives without either of his parents around. And Carruth will be in prison for a long time. He needs to look no farther than the mirror to see how his fate was sealed.

Contrary to popular belief, narcissists are not impervious to criticism, believing that they are above it all. Many live their lives trying to pretend they are impervious, using their egos as a way to hide their insecurities and vulnerabilities. Joe Theismann once said, "Ego is armor. People with the biggest egos, to a large degree, are probably the most insecure people you'll find. I know I am."

Did you ever wonder why a professional athlete who is attractive, rich, and charismatic would be involved in any type of sex crime? Is it because they are unable to find a willing partner and must take one by force? Some may be so narcissistic that they believe that any woman would want to be with them and therefore, if a woman says no, she really means yes. So they ignore what the woman says and then act somewhat surprised when the police come to investigate. "Well, it was consensual," he may explain. Funny, she did not experience it that way.

When people's egos are involved, especially when they are fragile, violence is a possibility because an insult may challenge a person's whole existence. Some people may respond violently, because in a distorted manner, they are defending their psychological lives.

ANTISOCIAL PERSONALITY DISORDER AND PSYCHOPATHY

Unlike many other diagnoses, ASPD is primarily a behavioral diagnosis, meaning that a positive diagnosis is given if the behavioral patterns listed here are present. The diagnosis does not speak to the reasons underlying why these behaviors exist. For the purposes of treatment and understanding the diagnosis, those reasons must be explored.

DSM-IV states that a diagnosis of ASPD results from a pervasive pattern of disregard for and violation of the rights of others occurring since age 15, as indicated by three (or more) of the following:

- Failure to conform to social norms with respect to lawful behaviors as indicated by repeatedly performing act that are grounds for arrest
- Deceitfulness, as indicated by repeated lying, use of aliases, or conning others for personal profit or pleasure
- Impulsivity or failure to plan
- Irritability and aggressiveness, as indicated by repeated physical fights or assaults
- Reckless disregard for the safety of self or others
- Consistent irresponsibility, as indicated by repeated failure to sustain consistent work behavior or honor financial obligations
- Lack of remorse, as indicated by being indifferent to or rationalizing having hurt, mistreated, or stolen from others

Antisocial Personality Disorders and Violence

1. Lawrence Phillips. What a physical talent! What a waste of talent. Given opportunity after opportunity regardless of the victims who lay in his wake, he never amounted to much as an NFL pro. The star running back for Nebraska came to the nation's attention in 1995 when beat his ex-girlfriend and dragged her down a flight of stairs. He pleaded no contest to assault charges and was put on a year's probation. After he paid $358.64 restitution and agreed to attend domestic violence counseling, he was allowed by then coach and now congressman Tom Osborne to play in the Fiesta Bowl.

Drafted in the first round by Dick Vermeil's St. Louis Rams, Phillips did not last long. Coach Vermeil, who also wanted to give Phillips a second (more like seventh) chance, waived him in November 1997 after Phillips skipped a team meeting and practice. He had gone AWOL after the coach stated that he planned to start another running back in front of him.

Because of his physical prowess, he was later given opportunities by the Miami Dolphins, San Francisco 49ers, and Montreal Allouettes of the CFL, among others. Never fulfilling his athletic promise, he presented increasingly as a serial offender with multiple arrests and an exceedingly poor prognosis of staying out of jail or having a long life. No matter how lofty the expectations of the coaches in charge, whether to win more games or to help build this young troubled adolescent into a mature man, they were not able to attain their goals. The fault is not completely theirs. By the time Phillips reached college, much of his personality and behavioral patterns were already set. Any chance for successful intervention would have required intensive, multisystemic intervention of the kind not provided to even the most talented young athletes, at least not yet.

Phillips—already wanted by Los Angeles police for domestic violence for allegedly attacking his girlfriend twice, once choking her into unconsciousness—was arrested in September 2005 after allegedly running his Honda Accord into three teenagers who argued with him during a pickup football game in Los Angeles. As a result, in October 2008 Phillips was sentenced to 10 years in a California state prison after being found guilty of seven counts of assault with a deadly weapon.

2. Wisconsin running back Booker Stanley faced battery and disorderly conduct charges incurred during a fight at a block party in April 2005. He was suspended from the team in December 2005 after his arrest following a fight with his girlfriend. In January 2006 he was charged with sexual assault, battery, and bail jumping in connection with a pair of alleged fights with his girlfriend.

All personality disorders require adulthood to finalize their diagnoses. The person must be 18 years old, but the personalities of all people, whether disordered or not, stem from what they were exposed to when growing up. But troubled people are not the result of having imperfect parents. Children are resilient. They do not need perfect parents; they just need "good enough" parenting, where they are raised in a stable, predictable household with structure and discipline, free from abuse. Many young athletes, unfortunately, do not grow up in that environment, putting them at greater risk for antisocial behaviors (as well as other emotional problems) as they grow older.

For those who grow up in the inner city seeing friends get killed and watching gangs recruit and threaten people, fighting can become a way of life. Compound that environment with a broken home in which domestic violence and drug use may occur, and the survival of some of these kids seems almost miraculous. For many, only a few roads lead out of that environment: education, entertainment, and sport.

This problem is not a race-bound phenomenon. Low SES (socioeconomic status) communities are a breeding ground for antisocial behavior because the environment can be a dog-eat-dog world. Many people develop paranoid personality disorders. They believe that their world is about to crumble down on them at any moment, and that fear is not delusional. Some develop an "I'll get you before you get me" view of the world. This orientation is not uncommon in people who have been exposed to repeated traumas; we see it as well in people who have endured long-standing physical, emotional, and sexual abuse. These people may be more likely to act out violently because that is how they learned to survive. That experience explains, but does not excuse, their antisocial tendencies.

Look at college and professional sports. Do you think that behaviors from these neighborhoods are present? Of course they are, and one of the things that get athletes to high-level sport is their drive to get away from the chaos in which they grew up. The fantasy to make millions of dollars and take their families away from poverty is pervasive. Unfortunately, leaving behind behavioral patterns engrained since childhood is difficult.

What is important to determine is whether people embrace that old lifestyle or whether they want to mature out of it and change their ways. Aspects to being a professional athlete can certainly propagate these problems. Promiscuity, misogyny, spousal abuse, and drug and alcohol abuse are problems that some professional athletes struggle with, regardless of where they grew up. That first point, whether a person wants to change or not, is the key to prognosis of treatment. People who have ASPD but are not proud of their behavior, who want to make lifestyle changes because they see the self-destruction that it is leading to, may benefit from treatment. Moreover, the younger they are when they come to that conclusion, the better the likelihood of their changing their behavior. But for people with a true hardened antisocial personality disorder injected with a steady dose of narcissism, for people who believe that they are above it all and can do what they want with the world, we are starting to look toward psychopathy—and for that, successful treatment is virtually nonexistent.

When people think of the word *psychopath*, most think of serial killers or Hannibal Lecter, and in the most extreme cases they are on target. Psychopaths often engage in criminal behavior, but psychopaths are not just the scary people whom you pray you never come across. Psychopathy, like other personality factors, occurs on a continuum. You likely come across people with psychopathic features with fair regularity.

In his 1993 book *Without Conscience: The Disturbing World of Psychopaths Among Us*, Dr. Robert Hare, the foremost expert in psychopathy, described psychopaths this way:

> *Psychopaths are social predators who charm, manipulate and ruthlessly plow their way through life, leaving a broad trail of broken hearts and shattered expectations without the slightest sense of guilt or regret. Their bewildered victims desperately ask, "Who are these people?"*
>
> *We often think of psychopaths as the disturbed criminals who capture headlines and crowd the nation's prisons. But not all psychopaths are killers. They are more likely to be men and women you know who move through life with supreme self-confidence—but without a conscience.*
>
> *Completely lacking in conscience and feelings for others, they selfishly take what they want and do as they please, violating social norms and expectations without the slightest sense of guilt or regret.*
>
> *He will choose you, disarm you with his words, and control you with his presence. He will delight you with his wit and his plans. He will show you a good time, but you will always get the bill. He will smile and deceive you, and he will scare you with his eyes. And when he is through with you, and he will be through with you, he will desert you and take with him your innocence and your pride. You will be left much sadder but not a lot wiser, and for a long time you will wonder what happened and what you did wrong. And if another of his kind comes knocking at your door, will you open it?*

Can you think of people who meet this description? Could they be doctors or high-powered executives on Wall Street? Could they be women? Could they be athletes? Yes, to all the preceding.

The lifetime incident rate of antisocial personality disorder for men is approximately 3 percent. For psychopathy, assessment is much more difficult because many psychopaths are never studied, but the lifetime incident rate is estimated to be about 1 percent. I once participated in a workshop on violence risk assessment conducted by Dr. J. Reid Meloy, one of the nation's top forensic psychologists. We were discussing psychopaths when he stopped and cautioned us that almost everything we know about psychopaths is based on the ones we studied after they were caught. Those out there who escape arrest or psychological study may be altogether different.

Dr. Hare developed an instrument to assess for psychopathy called the Psychopathy Checklist-Revised (PCL-R), the instrument of choice in forensic evaluations. Of interest here is to think about the presence in the athlete population of the 20 characteristics on which psychopathy is assessed.

Each characteristic is scored a 0 if it does not fit, 1 if it is a partial fit, and 2 if it is a reasonably certain fit. The highest score possible is 40. A score of 30 or higher rates the person as a severe psychopath, a score of 20 to 29 identifies the person as a moderate psychopath, and a score of 10 through 19 indicates mild psychopathy. These characteristics break down into two factors:

1. Aggressive narcissism
2. Chronic antisocial behavior

The psychopath is reptilian and can stare right through others with cold eyes. Psychopaths have little regard for the destruction that they cause. They are true predators. They stalk, and like a cat preparing to pounce, they are keenly aware and ready for action but not overexcited. These people can fake a lie detector test in their sleep, although they occasionally trip up because they become physiologically excited while enjoying their deception.

Table 5.1 Twenty factors assessed on the PCL-R, each scored from 0 to 2

Glibness, superficial charm	Promiscuous sexual behavior
Grandiose sense of self-worth	Early behavioral problems (before age 12)
Need for stimulation or proneness to boredom	Lack of realistic, long-term goals
Pathological lying	Impulsivity
Conning, manipulativeness	Irresponsibility
Lack of remorse or guilt	Failure to accept responsibility for own actions
Shallow affect (emotion)	Many short-term marital or romantic relationships
Callousness, lack of empathy	Juvenile delinquency
Parasitic lifestyle—lives off people	Revocation of conditional release (inmates)
Poor behavioral controls	Criminal versatility

Does anyone think that psychopaths make up the majority of those who participate in sport in the United States? Well, yes. Author Jeffrey Benedict, for one, seems to believe that many athletes are psychopathic. We explored this issue in detail in chapter 2, but I do not come to the same conclusion. In any case, the important point to come away with from the discussion of the PCL-R is that it has promise as a tool for exploring psychopathy in athletes. But no research to date has normed this instrument on athletes, and until this is done no conclusive statements can be made about a subgroup of the population.

I have spent a great deal of time discussing mental illness and its relationship with violence because those who work with athletes need to

- understand psychopathology better and know what it looks like should they come across an athlete with such problems,
- understand why such problems may or may not lead to violence,
- recognize the most violent forms of mental illness, and
- discard the idea that those who are mentally ill are more likely to engage in violence (addressed in the following section).

John Monahan and his colleagues studied the relationship between mental illness and violence. Their findings were well summarized in their book, *Rethinking Risk Assessment: The MacArthur Study of Mental Disorder and Violence* (Monahan et al., 2001). The MacArthur study produced a great deal of data by evaluating patients who were in acute civil psychiatric hospitalizations. The basic summary statement was that if substance abuse is removed from the equation, those who are mentally ill are at no higher risk for violence than those without mental illness. Even more interesting was the fact that patients without substance abuse did not differ from community controls without substance abuse in frequency of violence or other aggressive acts.

What does this tell us? A small handful of athletes may develop some form of mental illness, being an athlete does not necessarily protect a person from developing mental illness, and some athletes may develop mental illness and become violent. Overall, however, people with mental illness are not more violent than those without mental illness, unless substance abuse is added to the equation. Then things can get problematic. And that is where we go next.

SUMMARY

In this chapter, we reviewed a great deal of information about various types of mental illness, their treatment, the likelihood that athletes will develop a mental disorder, and, if they do, the probability that it would contribute to an increase in anger or related violence.

Ultimately, the incidence of major mental illness in athletes, especially those illnesses that may cause violence, appears to be rather low. When such illnesses do appear, they are usually so debilitating that they interfere with the ability to continue to participate.

More common are mood disorders. When athletes present with less severe symptoms such as a mild depression or generalized anxiety, they can be successfully treated and can return to play. Athletes are not immune from mental illness, although they may be less likely to report symptoms because of the perception of their excellent health. Most mental illness, even in athletes, does not lead to violence.

When an athlete has a problem with anger, however, an evaluation should be performed to determine whether an underlying mental illness is present. Only after treatment should anger management be considered.

CHAPTER 6

DRUGS, VIOLENCE, AND SPORT

Although we might like to believe that professional leagues and antidoping agencies restrict the use of performance-enhancing drugs because they care about their constituency's health, the truth is that regulatory agencies, which are (directly or indirectly) the arms of the sports governing bodies, want to ensure fair competition, a level playing field. The level playing field is what draws us to watch. On any given day, anyone can win.

Differences in talent alone can skew the field, although Major League Baseball somehow imagined that a huge luxury tax would deter George Steinbrenner from spending vast sums to get the best players, even if doing so did not always lead to championships. The bottom line is that sports are a multi-billion-dollar business, and the executives know it. If fair competition was removed from the game, many fans would not be so drawn to it. And if fans found out that the games were somehow slanted in one team's favor, many would turn their backs altogether.

The importance of fair competition is the main reason that gambling (see Rick Tocchet's or Art Schlicter's involvement), especially on games in which the gambler is involved (see Pete Rose, 1919 Black Sox scandal), and steroids (including other illegal performance-enhancing supplements) receive more attention than domestic violence and other transgressions by athletes. If athletes are bad, people still come to see them play. If athletes cheat, sales decline.

What about the relationship between drugs and violence? In this chapter we will discuss both performance-enhancing drugs and drugs of abuse, sometimes referred to as recreational drugs that are not used for performance reasons. Some popular myths will be challenged, and some unspoken trends will be attended to.

What may be most surprising about this chapter is that it is one of the shortest in the book. The reason is simple. Although drug use and violence often coexist, rarely can a definitive conclusion be made that drug use, whether recreational or ergogenic, has a causative relationship with violence. Can drugs be a contributing factor? Without a doubt—and this chapter will discuss which substances are most often linked to violence. But we surely cannot absolve athletes, or anyone else for that matter, of the responsibility for their actions by saying that they are violent because of drugs.

DRUGS OF ABUSE AND RECREATIONAL DRUGS

I once gave a presentation on violence in sports and was discussing, as I will shortly, the relationship between recreational drugs and violence. After the presentation, an athletics director approached me to inform me that he found my use of the word *recreational* in connection with drugs to be offensive. I was caught off guard and apologized because I intended no offense, but the incident led me to think a little more about my word choice. This issue is absolutely about semantics but is nevertheless worth exploring.

When we think of drugs, we often consider how they are abused. The implication here is that drugs have an appropriate use that some people are not attending to. Such people are thus misusing, or abusing, drugs. Well, cocaine was originally an anesthetic, specifically used in eye surgeries, and it was the base chemical of later developed and widely used anesthetics such as Novocain. So, if this is your point of reference, then yes, cocaine is abused. The same applies to cannabis, which has been found to be helpful in treating glaucoma and easing the nausea effects of chemotherapy. Therefore, cocaine and marijuana may appropriately be called drugs of abuse because people are not using them for their medicinal properties and are often abusing them to excess, at times leading to addiction.

But many people who use drugs never become addicted, neither physiologically nor psychologically. They use drugs as a leisure activity. Although they may be medicating underlying psychological conditions, many people who drink alcohol and smoke marijuana do so with friends to take the edge off after a long day of work. Can this activity inadvertently or while unmonitored escalate to an addiction? Of course it can. But considering the ubiquity of beer advertisements and high volume of beer sales, it would be safe to say that most drinkers do so for leisure, for fun, and for recreation. Thus, categorizing drugs as both recreational drugs and drugs of abuse is appropriate, acknowledging that such use can spiral out of control into full-blown addiction.

Alcohol

Anheuser-Busch reported in a 2004 study that beer was a $78 billion industry that accounted for more than half of all alcohol sales. These numbers should come as no surprise, because beer commercials pepper most televised major sport events. Sport and beer is a combination as American as peanut butter and jelly, unlikely to be separated.

In the Ron Artest fiasco, what substance led to a fight with fans? Beer. In the Gary Sheffield incident, in which a fan hit him when he was trying to field a ball, what substance was involved? Beer. In the Duke lacrosse team rape accusations, what substance was involved? Alcohol. Even the history of the celebrated Yankees franchise cannot be discussed without admitting to the severe alcohol abuse of two Yankees legends, Mickey Mantle and Billy Martin.

To separate beer and sport, we need a crowbar. Beer is woven into the fabric of the culture. Nearly every sporting event is "brought to you by" one beverage or another. Although limiting the quantity of alcohol that fans can consume at sporting events may reduce the number of alcohol-induced fights, the notion that alcohol is the solitary culprit is misguided. In soccer, a sport whose fan hooliganism makes a Bronx cheer look tame, the obsessive fandom cannot point at alcohol as the cause of violence; team identity paired with a team's success is often a more accurate predictor.

Nonetheless, we must consider sport psychologist Chris Carr's seminal studies (1990 and 1992) that examined alcohol use among athletes. Carr found that 92.3 percent of secondary and high school athletes and 90.4 percent of elite athletes reported using alcohol during the previous year. He also found that male athletes drank to intoxication more often than male nonathletes did. If we pair this finding with research that argues that frequent drinking, high-volume drinking, and weekly involvement in sport were significant predictors of initiating fighting attributed to alcohol use (Swahn & Donovan, 2005), we can see why alcohol and athletes can be a dangerous combination.

Note, however, that a 2006 study titled "Jocks, Gender, Binge Drinking and Adolescent Violence" (Miller et al., 2006) showed no significant differences between jocks and nonjocks in binge drinking. This finding suggests that the disinhibitory effect of alcohol itself is what leads to an increase in violence, not being an athlete who is intoxicated.

Research has shown conclusively that alcohol is associated with violence. My issue with this statement is that alcohol does not cause violence. Alcohol is one of many factors that have a synergistic effect on violence, meaning that when the factors are combined, the total effect is greater than the sum of the individual effects.

The psychoactive qualities of alcohol are variable based on individual temperament, quantity ingested, body weight, metabolism, tolerance, and an array of other environmental factors. Uniformly, alcohol is a central nervous system depressant, meaning that it slows everything down, not that it necessarily causes the person to become depressed. This concept is counterintuitive because people often think that alcohol causes them to become more excitable. Their being excitable results from a weakening of their inhibitions, not because they become physiologically stimulated, as they might when using amphetamines or cocaine. Security personnel in bars and nightclubs sometimes refer to "beer muscles." This term refers to people who drink a good amount of alcohol and then think that they can take on the world. They cannot fight any better, but their inhibitions diminish, their judgment becomes impaired, and they do not recognize their limitations. In fact, those who drink large quantities of alcohol, even when they become violent, are often not a threat because they are uncoordinated and disorganized. Security can easily sweep them up and show them the door.

A variant on the same theme, "beer goggles" is a term used to describe a distortion that causes people to look more attractive while the "wearer" is under the influence of alcohol. Again, this issue is one of judgment and inhibitions. Alcohol does not make people more violent, and it is not an excuse for violence. In legal terms, intoxication may be considered a mitigating circumstance that may lead to some leniency on the basis that the person would have shown better judgment if not intoxicated, but it is not an excuse.

Many people believe that alcoholism is a disease and use a disease model to explain the addiction. In fact, years of research has shown genetic predisposition to addictions. Although I appreciate the success that many in 12-step programs have found (the 12-step programs are the foundation of Alcoholics Anonymous and other popular group programs), we must be cautious about externalizing responsibility to the alcohol or the disease rather than the person. I have personally treated alcoholics who also suffered from mental illness. After AA meetings some of them would go to the bar with their sponsors and AA buddies and drink until exhaustion. Obviously, many people in self-help programs do not engage in that behavior, but ultimately the success of these programs comes from the individual and the support of a group focused on sobriety.

I believe strongly in empowerment. Just as I believe that we are responsible for our behavior when we do not control our anger and become violent, I believe that we are responsible for choosing to put an intoxicant in our bodies that may weaken our inhibitions and increase the likelihood of violence.

Another point worth making is that some people are happy drunks whereas others are angry drunks. When alcohol peels away the layers of ego, the vulnerable core of who people are is what remains. People who constantly feel as if they cannot get a break and that others are out to get them normally engage in self-censoring. When they drink, their inhibitions fade away and out comes Mr. or Mrs. Nasty. Similarly, people who are laid back and for the most part are at ease with themselves can, in most cases, drink and display more of the same.

One cautionary note, however, is that people's thoughts, moods, and behavior are multiply determined. Predicting how people will act when intoxicated is sometimes difficult. Past behavior generally predicts future behavior, but exceptions occur. People should always show caution in dangerous situations.

As we segue into discussion of other substances, I think it would be instrumental to recall a segment of Bill Cosby's performance in the film *Himself.* Cosby said that he asked a friend what the deal was with using drugs. His friend replied, "Well, they intensify your personality." In one of the few times in his career that he used profanity, Cosby quipped, "Yes, but what if you're an asshole?"

Marijuana

Most people do not realize that tetrahydrocannibanol (THC), the psychoactive chemical in marijuana commonly referred to as cannabis, is a hallucinogen. The most common effects of cannabis are a sense of euphoria, a heightening of sensitivity, and a slowing of the subjective experience of time. A common side effect is increased appetite (affectionately known as the munchies). Eye redness and dry mouth are not uncommon. Additional effects are cognitive and motor impairments that are both subtle and profound. The last person to ask whether he or she can drive a car is someone who is drunk, correct? Actually, people who have been drinking are more likely to admit that they cannot drive than are those who have been smoking pot. But marijuana intoxication causes impairment of motor skills that can remain long after the euphoria from the high dissipates.

At high dosages or in people who have a predisposition toward psychotic symptoms, cannabis can trigger perceptual disturbances in which the mind plays tricks. This effect is much more likely to occur with traditional hallucinogens such as LSD, PCP, and mescaline, but it can happen with cannabis. Users may become increasingly paranoid or think that they see or hear things that are not really there. In these states, people are more likely to become violent because they feel out of control and are often frightened.

Most people know, however, that "potheads" are much more likely to be sitting around the house not doing much other than snacking rather than ransacking the place and raising hell. Marijuana, in and of itself, has not been associated with violence. Although athletes as well as nonathletes use marijuana recreationally, it is neither performance enhancing nor anger inducing.

A closing point on cannabis relevant to athletes is that some people have argued that chronic cannabis abuse can lead to amotivational syndrome, a state of apathy or a long-term unwillingness to persist in a task. It is not clear whether that syndrome results from cannabis or from a set of character traits of those who chronically abuse marijuana. Athletes seeking to achieve at a high level should consider that cannabis use could negatively affect their motivation to adhere to training, and in turn, their performance.

Cocaine, Crack, and Heroin

Cocaine is a white powdery substance that is most often snorted through the nose but can be injected or smoked as well. Its use results in stimulation of the central nervous system (CNS). Cocaine can produce a sense of alertness, euphoria, and well-being. Additionally, it often decreases the need for sleep and food. Some users believe that cocaine enhances sexual performance. At higher doses or when used by people with a predisposition to psychosis, paranoia (the feeling that others are out to get them) and perceptual disturbances such as hallucinations (hearing or seeing things that are not really there) are more common. One expert (Jaffe, 1992) noted that cocaine has often been linked to physical aggression. He explained that because cocaine increases energy and confidence and can precipitate irritability and paranoia, the link between cocaine and aggression is logical.

I have separated the discussion of cocaine from the discussion of other stimulants because cocaine is not used as a performance-enhancing drug in sport. Many Wall Street traders can stay up days on end in a hypomanic but surprisingly productive state because of cocaine. At low doses it would likely be effective in the way that other stimulants are, but the ease of its detection (and being on the banned lists) and the intensity of the high make it less ideal for sport performance. Cocaine is almost exclusively a recreational drug.

Cocaine is both physiologically and psychologically addictive, but withdrawal is not as severe as it is with opiates such as heroin. Crack, which is a freebased form of cocaine (sometimes called cooked because of the process by which it is produced), is sold as "rocks." Crack has the same effects as cocaine, but the effects are more intense, including its addictive properties. Even one use of crack can reportedly lead to addiction because the high is so pleasurable that the user immediately wants to chase after it for the next high.

The physiological escalation that accompanies cocaine intoxication makes users extremely dangerous if they do become violent. A colleague who was a captain in the state police before becoming a psychologist recalled an illuminating story. While high on cocaine, a 16-year-old boy who was 5 feet, 3 inches (160 centimeters) tall and weighed no more than 135 pounds (61 kilograms) took on five state troopers, all of whom were well over 6 feet (183 centimeters) tall and weighed at least 200 pounds (91 kilograms). Just when they thought that they had him subdued (he was face down and an officer on top of him was preparing to cuff him), the boy grabbed a folding chair by the bottom of the leg and threw it across the room, striking one of the officers in the nose with enough force to fracture it. To understand how much strength this takes, lie flat on your back and try to lift a folding chair by its leg. The increased strength that this teen had while high on cocaine was remarkable. Imagine the situation if that teen had been a 6-foot-4-inch (198-centimeter), 265-pound (120-kilogram) football player.

Cocaine, historically, was a drug of the rich because of its expense. Although those in the lower socioeconomic levels use it, corporate executives, entertainers, and professional athletes use it as well. Some popular athletes who struggled with cocaine were Lawrence Taylor, Darryl Strawberry, Ken Caminiti, and Dwight Gooden.

As I have noted throughout this book, violence is multiply determined. Sorting out what is causative toward violence versus what is contributory is difficult. Substance abuse muddies the waters further because someone may be violent because of intoxication by the drug or because violent behavior is required to acquire more of the drug. "Crackheads" often engage in extreme behavior from prostitution to sudden, unprecipitated, and often brutal robberies to feed their addiction. I once heard a leader in an inner-city neighborhood explain that the world of violence completely changed with the appearance of crack. It was more than just the violence related to turf wars over where who could sell what. With crack, the users were craving so strongly that they would murder someone to sell the person's sneakers for a rock.

In this way, heroin and other opioids are similar. They are highly addictive and produce euphoria when ingested orally, intravenously, subcutaneously, through the nasal membranes, or when smoked. Tolerance to this euphoria develops rapidly; regular users may require significantly more drug than when they started. The ability of these chemicals to block pain, both physical and emotional, can also encourage abuse and addiction. Their psychophysiological effects are rarely associated with anger and violence, but their use may be a precursor to violence when the addict needs money to buy more of the drug. So heroin leads indirectly to violence, but not because of the neurophysiological effects of the drug.

Moreover, athletes do not commonly abuse heroin and opioids but to assume that they never do would be a mistake. Because of their painkilling properties, these drugs, like narcotics such as Vicodin, Percocet, and Oxycontin, may be abused by athletes who are recovering from injuries. Brett Favre has the dubious honor of the most publicized battle with painkiller addiction. His successful battle was public, but other athletes deal with this problem privately. Coaches, parents, athletes, and sport psychologists should be aware of this problem. Although it does not occur frequently, opioid addiction, in whatever form, can have tragic outcomes.

One such scenario occurred in April 2008 when promising Georgia Tech pitcher Michael Hutts was found dead in his apartment because of an accidental heroin overdose. Hutts had made the dean's list and was not identified as a young man known for substance abuse. Georgia Tech athletics director Dan Radakovich in a prepared statement noted, "It is the story of a young man who excelled in academics and athletics whose life was cut short by a very tragic mistake in judgment."

THE NEED FOR SPEED: STIMULANTS, AMPHETAMINES, CAFFEINE, AND NICOTINE

Through various chemicals, the different types of stimulants act in similar ways on the body. Stimulants have been used in sport for decades. These drugs have some obvious performance-enhancing effects, yet until recently they have received surprisingly little attention compared with steroids.

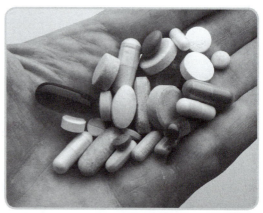

©PhotoDisc

©PhotoDisc

Although they may seem harmless, stimulants such as caffeine, certain medications, and chocolate can greatly impact an athlete's judgment.

The effects of stimulants include increases in heart rate, blood pressure, and breathing rate as well as greater alertness. Stimulants have bronchodilation and sinus-clearing properties (consider pseudoephedrine, which was implicated in the deaths of Minnesota Vikings tackle Korey Stringer and Baltimore Orioles pitcher Steve Bechler). They also lead to a decreased sense of fatigue, decreased appetite, and an increase in self-confidence. Stimulants may distort users' perception of reality and impair their judgment, leading them to place themselves at higher risk of injury when they need to rest. Other adverse effects may include stroke, heart attack, and psychosis.

The use of stimulants dates back to World War II when soldiers used them, but they have been around sport almost as long. When the deaths of prominent athletes, including cyclists Knut Jensen of Denmark and Tommy Simpson of England, were attributed to amphetamine use, stimulants became the first class of drugs prohibited by the International Olympic Committee (IOC). Included are amphetamines, nicotine, and caffeine, although the 2006 IOC and WADA (World Anti-Doping Administration) list of prohibited agents no longer includes caffeine or pseudoephedrine. Note that not all sports use this list.

Amphetamine abuse among student–athletes has been consistently reported to be in the range of 2 to 9 percent (Anderson & McKeag, 1985; Murphy et al., 1985).

First exposed in Jim Bouton's book *Ball Four*, the pioneer in behind-the-scenes baseball books, and then described in David Wells' *Perfect I'm Not: Boomer on Beer, Brawls, Backaches, and Baseball*, the ubiquity of amphetamine use in baseball has become common knowledge. Ken Caminiti told *Sports Illustrated* that only a couple of guys on each team did not take "greenies" (as amphetamines are affectionately called) before playing. Many baseball players have talked about the assistance provided by amphetamines in getting through the dog days of summer. In November 2005 Major League Baseball and the Players Association added amphetamines to the list of banned substances. Some expected to see higher ERAs, fewer games played, and more days on the disabled list (DL), figuring that amphetamines sometimes helped players play through nagging injuries.

In his September 8, 2006, article, ESPN's Jerry Crasnick noted the difficulty of assessing the effect of the absence of amphetamines. The hypothesis that teams with younger players and fresher legs, such as the Florida Marlins and Minnesota Twins, would have less need for the drug and would thus surge late in the season was countered by the late-season push of the San Francisco Giants, a team with an aging roster.

Crasnick noted that 10 major leaguers appeared in all 162 games in 2005, and that 7 might do it in 2006. Extending the comparison, 71 players appeared in 150 or more games in 2005, and that number looked to be closer to 80 in 2006.

With regard to the notion that players would spend more time on the disabled list, through the end of August 2006, major leaguers had spent a total of 18,720 days on the DL, which was a decrease from the 19,944 days in 2005 and the 20,699 days in 2004 at the same point of the year. Those figures would support the idea that amphetamines lead to more serious injuries. The rationale is that when amphetamines are unavailable, athletes rest minor injuries and do not end up on the DL.

Determining how the amphetamines ban has affected participation is difficult, but one does not get the impression that ballplayers are less amped up for the game and less likely to confront opponents with brushback pitches or other aggressive play.

The ubiquity of stimulant use is often understated because caffeine and nicotine have long been staples of everyday life. Many Americans start their day with a cup of joe, and little is said about the effect. Consumption of caffeine products is rising, and coffee is just one source. Gyms have for years been touting "energy drinks," which have caffeine as their most common ingredient. Jolt cola, which first appeared in 1985, had as its initial slogan "All the sugar and twice the caffeine." Caffeine has undeniable effects on arousal and performance, at least for short periods. Because it is legal and no limits are placed on the quantity purchased or used, the likelihood of abuse of stimulants is high. The potential for caffeine to contribute to the risk of violence has led many psychiatric hospitals and state prisons to restrict its consumption. Will Major League Baseball follow up its prohibition of amphetamines by banning Starbucks?

Smoking cigarettes is not helpful to aerobic health and is thus contraindicated in athletes. Seeing athletes smoking these days is uncommon, but the stimulant effects of nicotine should not be ignored, especially considering the fact that stacking stimulants can have synergistic effects.

Another aspect of stimulant use that can be associated with violence is the effect of withdrawal on irritability. People who are accustomed to drinking one or two cups of coffee per day can develop severe headaches and irritability when they do not have access to their fix. Consequently, they can be more prone to conflict. Athletes may therefore be more prone to violence not only while using stimulants but also when they do not have access to them.

Although stimulant use has been associated with violence, I could not find any case in which an athlete's violent behavior was directly attributed to the use of any stimulant. Nonetheless, any police officer who has responded to a call involving a person who is high on stimulants can readily describe how dangerously aggressive these people can be.

The take-home message for athletes, coaches, parents, and sport psychologists is that the use of stimulants can increase the likelihood of violence. Although the link between stimulant abuse and violence has not shown to be present in any highly publicized case involving athletes, we should not conclude that stimulants can be used safely. I believe that athletes who abuse alcohol or stimulants are more likely to become violent than those who abuse steroids. I will explain why in the next section.

STEROIDS—WHAT IS THE "RAGE"?

Examination of the effects of anabolic androgenic steroids (AAS) on violence is problematic because to learn anything about their effects, we have to study people who are using them illegally. Doctors cannot ethically or legally prescribe AAS to anyone who does not have a medical need for them.

Dr. James Shortt, a physician in South Carolina, was investigated by federal agents for prescribing steroids and other performance-enhancing drugs to members of the Carolina Panthers. He eventually pleaded guilty to conspiring to prescribe steroids illegally to several players and was sentenced to one year and one day in prison. As part of the deal, 42 additional counts were dropped. The South Carolina Board of Medical Examiners had previously revoked his license to practice medicine.

Much of the evidence about the effects of steroids on anger and violence are anecdotal, noncausative, or indirect. I am not implying that steroid abuse is innocuous and that using them is acceptable—quite the contrary. But in this discussion, I hope to illustrate that blaming athletes' violence on steroids does not clarify matters.

Before I begin, I would remiss not to refer you to the work of Dr. Charles Yesalis, who has been studying and writing about steroid abuse since the early 1980s. For a complete review of the history of the field, read his work. Specifically, *The Steroids Game: An Expert's Inside Look at Anabolic Steroid Use in Sports*, which he wrote in 1998 with Virginia Cowart, is an excellent, concise review of steroids from multiple angles over time.

What exactly are steroids? Anabolic steroids are a family of drugs that includes the male hormone testosterone (and many synthetic analogues), which has anabolic (muscle building) and androgenic (masculinizing) effects. Studies have shown various usage rates. Kaplan and Saddock's *Synopsis of Psychiatry* estimated that one million Americans have used illegal steroids at least once. They offered that male users outnumber females at roughly a 6-to-1 ratio and that about half of users started before they were 16 years old. They reported that the highest use was among 18- to 25-year-olds, followed by 26- to 34-year-olds. Kaplan and Saddock estimated that the rate of use by bodybuilders was 50 to 80 percent.

Estimates of anabolic steroid abuse among student–athletes have ranged from 4 percent (Murphy et al, 1985) to 20 percent (Dezelsky, Toohey, & Shaw, 1985; Toohey, 1978).

Some people have argued that the true prevalence of steroid abuse is practically impossible to measure and that we need look no further than how much they improve performance to understand why so many people abuse them.

Dr. Julian Bailes, coauthor of *When Winning Costs Too Much: Steroids, Supplements, and Scandal in Today's Sports*, separated those who abuse steroids into three classes. He wrote, "The first and most common use is by individuals who desire to be stronger with greater capacity for strength, lean body mass, and speed." He offered that by combining steroid use with weightlifting, experienced athletes could gain strength and increase their body weight by an average of 10 pounds (4.5 kilograms) after about a month. These are the more common users of steroids.

From there he stated, "They (AAS) are believed to increase the number of oxygen-carrying red blood cells in the body, an obvious benefit for any athlete, especially those involved in endurance activities." Early thoughts about steroids were that they increased muscle mass and possibly fast- and slow-twitch muscles that handle both sprints and endurance, but if they in fact increased oxygen availability to muscles, then endurance athletes would jump on board as well. People seeking to improve their performance are not likely to explore only a single avenue. In the cycling community, more scrutiny had been directed toward blood doping and the use of erythropoietin (a glycoprotein found in the body that leads to an increase in red blood cell production, thus leading to an increase in aerobic capacity) than steroid use until Floyd Landis was found to have an elevated ratio of testosterone to epitestosterone, indicative of testosterone use, and thus was forced to forfeit his Tour de France title. Endurance athletes are the second class of steroid users.

People who use steroids for the perceived positive effect on their appearance are the third class of steroid abusers identified by Dr. Bailes. This group is surprisingly large. I worked at a health club in the mid-1980s and remember the availability of steroids and the many men who were chasing the perfect body. These men were not even amateur bodybuilders; they simply wanted to perfect their bodies so that they could land as many sexual partners as possible. I was friends with some of the "juicers" and remember asking one of them, "Don't you know that stuff will kill you—shrink up your testicles, destroy your liver, give you brain cancer?" His response? "Hey, we all die eventually. When I die, I want to look my best." The low self-esteem that seems so central to these males is akin to that of females with anorexia who see themselves as fat no matter how much weight they lose. The limits that these men would go to and the things that they would ignore (severe acne that even the meanest tanning beds could not hide, balding, gynecomastia—breasts produced in males as a result of steroid use, sometimes unflatteringly referred to as "bitch tits") to chase that body were astounding. Even Lyle Alzado's death had little effect on them because they figured that it would never catch up to them. Alzado did not think so either, not until the end.

Considering the increase in the size and speed of professional athletes, the increase in the number of home runs hit (ignoring for a moment the issue of "juiced" baseballs—strange that we use that term for baseballs, huh?—and the dilution of quality pitching by the addition of more major league baseball teams), and the breaking of record after record, the influence of steroids on sport performance is unquestionable.

Since the BALCO scandal broke, many studies have examined various aspects of the effect of testosterone and steroids on performance. Some people think that steroids do more than just make people stronger. One argument would be that although steroids might allow a baseball player to hit the ball an average of 25 feet (8 meters) farther, he would still need to have tremendous eye–hand coordination just to hit the ball. Some people have hypothesized that increased testosterone assists with visual tracking, thus improving the ability to hunt, pointing to studies of the relationship of testosterone with visual mental rotation. Ignoring the fact that in some species the female is the better hunter, some of this is just mental gymnastics. Many baseball players started with exceptional eye–hand coordination. By adding power, their performance and statistical record would soar.

Of importance to this book is not the prevalence rate of steroid abuse or even their effect on performance, but their psychiatric effect.

On March 17, 2005, Dr. Kirk J. Brower offered testimony to Congress on precisely this topic. Citing other authors, Brower reported that the most frequently described adverse psychiatric effects of AAS are extreme mood swings ranging from mania to depression, suicidal thoughts and behaviors, marked aggression including homicidal thoughts and behavior ("roid rage"), grandiose and paranoid delusions, and addiction. Dr. Brower noted that mania, delusions, and violence were more likely to begin during steroid abuse and depression and that suicide was more likely to occur within three months of stopping. While noting that suicide is already the third-leading cause of death among young people (ages 15 to 24), Brower stated that adding steroids to the mix is "especially troubling."

He went on to state that the true rate of adverse psychiatric effects among AAS users is unknown—appropriately acknowledging the limitations of these types of studies. He recognized that studies often use a small number of subjects who may not be representative of all AAS users, that self-reports may not be accurate, and that the quantity of steroids being used could not be verified. Recognizing these limitations, Dr. Brower reported that studies show higher rates of psychiatric effects in AAS users than in comparable nonusers.

After citing research that he acknowledged as flawed, Brower explained what the gold standard is for research. He accurately explained how and why placebo-controlled, double-blind, randomized, controlled studies are important. He found four studies that used those methods and employed relatively high doses of AAS. He reported that "three of these studies indicate that *some* individuals will experience severe, adverse psychiatric effects after high doses of AAS are administered, although one study found no evidence of psychiatric effects."

Although illicit abuse of steroids may occur at doses of 10 to 100 times the prescribed therapeutic dose, the studies were ethically limited to doses of 5 to 6 times the therapeutic dose. Dr. Brower explained that these gold standard studies may underestimate the problem. We cannot make conclusions about steroid abusers who are not represented in these studies.

Dr. Charles Yesalis also discussed the issue of steroid use and violence, called roid rage. Reviewing the literature, he concluded that "although most scientists apparently agree that anabolic steroids, especially at high doses, seem to increase aggressiveness, not all studies reach this conclusion." Yesalis defined roid rage as "spontaneous, highly aggressive, out-of-control behavior where the police either were called or should have intervened." He noted experts in the field disagree and that some do not even believe that it exists. He recognized that many factors converge to lead to these episodes including a history of mental illness, a propensity for violence before steroid use, placebo effects (whereby the steroid abuser expects to become more violent and thus does), the actual biochemical effects of the steroids themselves, and other factors— making it difficult to put the total causality on the steroids themselves. Dr. Yesalis concluded that "if this phenomenon is real, it is relatively rare (probably less than 1 percent) among steroid users."

James Tedeschi and Richard Felson examined the research linking testosterone with aggression in their book *Violence, Aggression, and Coercive Actions*. In reviewing studies of criminal recidivism of castrated (surgically or chemically) sex offenders and those who took testosterone antagonists to reduce sexual behavior, they came to this conclusion:

> *It would not be surprising if the research on surgical or chemical castration indicated some relationship to sex drive and sexual misconduct. The general question here, however, is whether reduction of testosterone reduces aggressive behavior in general, not only in relation to sexual gratification. There is no evidence that castration will affect aggressive behavior that does not involve sexual misconduct.*

In essence, aggressiveness cannot be explained solely by hormonal causality.

One of the best depictions of the relationship between steroids and aggression can be found in an unheralded article written by Martin Sharp and David Collins. Titled "Exploring the 'Inevitability' of the Relationship Between Anabolic-Androgenic Steroid Use and Aggression in Human Males," the article appeared in the *Journal of Sport and Exercise Psychology* in 1998. The authors began by explaining the flaws in the simplistic causality model between AAS and aggression. They noted that the theory gained further support because the media treated it as fact.

This mistaken belief in the role of steroids in violence may have foreshadowed what occurred in 2006 when San Diego Chargers linebacker Steve Foley was shot by an off-duty police officer after he was seen driving erratically and suspected to be intoxicated. His blood-alcohol level was nearly three times the legal limit, and he had been arrested five times since 1999, including occurrences that involved alcohol or confrontations with officers. According to an affidavit for a search warrant, the prosecutors requested a sample of Foley's blood to test for performance-enhancing drugs. Dan Nordell, a criminal investigator, wrote this in the affidavit:

> *His history of aggressive and even violent contact with law enforcement indicates the possibility of more than mere alcohol involvement. . . . Steroids can cause erratic behavior in those that use them. This has been given names like 'roid rage for the uncontrollable outbursts and violence experienced by some users.*

This was all cited in a September 14, 2006, article in *USA Today*. Left out were the many other explanations for why someone would act that way.

In any case, going back to the Sharp and Collins article, the authors noted that although the causal link between testosterone and aggression is firmly established in certain animal species (Bernstein, Gordon, & Rose, 1983; Bouissou, 1983; Simon, Whalen, & Tate, 1985), the evidence is much less compelling for human males (Archer, 1991; Meyer-Bahlburg, Boona, Sharma, & Edwards, 1974; Tricker et al., 1996). They referenced an article by Blackmon and Pellon (1993) and concluded that "asserting that there is some underlying effect of a drug on behavior without taking into account the influence of variables which control behavior is as unprofitable as asserting that genetic influences . . . are somehow independent of the environment."

Further reviewing the literature, they stated that although a popular 1994 study by Choi and Pope found that AAS users reported significantly more fights, verbal aggression, and violence toward their significant others, prompting those authors to conclude that the wives and girlfriends of AAS users may be at heightened risk for violence, another study seemed to disprove the hypothesis that higher levels of testosterone increased the risk for domestic violence. Lindman, Pahlen, Ost, and Eriksson (1992) studied males who were arrested following spousal abuse and found that serum testosterone levels were not elevated in comparison with controls.

More evidence that questions the relationship was found in a 1992 study by Bahrke, Wright, Strauss, and Catlin (1992), who conducted studies on people who self-administered steroids. The researchers concluded that steroid use did not increase aggression in human males. Bahrke, in 1993, stated

> *a tiny percentage of AS using athletes appear to experience mental disturbances that result in seeking clinical treatment and of those who do, some may already suffer from existing mental health or other substance abuse problems. At this point, a cause–effect relationship has yet to be established.*

Two studies additional studies (Kouri et al., 1995; Tricker et al., 1996) were comparable in that they used the same high doses of steroids and similar methodologies. Kouri and colleagues reported results that they believed showed a "clear indication of a causal relationship between AS and aggression." On the other hand, Tricker and colleagues stated, "Our study failed to detect any significant effects of testosterone treatment on mood or the subsets of angry behavior examined."

The inconsistency of the findings points to the involvement of other mediating factors. One of the most intriguing possibilities is social mediation. Rejeski, Gregg, Kaplan, and Manuck (1990) studied the effects of steroids on cynomolgus monkeys because their social structure has been identified as being similar to that of humans. The authors found that the magnification effect of steroids was mediated by social status. Dominant monkeys became more aggressive, and less dominant monkeys actually exhibited an increase in passive behaviors such as paranoia, depression, and social isolation. Sharp and Collins summarized the study:

> *Even if some pharmacological effect does exist (and we recognize that it does, although the degree and mechanisms have yet to be demonstrated), social influence and group effects must represent an important facilitating— or perhaps for some groups inhibiting—factor in behavioral responding.*

It is alarming that the popular press, and even many professionals, speak with such certainty of the phenomenon of roid rage when the incidence of users having such reactions is estimated to be low or is nonexistent. Furthermore, some steroid users have traditional psychiatric symptoms such as psychosis or mood swings (mania or depression) that can be just as debilitating to them and people around them. The sensationalism surrounding roid rage may well have more to do with its promulgation by the media than the actual effects of steroids on anger and violence.

Returning to Dr. Brower's testimony to Congress, understand that I am not criticizing Dr. Brower because his job was to present to Congress what is known of the psychiatric effects of steroids and to do so in a powerful way to alert Congress about the potential damage that steroids can cause. Percentages and incidence rates do not matter in life-or-death situations. As with the lottery, even if the odds are extremely long, people will play if the prize is big enough. Even if the chance is less than 1 percent that a teenager who uses steroids will commit suicide, if that child is yours the odds do not matter. The problem is that we are uncertain about the effects of steroids on people's emotional well-being.

An interesting hypothesis that has not been well studied relates to Berkowitz' completion hypothesis (see chapter 1). Steroid abuse has been implicated in damage to multiple organ systems, such as increased risk of heart and cardiovascular disease, liver disease, liver cancer, and prostate cancer; thinning of connective tissue (increasing the likelihood of tendon and ligament tears); and possible havoc to the reproductive system. With such pervasive changes occurring in the body, becoming physically uncomfortable and irritable is both predictable and commonly reported. Applying the completion hypothesis, this irritability could lead to a negative affect state that would increase the likelihood for aggression to occur. Steroids could certainly be a contributory factor toward violence, even if the relationship is not purely causative.

TREATMENT IMPLICATIONS FOR SUBSTANCE ABUSE AND VIOLENCE

Rarely do substances alone cause people to become violent. Most commonly, those who become violent because of the effects of drugs, which either lower their inhibitions or elevate their fury, have physical aggressiveness in their behavioral repertoire in the first place. Because of the effects of drugs, psychotherapeutic interventions will have little influence during intoxication. Although techniques such as distraction, removal to a less stimulating environment, and physical restraint may be helpful, until the drug runs its course and is metabolized, calming people down while they are intoxicated is difficult. At times, hospitalization is necessary.

But treatment options are available. Substance abuse treatment, when the person truly wants to become drug free (many people who enter drug treatment are ambivalent at best and go only because others, such as family, loved ones, and sometimes judges, force them to), can be successful. Incorporated in such treatment, anger management can be extremely useful. One of the reasons that people abuse drugs is to control their moods. Likewise, a reason that they continue to use drugs is that they work! The addiction is both physiological and psychological. Drugs often make people feel better, so they are being reinforced for their drug use. The problem, however, is that drug use does nothing to address the underlying emotions that people are trying to manage. Furthermore, problems tend to grow when they are not addressed. So if people do not want to work on their issues now, they do not have to, but the problems will continue to grow and in turn will become more difficult to solve. Furthermore, other problems are often associated with drug abuse, such as financial troubles, social difficulties as the drug becomes increasingly important to the user, and ultimately criminal involvement.

These people need to be taught anger management skills. Practice is essential to developing a reflexive ability to self-regulate. Simply stated, as people become more proficient at recognizing their moods, they begin to use their tools earlier and become more successful at managing situations. Increasing their confidence and competence in doing so, as part of substance abuse treatment, can attack the problem from multiple angles.

Ultimately, the best treatment is prevention. A long-held illusion is that athletes are so involved with their health that they would not risk harming their bodies by ingesting chemicals. Through years of research, we know that this is not true. In fact, athletes may be at greater risk because of their feelings of invincibility, the pressures that they are under to perform their best, and the mixed messages that they receive about performance-enhancing drugs.

The Association for Applied Sport Psychology held an Anti-Doping Congress in Louisville, Kentucky, as a precursor to its annual conference in 2007 to focus on the significant effects that drugs are having on athletics. Increasingly, we need to see proactive approaches to education. Reaching athletes at an early age is crucial. We need to appreciate physical fitness. We can admire the feats of elite athletes, but we also need to return to hard work, discipline, good nutrition, and proper training. Most important, we need to cease our hero worship of athletes who are involved in drug abuse (performance enhancing or otherwise) and crime. These people need help. Sport psychology has a responsibility to develop innovative and progressive ways to help athletes who abuse drugs.

SUMMARY

Drugs are rarely the sole cause of anger, aggression, or violence. Some substances have a contributory or additive influence on potential for violence, but some do not. Marijuana is rarely associated with violence. Heroin and opioid intoxication rarely cause violence, although criminal activity is sometimes necessary to support a habit.

Cocaine and stimulants place people at higher risk for violence. Although their abuse may be more accepted in some realms of the athlete culture (stimulants more so than cocaine), the potential for increased violence, especially in those who are temperamentally angry, should not be understated. This notion applies as well to caffeine, a substance whose psychoactive effects are often ignored.

Because of its pervasiveness and profound effect on lessening people's inhibition, alcohol is perhaps the most common contributor to athlete violence. Note that this alcohol-related violence is not an athlete-specific phenomenon. Alcohol can increase violence risk for all people for the same reasons. The point is that athletes should not believe that they are immune. Extra care should be taken to educate athletes about this potential.

Anabolic steroids present a much cloudier picture. Some research points to an increase in testosterone leading to an increase in aggressiveness, but other research challenges this premise. The concept of roid rage has similarly been argued. Increasingly, steroids are seen more as a contributory factor to violence than a causative factor.

Moreover, treatment protocols for anger management will have little value while people are actually under the influence of drugs. But anger management can and should be an integral part of substance abuse treatment for athletes who have been involved in violence.

Ultimately, despite recent efforts, the field of sport psychology is still lagging behind in addressing the problems related to substance abuse and sport. Because anger and violence has also been understudied, together they represent overlapping domains that require greater attention by professionals in the field.

CHAPTER 7

DEVELOPING AND USING ANGER MANAGEMENT PROGRAMS FOR ATHLETES

The culmination of the previous chapters leads us to the "How To" of anger management. As should be clear by now, getting angry in and of itself, is not a problem. It is the high levels of anger that lead to reactive aggression. The program that is outlined below provides guidelines on how to recognize one's emotion levels and control them. This is done by becoming aware of one's body, how it changes when one is very angry, and different methods to both calm down when very angry as well as ways to avoid getting so angry in the first place. These techniques are truly cognitive and behavioral skills.

PRESCREENING FOR ANGER MANAGEMENT PARTICIPATION

Certain groups of people should be evaluated before they are enrolled in an anger management program. When I say evaluated, I do not mean unilaterally ruled out, but prescreened. Certain kinds of people are more likely to benefit than others are from this type of work, and determining who they are is important before beginning any anger management work.

The first question should always be this: Why are you here? If the person is self-referred and motivated—great! If the person shows up because someone said that he or she had to be there—beware! Mandated therapies are notoriously difficult, particularly when people are getting help for behavioral patterns that may be ego syntonic (they like acting that way). People who are doing this work are more likely to benefit from it if they are there because they chose to be there. I am not opposed to discussing with clients the benefits that they can get from anger management training, which certainly includes satisfying the mandate of whoever made the referral. Ultimately, success or failure will come from the client, not from the leader, so the person has the choice of how to proceed. Often, when the issue is posed that way, the client will concede and stay, at least to check it out. If you demand that they stay and participate, you may be wasting each other's time. Sometimes, people do better by delaying their participation until they are ready to do the work.

The second question is this: Who is the client? As in all sport psychology interventions, this question is critical. The issue is about more than knowing who is going to sign the check. The more important issues involve who is expecting results and how they are going to know about them. Sorting this out ahead of time is necessary to avoid confidentiality concerns and ethical conflicts as well to create a safe therapeutic space for the work to be done.

The last area of prescreening, which may include pretest questionnaires or other psychological testing in rare cases, is whether the likely problem for the individual is a skills deficit or severe psychopathology or even psychopathy. Refer to chapter 3 for instruments that may help make this determination.

When I receive an anger management referral, whether clinical or sport related, I ask for information about a recent medical examination and any counseling history. The screening should ask direct questions about past or current pathology, including substance abuse, to ascertain whether the client would be best served in a more controlled arena, such as in individual sessions where clinical problems can be addressed along with the anger issues. If you are not psychologically trained, you should refer the client to someone with the proper background before you start down this path. It could quickly go to places that you never expected.

INDIVIDUAL VERSUS GROUP

As Bruce Hale and I explained in our chapter for Shane Murphy's *Sport Psych Handbook*, both individual and group interventions have pluses and minuses. These attributes should be considered when deciding how to implement anger management skills.

Individual counseling sessions allow greater exploration of incidents and issues that may be embarrassing if addressed in front of others. Furthermore, if a hidden psychopathology may present, especially a trauma-related issue, a group setting could be not only humiliating but also damaging. In addition, current teammates may soon be on opposing teams. Sharing thoughts and feelings may leave a person feeling vulnerable. Exploring those thoughts and feelings one-on-one in a safe environment may promote greater honesty; the lack thereof is a considerable obstacle to progress.

Group interventions offer the opportunity for a group of athletes to learn the skills together. This aspect may be particularly valuable when the intervention is for a whole team or parts thereof. Reinforcement can then occur outside the leader's office, and what is learned can be extended to new environments. In my experience, group sessions can have a significant team-building effect. Athletes learn more about how other athletes think. Through role playing, they can see how their peers react to situations that may also develop in other venues. This area would be another good topic for research. In research on these types of interventions, measures of team cohesion may provide some useful information. By learning each other's triggers, players can help their teammates regain composure and self-control in volatile situations rather than react in a destructive manner.

In no case, however, do I assign any athlete to be responsible for the behavior of another. I do believe that athletes influence each other and contribute to the culture in which decisions are made, but people must ultimately take responsibility for themselves. Collectively, the team takes responsibility for the team.

Finally, although role playing is an excellent way to teach the lessons that follow, and it tends to be more effective than a lecture-based format, the leader must strive to make the program exciting, interactive, and fun. People learn better when they are having fun.

ANGER MANAGEMENT

Hey, how do you feel?

Good?

Fine?

OK?

Not bad?

No, how do you *feel*?

Several basic elements can hinder the effectiveness of anger management programs. The first is that most people do not know how to label their emotions. Any emotion management program must begin with teaching people how to recognize how they feel. Just as important is to recognize that the purpose is not truly to manage anger. The real purpose is to manage behavior associated with anger, or reactive aggression management. The place to start is with emotion labeling because as arousal increases, controlling emotions and related behavior becomes increasingly difficult.

Emotion Labeling

In my opinion, the deficit in emotional labeling has reached epidemic proportions in the United States. The cause may be our susceptibility to the more-is-better approach: "If one is good, then give me a thousand." We have great difficulty identifying how we feel and how much we feel. After all, emotions have their own experience, which varies slightly from person to person, but they can also be experienced at different intensities, frequencies, and durations.

Nothing about any emotion is inherently good or bad. The judgment that we place on them is the single greatest obstacle to managing them. To expand, parents often tell their children that being angry is not good. Men are socialized as boys to hide their emotions, especially their fears and sadness, although they may be simultaneously confused by the intense football coach who encourages their anger and aggression. The 12-year-old Pop Warner football player who cries may be called a sissy, a girl—as if being a girl is a bad thing—or worse. I will focus more on communication between coaches and athletes later, but at the onset, we must divorce ourselves from the idea that having a particular emotion is good or bad. Making that sort of judgment is complete nonsense.

The way to go about teaching athletes to label their emotions is twofold. The easier way to start is to teach them how their bodies react during emotional changes. They have their bodies with them all the time, they tend to pay close attention to their bodies (in my experience, the only group of clients who pay more attention to how their bodies feel are substance abusers), and they can gain tangible results from controlling the physiological changes associated with emotion.

Ask your athletes to imagine for a moment that they are not young human athletes but instead cute fuzzy bunnies in the woods. (Expect some groaning from your young male athletes, but proceed anyway.) Set up this scenario. You are hopping along and out of nowhere, a giant grizzly bear pops out with its claws bared and saliva dripping from its fangs. It growls as it moves toward its next meal . . . you.

Are you scared?

You bet your butt! How do you know? Think about how your body feels. What must you do to survive? You need either to run or to get ready to fight. In either case, your body needs to prepare for action. The autonomic nervous system is the automatic, involuntary part of the nervous system. It has two parts. The sympathetic nervous system is responsible for the increase in the following functions, and the parasympathetic nervous system controls the decrease. A loose analogy would be that the sympathetic nervous system is the on switch and the parasympathetic nervous system is the off switch. It is not quite that simple because some bodily functions do not abide by those rules, but in a fight-or-flight situation—in which you must either run or fight to survive—the sympathetic nervous system kicks in full force.

All the physiological changes that occur during the sympathetic response have survival value. Muscles tighten so that they are ready for work. To operate, they need glucose and oxygen. The shakiness that people feel is associated with adrenaline, the hormone or neurotransmitter used by the nervous system during these changes. The amount of glucose being released into the blood stream increases. The breathing rate increases so that more oxygen gets into the body. The heart rate and blood pressure increase to move the oxygenated blood to the muscles. Perspiration increases as well.

Sweating has three main functions that aid survival:

1. It cools you down to counter all the muscular activity.
2. Your body becomes slippery. If a predator is trying to grab you to make you its lunch, you become harder to catch.
3. You stink! Animals tend to leave things alone that have a foul odor, especially food.

Our bodies are designed for survival. No thought is necessary. All these things just happen. I have presented on this topic hundreds of times. Every time, people fail to realize the adaptive value of this response. When you understand why your body is reacting this way, it becomes normalized and controllable.

Before we move on, I want to outline two interesting points about the relationship between autonomic nervous system arousal and anger.

First, recall that the on–off analogy is imprecise. Although the parasympathetic nervous system turns on digestive and eliminative functions, the autonomic nervous system is at times so shocked that the parasympathetic nervous system releases control of the anal sphincter and bladder, causing the elimination of feces or urine. If you have heard of the phrase "scared shitless" or that someone was so scared that he peed in his pants, this is precisely the reason why.

This reaction also has survival value. For the fuzzy animal in the woods, the bodily waste left behind can be repugnant to predators or serve as a type of smokescreen that can assist with escape. In addition, if the bladder or bowel were ruptured by a blow to the abdomen, the contents entering the abdominal cavity could lead to infection and death. Elimination prevents this from occurring.

The second issue is a phenomenon called parasympathetic rebound (figure 7.1). Generally, every action has an equal and opposite reaction, but the sympathetic nervous system can occasionally spike so quickly that when the parasympathetic nervous system becomes active (and works significantly slower than the sympathetic system), it slows down the body to an even greater degree.

This parasympathetic rebound can slow down the body so much that the heart stops. This is believed to be what happens when someone is "scared to death." Actually, the person is relaxed to death because the body overreacts to the intense arousal by slowing itself down too much.

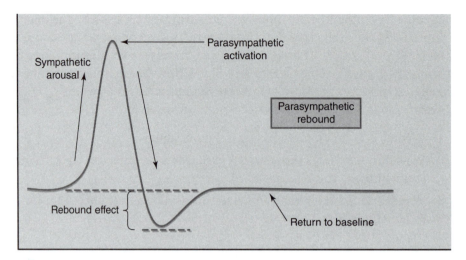

Figure 7.1 Parasympathetic rebound.

Parasympathetic rebound is common, but lethal outcomes are extremely rare. It more commonly presents itself in the experience after an episode of arousal. Think about how tired you were after the last time you became furious or how drained you felt after you cried subsequent to being scared or hurt. This feeling is likely a result of the parasympathetic rebound.

Returning to our original premise of emotion labeling, one way to identify how you feel, specifically when you are angry or anxious, is by paying attention to how your body feels. All animals have the same sympathetic arousal. You can even tell how other people are feeling by observing how their bodies change, including their facial expressions.

Just as you can recognize a potential attack by a dog by its raised shoulders, laid-back ears, bared teeth, and bristled hair, you can identify aggression in humans by changes in their posture. You may see it in the form of clenched teeth or tight fists. You may see their eyes widen or their shoulders rise a little. Their arms become tenser and float away from their bodies as if they are getting ready to strike by themselves. Some people start to pace, showing what is known as psychomotor agitation—the inability to stay still. If they are talking, the speed and volume of their voice may increase. Some people shift their eyes quite a bit, but others lock on their target and are unable to shift their visual frame. If you want to de-escalate someone, do it early, because after people reach a certain point, defusing them is virtually impossible.

Figure 7.2 illustrates a normal progression of escalation. Each letter shows the culmination of an individual event or provocation. The time between letters A and D corresponds to the length of the person's fuse. Although some people explode at A or B whereas others can reach L or M, what is depicted is that each time someone's anger increases, returning to baseline becomes more difficult. Every person has a personal explosion threshold,

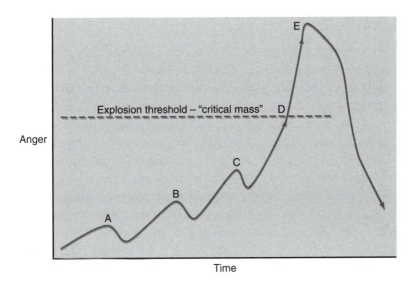

Figure 7.2 Explosion threshold.

but it is dynamic, meaning that various factors can influence it. Yes, certain people have longer fuses than others do, but even for those with a long fuse, certain issues may considerably lower the threshold, such as a loved one being in danger, real or perceived. In addition, because some people are more comfortable being angry than others are, more may be required to cause them to explode.

I sometimes refer to the explosion threshold as the critical mass. I pilfered the term from physics, which defines critical mass as the amount of fissionable material needed to sustain a nuclear chain reaction. The analogy is that after a person develops a critical mass, the quantity of anger available is sufficient to feed on itself until either it runs its course or a significant force interferes with it. I believe that when someone reaches this point, reason or verbal interaction will have little or no effect. Only four things will stop the person at that point:

1. Physical restraint

2. Medication

3. Distraction

4. Discharge of energy

These are the only options when a person reaches the critical mass. Anyone who has worked security in a nightclub or worked in a prison or psychiatric hospital can confirm this statement. At that point, all reason goes out the window. People who reach their explosion threshold think that they are invincible, do not care about the consequences, and often sacrifice themselves physically to attain their goals.

Relaxation Techniques

Athletes have heard about the value of relaxation since they started playing. Most incorporate some form of relaxation exercise into their precompetition routines. Probably the greatest value of the superstitious routines that athletes engage in is that they believe their routines lead to success. They worry less about failing and can calm themselves down to focus on the task at hand. Whether standing at the free throw line or standing on the mound looking in to get the sign from the catcher, athletes often consciously take a couple of deep breaths to calm themselves down.

One of my more embarrassing moments as a sport psychologist occurred with this issue when I was working with a high school basketball team. The coach asked me if I could work with one of his players, Dwayne, who was shooting miserably from the free throw line. I watched him for a time in both practice and game situations before I started working with him. I could not detect any variation in his routine in either situation, so I assumed that the problem was that he was tightening up. I thought that if I taught him to relax, his free throw shooting would improve. I taught him diaphragmatic breathing and paired it with imagery and visualization (which I will discuss more in a moment), and he reported that he was able to achieve a good relaxing state, almost like floating. He was eager to try the new approach in practice and then in games.

Initially, he seemed to be improving. He hit seven of his first eight free throws. Momentarily proud, I was pleased with his newfound success. But then we tracked his performance over time. After the first stretch, he returned to form and wound up shooting about 15 percent less from the stripe. So after working with me, Dwayne's performance was worse! I reviewed what we did but could not figure it out, so finally I just asked him. What I learned was that my installing a relaxation program threw him off the routine that he used to relax: dribble the ball twice, spin it in his hands, take a deep breath, dribble twice again, spin it in his hands, take a deep breath, and then shoot. His coach later brought in a shooting coach who identified Dwayne's problem as a technical issue with his release and follow-through. His problem was not about relaxation, so my intervention made things worse for Dwayne rather than better.

The moral of the story is not to assume that you know how to relax people and that they do not. Find out what people use first and determine whether tension is truly the issue. Dwayne's problem turned out to be a technical issue that I could not fix and only made worse by changing his relaxing preshot routine.

Using the body as the starting point for anger management with athletes makes sense because athletes are body conscious and kinesthetically aware. They tend to notice subtle changes in how their bodies feel. After they are cued into the changes that occur when they become angry, they can mobilize a plan to de-escalate. Incidentally, anger and anxiety are similar physiologically, so the techniques used to control bodily escalation for anger are similar to those used in anxiety reduction. Several physiological changes correspond with anger arousal:

- Breathing rate increases.
- Heart rate increases.
- Muscle tension increases.
- Sweating increases.
- Urge to urinate increases.
- Blood pressure increases.

From the preceding list, check off the ones that you can control directly. The only items that you can control directly are breathing rate and muscle tension. Fortunately, if you slow either of those, the rest will follow. Therefore, relaxation techniques should focus on these two changes first.

Diaphragmatic Breathing

Do not be alarmed by the fancy scientific terms. Diaphragmatic breathing is simply deep breathing. The proper technique to gain maximal benefit from each breath is to slow the rhythm and take as much oxygen as possible into the lungs on each inhalation.

When you ask people to calm down and take a couple of deep breaths, they often breathe in and out quickly, huffing out the breath and moving their shoulders up and down. But you do not breathe with your shoulders; you breathe with your lungs. If the shoulders are moving, you are not breathing correctly.

To ensure that you are performing the technique correctly, start by imagining that you have a balloon in your stomach. The goal is to blow up the balloon as you inhale. The diaphragm is a curved muscle below your chest, immediately below your ribcage. When you take a deep breath, the diaphragm pulls down to expand the space in your chest for your lungs. Simultaneously, it pushes out your belly. You can observe this by sitting in a chair with your back placed squarely against the back of the chair. Maintain good posture but be relaxed. Sit with your feet comfortably on the floor and place one hand on your belly, between your sternum and your navel.

As you take a slow, deep breath, your hand should move outward. If it is not, reposition yourself, get comfortable, and take a slow, deep breath. Allow yourself to find a comfortable rhythm. Do not force things; just allow your breathing to be nice and slow. Count to three slowly to yourself as you inhale, hold your breath for a count of one or two, and then slowly exhale for a count of five. Wait a couple of seconds and then begin again. I find it easier to slow down by breathing in through my nose and out through my mouth. If you have sinus problems or do not find it comfortable, you can inhale and exhale through either your nose or your mouth. Just be mindful to take slow, steady breaths and allow yourself to relax. Do not fight against yourself; doing so only makes it harder to relax.

The strange thing about relaxation is that the harder you try to achieve it, the more difficult it becomes. As with the Chinese finger trap, which traps the fingers (often the index fingers) in both ends of a small, woven cylinder, the more you struggle, the harder it is to have success.

Although breathing is part of life, when people pay attention to it they often interfere with their own rhythm. This is normal. We change many things in life by paying attention to them. But by learning to control our breathing, we learn the basic skill of slowing ourselves down and relaxing.

Progressive Muscle Relaxation

To relax your muscles, the first step is to determine where the tension lies. For most people, tenseness occurs in a particular muscle group. For me, it occurs in the trapezius muscles, which connect the neck to the back and shoulders. This location is a common area of tenseness, but some people notice it in the calves, in the lower back, or in the facial muscles around the jaw or forehead. The first step is to scan your body from head to toe, paying attention to what is tense and what is not. The next step is to learn how to relax those muscles.

Progressive muscle relaxation (PMR) is a method of relaxing your body by deliberately tensing a muscle group and then relaxing it. This is done one muscle group at a time. Becoming proficient in the technique can take a significant amount of time. When you become proficient and know where your tension tends to accumulate, you can relax your whole body by relaxing that one muscle group, which may be the trigger point that either turns on or turns off muscle tension. When athletes learn PMR, they can use it in several situations: to assist with falling asleep, to ease precompetition anxiety, and ultimately to fine-tune their tension during participation.

Athletes should also be aware that tension related to anger or anxiety should not be confused with soreness from strenuous exercise or injury. If they are aware of any injuries, they should consult a sports medicine professional to make sure that no contraindication is present in their situation. We certainly do not want to add to a problem.

The goal of learning these skills is to be able to turn the excitation volume up or down. The goal is not to put athletes in a relaxed, sedated state in the midst of competition because they cannot be successful in sport when they are underaroused.

Finally, before I give a script for PMR, I recognize that this skill, like physical skills, requires practice and repetition. Rarely does someone master the skill on the first try. When psychologists work with clinical problems, several sessions of honing are normally required before the client becomes marginally proficient with these skills. The goal is to become increasingly aware and in control of muscle tension. On certain days calming the body may be easy; on other days PMR by itself will not be enough. Athletes should use as many tools as they have in their repertoire. PMR and the other tools mentioned in this section are excellent sleep aids for those who have difficulty getting enough rest because they are too keyed up.

PMR Script

Now, I want you to get yourself comfortable in your chair. Sit with good posture but without being stiff. Place your back against the chair, let your arms hang loosely at your sides, and place your feet on the floor in front of you. Good. Now prepare yourself for this exercise by beginning with your breathing. Breathe in through your nose nice and slow, hold it for a couple of seconds, and then slowly exhale through your mouth. Nice and easy, in and out. If you like, you can close your eyes during this exercise, but it is not necessary. Some people benefit by imagining things as they breathe. People might imagine their breathing being in sync with waves coming up on the sand and then returning to the ocean. They take a deep breath in with the water coming up and release their stress and tension with the water as it returns to the sea. Do this a few times yourself to begin to become comfortable and relaxed . . . slow everything down . . . nothing else in the world matters at this moment. This is your time, your time to control your body and how it feels. Excellent. Enjoy the feeling of the tensions of the day washing out of you.

OK, now we are going to begin going through your muscle groups—deliberately tightening them, noting the tension, and then relaxing them. When you are ready, make tight fists out of both hands. Squeeze hard enough to bring slight discomfort. Feel your fingernails sticking into your palms, feel the muscles in your forearms slowly shake from the strain, and hold them tight without relenting. Maintaining this tension is important to learning about your control over your muscles. Hold it for a slow count to 10. Begin . . . 10 . . . 9 . . . 8 . . . 7 . . . 6 . . . feel the burn . . . 5 . . . 4 . . . 3 . . . 2. When you reach 1, release your fists and let your hands fall gently back to your sides. Pay attention to the warmth coming over your hands. You may even experience a slight tingling and a cooling sensation, perhaps noticing that your hands are cooling off as the blood flows out and the perspiration in your palms starts to dry. Your hands may feel heavy. I want you to notice the difference between the tension you felt a moment ago and the relaxation that you feel now. Continue to breathe slowly and enjoy feeling the difference . . . the relaxation . . . you did this . . . because you are in control.

(continued)

After breathing slowly and rhythmically for a couple of moments, gently nod your head when you are ready to continue. Good . . . we will move on. Now I want you to lift up your arms and bend them at the elbow, bringing your fists toward both sides of your head as you did when you were showing off your biceps as a kid. Tighten those biceps and at the same time expand your chest and push your elbows farther back like a butterfly slowly moving its wings backward. This movement should create some tension in your upper back as your shoulder blades are pushed together. I want you to focus on the overall tension that you are feeling in your upper body . . . perhaps in muscles that you do not pay much attention to during the day . . . maybe where your stress goes to accumulate and hang out, weighing you down. Again, hold on to the tension . . . welcome it because you control it, you brought it, and you can make it leave whenever you want. You may feel the muscles start to fatigue a little bit . . . this is good . . . the relaxation feel will that much better. As the muscles are swelling up from the blood rushing to the area, I want you to slowly relax your biceps . . . let your hands fall toward your lap, but before you focus on those biceps relaxing, raise your shoulders up as if you are trying to touch your ears with them. Feel the tension move up your back from your shoulder blades to those traps, the muscle that connect your neck to your shoulders . . . tighten them up. This is another place where a lot of stress accumulates . . . push those shoulders up toward your ears . . . feel the tension . . . hold it. I know that the muscles are getting tired . . . just for a couple more seconds . . . OK, now slowly let them fall lax. Let your shoulders droop down . . . let the blood flow out of them . . . enjoy the difference in the tension . . . become familiar with it . . . master it. Center yourself again and refocus on your breathing . . . nice and easy.

After a couple more moments we are going to move on to your face muscles. Just keep breathing and notice the tension leaving your body. You should already be feeling more at ease than before . . . but if not, no worries . . . you are learning more about your body, and the more familiar you become with it, the greater control you have. In . . . out . . . breathing slowly. Waves come in, inhale . . . hold it, thinking about the waves breaking on the sand . . . and then gradually release, sending your stress out to the open sea that can hold all of it for you . . . OK, now are you ready? Whether you realize it or not, your face has many muscles, and your emotions tend to spend a good deal of time there. Laugh too long and your cheeks hurt; be angry too long and your brow is tired at the end of the day. We are going to cleanse your face muscles from the emotional tension. First, spend a moment exploring those muscles . . . open your mouth wide . . . hold it and then release. Smile big . . . hold it . . . and release. Then I want you to raise your eyebrows up . . . high, as if you are trying to touch the ceiling with them . . . hold them. If you want to, feel the skin on your forehead, which may be wrinkling a little bit with the pressure . . . hold it . . . now slowly bring them back down but do not relax them . . . bring them all the way down so that your brow is tight, you look angry, and your eyes are squinting. Your eyebrows are practically touching, and your forehead is tightening. At the same time I want you to tighten your jaw and clench your teeth together as if you are holding on to something. Your jaw is now like a vice. Imagine that as your teeth are tightening and your brow is pulled down that you are trying to make your bottom jaw and your eyebrows somehow meet. This is the face of tension . . . the face of anger . . . the face of rage . . . and you can make your face this way . . . you can control all your muscles in your face and all the tension that you are feeling. Your face is a contorted knot, and you made it happen because you are in control . . . feel your teeth pressed together . . . feel your face becoming tired. Now when I count down from three to one, slowly relax the muscles in your face . . . three . . . two . . . get ready to relax . . . one. Good . . . now release all the pressure from those muscles and let them relax . . . refocus on your breathing. It might have increased during this relaxation exercise. It is OK . . . you can calm it all down . . . let your tongue sit comfortably in your mouth. Your jaw is no longer clenched, and the strain in your muscles just drops down from the top of your skull and out the bottom of your jaw. Just let it all go . . . excellent . . . enjoy this for a moment or two . . . just breathe and relax.

As you continue breathing, we are going to use this steady process as way to experience tension as well. Breathe slowly, in and out. Now I want you to take in a very deep breath and hold it. Notice the discomfort and the muscles in your expanded chest. Hold on just a little longer, not to the point that you get dizzy, but so that you can feel that your body wants to release the heavy, carbon-dioxide-filled air and replenish it with cool, oxygen-rich air. And then . . . release slowly. Your body will breathe quickly at first. This is normal . . . do not worry . . . help your body regain control of your breathing, slowly and steadily.

OK, now we'll go down the torso to the abdomen. Although these muscles do not usually hold a great deal of our stress, we want to experience the difference between tension and relaxation in all parts of the body. Slowly, I want you to pull your abdomen in as you did when you were young and tried to show everyone how skinny you were. Suck it all the way in toward your spine. Hold it for a moment, but not too long because breathing in this position is next to impossible. But hold it long enough to feel the strain on the muscles. Now slowly relax with an exhale and return your breathing to a slow, steady rhythm.

Continue down to the lower abdomen. We will now tense and then release those muscles, along with the muscles of your hips and upper thighs. Remember to continue breathing between the exercises . . . nice and slow . . . it is about balance and rhythm. Now I want you to place your hands on the sides of your chair for support and then squeeze your knees together as if a balloon is between your legs. Then pull your legs up toward your chest. You will feel tension in your hips and lower abdomen, as well as in the muscles on the inside of your thighs. You may not be accustomed to focusing on them, so

(continued) ➡

they may tire quickly. If they do, hold it for as long as you can. If they do not tire, hold it until you feel the burn. Then, like before, slowly relax and place your feet back on the floor, paying attention to the sensation of relaxation . . . of how heavy your legs felt while you held them up and now how nice it feels for them to be supported by the floor. Continue breathing. Relax.

Now we will move on to your legs. We are going to tighten your thighs and calves now. When you are ready, lift your lower legs up so that your legs are straight, as they are when you are doing leg extensions in the gym. You should feel your thighs tighten, and you may be able to feel the cuts in the muscles of your legs as they contract. Enjoy that tension . . . feel the blood filling the muscles . . . continue to breathe nice and slow. Keeping your legs straight, point your toes out straight ahead. Think about a diver in pike position or a gymnast pointing the toes in midflight. Holding your toes straight as an arrow, push your feet downward and feel the tension building at the bottom of your calf now too. Hold it for a couple of moments, notice the tension, and notice the difference from relaxation. Hold it a little longer . . . OK, now slowly let your feet find the floor and pay attention to the relaxation that you feel throughout your body . . . feel the control . . . feel the power that you have over your body . . .nobody makes you tense . . . only you do and you can stop it . . .you are learning how.

We'll move on to the last muscle group now. Your muscles may be getting tired . . . this is good . . . they cannot be tense and tired at the same time. Enjoy the exhaustion . . . you made it happen . . . it's the same as a good workout . . . you work the muscles and then they relax after being used, but they become tired. OK, now place your heels into the floor and raise your feet up on an angle. Try pulling them toward you . . . no hands . . . just the muscles in your ankles and legs. Point your feet up to the sky . . . feel the tension in your lower shin . . . pay attention to the tension spreading through your feet . . . enjoy the tension. After holding for 10 to 15 seconds we are going to let it go. Then relax . . . you are feeling great . . . doing a great job.

Now before we finish, scan your body from head toe. Go through the muscle groups one by one. What is still tense? Anything? If so, repeat or just remember that this place might need more work. You are going to practice this everyday, maybe more than once a day until you become really good at it. Then you will be able to do a quick body scan and relax the culprit, the muscles where the tension is. Eventually, you'll be able to relax everything by just hitting the target muscles. You can do this . . . you did do this . . .you did a great job.

Imagery and Visualization

The relaxation exercises incorporated small elements of imagery and visualization, a valuable tool that can be extended further. I provide here an introduction to the world of visualization in sport psychology and the role that it can play in anger management.

Surely by now you have heard of football teams spreading out on a field while a sport psychologist walks them through an imagery exercise. Although this process may work, it should not be the first foray into the world of imagery. Before these powerful mind games are incorporated into athletes' mental skills training, certain cautions should be considered.

Although the idea may seem innocuous, in imagery and visualization exercises the leader walks around inside the minds of others, entering a place without permission. You should always ask participants whether they are comfortable with these types of exercises before you start. Ask them honestly and do not exert pressure. Obtain informed consent. Tell them what to expect, what they might gain. Inform them that they have the right to stop whenever they are uncomfortable. After obtaining their consent, you can begin.

Be aware that some people have adverse responses to these exercises. Specifically, people who have been traumatized (a possibility among your athletes, as noted in the chapter on mental illness) find that their imaginative world can be a terrifying place because the flashbacks from abusive events reside there. A subset of those people may be prone to dissociation, in which they disconnect from reality and become immersed in the imaginative scene. If you suspect that anything strange is occurring, you have a responsibility to protect the affected participants. Try to talk such people down. Ask them to focus on your voice. This kind of episode can be frightening to them, to you, and to everyone nearby. This possibility is all the more reason for obtaining consent beforehand.

Assuming that all the participants check out and sign on, think of imagery in several steps:

1. Teach participants about the power of imagery and visualization.
2. Use imagery and visualization as a relaxation exercise—take them to a happy place.
3. Teach participants to imagine perfect performance.
4. Use imagery and visualization as a training exercise and problem solver.

Teaching About the Power of Imagery

Imagery was described by Weinberg and Gould (2003) as a form of simulation. It is similar to a real sensory experience, but the entire experience occurs in the mind. Imagery has become a staple in the sport psychology world. Dr. Shane Murphy and his colleagues (Jowdy, Murphy, & Durtschi, 1989) at the United States Olympic Committee (USOC) conducted a survey of the athletes and coaches at the Olympic Training Center in Colorado Springs. The researchers found that 90 percent of the athletes and 94 percent of the coaches used imagery in their sports. Twenty percent of the athletes reported daily use, and 40 percent used it three to five days per week. Eighty percent reported that they used imagery to prepare for competition, 48 percent to fix technique errors, 44 percent to learn and perfect new skills, and 40 percent to relax. All the coaches and 97 percent of the athletes stated that imagery improved performance.

A great deal of research is available about imagery and visualization. For further information, I recommend reviewing the work of Richard Suinn, Dan Gould, Lew Hardy, and Michael Mahoney.

Imagery is almost magical. We can close our eyes and go anywhere. Sport psychologists have known for years that when people engage in an imagery exercise, even when they are not physically doing anything but visualizing a scene, their brain responds. PET scans and functional magnetic resonance imaging (fMRI) instruments can take pictures of the brain and identify which parts of the brain are at work. Jean Decety at the University of Washington's Center for Mind, Brain, and Learning found in his research that when someone imagines starting a movement, the corresponding parts of the brain that control the body parts become active: the premotor cortex as the action is being prepared, the prefrontal cortex as the action is initiated, and the cerebellum during control of the movement sequences that require coordination. Thus, to the brain, imagining an event is analogous to doing the event.

A factor related to the effectiveness of imagery is the vividness of the image, how real it seems. Incorporating as many sensory modalities as possible helps athletes attain the totality of the experience. You should guide their first foray into imagery so that you can teach them what to focus on. Recognize, however, that what they do in their minds is ultimately up to them.

Using Imagery and Visualization as a Relaxation Exercise

At risk of sounding corny, I try to avoid using the phrase "going to a happy place," but it is hard to state it any better, because happy can be exhilarating. The tone of voice used is similarly important. The pace of delivery should be slow and steady, at a low but easy-to-hear volume and at an even pitch, though not a monotone. Do you remember the TV show with Bob Ross, the painter, who talked as he painted beautiful landscapes? His voice was almost hypnotic as he added a "happy tree" here or there. If you remember that, use it as a model when you are teaching relaxation through imagery. Several tapes and CDs on the market are helpful. Clinical psychologist Dr. Arnold

Lazarus has a 37-minute tape that does not include imagery but does teach PMR. The tape is available for purchase through the Albert Ellis Institute in New York City (www.REBT.org).

The two scenes that I use most often are a beach scene and a mountain scene, but before I impose where people go in their minds to relax, I ask them to tell me about the type of scene that reminds them of a safe, relaxing place. I once worked with a mountain climber who was able to describe in vivid detail the serenity at the top of a peak in Arizona. Although it was extremely hot down below, she felt a cool breeze where she sat looking over the expanse of red orange cliffs around her. As people become more comfortable, they have less need for guidance. Instead, you can ask them sensory questions to help them attend to the cues that make an experience feel more real.

The following transcript of a visualization exercise focused on relaxation with a collegiate female soccer player who felt stressed all the time. She had used imagery and visualization in the past to hone her skills but not to relax. She told me that she was most relaxed when she was alone at the beach.

MA: OK, are you ready? Are you comfortable in your chair? Just sit comfortably with your feet on the floor and your hands relaxed in your lap or at your side. Take a couple of deep breaths as we've discussed previously—in through your nose, hold it, and then out through your mouth. Nice and slow. Gently nod when you feel yourself slowing down and you are ready to begin.

KK: [After a few moments, her breathing is slow and steady, and she nods.] OK, I'm good.

MA: Now I want you to remember that I will be guiding you, but this is your world and you are free to change things to whatever makes it most real and most relaxing. We are going to the beach now. [A short pause.] Let's begin by tying your breathing to the waves, to keep you grounded and in a good rhythm. Time your breathing with the waves. As a wave comes in, take a slow, full breath, blowing up the balloon in your stomach. Hold it while the white foam rolls up on the sand and then release it as the water goes out . . . taking any stress you have with it. When I ask you questions, you can nod gently or respond, whichever you prefer. Time your breathing . . . [A couple of cycles occur.] . . . Can you hear the wave gently crashing on the sand?

KK: [She nods.] I can see the water coming up toward my feet.

MA: OK, good. Tell me about the temperature of the air.

KK: It is hot . . . it must be summer.

MA: Great. Is it uncomfortable hot? Remember, you are in control.

KK: No, it is nice . . . I can feel the sun warming my skin . . . and it isn't humid. It is dry and warm.

MA: Can you see the light from the sun coming through your closed eyelids?

KK: Yeah, I am looking up at the sky and feeling the sun land squarely on my face.

MA: OK, is there any breeze?

KK: Yes, it is refreshing. Cool, not cold.

MA: Pay attention to how it feels on your skin. Notice subtleties. Maybe the wind is moving the little hairs on your arm, or cooling little beads of sweat are accumulating on your forehead. Pay close attention to how everything feels.

KK: I am . . . it feels great.

MA: Excellent. While you are still paying attention to that, I want you to imagine that you are looking down toward your feet. How far are you from the surf?

KK: About 10 feet. The sand is warm. It is fine but has a little coarseness to it. It feels good to dig my toes in to it. It is warm but not hot like afternoon . . . it is just heating up and the beach is practically empty. It must be around 11:00 in the morning. I can feel the difference in the sand when I dig my toes in and the sand underneath is cold and moist. It is a refreshing difference.

MA: Very good. Pay attention to exactly those types of things. How are you feeling?

KK: Hungry . . . I can smell food coming from the Boardwalk . . . beach food . . . hot dogs and french fries. But there is a calmness . . . there is nothing I have to do right now.

MA: Can we return to the food later, or are you kind of locked into the smell?

KK: No, I think I can enjoy it as part of the big picture . . . no need to focus on it.

MA: When you mention your toes in the sand, do you feel anything else? What do you see?

KK: As I look down, I see the waves coming in right in front of me. I undig my feet and stand in the warmer sand for a moment . . . letting myself warm up.

MA: Do you hear anything in particular?

KK: Yes, I hear the waves coming in and out . . . I hear seagulls in the distance . . . they are squawking as they dive for fish . . . it isn't annoying . . . it feels so natural . . . I can actually hear them crashing into the water and see them coming out with fish. I love nature . . . it always makes me feel so balanced.

MA: Anything else?

KK: I can hear children playing in the distance . . . but there is no stress . . . they are laughing and having a good time.

MA: Besides the food, do you smell anything?

KK: Yes, I noticed it as soon as we started. I can smell the salt in the air, you know the way an ocean smells . . . and it immediately calms me down . . . always did.

MA: How does your body feel?

KK: Kind of weird. I had an Achilles injury that I was rehabbing and when I was digging my toes into the sand, I felt some tightness in the area, although I wasn't moving.

MA: And now?

KK: It kind of relaxed. I focused on other things . . . my whole body feels much lighter now.

MA: I want you to pay attention to all the details that we discussed. Take a moment to take them all in. If you want extend the scene, walk down to the water, feel the coolness on your legs . . . but just take a moment to be completely immersed in the experience. [A pause for a couple of moments.] When you are ready, you can slowly open your eyes. [She continues and smiles softly. Her breathing continues to be nice and easy. Her chest expands and then slowly releases until she finally opens her eyes.]

MA: Well?

KK: That was unbelievable. I feel as if the weight of the world came off my shoulders.

MA: Good. Remember that you can make that happen whenever you want. What specifically helped you get into the scene? People struggle at times.

KK: Absolutely focusing on the things that I saw and heard and felt. I felt as if I was right there, not in your office. I can use this to help me get to sleep at night, or before matches. I think I had this all along and just didn't use it . . . as if I could have had the best equipment but was playing with cheap stuff. Why didn't I know this before?

MA: Kathy, first off, this is new and with practice it can be a useful part of your skill set. You will find many uses, but the most important thing to remember is that *you* are the vehicle for change. You control your mind and your body. These skills can be as powerful as your physical skills.

KK: Wow, I feel like I am much more powerful.

MA: Wait, it gets better. We can use this as a training ground. You need to work on it, but when you get proficient, you will improve your ability to relax and unwind.

KK: And can I use things to help the process of relaxation? I am thinking about one of those CDs with the ocean waves, and maybe scented candles.

MA: Absolutely. Anything that assists with the process, especially the sensory process, can make it more vivid and better.

KK: Cool. Thanks . . . I can't wait to learn more of this stuff.

Teaching Participants to Imagine Perfect Performance

The idea of imagining the perfect stroke or perfect pitch with perfect mechanics is at the heart of most imagery and visualization exercises, and for good reason. If people can visualize it, they can make it happen. Of course, it is not always that simple. I can throw a baseball 80 miles (130 kilometers) per hour, but I cannot throw a sinking fastball at 92 miles (148 kilometers) per hour with pinpoint accuracy just because I can imagine it. If what is being imagined is within a person's skill set or within reach of his or her capability, the imagery playground is the stage for getting closer. Avoid the pitfall of setting up extremely high expectations. Do not lead athletes to believe that because they can see it with imagery, they can always do it, especially because when people are overaroused they often struggle with even simple things.

Some tennis players visualize their opponent's style or anticipate how the match will be played. Others become so in tune with the game (flow states) that they can anticipate what will happen next. Wayne Gretzky once said that he does not go to where the puck is; he goes to where the puck is going. So in their minds, in your office, athletes can hone their skills, imagine the impossible as possible, and with the help of technical coaches use the mind as the practice field to improve technical imperfections.

Using Imagery and Visualization as a Training Exercise and Problem Solver

After athletes become comfortable with the use of imagery and visualization, they do not always respond as you hope they will in real-life competition. When I hear about sport psychologists who use imagery and visualization to prepare an athlete for the perfect performance, I am concerned about what they will do with the athlete afterward when the preparation does not work. It is not that imagery and visualization never work; it's just that life is not that convenient. Invariably, a gust of wind will distract you during your backswing, a fan will yell something as you are awaiting the pitch, and everyone behind the backboard will be waving those darn foam noodles—you have to be able to adapt.

The perfect model is only the starting point. A tailback can be found before the game, sitting in a corner of the locker room with his mp3 player on visualizing the plays unfold before him, looking for the hole to open up so that he can dart through to the second level of the defense. Increasingly, athletes develop the skills all by themselves. I remember all the way back to Little League when I was so disappointed with a rainout that I imagined myself and the rest of my team of nine-year-olds playing the scheduled game—pitch by pitch, at-bat by at-bat. I even deliberately had our team make errors and sometimes lose, to add greater realism. Many athletes do not just play sports; they live sports. When they cannot be out there on the field, they take it to the playground, ball field, arena, or stadium of their mind.

Taking it to the next level, you want athletes to use imagery and visualization as an opportunity to deal with adversity, to learn to expect the unexpected and, in their minds, to cope with a situation and persevere even when things are not going according to plan. They should understand the benefits of having a quiet, balanced mind that can accommodate changes rather than a stubborn, rigid mind that can execute a game plan but cannot adjust if the game plan does not work.

I believe that pure physical athletic talent can take an athlete to a certain level. For many, talent can take them to the highest levels, but elite athletes have the mental skills, creativity, and confidence to adapt. Consider Bobby

Knight—not for his angry antics but for his tactical coaching ability. He is arguably one of the best technical coaches in the history of college basketball, but it is surprising that more players of his players did not move on to successful pro careers. His players play in his system, his way, and if they deviate from that, he has no problem letting them know. When the execution produces the planned results, everything is fine, but if his team plays an opponent that is better prepared or neutralizes the strong points of Knight's system, his players have to adapt on the floor. Their creativity will make the difference. If they are anxious about what will happen if they take a chance and fail—being berated or publicly humiliated—they will be unlikely to take those chances. When the system works, the team looks like a well-oiled machine; when it does not, it seems as if players are running in different directions.

Imagery presents an opportunity for athletes to take chances, build their confidence, and study how their decision-making skills change when their emotions change. Sometimes, the most helpful action is to incite an angry storm inside the athlete. By exposing people to anger, under controlled circumstances, they become more comfortable with the emotion, understand it better, and learn to manage it better. Through visualization, athletes can conjure up the images that have made them angry and rile themselves up. If you then ask them to repeat the multiplication table, they often struggle. Why? Intense emotion interferes with cognitive processing. Concentrating on a task and making good decisions become more difficult.

The skills build on and complement one another. To teach athletes how to manage their anger in game situations, invoke anger responses in mental exercises and instruct them to use the growing number of tools that they have to modulate their emotions so that anger helps them rather than hurts them.

Two movies are helpful in discussing anger and imagery: *The Program* starring James Caan, Omar Epps, and Halle Berry and Adam Sandler's *The Waterboy*. In both movies, you can see how athletes use imagery and even play mind games with themselves to psych themselves up using anger.

In *The Program*, one of the characters is a star linebacker named Alvin Mack, who is known for his ferociousness. In game scenes, he gets himself amped up before each play by trash talking at the opponents, accusing them of doing various misdeeds to his family, motivating himself to maim them.

In one scene, he accuses the opposing tailback of shooting his mother. In another, Mack blames the quarterback on the other team for "ratting out" Mack's brother and sending him to jail. In yet another, he identifies an opposing player as the guy who impregnated his baby sister.

Of course, Mack's brother is not in jail, his mother was not shot, and his baby sister was not pregnant. He imagined those scenarios to motivate himself on the field, to ignite his rage. But Mack was so focused on his target that he became vulnerable to an offensive lineman who takes out his legs, yielding a compound fracture that ends his playing career. This scenario offers an important lesson. An athlete who focuses too much on one area becomes susceptible to other threats. Mack got himself into a seething rage, intent on retribution, but he did not recognize that although some parts of his game would benefit, others would suffer.

Although an unlikely ally, Adam Sandler has provided great material for the sport psychologist who is focusing on anger. From *Happy Gilmore* to *Anger Management* to *The Longest Yard* to *The Waterboy*, several of Sandler's movies have dealt with the sport arena. His character Bobby Boucher from *The Waterboy* depicts a not-too-bright waterboy in Louisiana who lives with his overprotective mother in the bayou. The hapless local team stumbles on Boucher's untapped potential by accident when he spears a player who insults him one too many times.

Coach Klein, played by Henry Winkler, encourages Bobby to fight back and unleash his pent-up frustration from past abuses. Asked for a demonstration, Boucher cannot duplicate it, leaving Coach Klein to ask, "Where was the intensity?"

Bobby responds, "I was just thinking about all the people who were mean to me over the years."

"They are going to be your tackling fuel . . . visualize all those people and then attack them," his coach instructs.

And so, a tackling monster is unleashed. Not surprisingly, Bobby has difficulty knowing when and how to let it out. When he is in a biology class and a professor who resembles Colonel Sanders ridicules Boucher's answers to science questions about the origin of anger and aggression, Boucher loses it and tackles the professor with the same ferocity he would use on the field.

"It's OK to fight back. Coach Klein said I could," Bobby says as other students pulled him off the professor.

Obviously, this near-cartoonish depiction exaggerates the relationship between anger and imagery, but it illustrates some salient points. People do in fact use mental images as fuel and motivation. Think about slights by the opposition that end up as bulletin board material for a team to rally around. Incorporating these thoughts into imagery can change motivation levels. Although athletes generally perform best when they are self-motivated, coaches make pep talks to arouse players when they are flat.

DISTRACTION

When people become agitated and prepare for a physical confrontation, they often lock eyes with their target. Like boxers who stare down their opponent at the beginning of a boxing match, they do not take their eyes off their adversary for a second. This action can serve several functions. A person who can significantly intimidate another can win the fight before it occurs. Locking on to the target also promotes vigilance; by focusing on the other person, a person is less likely to be taken by surprise. Usually, the stare down leads to intensification of the conflict, a crescendo that culminates in a physical fight.

An effective way to de-escalate such conflicts is to distract one or both of the participants. Security personnel in nightclubs move themselves between combatants before the situation progresses to fisticuffs. They disrupt the stare down and lead the adversaries away in different directions. Sometimes they tell one of the people a joke that requires the person to shift attention away from the provocateur. That second of distraction provides the person with an opportunity to consider alternative methods of handling the problem.

This approach is useful not only when someone is on the verge of a fistfight. When people recognize that they are escalating, by removing themselves or shifting their attention to something other than the provocative stimulus, they create the distance necessary to calm down.

One client whom I worked with on anger management offered that he read a book to calm himself down when angry. Even intellectuals have difficulty concentrating on what they are reading while they are furious. What he explained, however, and he was not someone whose anger spiked very high to begin with, was that reading gave him the opportunity to take his mind to a different place and to stop ruminating on what was frustrating to him.

In fact, distraction can be effective both in the moment when someone is extremely angry (when the security staff separates two people preparing to fight) and when someone's anger is just starting to build. Some tools that can be effective in distraction include reading, listening to music (depending on the type of music, of course—some can add fuel to the fire), taking a walk, watching television, exercising, or a combination of these activities.

EXERCISE

As mentioned in chapter 1, reciprocal inhibition is the theory that explains how two opposite experiences inhibit one another. As an example, if you are physically exhausted you may have thoughts of anger, but your body may be unable to produce a traditional anger response. Being furious and exhausted at the same time is difficult.

Thus, when someone is angry, an intense bout of exercise can be just the remedy. Whether it is a challenging run, weight training, or a game of pickup basketball, exercising to exhaustion can significantly reduce a person's anger. Three theories or psychological concepts support this solution. The first is the reciprocal inhibition theory mentioned earlier. The second is catharsis, also mentioned in chapter 1, whereby a person expends pent-up energy, thus relieving the building emotional pressure. The third is the concept of sublimation, a method by which a person refocuses mental energy (which Sigmund Freud believed was limited) away from negative outlets toward positive ones.

A cautionary note applies to exercise as sublimation. If the exercise used to achieve de-escalation involves behavior that can be used for violence, the likelihood of future violence can actually increase. To explain, imagine that you are feeling frustrated following an argument with your boss. You choose to hit the heavy punching bag to dispense the excess energy. You will feel better, as catharsis would explain, but the next time you are angry and do not have a punching bag available, you will be more prone to hit because you were previously reinforced for using that behavior. So, those who use exercise to calm themselves down must be mindful to engage in exercise that will not translate into violence the next time they become angry.

TRIGGER RECOGNITION

As you are developing athletes' de-escalation skills, you also need to show them when to use the techniques. As mentioned previously, by the time people recognize that they need to calm down, it is usually too late. For that reason we need to teach them to recognize the cues earlier.

So far, we outlined the physiological cues associated with arousal. They represent a good place for athletes to start in noting their escalation, but they are not the only sign.

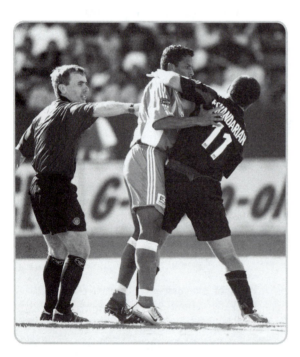

Most of the experts who have developed anger management programs in the clinical world, such as Dr. Eva Feindler, my mentor at the C.W. Post Campus of Long Island University, Dr. Howard Kassinove of Hofstra University, or Dr. Jerry Deffenbacher at Colorado State University, discuss the need to identify triggers to implement de-escalation skills sooner rather than later.

Kassinove and Tafrate (2002) define triggers as the external or internal stimuli that set the stage for the anger response. Triggers have been categorized by modality: verbal, motor or visual, or direct or indirect.

When differentiating by modality, verbal triggers may be insults, rudeness, cursing, accusations, unwelcome criticism, or prejudicial comments. Motor triggers may present in the form of a punch, a kick,

Motor triggers, like the physical contact between these two soccer players, could lead to a serious physical fight. One of these players may respond differently to these triggers, though, and be able to walk away from the provocation without allowing it to escalate further.

©Andy Mead/Icon SMI

a shove, or being restrained. Visual triggers may be a dirty look, seeing someone mistreat another, or even seeing a family member do something embarrassing. These modes are direct triggers. Although some would likely produce a nearly universal response (most people would agree that being punched would lead to an anger response), there is still room for individual variation. What one person sees as provocative another may not.

When teaching athletes about triggers, the direct triggers are easier to train on. When you ask people to think of things that make them angry and would likely lead to a response, the direct triggers readily jump to mind.

The indirect triggers are more elusive. Indirect triggers can arise from many sources, but commonly they result from the athlete's misinterpretation or misattribution of events, which is the result of a faulty appraisal system. Indirect triggers may include observed injustice or unfairness. They can come from within as well, taking the form of negative self-statements (misattributions or misperceptions), and can heighten a conflict.

For now, the goal is for athletes to learn what their triggers are. Later, triggers will be the cues that athletes either learn to avoid, to disempower (so that they do not lead to escalation), or to use as a prompt to employ relaxation exercises that prevent their becoming agitated. One way for people to identify their triggers is to think about the people who always know how to push their buttons. How do others know their buttons better than they do? Because they pay more attention to the person than he or she does. Athletes need to think about what sets them off so that they can prepare for their occurrence.

Some common indirect triggers in the sports world include

- poor sportsmanship,
- inconsistent effort,
- inconsistent officiating,
- blaming others,
- cheating, and
- trash talking or taunting.

In fact, athletes who are well acquainted with their triggers are nearly impervious to trash talking. Athletes can practice by thinking about how they would trash talk at themselves. What would they use on themselves to throw them off their game? This exercise should point them in the right direction to recognize their triggers.

PROBLEM SOLVING

Basic problem-solving skills are not universally present in people or athletes. People often become frustrated when they cannot solve their problems. Failing at this task can precipitate anger and acting out. Teaching problem-solving skills is teaching life skills. Athletes who develop their problem-solving skills will perform better in both the sports world and everyday life. I use two models to help teach problem solving.

Before they can solve a problem, people have to be able to identify its components. Using the proverbial five Ws and one H can give people a great deal of information about their struggle.

- Who is involved in the problem?
- What is the problem? What are the important details?
- Where is this all occurring?
- When does it occur, and when do I need to solve this?
- Why is this a problem for me, and why is it difficult to solve?
- How did this become a problem, and how am I going to solve it?

The next step is to generate a list of possible solutions. People might be surprised that they have difficulty doing this, but many people have problems generating possible solutions. At first, they should fire out as many solutions as possible without worrying about how bizarre they are or how unlikely they are to succeed. Use sports scenarios here because athletes tend to be pragmatic and they realize that there are more possibilities than it initially seems. When stuck, I refer to the option play in football. What are the options?

Well, depending on what the defense is showing, the quarterback can either hand off to the fullback or pull out and start running the option with the tailback trailing him. He can then decide whether to run it or lateral to his trailing tailback. Is that it? Well, no. In theory, if there is no opening for either runner, the quarterback can still look for a receiver downfield before he passes the line of scrimmage. The point is that many options or solutions are available. After all, game planning is all about premeditated problem solving—figuring out what the other team will present (the problems) and how to outstrategize them (the solutions).

After your athletes develop a list of solutions, they should rank them by their probability of success. They can then pick the solution that produces the highest probability of solving the problem. The next step is to implement the solution.

By the way, picking the right solution does not guarantee success. Effective execution is required, but going through this process will improve the athletes' chances for success. Keep in mind the influence of emotions on this process. The angrier a person is, the harder it is to execute the process. Furthermore, the process is reflexive because the less successful a person is, the angrier the person is likely to become.

So the place to start is to pin down the details of the earlier questions to

Situation or Problem?

A therapist once asked his client, "Why do you look so troubled?"

The client responded that he had a lot of problems, a lot on his mind.

The therapist responded, "Now I know why you are struggling . . . but you don't have problems, you have situations."

The client, confused and slightly perturbed that his struggles were being minimized, retorted, "Oh, I don't have problems? I only have situations? What exactly is that supposed to mean?"

The seasoned counselor smiled knowingly and replied, "I am sure you think these situations will be difficult to resolve and perhaps you are right, but by identifying a situation as a problem before you even tackle it, you are identifying it as more difficult to solve, and thus making it so. There are only situations. Some are more difficult to navigate than others, but don't decide your likelihood of success ahead of time. You only make the hill you are trying to climb steeper."

When you identify a situation as a problem, you are already rooting against yourself, unless you like being the underdog. You believe that this situation will be hard to remedy. Perhaps you are right; perhaps you are not. Why not just get at it and see how you do?

produce a roadmap of how to find a solution. After recognizing that he or she is angry, the athlete must stop, pause, think, and then answer the next set of questions, which arise from those mentioned earlier:

- What is the problem?
- What can I do?
- What will happen if . . . ?
- What will I do?
- How did it work?

Encourage brainstorming. You want your athletes to generate as many solutions as possible. A nonsport exercise can be used initially to demonstrate how it is done. Consider the following scenario:

Earl is stranded on a highway alone, 20 miles (32 kilometers) from civilization, and has no phone. What should he do? Well, he (and you and the athletes) should go through the problem-solving routine.

You can then use the hassle logs discussed in chapter 3 to identify athletes' situations that can demonstrate the problem-solving process. Where there is a will, there is a way. Remind the athletes that whether they realize it or not, they use these skills all the time during competition. They need to master the skills so that they can apply them to various situations and avoid the negative effects of emotional peaks.

COMMUNICATION AND ASSERTIVENESS TRAINING

How people say something is often more important than what they say. People respond to tone of voice, body language, words chosen, and attitude projected. Athletes who are mindful of these things will achieve more success in sport and in life. This is true for high school athletes presenting themselves to coaches on recruiting trips, coaches trying to recruit young athletes, professional athletes dealing with the media, or athletes seeking to join a business venture. How people carry themselves says a lot about how they see the world, how they see other people, and most important, how they see themselves.

People who are angry do have to display it. Furthermore, people who let others know that they are angry may get what they want through intimidation, but those who are too emotional are cueing in others that they are not thinking clearly. They are, in fact, less likely to win an argument. Athletes want to control their emotions and stay calm even when angry so that they can maintain focus on their goals. Those who allow their anger to disrupt their communication patterns are less likely to meet those goals.

In chapter 1, I discussed the inappropriate use of the word *assertiveness* to describe instrumental aggression. But assertiveness is appropriate when athletes communicate to others, especially to those in a position of authority. Being assertive is communicating what they want in an appropriate way and standing up for their rights to be heard, although they do not necessarily have the right to get what they want.

Case in Point

A senior forward on the girls' high school basketball team swings open the door to the coach's office.

"Damn it coach, I have been busting my ass for you for the past four years, we're halfway through the season, and I only get 5 to 10 minutes per game. I am better than the two girls in front of me. They stink, and you won't give me any light. What the hell is wrong with this picture?" she asks her coach.

Another approach:

Knock on the door.

"Hey coach, can I talk to you for a minute?"

"Sure," she responds.

"Look, as you know, this is my last year playing here and I love being part of this team. I want to do well personally and I want us to do well together. It's just that I am getting a little frustrated. I have done everything you have asked me to, worked on all the parts of my game that you said needed improvement . . . and I haven't seen a corresponding increase in playing time. It is really important to me and I think I can help the team if I am on the floor for more minutes. Is there anything you think I need to do to prove to you I deserve that? If not, I would really like the opportunity. What do you think?"

She may be thinking the same thing in both situations, but which scenario is more likely to be more successful in getting the coach's ear and persuading her to consider the player's request? Obviously, the second one. Athletes, especially those who compete in team sports, know the value of communication, but they may not appreciate the value of different types of communication.

Similarly, athletes should learn about differences in posture. You can show them how facial expressions can give away their emotions to their coaches, their teammates, and even their opponents. Revealing that information can sacrifice power because opponents who can play off a player's emotions may gain an edge.

Remaining calm and communicating in a way that allows the best chance of success is not always easy. Athletes should use the methods mentioned earlier in the chapter to modulate their emotions so that they communicate effectively.

COGNITIVE RESTRUCTURING

People often have thoughts, cognitions if you will, that either cause or contribute to their problems. Several common types of cognitive distortions require restructuring. This section is divided into two parts. The first discusses common cognitive distortions that appear in anger-filled scenarios, and the second discusses how to dispel those destructive thoughts.

The relationship between thoughts, feelings, and behavior is complex but undeniable. They cause each other, affect each other, and can change each other. When you ask people how they feel, they often tell you what they are thinking or what they want to do. The latter two are important but undeniably different. To know when an intervention is necessary and what intervention to choose, athletes must first know what they feel. Refer to the discussion earlier in the chapter on this topic. Not knowing what you feel and hoping to know what to do about it is akin to treating a disease before you know the diagnosis. It may work, but it is not likely.

Moving on to the question of cognition is the natural next step because it often determines how someone is processing a situation. Examining the athlete's thoughts can help the sport psychologist realize that the way in which the person is thinking about a situation may have nothing to do with the facts. It could be based on extraneous details of the person's life, it could be based on a previous experience with the same person or a similar situation, or it could have nothing at all to do with the situation at hand. The scenario may simply present an opportunity for the person to act out about other issues that may be completely unrelated.

One school of psychotherapy that deals with cognitive distortions that lead to struggles is rational emotive behavior therapy (REBT), developed by Albert Ellis. Ellis was known for his willingness to confront the irrational thoughts that lead to emotional responses and resultant behavior. Clients needed a good amount of ego strength to withstand his aggressive challenging questions (by the way, Ellis did not work with athletes). Ellis worked to dispel the "tyranny of the shoulds," first coined by psychoanalyst Karen Horney. Ellis described it is as taking perfectly appropriate preferences of behavior and selfishly or foolishly turning them into what must be, what should be, and what ought to be.

Never missing an opportunity to play on words, Ellis categorized these thought patterns with catchy questions such as "Why do you should on yourself?" (to understand the play on words, replace *should* with a synonym for excrement) or "There you go, engaging in musturbation again," not the good kind, but the self-punishing kind.

The goal in REBT is to turn that thinking around. When people say what they should do or how things ought to be, the statement needs to be reframed. From his lectures I can still hear his loud, whiny, high-pitched voice challenge, "Sure, it would be nice if you could always get what you want. It would make you happy if you could get that, but who the hell says that it *has* to be that way?"

We generate many expectations and impose unfair rules on ourselves when we live under those circumstances.

I met Dr. Ellis early in my career when, to my surprise, I found him sitting alone at the American Psychological Association's annual convention reading the program. Wanting to introduce myself and thank him for the influence that he had on my thinking (I embraced the idea that people need to stop complaining about how things are supposed to be and instead take charge of their own lives and destiny), I timidly walked up to him and introduced myself.

"Hi, I am Mitch Abrams. I'm a psychologist and I really learned a lot about how to change people's thinking through your methods, but I must admit I am a bit surprised to find you sitting here by yourself without a gaggle of students waiting on your next word," I said.

He looked up from his book and said, "Nice to meet you, Mitch. Can I ask you a question?"

"Sure." I was pleased that a conversation was unfolding.

"You said you were surprised I was sitting here alone, like you wouldn't expect that or it shouldn't be that way," he said.

"Yes . . . something like that," I offered, knowing that I was being set up.

"Well, why the hell not? I am really not that important that I *should* have someone around me every damn second of the day, am I? I mean really, kid, who *ought* to be holding my hand and keeping me company. I seem to be all right. Do you think I am not?" he asked as he threw the last verbal punch. A slight wry smile hinted at the corner of his mouth, and his eyes twinkled.

"Thank you, Dr. Ellis . . . point made," I said.

"Al . . . call me Al," he ordered. "If you call me Dr. Ellis, I assume that you don't see me as a colleague . . . and I wasn't trying to give you such a hard time, just showing that we all do it all the time . . . even a smart young psychologist."

I realized that the lesson was over. To this day, I carry it with me—especially with athletes. Sport and expectations go hand in hand. Sure, you want to win the Stanley Cup. Sure, you need to work hard to make it happen, but will you die if you do not win it? No. Deciding how you want things to end up and differentiating them from how they should end up or how they must end up are completely different.

When setting goals, athletes should identify them as goals. They should make short-term goals and objectives to meet, as well as long-term goals. They should develop plans that spell out how they will achieve their goals. But most important, they should understand them as goals, not as musts. Believing that they must achieve something puts too much pressure on athletes or teams, and this pressure can interfere with reaching those goals. Unexpected events occur all the time, and these sometimes require people to change their expectations to match the situation. Setting goals as what has to be increases the difficulty of achieving them.

A good example of this was the 2005 New York Jets. Media prognosticators were almost unanimous in their preseason predictions. The Jets would be going to the playoffs and would likely make it to the Super Bowl. But how did those goals sound when both the first- and second-string quarterbacks (Chad Pennington and Jay Fiedler) were lost for the season with shoulder injuries? The third-string QB was unproven, and the team had to bring back a 40-year-old veteran who quickly showed that his best and healthiest days were behind him. The third-string quarterback was reinserted into the starting role. A steady flow of starters (seven total!) found their way to injured reserve. Did any team in the league have the depth to withstand those types of losses? Furthermore, who could have predicted that so many starters would go down? The point I am making is that despite the fans wanting ownership's head for going 4-12, stating that they *should* have done better is unreasonable. The Jets had lofty goals, and I am sure that they wanted to reach them. If we are going to participate in sport we need to remember that our goals are what we want to have, not what we must have. When goals are about *must*, no exceptions or circumstances permit us to tolerate anything else.

Jerry Deffenbacher of Colorado State University is one of the nation's experts in adult anger management. He has written extensively, including in manual development, about common cognitive distortions and the need to restructure them to improve coping. In a book that he wrote with Matthew McKay titled *Overcoming Situational and General Anger: A Protocol for the*

Treatment of Anger Based on Relaxation, Cognitive Restructuring, and Coping Skills Training (2000), he described cognitive distortions that are commonly associated with anger and offered antidotes to the thinking. The following is a summary of this work:

1. *Magnifying or catastrophizing* is the tendency to think that things are worse than they really are. Most often occurrences that seem to be the worst thing that could happen or are thought to be awful or terrible tend to be merely inconvenient, frustrating, or disappointing. They certainly are not going to kill you.

Deffenbacher and McKay explained that lying to yourself and pretending that a negative situation is a positive one is not helpful. The recommended action is to assess it accurately. When you receive a bill that is outrageous, avoid using that language. Instead be more precise: "Man, it's 40 dollars more than I expected—that sucks." That statement explains the frustration but does not overreact.

Helpful Coping Thoughts for Magnifying or Catastrophizing

- It's not the end of the world. It's just frustrating.
- It's not worth getting so pissed off about.
- Shit happens, but I can develop a plan for how to deal with it. Getting all upset will just keep me from solving the problem.

2. *Overgeneralization* is expanding a problem beyond its true boundaries, sometimes making it seem bigger than life. The authors recommend not using generalizing terms such as *always*, *never*, *totally*, *everybody*, *nobody*, and so on. Again, be accurate about describing the problem and look for exceptions to the rule. When you think, "Man, she is always late," think again. Really? Always? Can you think of one time that she was not late? Well, if you can, she is not always late. Of course, you can be annoyed with someone for being late, but overgeneralizing only fuels your fire and causes you to be more likely to act out.

Helpful Coping Thoughts for Overgeneralization

- C'mon now, how many time has this *really* happened?
- Sometimes things go a lot better than this. This does not happen *all* the time. This is an inconvenience and it stinks, but I can deal with it.
- If I don't make this bigger than it is, I can relax and let it blow over.

3. *Demanding or commanding* is similar to what was described earlier in rational emotive behavior therapy. In this pattern, you put unrealistic demands on yourself or the world and then become angry when things do not go your way. Deffenbacher and McKay note the following pervasive themes:

- Perfectionism: I or others should do it perfectly. Errors are not acceptable.

- Others should love me: Certain people should approve of me or give me support in the manner that I deem appropriate. In effect, they do not have the right to feel whatever way they want.

- Others should not dislike me (similar to the previous point but not the same): I believe that people should not think or say anything negative about me. This expectation is unrealistic. It would be wonderful if people behaved that way, but they do not.

- Things should be fair: This is one of the more common demands that we put on the world. Although we still hear our mothers in the back of our heads saying, "Well, life is not fair," many hold on to this fantasy.

- Bad things should not happen to me: I should not have to deal with this frustration, delay, pain, or whatever. This viewpoint is grandiose. Curveballs are thrown to all of us. The situation is not the bad thing; how we deal with it is what matters.

The following are some examples of cognitive distortions that you might see in sport. They are followed with restructurings of those notions to yield a thought pattern that can lead to better decision making and ultimately a more rational view of the situation. This sort of restructuring can be the springboard to solving problems with coaches, teammates, and others involved in sport.

- Coach should have known that his pulling me for a pinch hitter would have hurt my feelings. Man, he didn't even care.
  - I know that Coach was caught up in the game, but it would have been nice if he has thought about how I felt before he pulled me. He might have still done it, but I would have preferred that he showed he cared a bit.

- They were killing us by three goals with only two minutes left. They shouldn't have been trying to score.
  - OK, good sportsmanship would dictate that they would just kill the clock and finish the game. I would prefer to play against a team that has good character, but that will not always happen.

- This is my fourth year on the team. I am a senior and the leading scorer, and the other girls have to vote me in to be captain.
  - Being popular is great and I hope that my team supports me, but people vote the way they do for many reasons. Some people may be better leaders than the best athlete is. It is not helpful to demand that I must be a captain. It would be a privilege, but I will give my best effort no matter what.

Helpful Coping Thoughts for Demanding or Commanding

- There is no guarantee that I will get what I want. Sometimes I do and sometimes I don't. I want to stay cool about it.
- People do what they want to do, not what I need them to do.
- This is not my preference, but I can make the best of it.
- I need to forget the shoulds; they only get me upset.
- Problems, fears, and needs influence the behavior of others.
- There is no reason why they should do it my way except that I want it that way.

4. *Inflammatory or global labeling* is a sweeping negative judgment that explains the totality of a person's character based on one or several acts. Engaging in this distortion distracts you from focusing on the behavior at hand. The authors note that the distortions can be humorous at times because of how inaccurate they are. Consider the following examples:

- That referee is an idiot. He doesn't know anything.
- Did you see what he just did to his teammate? He is such an asshole.
- She is a complete bitch, that coach.
- That team is run by a bunch of morons. How many bad draft picks can one team make?

The counter to this tendency is to be more specific. The preceding judgments may be based on facts, but the focus should be on those facts, not an extrapolation of them to the person's total character. You may even want to think about the literal translation of what you are saying. For instance, if the referee was truly an idiot, how does he know any of the rules? Oh, he didn't give you a call and therefore has a low IQ? Or the player is an asshole, huh? Really? Nope, the whole body is not out there on the soccer field, just an asshole. She is a complete bitch. Well, a bitch is a female dog, so I am guessing that previously she was missing a leg or a tail or something, but now she's a complete bitch. And finally, yes, the team has no intention of winning; they try to hire the dumbest, least qualified staff members to make the worst decisions just so they can have a bad draft. That sounds about right.

Helpful Coping Thoughts for Global Labeling

- The person is not really an asshole or a bitch or whatever I said. He or she is just a person with whom I have a disagreement.
- No one is really *all* bad. People generally do the best that they can.
- What am I really angry about when I am focusing so much on one person? I can handle this.
- I'm pissed off and it is a pain, but it is not the first time that I dealt with adversity. I've got this covered.

- People make mistakes—it's how they learn. But, man, are they doing their job well!

5. *Misattributions or single explanations* occur when you attribute someone's behavior to a single negative cause without much evidence and are unwilling to consider alternatives. You seem to think that you can read the minds of other people and know their intentions. A certain paranoid flavor affects your thinking: He is doing that just to piss me off; the only reason she did that was to embarrass me; the ref has had it in for me for a long time. The easiest way to confront this distortion is to find a way to challenge the truth of your belief. Explore alternative explanations to the situation other than the desire of people to hurt you. If you have the courage, ask other people how they view the situation. Be open to their response. There is no easier way to look foolish than to believe that your explanation is the only one possible.

Helpful Coping Thoughts for Misattributions

- Checking out the facts first can prevent me from jumping to conclusions.
- Other explanations may be plausible; I'll try to slow down.
- I am less likely to sort out the situation if I am furious.
- What evidence do I have for my explanation of the situation?
- I can stop the mind reading and quit assuming that everyone has an ulterior motive.

6. *Blaming* is not a hard distortion to explain. Blaming comes from the belief that the other person did it to you on purpose and should pay for it. Although blaming someone may feel good temporarily, you are often left feeling helpless and in turn even angrier. You forget the choices that you make, both the choices that led to the situation and the choice of what you will do in response.

I remember a George Carlin skit about losing things. He asked, "What's the first thing you ask when you lose something? Is it 'Gee, I wonder where I put it?' Nope, the first thing you say is, 'Who stole it?'" And he was right. Most of us cannot accept the fact that we are stupid enough to lose something all by ourselves. Carlin joked further that the item could be something that no one would ever want: "Yep, they got my banana guacamole and my collection of used bandages."

Deffenbacher and McKay also noted that you become judge, jury, and executioner when you blame. You attack and punish angrily. People either pull back or counterattack, so the cycle begins to escalate.

Some examples of blaming in sports are the following:

- Whenever we are playing doubles, you jump around in front of me to distract me and make me blow my serve.

- If it weren't for your need to swing for the seats all the time instead of just putting the ball in play, maybe we could move the runner into scoring position and make my job easier.
- I saw you looking at me that way. It's your fault that I missed the layup— you put too much pressure on me.
- How did I miss the empty net? You made me miss by telling me how easy it is to hit. You made me break my concentration.

Helpful Coping Thoughts for Blaming

- I am not helpless; I can take care of myself in these situations. I am in control, not them.
- I need to focus on the things that I have control of and master them.
- It may be frustrating, but even if it *were* someone else's fault, I still have to deal with it and I can excel.
- If I dish out punishment about this, I can get tossed. I cannot contribute to the win from the locker room. I need to make sure that I don't let anyone take me off my game.

After reviewing common cognitive distortions and how they can play out in an athlete's mind, it is helpful to move to a discussion about personal power. People will often have justifications rooted in these distortions for why they must argue or fight; and for many, they believe their pride is at stake. If they don't fight, they will be seen as weak and powerless. The toughest guy in prison never has to fight because all the inmates know of his power and they realize that testing him could be fatal. Those who have ultimate power do not have to use it. Occasionally someone will want to take a shot at the champ, but a truly powerful person is never challenged.

When I was in graduate school, I co-led an impromptu workshop and debriefing with my mentor, Eva Feindler, in response to an attack by a group of adolescent males on two smaller teens in their neighborhood. This event occurred in a predominantly Jewish but multiethnic neighborhood on Long Island. The details of why the teens did it were not as crucial as the misattribution of power that the assailants claimed. We met with the young men, sat in a circle, and asked for the details of the attack so that we could process the event. Rather indignant, they rationalized their behavior. One said that they were taunted first. Another said that the victims were where they should not have been. Some said that they had to demonstrate that they could protect their neighborhood, that the attack was a display of power.

This discussion went on for a while until we asked whether 10 guys beating up 2 guys was really a fair fight and how the 10 guys winning demonstrated power. We suggested that the attack was a sign of weakness because it took so many to beat so few.

This incident recalls the little guy–big guy dynamic. The big guy always loses because even if he wins the fight, he was supposed to and he must be a bully. But if he loses, he is a wimp who got beat up by a weakling. Similarly, if the smaller guy loses, he was supposed to, but if he wins, he took down the champ.

The point was finally driven home when the young men were reminded of what sort of power they had. Those 10 teens were in school on a Saturday morning when they should have been in temple. The only reason they were not arrested and in a juvenile detention center (the injuries were severe) was because their parents were on the PTA. Finally, although the two victims had been injured, they were home and free to do what they wanted to do, while these 10 guys were going to deal with all types of consequences. Who really wound up having more power?

When anger and violence are abound, people often get hurt. Afterwards, if someone apologizes, societal graces dictate that the apology should be accepted and the person forgiven. A critical theme to remember is that forgiveness is always a choice. While working in prison, I had the good fortune of working with an amazing social worker who ran a forgiveness group. No one has taught me more about this topic, not only by the details of the resources that she uses but also by the sincerity, genuineness, and compassion with which she delivers the material. LaWana Darden, an African American woman, daughter of a minister, and now herself ordained, has the unique ability to give inmates a fresh slate every day. She does not forget when they challenge a rule, but she does not hold a grudge and gives them a chance to show their goodness each day. She can take on a caring but firm maternal role. She will do everything she can to help the people whom she is working with, but if they cross the line, she lets them know and backs them up. The next day, they start over. Much of what follows is a summary of what she taught me.

First, when you act out and hurt someone, you may be hurting yourself at the same time. Sometimes you act impulsively in the heat of the moment, sometimes you overreact to misinformation, and sometimes you get it right on the money, but you still go too far with your response. At times, because of your actions, you alienate people who might have turned out to be allies or friends in the future. Then you want forgiveness, so you apologize. People seem to expect that if they apologize their apology has to be accepted and that life should move on as if the event never happened. This expectation is both unreasonable and unrealistic.

In some ways, apologizing is the worst thing that you can do when you hurt someone because after societal expectations are satisfied, what else can the victim do? To illustrate, let us say that I punch you in the nose. You are likely angry, embarrassed, and hurt. Then I apologize. Do you feel better? Maybe a little bit, but you are probably still upset and appropriately so. You do not have to accept my apology, but because I have fulfilled what etiquette dictates, you are left with your frustrations and I can move on to other matters. Apologies are not always accepted, and saying that I am sorry does not make things OK. All of us have the right to decide whether we want to forgive. Moreover, like the old saying goes, "I may forgive, but I won't forget." Forgiveness does not mandate forgetting. In fact, from a survival point of view, remembering who has wronged you can help you prevent it from happening again.

Understand that an injury to pride or feelings can take longer to heal than a physical injury. Many survivors of abuse state that they would much rather be hit than have their emotions invalidated. Think about this before you act out on your anger. A momentary outburst can have long-lasting consequences with people whom you care about.

Some people think that tolerating someone's behavior is a sign of weakness. The other person will then think that he or she can do anything to you. Exactly the opposite is true. Tolerance, allowing someone to start over, is a sign of strength and courage. Only a strong person can consider this. A weak one would be too terrified to take the chance.

Ironically, the longer you hold on to something that was done to you, the more power you give the person who did it and the more damage you do to yourself, especially if that resentment takes the form of anger. A large body of literature illustrates the connection, and arguably causality, between chronic anger and cardiovascular disease. Some people use the phrase that failing to come to peace with grudges will just "eat you up inside." Whether that is literally true or not, optimizing performance and happiness is difficult when you have the weight of previous wrongs pulling you down, impeding your forward progress. Holding grudges is similar to running sprints with a parachute on your back. You may become stronger and improve your stamina, but you could probably use that energy for more positive things. After all, training with a parachute is designed to make you faster when the drag is removed.

You may want to remind yourself that some of the problems come from how you see the world. As mentioned earlier, we believe that people are supposed to act in a certain way, that we can trust certain people, and that the world is a fair, just place. This is not true. When we hold high expectations for people, we will occasionally be disappointed. Remember this truism when dealing with someone who has wronged you. People are who they are and do not always want to change. They will do what their character predicts they will do. A classic Aesop fable illustrates this beautifully.

PREDICTION OF CONSEQUENCES

Is the world a predictable place or not? Fortune tellers have been around for hundreds of years. Psychics say that they can predict the future. Although

The Scorpion and the Frog

A scorpion and a frog meet on the bank of a stream. The scorpion asks the frog to carry him across on his back. The frog asks, "How do I know you won't sting me?" The scorpion says, "Because if I do, I will die too."

The frog is satisfied and they set out, but in midstream the scorpion stings the frog. The frog feels the onset of paralysis and starts to sink, knowing that both of them will drown. He has just enough time to gasp, "Why?"

The scorpion replies, "It's my nature."

choosing the winning lottery numbers may be impossible, many things in life are predictable.

What would happen if you hit a police officer? Do you need to be a psychic to know the answer to that question? What would happen if you cursed out an umpire? Similarly, you could guess the result. Maybe a better question is this: If you do know what the consequences are, do you care?

In prison, many inmates who committed a crime openly admit that they did not think that they would be caught so the consequences did not matter. Other inmates committed a crime impulsively and did not care about the consequences in the heat of the moment. This circumstance is reminiscent of the "blacking out" discussed in chapter 5.

And some athletes believe that they do not have to deal with consequences because a coach or a parent or someone is going to fix things for them. Athletes must be taught that they cannot rely on others and should live their lives preparing for the consequences in the worst-case scenario.

If a Division I athlete attends a party where alcohol is being served, everyone is drinking, and a fight breaks out, all may be arrested, but the athlete may be suspended, lose his or her scholarship, and be expelled. Athletes should always consider the worst-case scenario, predict it, and act accordingly. Paranoia is almost understandable because athletes are often singled out; they should not assume that they will get a fair shake. They will be blasted by the media before any details of the incident emerge. If they consider what the consequences could be in the worst-case scenario, they are less likely to make bad decisions when they are angry and thinking less clearly.

An effective way to teach athletes to become more proficient in predicting consequences is to have open discussions in which a leader (coach, sport psychologist, team captain) writes down potential situations and possible outcomes on a blackboard. For example, the leader could describe a scenario in which a member of the team is in a bar and is approached by a "fan" who appears to be inebriated. The person starts criticizing the player's performance. What are the different ways in which this scenario could play out? Create a list. What are the different ways in which the athlete could handle the situation to prevent a bad outcome from occurring? Create a list. You want athletes to gain experience in analyzing situations and making good decisions before they face a situation in real time.

Another angle on this theme is that athletes should know how they respond when they are angry. Do they have a short fuse? Are they easily provoked? If this is the case, until they can improve their anger management skills, they should enlist teammates and friends to help them defuse situations, not those who would encourage them to flush their future down the toilet.

I once discussed with a woman who worked at Rahway State Prison the tragedy of some of the lifers who not only killed or severely injured other people but also destroyed their own lives in the midst of a single impulsive, youthful, and sometimes drug-induced act. They threw everything away because they did not consider the consequences. Young people often do not know whose advice to listen to—that of their parents or coaches or that of their peers, who often do not know any better.

When Tony Dungy's son committed suicide, the sports world wept because the child of a well-respected, good man was gone. Despite his tremendous grief, Coach Dungy gracefully modeled what an amazing person he was. During his painful time, he spoke and taught. Profoundly, in his eulogy, he quoted a surprisingly insightful source, "My daughter Tiara said it best the other day. She said, 'I just wish he could have made it until he was 20. Because when you're 17 or 18, sometimes the things you guys say to us don't always make sense . . . When I got to 20, they started making sense again.'"

People, especially young people, can become lost and engulfed by their emotions—whether it is depression, anxiety, or anger (or any combination thereof). During those times, they have difficulty thinking about how things will turn out, what the consequences of their actions will be, how what they do will affect them and those around them. The time to predict those consequences and choose the right path is before they are in those emotionally intense periods that could have tragic outcomes.

MORAL DEVELOPMENT

Sport researchers have written a great deal about the importance of moral development and sportsmanship. The two concepts are arguably joined at the hip. The two names most commonly associated with this work are Brenda Bredemeier and David Shields. They noted the potentially negative influence on moral development that occurs when aggressive and competitive behaviors are sanctioned in sports (Bredemeier & Shields, 1987, 1995). They noted the importance of devoting explicit attention to moral training and have taken the position that such character development should not be left to chance in young athletes.

In one study (Bredemeier et al., 1986) children in a summer sports camp were exposed to one of three conditions:

1. A social-learning model in which moral principles were taught through modeling and vicarious and direct reinforcement

2. A structural-developmental model that used dialogue aimed at resolving interpersonal disruptions and conflicts among children as a vehicle for promoting growth

3. A control group, that is, a normal camp program

Both the first and second conditions yielded significantly positive changes in moral reasoning, whereas the third group showed no change on posttest analyses.

The late Arnold Goldstein, founder of the Center for Research on Aggression at Syracuse University, was one of the pioneers of anger management work. In the program that he developed, aggression replacement training (practiced in over 20 countries throughout the world), he noted the need for both anger control training and moral education, basing his work on Kohlberg's research on moral reasoning (read Kohlberg's work for an explanation of his theories, including interesting cross-cultural validation from the 1960s and 1970s). The research evidence suggests that moral dilemma discussion groups can successfully enhance moral reasoning stages (Goldstein & Glick, 1987, p. 114).

Asking athletes to consider moral dilemmas can improve their self-awareness about their morals and possibly improve their morals as well. Weiss (1987) offered that coaches can pose these dilemmas to young athletes during practice:

- Not putting out enough of the best equipment for all athletes
- Devising a drill with unequal opportunities for practice, such as having one person always on defense
- Devising a drill in which players might be tempted to hurt with words (laughing, yelling), such as having someone demonstrate weak skills or having unfair relay teams
- Devising a drill that provides possible opportunities for rough play, such as the hamburger rebound drill, in which two people block out one person simultaneously and go for the ball

Coaches should follow up the activity with discussion and continue such exercises over time.

The following three scenarios can be used in such discussions. The first was taken from Weinberg and Gould's (2003) *Foundations of Sport and Exercise Psychology* textbook (p. 537):

MORAL DILEMMAS

Taking Advantage of Injury

Rodd and Kevin are two evenly matched 150-pound (69-kilogram) wrestlers involved in a close match. Rodd injures his left knee, takes an injury time-out for treatment, and then returns to the mat. He is in obvious pain, and his movement is greatly constrained. He cannot place weight on his injured leg. Imagine that you are Kevin. Respond to the following questions:

- Should you execute moves to the side of the injured leg because it will be easier to score points?
- After you are in contact with your injured opponent, should you put extra pressure on his injured leg to cause him pain so that you can turn him to his back and pin him?
- Should you avoid executing moves toward his injured leg unless the match is close in score?
- Should you avoid executing moves toward his injured leg entirely and try to beat him at his best?

Report the Juice?

One day Richie walks into the locker room and discovers that the team's defensive captain and middle linebacker, Pete, is injecting a defensive lineman with what Richie assumes to be steroids. He knows that steroids are against the rules and illegal, but he also knows that better performance by his teammates can help the whole team. In addition, Richie does not want to be singled out as the rat that turned on his team.

- What should Richie do?
- Does it matter, or should it matter, that Richie does not know for sure what is in the needle?
- Would it matter if Richie went to the same school but played for a different team?
- Which is the most central point and why: that using steroids is wrong, that Richie does not want to snitch on his teammates for fear of rejection, or that Richie does not have the authority to enforce the rules and should report what he sees to someone who does?
- Is the issue that Richie does not know whether the coach is aware of this? Does that circumstance even matter?

Academic Fraud

Lisa noticed that one of her teammates on the softball team, Nicole, just received a paperback from their English literature professor and received an impressive B+. Noting that Nicole was always floating on the cusp of ineligibility, Lisa was understandably suspicious, especially because she got a B−, which was conspicuous by comparison with her normal straight As. When she congratulates Nicole and asks what led to the turnaround, Nicole states that she got the paper from her tutor. Assuming that Nicole means that her tutor helped her with the project, Lisa asks which parts she needed the most help with, the content or the writing style. Nicole responds, "No, I got the whole paper from my tutor at the Academic Support for Athletes Center. Don't tell anyone, OK?"

- Should Lisa ask Nicole if anyone else knows, especially the coaches?
- Lisa takes pride in her work. Should she blow the whistle on Nicole?
- Does it matter that they are part of an NCAA Division I program that could receive harsh sanctions for the school if this is discovered?
- If Lisa decides to report what she was told, to whom does she report it and why? The coach? The director of the Academic Support for Athletes Center? The NCAA? Why?
- Lisa knows that Nicole is the team's best pitcher. How does this enter into her decision?

Date Rape

After much scandal about allegations that a second-string small forward on the school's basketball team, David, committed an acquaintance rape, no charges are filed because the victim is frightened about the process of the trial, including the potential ridicule and retraumatization. The team trainer is taping David's ankles when he breathes a sigh of relief, stating, "Thank God, the bitch didn't want to take this any further. She was all over me and then when I gave it to her, she cried rape the next day. She said no, but you could tell that she wanted it." Shocked, the trainer looks at the next table over and sees the team's captain just shaking his head in disbelief. David, all 6 feet 7 inches (200 centimeters) and 260 pounds (118 kilograms) of him, jumps off the training table and walks out of the training room as if he was just reviewing his stat line from a game. The starting point guard and team captain, Shawn, is still in disbelief when he looks at the trainer and says, "Man, everyone was backing him, like he was set up. But he did it . . . he really did it."

- If you are Shawn, what do you do now and why?
- The reputation of the team, the coach, and the university are all based on a lie. Do you have the responsibility to report what you know, and if so, to whom?
- It turns out that your sister is best friends with the victim. Does this change your decisions, and if so, why?
- David is physically imposing and has a history of violence, possibly even gang affiliation. Does this affect your decision about how to handle this situation?
- Does doing nothing equate with implicit approval?
- What do you hope to achieve by your decisions?
- The team may not support anyone going against a member of the team. How does this dynamic affect how teams manage sensitive subjects?

EVALUATION AND MODIFICATION

The last piece of the puzzle includes a specific focus on evaluation and modification. I am not aware of any person who handles every situation perfectly. Learning new skills and implementing them is part of the process, and this is true for all involved—for athletes learning the skills as well as for coaches and practitioners teaching the skills and installing a program. Expecting perfection, especially before these new skills are mastered, is a monumental mistake. Players should allow themselves to be human. If they get it right and avoid bad outcomes, they may want to reward themselves, perhaps with verbal self-praise, an extra scoop of ice cream, or a day to do whatever they want. The point here is that by rewarding themselves, they are more likely to repeat the positive outcome. They want to make the connection between handling situations well and increased peace and happiness in their life.

Along the same lines, if they struggle, they should own it. Failure does not occur for those who keep trying. Athletes should figure out where the mistakes were, forgive themselves for being human, and plan how to deal with things better the next time. The athlete's hassle log (see chapter 3) can be particularly helpful here. By running through their skills, athletes can figure out where they went wrong and correct it for the next time. Dwelling on mistakes is not helpful. Obviously, the severity of the outcome will affect this. If an athlete loses his or her cool and is arrested, the consequences are much bigger than if the athlete blows up at the referee and receives a red card. The lesson to be learned is that if athletes make the same mistakes repeatedly, they will make no progress. They need to learn from those mistakes so as to avoid repeating them. Athletes should value them as opportunities to better themselves.

The process of evaluation and modification is a lifelong process in any skill. Athletes at the top of their game never stop practicing to perfect their craft—from ice skaters to skiers to pitchers. They must not be fooled into looking only for the results. The results will come when the process is right.

SUMMARY

This chapter covered the how to of anger management for athletes. To begin, the different modalities of intervention such as group versus individual psychotherapy were explored. Tailoring a program to the athletes with whom the coach or practitioner is working is crucial. Athletes need to learn several skills. Emotion labeling was the starting point because people will not use the skills unless they are able to recognize when they are needed. Bodily changes associated with anger were delineated. Specifically, the activation of the sympathetic nervous system was explained, and this discussion led to an explanation of methods to reverse this activation and thus de-escalate anger.

The de-escalation techniques that were introduced included diaphragmatic breathing, progressive muscle relaxation, imagery and visualization, distraction techniques, and exercise.

By identifying personal triggers and learning to recognize them early, athletes can initiate calming techniques early, when they are most likely to be effective. Furthermore, a source of frustration for many people is their inability to solve problems. This circumstance is compounded by the fact that problem solving becomes more difficult when a person is angry. Therefore, anger escalation and difficulties in problem solving feed off one another. Deficits in problem-solving skills are common, and teaching those skills can significantly affect both the frequency of becoming angry and the ability to solve problems, which would in turn reduce anger.

The importance of good communication skills was described as were methods to improve athletes' interpersonal effectiveness and ability to manage potentially conflictual relationships.

The common cognitive distortions associated with anger were introduced and were followed by a discussion of the methodology of restructuring thoughts to improve the emotions and behavior associated with those negative thoughts.

When angry, people often do not consider the consequences of their actions and then are somewhat perplexed with the negative outcomes that follow. The world is not that unpredictable, and the ability to predict the consequences of one's actions is a teachable skill that athletes can greatly benefit from.

From there, we progressed to exploring the topic of moral development in sport. Exercises were introduced that may help raise athletes' consciousness about moral issues and advance their moral development.

The chapter culminated with a discussion of the importance of including evaluation and modification of any program that is implemented. No one learns skills instantly, especially when deviant behaviors may have been reinforced for years. Athletics programs must set up mechanisms to monitor how their athletes are doing and modify their programs to target specific skills deficits among athletes that may require greater attention.

CHAPTER 8

SYSTEMIC INTERVENTIONS FOR ATHLETES

Very often when I am contacted to do anger management work with athletes, an incident has already occurred and the organization hopes to undo what has transpired. Obviously, no one can change the past, and intervention requests are often related to damage control and public relations. I can appreciate that position because no coach wants the negative press associated with an athlete's transgressions nor do they want the behavior of a single athlete to smear the image of the whole team.

The consequences that can occur to an organization following an athlete's poor behavior span a wide spectrum. Many have economic ramifications. For instance, just as winning the NCAA Basketball Championship can bring in a great deal of money, endorsements, and recruits, a negative image can hurt overall recruitment for an institution. Universities worry not only about athlete recruitment but also about overall student recruitment. When an athlete accused of rape is supported by the university, recruitment of female students becomes more difficult. Would you want your daughter to attend a university that tolerates such behavior?

Parents these days are doing more research on the colleges that their children want to attend. Many ask specifically about life skills programs. The NCAA's CHAMPS Life Skills Program has great promise for both student–athletes and the student body at large. The implementation of the program varies tremendously from one school to another. At university A, the program might be soundly endorsed by the entire athletics department, and coaches may mandate their athletes' participation. At university B, the program may consist of a binder collecting dust in a file cabinet.

The NCAA does not require all teams to participate in this program. In fact, teams have to pay to participate. The university's involvement in this program or others with similar goals is variable. But universities are apparently not aware of a growing trend. When bad things happen and people want justice, they have to accept that the judicial system does not always provide it and cannot change what has happened. For this reason, justice is often meted out in dollars and cents. People seek more than justice. They also want revenge. And the deeper the pockets are, the sweeter the revenge can be.

In several cases in which athletes were involved in criminal activity, the victim sued the school for the athletes' behavior. The argument is that had the school not provided the athletic scholarship, the athlete would not have been at the school and thus would not have committed the crime. College athletes rarely have riches. Although they may have the potential to earn big money, they have not yet officially earned a dime. (If they had, they would lose their amateur status and be scrutinized by the NCAA.) The school, however, has a great deal of money.

The Christy Brzonkala case demonstrated just how far this could go. In fall 1994, while enrolled at Virginia Polytechnic Institute, Brzonkala alleged that Antonio Morrison and James Crawford, both varsity football players, raped her. She sued for $8.3 million. She sued both the alleged rapists and the school.

In this case, Ms. Brzonkala did not initially go to the police. Traumatized, she became depressed and withdrew. Court papers indicate that

> *she changed her appearance and cut off her long hair . . . ceased attending classes and eventually attempted suicide. She was treated by a Virginia Tech psychiatrist who prescribed antidepressant medication, but neither the psychiatrist nor any other Virginia Tech employee or official made more than a cursory inquiry into the cause of Brzonkala's distress.*

A few weeks after the assault, Ms. Brzonkala confided in her roommate about what had occurred, but she was still too fragile to discuss the incident in depth. She never pursued criminal charges because she thought that a conviction was impossible without the collection of physical evidence (rape kit, clothes with evidence, and so on). Ms. Brzonkala identified her assailants and filed a complaint against them under Virginia Tech's Sexual Assault Policy in April 1995. After several hearings, the school's judicial committee found insufficient evidence to take disciplinary action against Crawford but found Morrison guilty of sexual assault. Remember that the ruling body was the school's judicial committee, not a police department or a city, county, state, or federal court.

The punishment started with Morrison's suspension for two semesters. After several appeals on the grounds of due process violations, his suspension was eventually set aside and he returned to Virginia Tech on a full athletic scholarship in fall 1995. Brzonkala learned about this from the *Washington Post*, not from the school.

Many legal proceedings later, including being heard on appeal by the United States Supreme Court, the university eventually settled the case, agreeing to pay $75,000 to Brzonkala.

On what grounds could a woman sue a school for the bad behavior of some of its students? Apparently, Title IX was the justification. Most people think that Title IX was designed just to give more female athletes the opportunity to participate in collegiate sports. Title IX of the Education Amendments of 1972 states "No person in the United States shall, on the basis of sex, be excluded from participation in, be denied the benefits of, or be subjected to discrimination under any education program or activity receiving Federal financial assistance."

Some cases have found legitimacy in the argument that schools that receive federal funding can be held civilly and financially liable for the behavior of students at their institution (Davis v. Monroe County Board of Education, 1999; Kelly v. Yale University, 2003). Critical for a finding supported by Title IX is evidence that the university had knowledge of a risk and was deliberately indifferent to this known risk.

In 2001 Lisa Simpson and Anne Gilmore reported being raped by University of Colorado football players and recruits. They sued on the basis of Title IX.

After the plaintiff's attorneys in the Simpson v. University of Colorado were granted a motion for summary judgment (in which the lawyers ask to forgo a trial and request a finding by the judge) in 2004, the Honorable Judge Robert E. Blackburn concluded that "it is not disputed that the plaintiffs were subjected to severe and objectively offensive sexual harassment on December 7, 2001," but evidence was insufficient to substantiate deliberate indifference by the university.

Historically, in the collegiate sports world, Title IX was used to level the playing field for athletic funding for male and female sports. Although the goal was to increase the number of opportunities for women to participate in sport, many universities, to cut costs, cut some of the men's sports. Most susceptible were the non-revenue-producing sports.

Other cases since then have used Title IX as the basis of such lawsuits against institutions. Although success has been limited, the fact that this mechanism of pressing charges has received an audience from the highest courts in the land lends support to the notion that the trend will continue, or more likely increase. Eventually, some success may result, and then "You could see hundreds, even thousands, of silent victims come forward" (Abrams in Feldman, ESPN Out of Control, May 30, 2002).

The guilt or innocence of the athletes involved is not the issue. Simply from a revenue point of view, universities cannot afford to have any students, particularly high-profile scholarship athletes, engage in behavior that could spawn a lawsuit.

YOUTH SPORTS

The best place to start is with youth sport. Research has repeatedly shown that the younger the recipients of interventions are, the more successful the interventions will be. An element of truth is contained in the premise that you cannot teach an old dog new tricks. So if we are going to reduce violence, we need to teach the lesson consistently, early, and often. No program or league should tolerate parents who abuse coaches, referees, each other, or especially children. Let us start with the important factors in developing a code of conduct for youth sports.

Code of Conduct

A code of conduct must be simple and enforceable. Otherwise, the code is not worth the paper that it is printed on. All participants in the sporting activity must be mandated to uphold the code. Unless they do so, they cannot participate. The rule must apply to everyone—no exceptions! The National Youth Sports Safety Foundation has developed an excellent code of conduct.

Sport Parent Code of Conduct

Preamble

The essential elements of character building and ethics in sport are embodied in the concept of sportsmanship and six core principles: trustworthiness, respect, responsibility, fairness, caring, and good citizenship. The highest potential of sports is achieved when competition reflects these "six pillars of character."

I therefore agree:

1. I will not force my child to participate in sports.
2. I will remember that children participate to have fun and that the game is for youth, not adults.
3. I will inform the coach of any physical disability or ailment that may affect the safety of my child or the safety of others.
4. I will learn the rules of the game and the policies of the league.
5. I (and my guests) will be a positive role model for my child and encourage sportsmanship by showing respect and courtesy, and by demonstrating positive support for all players, coaches, officials, and spectators at every game, practice, or other sporting event.
6. I (and my guests) will not engage in any kind of unsportsmanlike conduct with any official, coach, player, or parent such as booing and taunting, refusing to shake hands, or using profane language or gestures.

7. I will not encourage any behaviors or practices that would endanger the health and well-being of the athletes.

8. I will teach my child to play by the rules and to resolve conflicts without resorting to hostility or violence.

9. I will demand that my child treat other players, coaches, officials, and spectators with respect regardless of race, creed, color, sex, or ability.

10. I will teach my child that doing one's best is more important than winning, so that my child will never feel defeated by the outcome of a game or his or her performance.

11. I will praise my child for competing fairly and trying hard, and make my child feel like a winner every time.

12. I will never ridicule or yell at my child or other participants for making a mistake or losing a competition.

13. I will emphasize skill development and practices and how they benefit my child over winning. I will also deemphasize games and competition in the lower age groups.

14. I will promote the emotional and physical well-being of the athletes ahead of any personal desire I may have for my child to win.

15. I will respect the officials and their authority during games and will never question, discuss, or confront coaches at the game field, and will take time to speak with coaches at an agreed upon time and place.

16. I will demand a sports environment for my child that is free from drugs, tobacco, and alcohol and I will refrain from their use at all sports events.

17. I will refrain from coaching my child or other players during games and practices, unless I am one of the official coaches of the team.

I also agree that if I fail to abide by the aforementioned rules and guidelines, I will be subject to disciplinary action that could include but is not limited to the following:

- Oral warning by official, head coach, or head of league organization
- Written warning
- Parental game suspension with written documentation of incident kept on file by organizations involved
- Game forfeit through the official or coach
- Parental season suspension

Parent or guardian signature

_____

Reprinted, by permission, from National Youth Sports Safety Foundation.

COACHES

Before children are even introduced to the code of conduct, coaches need to be lectured on it separately. The influence of coaches on children is undeniable. Coaches must set the example of what is expected. They need to be respectful of each other, officials, children, everyone. The administrators of the league must be prepared to remove any person who violates the code of conduct.

Although removal needs to be a real consequence for transgression, the threat of this action should not be the reason that coaches comply. The code of conduct should be presented in a meaningful way that underscores the message that parents are entrusting the coaches with their children. Coaches have a responsibility, an honor, to teach children about the sport. This teaching should include having fun (always the most important thing for children) and learning sport skills.

The age at which youth programs should begin to focus on winning and losing has been a topic of debate for a long time. Some people believe that children should learn to compete when they are very young because competition teaches them to deal with adversity. I believe that seven-year-olds who are more interested in their batting averages than whether or not they had fun playing are likely to quit as soon as they reach a competitive level where they struggle. For younger children, whether the sport is soccer, cheerleading, or basketball, the focus should be on having fun and learning new skills.

In my experience, children's physical skills tend to crystallize by age 8 or 9. Their physical dexterity seems to come into balance with their mind–body control, even for the late bloomers. For this reason, I use the 10-year rule. By the time children are 10 years old, they are physically, emotionally, and mentally prepared to compete and deal with the trials and tribulations that go along with it. I use this age as a safe guideline. Many children are ready at around 8 years old, but I do not want any child to lose face and be embarrassed. The later the cutoff age is, the less likely it is that a child will be embarrassed and turned off to sport. Certainly, many established experts disagree with me. I urge you to gauge the development of the children with whom you are working and assess what you think they can manage.

PARENTS

Ah, what to do with them? Some leagues ban them from the playing field altogether. One bad incident can overshadow the constructive support of hundreds of parents. Do parents have any greater feeling than watching their child perform well and then look to them for their proud acknowledgment? I have seen children literally stop in the middle of what they were doing and look for that smile from their parents. We do not want to throw the baby out with the bath water, but parents can be a major obstacle to a successful sport program.

Children who demonstrate difficulties managing their anger often learned their behavior from mom and dad; the adage that the apple does not fall far from the tree may apply here. Parents also need to attend a workshop that outlines the code of conduct. Their being permitted to attend games is contingent on their obeying the code. What do you do if a parent breaks the rules? Do you punish the child as well? You want to be flexible and not punish a child for the behavior of his or her parents. One way to deal with it may be to allow the child to participate but bar the parents from the arena or stands because of their behavior.

Just as some children never develop the skills necessary to manage their anger, some parents have the same deficits. In a study that examined youth soccer players, Jay Goldstein discussed his concept of sideline rage and analogized it to road rage.

When parents have difficulty controlling their temper, simply asking them to stop will not work. You could recommend that they read a book such as this to give them tips on how to control their anger; the advice offered in the anger management program works for parents as well. Another option is to have a speaker provide anger management workshop for parents. In exploring this strategy, you need to know ahead of time that some people will not benefit from learning anger management skills because their problem is not a skills deficit. Furthermore, parents will be resistant if the workshop is mandated, and it is thus less likely to be successful. If you suspect that anger among parents is already or could be a problem in your league, your best bet is to have everyone attend. If you have the space, make it a large presentation. You can charge a nominal admission that will both pay for the speaker and raise funds for equipment. That kind of approach gives a positive spin to an event that some may see as punishment. The promotional strategy would be to highlight the expertise that will be presented. An added bonus is that this approach is proactive. Organizations are always in a better position by offering these presentations before an incident happens rather than after the fact.

Remember that single-session interventions do not have lasting effects in skill building and personality change, but they do raise consciousness about the issues. Sometimes just making it something that people talk about has a significant effect.

If you have offenders whom you suspect will require more intervention than a parent workshop, be sure to have professionals whom you can refer to. Those professionals should have training in anger management and a solid understanding of athletics. You should look for a sport psychologist, ideally one who is licensed as a psychologist, not someone with a doctorate in sport science or kinesiology, because the licensed psychologist would be more qualified to deal with serious emotional problems.

KIDS

A recurring theme with any intervention for children is that it depends on where the child is developmentally. Several theorists have discussed the stages of moral development (Kohlberg, 1968; Kohlberg & Diessner, 1991; Kohlberg & Elfenbein, 1975; Kohlberg & Puka, 1994; Weiss & Bredemeier, 1991; Bredemeier, 1994; Bredemeier et al., 1986; Weinberg, 2003) both in sport and not, and all agree that moral development does not correlate directly with age. Furthermore, some people never attain the highest level of moral development, generally accepted to be what is best for all involved. That being said, what children are taught will depend on their receptivity, which will be affected by their age, maturity, moral development, and other factors. From a purely behavioral point of view, the efficacy of a code of conduct will be shaped by the consistency of its enforcement—hence the push to have the adults buy in to it first.

How a code of conduct is drafted for children must take all this into account. Simple points to consider are the following:

1. Keep the reading level as low as possible. This approach is not intended to insult anyone but to make it useful to children of different ages and abilities.

2. Base rules on behavior as much as possible. Younger children do not always understand right from wrong. Spelling out behaviors as specifically as possible can help. Consider the following examples:

    a. Avoid the following:

        i. No unwanted physical contact.

           Children may not know what the term *physical contact* means, and they barely know what they want, let alone what someone else wants.

        ii. No hitting, punching, or kicking.

           Be careful about giving what looks like an exhaustive list. One kid will say, "Biting isn't on the list, that must be OK."

        iii. Don't be a sore loser.

           Losing hurts. Kids are often sore after they lose. Kids take things literally and may not know what this guideline means. Instead, promote sportsmanship. They may not know what that word means either, but encouraging sporting behaviors will offer the opportunity to discuss it.

    b. Give these a try:

        i. Respect all people in the game, including the adults. Respect means not hitting, kicking, yelling at, or doing anything else that would hurt your feelings.

This guideline teaches empathy. If you want a child to think about what behaviors to engage in, ask her or him to imagine being the recipient. The child may think twice.

ii. Be a good sport. Keep your head up and shake hands after the game whether you win or lose.

This guideline teaches self-respect and losing and winning with dignity. Looking forward to tomorrow is difficult with your eyes facing the ground.

These pointers should give you some ideas about developing expectations for kids. Never forget that they are always watching and will do what they see others do. When I was young I emulated Earl Weaver and Billy Martin, managers of the Baltimore Orioles and New York Yankees respectively. Those men argued with umpires in dramatic fashion. I remember George Brett running up to the umpire in 1983 and going face to face with him when he was accused of doctoring his bat with pine tar. Playing stickball in Brooklyn, we used to duplicate the batting stances of those we admired. The kids are watching; adults need to demonstrate what we expect from them.

With cases that require more assessment or interventions, consider the topics discussed in chapter 7.

HIGH SCHOOL SPORTS

Significant developmental variability is present in high school sports, but stability is present as well. High school sports are often the first level where complete organization is in place. Sure, we have sandlot and Pop Warner, local cheerleading troops and club soccer teams. But the path to collegiate sports, if the athlete is so motivated and meets the athletic necessities, is high school athletics. High school competition may be the last bastion of pure athletics before money starts corrupting things. We might think of high school sports as the bottom of the ninth when we are down on runs and have one last chance to win the game. For this reason, along with the fact that our youngsters are becoming young adults during this time, having a model program is crucial.

Drill training in high school sports can keep athletes focused on competition and be a great tool for keeping students safe from negative influences like drugs, alcohol, and violence.

Our adolescents can find lots of trouble during this time. Hormones start pumping. Young men try to prove that they are men. Young women try to prove that they are no longer little girls. Sexual exploration occurs. Gang recruitment occurs (at even younger ages in some neighborhoods). What can we do to protect our athletes? One thing we can do is keep them involved in athletics. Many adolescents find trouble when they have a lot of free time on their hands. Keeping them busy will keep them out of trouble.

Many studies, such as Donaldson & Ronan (2006) and Finlay & Coplan (2008), demonstrate the longitudinal benefits of sport participation. One way to help our athletes is to keep them involved in sport where they can learn how to deal with adversity, manage their emotions, gain confidence, appreciate teamwork, and so forth. Simultaneously, we must ensure that they get a steady dose of discipline, structure, and accountability.

Most often, by the time star athletes reach high school, they have already been recognized as different. They have been doted on and given special privileges. In some cases, this treatment is appropriate. Without such support, they would not be able to compete consistently at that level. Paired with chronic winning (as mentioned in chapter 3), this special treatment can create a monster in the making. To prevent the swelling ego from turning the athlete into an out-of-control kid who winds up embarrassing or hurting him- or herself and others, we need to drill home the value and need for discipline and sportsmanship.

Acting out cannot be tolerated because fixing the problem only spawns more problems. Of course, you want your athletes to be able to play. Academic eligibility rules start taking form in high school. Athletes must pass their classes if they expect to play.

Let us not forget how difficult it is to transition into high school in the first place. Although students may have learned about moving from classroom to classroom each period in middle school, now they practically need a map to get from one place to another, and they have significantly more obstacles to steer around. They will be tempted to socialize, be truant, experiment with drugs, and navigate romantic relationships. High school age is a tumultuous time. Adolescents look to adults for guidance, and they need a consistent structure to feel safe.

Many families have come to me to help them with their adolescents' passage through one form of emotional crisis or another. Adolescents may be outwardly demanding their freedom, but inside, whether they are aware of it or not, they have some fear. People have a greater feeling of invincibility in their teen years than they do at any other point in their lives. Many teenagers think that they need to act as if they know the way, although they do not. Athletes are even more prone to this behavior, because they are expected to be confident. Many of them are, but that confidence may not apply to all areas of their lives.

Children need reliable boundaries, or as I like to call them, padded fences. Teams, like families, should have ground rules. Although negotiating more of the ground rules becomes appropriate as adolescents reach their late teens, those in charge should determine what is open for negotiation and what is not. Many athletes get an added sense of discipline from their coaches; some get it only from their participation in sport. If we want them to be well-rounded young adults, all aspects of who they are must be developed—physical, mental, social, and emotional.

So why do we have the padding on the fences? We want young people to be able to learn lessons by running full speed into immovable fences but not be seriously hurt in the process.

High school athletes, especially those who live in areas of high crime, high poverty, and few resources are particularly susceptible to struggles of all sorts. An excellent program developed by the National Football Foundation is called Play It Smart.

Play It Smart

In 1998 the National Football Foundation created Play It Smart, an educational program targeted at kids from tough inner-city environments where family and community support are generally lacking. The program, designed to take student–athletes' passion for sport and dedication to their team and transform it into a force for greater good in their lives, has exceeded expectations. At less than a dollar a day per student–athlete, the program has sent 80 percent of its participants on to college. (www.playitsmart.org)

The Academic Coach and Springfield College

At the heart of the program is the Play It Smart academic coach, equal parts mentor, advocate, counselor, teacher, coach, and friend. Each academic coach receives special training and support from the National Football Foundation Center for Youth Development Through Sport (NFF Center) at Springfield College (Massachusetts).

The academic coach works with the kids for the entire school year—in ways that their head coach cannot. The academic coach brings the kind of extra attention to the player's off-field development that most head coaches would like to provide if they had the time, training, and resources. But the head coach's enthusiasm and support are essential to making the academic coach effective by giving him or her the same authority as the other assistant coaches.

Besides noting that 80 percent of the participants enroll in college versus the 64 percent of their peers as the same schools, Play It Smart also reports that 98 percent of their students graduate from high school versus a national average of 86 percent. Furthermore, these student–athletes take the SAT or

(continued)➤

Play It Smart *(continued)*

ACT at twice the rate of their classmates. On average, their teams perform more than 500 hours of community service each year.

Although this program is specifically for football, there is talk to expanding it to other high school sports. Dr. Al Petitpas, who is the director of the NFF Center for Youth Development Through Sport at Springfield College, is one of the most generous, compassionate, and humble leaders in the sport psychology world. The success of this program is proportional to the quality of the people involved, like Al.

The Play It Smart Program, initially directed by Jim Presbrey and now directed by Charles Gomes, has not skipped a beat in making this a prototype for programs to develop well-rounded student–athletes.

Quality programs like Play It Smart can provide effective support to struggling high school sports programs. But even with the resources that the NFF and Play It Smart bring to the table, the ground floor is where it starts. The commitment of coaches, athletes, and parents is crucial to helping athletes live up to their full potential in all aspects of their lives.

COLLEGE SPORTS

Trivia question: What were the circumstances that led to the creation of the NCAA?

Answer: Too many violent deaths in football.

At the turn of the century, violent play in football grew to such proportions that President Theodore Roosevelt took an interest. In 1905, 18 deaths and 159 serious injuries occurred in college football. He called together representatives from Harvard, Princeton, and Yale to discuss the issue. One outcome was the formation of the Intercollegiate Athletic Association of the United States (IAAUS) to regulate the violent rules of football. Football was almost abolished. In 1910 the organization changed its name to the National Collegiate Athletic Association (NCAA) (Fleisher, Goff, & Tollison, 1986). The very organization that governs collegiate sport was originally instituted to curb violence in sport.

The NCAA developed the CHAMPS Life Skills Program. As of August 2005, 513 NCAA institutions, about half of the total membership, participated in the program. Although the NCAA has expectations about establishing codes of conduct and preventing violence, it is somewhat surprising that the program does not mandate anger management as a component of CHAMPS (the institutions have latitude to implement the program to meet their needs).

Universities are a segment of our society that requires special attention. Young adults are on their own, often for the first time, and are subject to significantly less supervision than they had previously. Some students take this freedom to an extreme, which can include criminal behavior.

Crimes committed on college campuses are often handled differently from crimes committed in the outside community. Whom does campus security report to? Are they law enforcement agents? Are they sworn police officers who have a responsibility to uphold the law?

In 1995 the Bureau of Justice Statistics surveyed campus law enforcement agencies that served four-year universities and colleges with 2,500 or more students. More than 90 percent of public institutions used sworn police officers compared with less than 50 percent of the private institutions.

The enforcement of law on college campuses is tricky because the question arises about the loyalty of the law enforcement agency. Is the agency loyal to upholding the law or loyal to the institution? I argue that on any campus where security is not made up of sworn police officers, crime reporting is more likely to go through administrative channels before the judicial system becomes involved. We know that crime is underreported anyway, but placing more obstacles in the way, especially those related to good public relations rather than justice, results in more criminal behavior going unpunished.

Administrators who want to reduce crime on campus, including crimes that may be committed athletes, should have sworn officers perform investigations. In some cases, reports of rapes and assaults have never made it to the police.

Furthermore, cases such as that involving O.J. Simpson demonstrate how the lack of proper police practice—securing of a scene, ensuring the integrity of evidence—can make a conviction extremely improbable.

Another area of concern is the discrepancy between criminal and institutional investigations. When a university has a documented student conduct policy (most do), it must be enforced. Someone needs to explain to me why a student who inappropriately cites a previous author's work can be expelled for plagiarism, whereas a student who gets into a fight at a bar after attempting to assault a woman sexually while drunk does not even miss Saturday's game, much less lose a scholarship or be expelled.

I believe in the value of sport, and I think that academicians who argue to do away with athletics completely miss the boat, but how can we stand by and say that the previous scenario makes sense? The reason is simple: It does not make sense; it makes cents—lots of them. The issue ultimately becomes about money. The amount of money that universities receive as a direct result of successful athletics programs is obscene.

In the early 1980s, Patrick Ewing accounted for about $12 million in increased revenues for Georgetown University. Similarly, stars like Bo Jackson at Auburn University (where the school added an entirely new football seating section) and Doug Flutie at Boston College have added several million dollars to revenues for their respective schools (Fleisher, Goff, & Tollison, 1986). According to Department of Education statistics, the University of Louisville, in the 2002–2003 year, had revenue of almost $15 million from its basketball program.

As revenue increases, more is at stake, which is all the more reason to develop proactive anger management programs at the college level. Sexual violence prevention should be a component of these programs. To be effective, these programs cannot be single-day presentations. Information just does not stick that way. A culture change must occur. Criminal behavior outside the lines cannot be tolerated.

Some universities fund such programs simply for the liability protection that they offer. If an athlete engages in an assault after the university has already instituted a comprehensive program, the institution is better able to use the "bad egg" excuse. The standard defense is this: "We tried to give these athletes the programming that they need. This one was just a bad egg. His needs went above and beyond what we provide." Legally, the university would argue that the student–athlete's individual circumstances were severe enough to cause the proactive, preventative services to be ineffective. The argument absolves the institution of responsibility and thus financial culpability.

One school of thought says that college sports are a form of slavery. Because of rules that prohibit athletes from turning professional until a specific age, almost all American athletes choose to attend college. Regardless of the fact that many sports people, such as Billy Beane and others, believe that completing college gives young athletes a better chance to adapt to the pros, some argue that universities exploit collegiate athletes to make vast profits in exchange for about $120,000 worth of education and housing. Universities tend to be good stewards of their investments, as long as they continue to produce dividends. Would Lawrence Phillips have been allowed on the field after assaulting his ex-girlfriend and dragging her down a flight of stairs if the University of Nebraska did not stand to gain from his participating in the Fiesta Bowl shortly after he completed probation? Phillips rushed for 165 yards and scored three touchdowns as Nebraska beat Florida 62-24. The university made a bundle on the game.

Just as a tailback with a torn ACL gets knocked down a notch, athletes need to be aware of other pitfalls. Behavior that can cause a player to be ineligible to participate or conduct that tarnishes the reputation of the institution will not be supported. The issue becomes a financial one, and athletes are measured on a ledger. Do the profits outweigh the loss, do the benefits outweigh the risk, and do the plusses outweigh the minuses? Decisions are made in that way, not by whether the coach likes or dislikes the athlete. Athletes are useful to business as long as they produce revenue. If they do not add income or if they detract from it, they are going to go. It's the American way.

No, it is not fair. Neither is it fair that poverty stricken high school students who really want an education cannot afford to get one, although athletes have that opportunity because they can run fast. The issue is not about fairness. A lot of things are not about fairness.

PROFESSIONAL ATHLETES

As discussed in chapter 7, I do not agree with the perception that professional athletes are more violent than nonathletes are, but I do believe that they are an at-risk population. As such, more programs should be available to teach them ways to avoid trouble. But more than just sport psychology interventions are involved; how leagues handle transgressions is also an issue.

Highly paid professional athletes probably have a different perspective on financial matters than their nonathlete peers do. Therefore, when transgressions occur, fines have a limited effect on athletes. For example, Randy Moss, then of the Minnesota Vikings, received a $10,000 fine for simulating pulling his pants down and mooning the crowd at Lambeau Field after scoring a touchdown against the Packers. Asked by reporters about the fine, he said, "Ain't nothing but 10 grand. What's 10 grand to me?" Bringing in a salary of $5.75 million, Moss had asked a fair question. KARE-TV of Minneapolis recorded the exchange between Moss and reporters outside the Vikings' practice facility.

Reporter: "Write the check yet, Randy?"
Moss: "When you're rich you don't write checks."
Reporter: "If you don't write checks, how do you pay these guys?"
Moss: "Straight cash, homey."
Reporter: "Randy, are you upset about the fine?"
Moss: "No, cause it ain't [expletive]. Ain't nothing but 10 grand. What's 10 grand to me? Ain't [expletive] . . . Next time I might shake my [expletive]."

To professional athletes, fines have to be meaningful to yield results. The $10,000 fine was an insignificant fraction of Moss' salary. How could he take that seriously? Fines may not be the best choice for punishment, at least not as the only punishment.

A point to remember is that the athlete who does not love to play is rare indeed. In fact, the wealthier the stars are, the more they want to show dominance over their peers.

Chad Ocho Cinco (formerly Johnson), a wide receiver of the Cincinnati Bengals, listed all the star cornerbacks that he would play against during the 2005 year on a sign with yes-or-no check boxes to denote who could cover him. Such public display is related to his need to show how good he is at what he does. He could not check either box if he was not on the field playing.

If leagues want to change behavior, they must suspend the offending athletes. Taking away their opportunity to compete is like taking away their air. This kind of punishment quickly gains their attention. For good measure, suspension without pay is recommended. After all, if the team cannot benefit from having the athlete on the field because of the behavior that the athlete engaged in, they should not have to pay for work not performed. Furthermore, the league should levy the discipline, not the team. The team has a vested interest in being lenient to their star players.

In November 2005 the Philadelphia Eagles finally had enough of star wide receiver Terrell Owens's criticism of teammates, management, and the organization. After numerous interventions resulted in zero change (in fact, Owens further escalated his antics), the team decided to take a bold stand. They suspended him for four games because of "behavior detrimental to the team" and intended to make him inactive for the rest of the season. Coach Andy Reid clarified that the team took that action after a "large number of situations that accumulated over a long period of time" and that Owens was "warned repeatedly about the consequences of his actions." Not even a day later, Owens, hoping to overturn the dismissal, apologized publicly for his behavior. Acknowledging that his "mentality . . . (that) can be his greatest strength can also be my (his) greatest weakness."

"This is very painful for me to be in this position," he said. "I know in my heart that I can help the team win the Super Bowl and not only be a dominant player, but also be a team player. I can bring that" (Owens apologizes to Eagles, McNabb and fans, Rob Maaddi, AP Sportswriter, November 9, 2005). What stung him most was that he was not going to play the game. When this possibility became a reality, the apology soon followed.

In his book *Bloody Sundays: Inside the Dazzling, Rough-and-Tumble World of the NFL*, Mike Freeman attempts to tackle this problem by developing guidelines to curb domestic violence, specifically in professional football. He offers six interventions to elicit a decrease in this behavior.

1. An initial conviction for violence against a woman, domestic or otherwise, or a plea bargain involving such a crime, would result in a year-long suspension without pay. During the suspension the player would receive extensive counseling, the league would monitor his compliance with protective orders, and the player would pay for the victim's counseling.

Does this punishment seem excessive? Consider that a first-time steroid abuser in the NFL is suspended for four games.

2. An accused player who believes that he has been wrongly convicted in court can appeal to an independent arbitrator agreed on by the union and the league. The arbitrator would investigate, with expenses paid by taking 1 percent of the league's television revenues, which are $17.5 billion, and placing the money in an interest-bearing account. This sum would provide

an arbitrator with a budget of millions of dollars per year to fund expenses and an investigative staff. The arbitrator would rule on the player's administrative appeal, or in essence, his fate. Finally, the arbitrator would have domestic violence training.

If the arbitrator upholds the court verdict, the player would be suspended. But if the arbitrator uncovers convincing evidence that the player should not have been convicted, the league would have to pay the player damages for his pain and suffering. The NFL would take out full-page newspaper advertisements and television spots in the player's NFL city to report the league's findings.

Lie detector tests would be used to prevent the unthinkable: a couple faking an attack to collect money from the NFL. Such examinations are not infallible, but when performed by a competent investigator, lie detection testing can be an invaluable tool.

This second step is necessary because, even in domestic violence cases, the court system can make mistakes. Witnesses lie, and evidence is tainted and fabricated. In the case of black players, America's courts have historically treated African American men more harshly and unfairly, O.J. Simpson aside.

3. A second conviction or guilty plea for domestic violence would result in a lifetime ban from the sport. The same appeals process would apply.

4. If a team signs a player with a previous conviction or suspension for domestic abuse and the player is convicted a second time, the team would face a $5 million fine and $5 million salary cap hit. Hitting teams in the pocketbook should persuade them to become more accountable. Many still gamble on players with questionable backgrounds. These players tend not to be weeded out. Instead they circulate throughout the leagues, like stale air in a house.

5. The league would develop a hotline for victims of domestic violence. An independent office such as the Miles Foundation would run it, and any accusations would be quietly investigated. The player's team would not be notified unless the investigators discovered evidence of abuse. People specifically trained in the field of intimate partner violence would operate the hotline and would offer resources to victims, including shelter, support, referrals, and advocacy.

6. The NFL would track the names of players under restraining orders. Already, the league attempts to keep the identities on file, but the effort is not particularly organized. And police and the league do not coordinate with one another.

When Mike Freeman was writing his book, I was one of three experts whom he asked to respond to the plan. He included some of my response in his book, but the following was my entire response:

I want to begin my response to Mike Freeman's proposal by thanking him for the opportunity to discuss this in an open forum and commend him for having the courage to tackle the difficult issues facing NFL players—especially with regard to violence. As a sport psychologist who is clinically trained and licensed, my views may not be representative of the field, but I hope they are helpful in advancing this necessary discussion ahead.

There appear to be three major issues involved here. First is the issue of the context of the violent behavior (directed at women or others). Is this behavior a manifestation of mental illness or learned behavior? Directly connected with this is the question of what types of interventions would likely be effective and prescribed. Associated as well would be reasonable expectations of the qualifications of those delivering services to these men.

The next issue relates to the culture of athletics and to what degree the NFL inherits a problem that really needs to be addressed at a much earlier age.

And finally, my comments on the specifics of the plan proposed by Mr. Freeman will be offered as both reinforcement and recommendations for his plan.

If one examines the research in the sport psychology literature regarding violence, despite its descriptive value, there is no consensus about what definitively causes it. Violence is not a problem solely owned by the professional athlete, and the place to start is violence research in general. It is safe to assume that three places that violence generates from are biological predisposition, learned behavior, and the result of sociopathy.

When I say biological predisposition, I am referring to people who are prone to violent outbursts due to a neurophysiological condition (which could be caused by brain injury or neurochemical imbalance). People with this variety of problem often require medications to assist with impulse control problems and are likely to have generalized violence problems in many different venues (meaning not just in relationships, but on the field, off the field, with anyone). We have an assumption that professional athletes are immune to psychopathology. Athletes contemplating suicide and engaging in such risky behavior are clearly pathological, and cases such as Irving Fryar's and Tito Wooten's cry for help and intervention. There is no reason why an NFL player could not manifest symptoms of severe mental illness— and though it seems to be rare, this should never be ruled out. There is such stigma around identification of an emotional problem that treatment is often not pursued until symptoms become largely unmanageable.

The most common cause of violent behavior is learned behavior. This occurs when the young athlete observes the use of violence to get what one wants as a child. It could include watching his father physically abuse his mother. Coaches provide very powerful modeling images, and those who advocate violence are likely to produce violent athletes. We know that athletes with anger management problems often have basic skills deficits. They may have difficulty identifying what emotion they are experiencing— rendering them helpless to manage the situation. They may have difficulties offering alternative accounts for why someone did something toward them other than provocative explanations. At times, they will lack other options on how to deal with a problem other than with violence. Further, this is complicated by the fact that violence in our society is reinforced. There is not a great deal of differentiation encouraged between provocative and nonprovocative stimuli. This can lead to great difficulty in knowing when and how to turn it on or off.

The lack of consequences for violence cannot be understated. Athletes love to play, and though it is a business where hitting them in the pocket- book can have power, I believe the greatest deterrence for athletes (short of incarceration) is removing their opportunity to play the game that they love—and at the same time they don't get paid as a result. Comments such as "Coach'll fix it" or "Do you know who I am" reek of a sense of narcissistic entitlement that was engrained in the star athlete way before he got to the pros. The culture of sports in universities is larger than life. If people are not aware that the campus police's loyalty is most often directed to the university before other law enforcement agencies, then they need to take a closer look at college life.

Finally, sociopath or psychopath (sometimes used interchangeably) is not a title that is reserved for serial killers like Ted Bundy and Jeffrey Dahmer. Sociopathy (as discussed earlier) refers to a personality struc- ture that is unconcerned with the rules and expectations of society. These people are narcissistic in nature and care primarily about getting their own desires satisfied. There is great controversy into what leads a person down the road to sociopathy, but we do know that most often this is a one-way street. That means that a professional athlete who is also a sociopath is not likely to change with any intervention one comes up with. The answer most often is incarceration. Simply stated, an athlete who is a sociopath has to be handled by the criminal justice system when he acts out. As Bill Parcells was quoted as saying (and quite accurately, I agree), "If Charles Manson could play, someone would take him."

And why shouldn't they? If there is no consequence, why not take a player who may be a "bad character guy"? A couple of reasons from a sport psychology perspective. First, "bad character guys" often find themselves in trouble with the law. If they had problems in high school and college, it will only worsen under greater scrutiny, greater competition, and greater sense of entitlement with their new-found fortunes from an NFL contract.

Athletes who are in jail cannot perform for you on the field. Probably most significant, however, is the fact that it is only a matter of time before a sports team or organization is sued for the behavior of one of its employees. The money that could get involved is scary.

American culture encourages aggression. From the NFL player to the woman on Wall Street working toward a promotion, our society reinforces aggressiveness without much regard for teaching skills that are necessary to manage the emotions that often accompany such behavior. Athletes tend to be the most popular people in school and often get preferential treatment. When this is engrained from such an early age, it is going to be very difficult to change. It is the main reason why so much attention is given to youth sport. Coaching seminars and parent workshops given by sport psychologists to educate adults on the effects of sport (both positive and negative) are crucial to avoid perpetuation of these tendencies that don't serve the athletes well over time. Sure, confidence helps them, but without the necessary reality checks and encouragement of hard work, they are ill prepared for later life.

It is also worth noting that different coaching styles have proven effective for different people. In general, authoritarian styles that use fear as the motivating factor often curtail athletes' potential by making them too afraid of consequences to be creative and figure out how to go to the next level.

So, who is going to work with these athletes? My personal opinion is that if you are going to address the issue of violence with athletes, you need qualified individuals. To me, qualified means there must be some standard of training. The best fit would be sport psychologists who are licensed as psychologists—doctoral level personnel who are trained in assessment and diagnosis of more severe mental illness and at the same time are educated in and familiar with athletic context. These professionals should be able to discern when a referral to a psychiatrist may be necessary (should medications need to be considered) and identify more severe psychopathology. Sport psychologists doing this work must be familiar with the nuances of sociopathy, impulse control disorders, abuse, violence, and substance abuse.

Finally, the "Freeman Anti-Domestic Violence Plan" deserves significant credit for its creativity and courage. Overall, I believe you would see significant and expedient results from such a plan. I have a couple of comments that I think are worth considering.

Point 1: The issue of requiring a conviction is a sticky point. Gaining a conviction in a domestic violence case is notoriously hard. Certainly, suspensions are the way to go because they remove players from the field that they love and they take a hit in the pocketbook. This seems to be the most likely way to effectuate change with NFL players. One might ask the question, however, whether it should be only charges of violence against women that lead to consequences or whether discipline should be levied for off-field violence in general.

Point 2: This was a well-thought-out idea—having a neutral arbitrator that the NFL pays for. I would also recommend that a player's suspension should be active until an appeal is heard. Otherwise, it is possible for a player to stave off an appeal for a period of time. If there is enough evidence for an investigation, have the player wait until it is resolved.

Point 3: As an advocate of sport and at the same time someone who would like to see a reduction in violent crime amongst athletes, even I thought that this was a rather severe idea. It certainly would seem to act as a deterrent to violence. What needs to be included somewhere before this point, however, is the mandate for treatment.

Point 4: This point is inventive and hits right at the core of the system that refuses to deter athletes from acting out. Now the team has to think twice about the players they invest in. You want to invest in a player, fine, but you may lose your investment, and then some.

Point 5: While there is no evidence that rape or domestic violence is false reported with any greater frequency than any other crime, I would be concerned that this hotline number may be ringing off the hook by people who look to take advantage of the dollar amounts involved in the NFL. Nonetheless, this is a crucial facet of a comprehensive intervention package.

Point 6: The notion of the NFL babysitting their players with restraining orders is a nice idea but probably not something that will yield a great deal of success.

Overall, Mike Freeman suggests an excellent program. I would want to know, in addition, what the NFL thinks about gang affiliation. This is likely an underattended-to-factor involved in athletes' legitimization of violence.

And, to offer insight into what a treatment program might look like to be available in conjunction with the plan, these thoughts and factors come to mind:

1. *Anger management—as it applies to athletes*

2. *Domestic violence—group and individual psychotherapy*

3. *Who pays for the treatment? And more important, who pays for the treatment of the victims? This should come directly from the player's salary.*

4. *Who is treatable and who isn't? What clinical presentations are amenable to treatment and what behaviors are primarily sociopathic and should be handled solely by the criminal justice system? This should be determined by a licensed psychologist or psychiatrist.*

To summarize, Mike Freeman has certainly taken on a huge challenge by trying to tackle this problem, and for someone without clinical training, he demonstrated a good grasp both of this problem and the types of interventions that may be effective. My comments and recommendations are to provide the clinical framework to a pioneering project. I believe that this program would improve the reputation of the NFL, provide treatment options for those who need it, change an environment that does not condemn (and at times condones) violence off the field, and call to action interventions before an athlete throws away his career or causes innocent people to be hurt.

Freeman's proposal is an important start, but it should be only the beginning. Many opportunities are available before, during, and after transgressions. One such opportunity that the NFL deserves credit for pioneering is their rookie symposium, which they hold every summer to orient the new rookies to life in the big time. They try to pack a great deal of information into a short period. Included in the symposium are life skills training, financial advising, information about substance abuse, personal conduct policy, and more. Anger management and specific education about violence (including sexual and domestic violence) could be added to the program. Other professional leagues would benefit from instituting such a program and expanding it as well.

One of the major problems with interventions such as this, however, is that single workshops rarely have lasting effects. Considering the amounts of money involved, professional teams would be prudent to have annual presentations for their team on these issues, as well as have professionals available to deal with these issues if incidents arise.

From a legal point of view, organizations at all levels will be held more accountable if they recognize a problem but do nothing. Institutions need to show that they are addressing the issue by implementing a program. Then, if a transgression occurs, an institution can argue that the athlete needed more services than it could provide. Of course, organizations should also have a mechanism for assessing this possibility and referring out to clinical professionals when indicated.

TEAM SPORT PSYCHOLOGISTS

Increasingly, sports teams are employing sport psychologists to improve sport performance. The United States Olympic Committee has had sport psychologists helping their athletes for many years now. Slowly, this approach has permeated both professional and college sport. The main goal is to help athletes improve their performance through mental skills training by removing the mental obstacles that interfere with performance.

Many teams and organizations do not realize that sport psychologists are not a homogenous group. They come from one of two major training environments. Some are trained in the sport sciences like kinesiology, and others are trained in psychology. Both are supposed to have fundamental knowledge of both domains, but those trained in the sport sciences are less well prepared to handle significant emotional problems. Even those who may be inclined to refer out problems that are beyond their expertise need to have a good background in identifying those problems. For this reason, those who are grounded in psychology are better equipped to identify and handle severe emotional problems.

Furthermore, the word *psychologist* is a legally protected word. Only those licensed by their state board or parallel governing body can call themselves psychologists of any type (sport or otherwise). Because sport consultants with either background can enhance performance, I believe that those who are also licensed psychologists give the team or organization both the highest level of training and the widest array of competencies. Of course, some sport science professionals achieve excellent results, and some licensed psychologists are ineffective. Exceptions occur on both sides, but the most prepared sport psychologists are licensed psychologists who have specialized training and experience working in sports.

As organizations continue to hire sport psychologists to handle the many mental aspects of athletes' lives, I believe that consideration should given to those who have expertise in the treatment of violence as well as clinical disorders that may increase the risk of violence.

One of the functions of sport psychologists is to assist professional teams with personality and character assessment in the predraft evaluation. Those doing the evaluations to be knowledgeable about violence, criminal behavior, substance abuse, and methods of risk assessment that are commonly used in the forensic world to predict future behavior.

ENTOURAGE TRAINING

Many celebrities, athletes and otherwise, believe that they are targets for exploitation, that their fame and celebrity status makes them targets for people who see dollar signs and want a piece for themselves. Many recent cases support the premise that athletes are targets.

In January 2007 Darrent Williams, cornerback for the Denver Broncos, was leaving a New Years party in a Hummer H2 stretch limousine with then teammates Javon Walker, D.J. Williams, and Brandon Marshall, when the limo was sprayed with bullets coming from another vehicle. Darrent Williams died as a result of the gunshot wounds. Willie D. Clark, identified as a member of the Crips street gang, was indicted in October 2008 on 39 counts, including first-degree murder, related to the incident.

Washington Redskins safety Sean Taylor died after being shot during a botched burglary in his home in November 2007. He was targeted by young men who knew that he was wealthy and had property worth stealing.

In September 2008 Jacksonville Jaguars tackle Richard Collier was shot more than a dozen times while he and a former teammate waited outside an apartment building for two women they had met at a nightclub. He was left paralyzed, and one of his legs was amputated.

Regardless of whether or not athletes are targets, is it not surprising that they do not do more to avoid these incidents? Why do they keep finding themselves in these situations? Several explanations have been offered:

1. They look for the excitement of situations or locations that may be ripe for trouble and then become caught up in it.
2. The people who are trying to exploit them are a lot smarter than they are.
3. They believe that they are above it all, that they are invincible, and that no one can harm them.
4. They are either not paying attention or do not know what to look for, or more accurately what to avoid, to prevent themselves from falling into these traps.

Assuming that celebrities do not enjoy giving away their money, being caught up in scandal, or being arrested for situations that quickly escalate out of control, they would be prudent to invest in measures to prevent these incidents from happening. After they are arrested, their resources go toward legal defense, public relations, and damage control, and these services can cost a lot of money. For much less money, they could learn the skills necessary to recognize bad situations and avoid them.

When I was young, growing up in Brooklyn, I had a friend, Milton Love, who always seemed to know when things were going to get out of hand, and he got himself away from the action before trouble arrived. Thinking back, I too knew a lot about avoiding trouble, and I honed that understanding when working security at clubs in New York City while working my way through college. This awareness can be taught.

These days, professional athletes have a large number of people in their inner circles. The circle may consist predominantly of people whom the athlete grew up with; or a security staff; or the athlete's agent, manager, accountant, personal assistant, or personal trainer. The point is that with so many people around, would it not make sense for one of them to be charged with keeping the athlete out of trouble?

The concept of entourage training is to teach one person from the entourage the necessary skills to keep the athlete out of harm's way. These basic skills include anger management and conflict resolution. Because athletes, like all of us, are human, the greater the number of people who are able to keep their emotions under control and avoid an explosive escalation, the better the outcome is likely to be.

As mentioned earlier, we can tell when someone is escalating, just as we can notice the change in a dog's posture before it attacks. Recognizing nonverbal cues is critical to knowing early when a de-escalation will be necessary, and the earlier the intervention is, the more likely it will be to succeed. Recognizing the physical signs of intoxication by alcohol or drugs can provide much information about the likelihood of reasoning with people, their coordination, and their energy. For example, although some people think that they can fight better when they are drunk (a phenomenon sometimes referred to as beer muscles), people who are inebriated are poorly coordinated and easy to knock off balance, although they may be mildly anesthetized to pain. People who are high on cocaine, amphetamines, or PCP may be several times stronger than normal, but they often are uncoordinated and have difficulty thinking clearly, making their management possible despite their increased strength.

In any case, being able to size people up and assess both the likelihood of their initiating violence and the potential danger associated with it is a necessary skill.

Another necessary skill is gang identification. As Paul Pierce can attest from the incident in which he was stabbed several times and nearly died, being able to identify gang members, when in their domain, and make a quick decision to leave the scene can be the difference between life and death. Of course, some high school, college, and professional athletes either are gang members, were gang members (rarely do you get to resign from such affiliation), or are friends with gang members. The dangers of gangs should be obvious. Gangs take themselves seriously, are sensitive to turf issues, and will either (a) not be impressed with an athlete's fame and fortune because they have their own riches and power in their arena, or (b) will feel threatened by the famous intruder and attempt to remove him. Information about gangs is useful. Although it may seem redundant to some, it is worth reviewing.

Back in the old days, celebrity sex symbols worried that when they checked into a hotel room, they would find a woman who would state that she was victimized and then blackmail them for money. So such stars used to have someone on their staff check the room before they entered. Athletes who worry about entrapment can have "their people" check their rooms before they enter and be on the lookout for groupies. Certainly, some groupies offer sex in exchange for being around popular people. Do I believe that hordes of women are doing this and then falsely reporting rape? No. But it can happen, so athletes must avoid such situations. When women are throwing themselves at an athlete because of his money or notoriety, he must either steer clear or trust the person in his entourage to be the voice of reason, to offer a reality check. If the person tells the athlete to stay away, he should stay away. And if the team identifies an area of town or specific clubs, bars, or restaurants to avoid because of the trouble that often occurs there, athletes should heed the warning.

In October 2005 Seattle Seahawks safety Ken Hamlin ended up in intensive care with a fractured skull and a blood clot on his brain. He had been assaulted in a nightclub in an area of town that coach Mike Holmgren had warned his players about. After the incident, the team changed its warning to an edict prohibiting its players from being in that area. I am not implying that Ken Hamlin is responsible for being the victim of a crime by being somewhere he was advised to avoid, but athletes need to be aware that they often have more to lose than to gain and that they can be targets.

Athletes who believe that they are targets want to protect themselves, and many carry handguns. Athletes are often found with weapons—when going through airport security, during police stops to assess for driving under the influence, or following an embarrassing and dangerous episode of accidentally shooting oneself, as Plaxico Burress of the New York Giants did in November 2008 (which later led to his release from the team). They may be carrying handguns that they are licensed to carry as concealed weapons, but often they are not licensed. Athletes certainly have a right to bear arms, but those who intend to possess a handgun must obtain proper training and become licensed. As an alternative, athletes may choose to hire professionally trained bodyguards. A more hazardous option is to delegate security responsibility to the toughest member of the entourage. If an athlete really wants a member of his entourage to serve that role, that person should receive formal training. An athlete should not gamble that his buddy can handle a life-or-death situation.

The types of professionals who can help in this arena include police instructors and security experts who specialize in management of details to protect potential targets. Self-defense training that focuses on tactics to neutralize and escape from an opponent can be useful, although many athletes have egos that impede their utilization of those skills. Finally, psychologists trained in threat assessment, anger management, and developing emotional intelligence can assist athletes, as well as members of their entourage, in learning methods to identify escalating situations that may lead to conflict, skills to prevent bad decision making in chaotic environments, and techniques to manage interactions that can lead to win–win outcomes.

The preceding are some of the possibilities that could be offered in entourage training. They represent a subset of the sorts of skills that can help keep athletes on the field and avoid problems.

SUMMARY

In this chapter we reviewed the complexities that organizations face when dealing with the transgressions of athletes. We explored how Title IX, originally proposed to create gender equality among federally funded institutions, provides the grounding for cases in which universities can be found responsible for the behavior of scholarship athletes if they create an environment that is not free of sexual harassment. Logically, this potential increase in financial and legal vulnerability should lead sports programs to create better mechanisms to prevent transgressions by athletes.

This topic led to an exploration of systemic interventions across age and competition levels. A review of codes of conduct was provided. Coaches and parents must model the behavior outlined in the codes of conduct.

Codes of conduct, which are becoming more common in youth sport, are only the starting point for rule enforcement. The Play It Smart Program, which provides academic coaches to high school football players, offers both academic support and character development. The argument was made that as athletes grow older and reach higher levels of competition, they need more, not less, support.

The NCAA CHAMPS Life Skills Program was reviewed. Rules enforcement at the professional levels was discussed. Although professional sports organizations are attempting to address the problem of athletes' involvement with the law, their efforts need to be reinforced. A strong argument was made in favor of using suspensions along with docking of athletes' salaries rather than fines alone if leagues hope to deter athletes' poor behavior.

Mike Freeman's plan to address NFL players' criminal behavior, which he offered in his book *Bloody Sundays*, was analyzed. Recommendations to bolster its interventions were provided.

Hiring sport psychologists to assist in the development and implementation of intervention and prevention programs was strongly urged, but it was also advised that those sport psychologists be competent in managing and treating deviant behavior.

Finally, the concept of entourage training was introduced as a means to have athletes' trusted circles protect them rather than place them in questionable situations. Although athletes may not appreciate its value, entourage training should receive strong support by agents who have a great deal of money to lose and by teams that cannot benefit from the athletes' skills if they are not available to play because of their transgressions.

Ultimately, the goal of this chapter was to illustrate the need for systemic interventions in sport and to offer various examples of the components of those interventions.

CHAPTER 9

PREVENTION OF SEXUAL VIOLENCE

Whether we use the words *dating violence, sexual violence, rape,* or any other euphemism to denote forced or coerced sexual contact is really a matter of semantics that has more to do with the comfort level of those discussing the issue than the difference in terminology. Sex is everywhere around us. It pervades the beer commercials during TV time-outs. The sport arena is not alone in using sexuality as a vehicle for commercialism—watch an episode of *Desperate Housewives.*

Nonetheless, with the ubiquity of sexual images, it is no wonder that people become confused about what is acceptable and what is not. Among young men, whose hormones are raging and whose social status is related to sexual conquests, it is not surprising or new that they plan to achieve sexual encounters by cooperation, by coercion, or even by force (note too that women can be perpetrators of sex crimes and that the phenomenon is by no means strictly heterosexual).

Some men believe that if they spend a great deal of money on a woman, by taking her to nice restaurants and by buying her gifts, then sex is the repayment—quid pro quo, this for that. Sorry guys—if you think that she has to "put out" because you spent all that money, you made two mistakes: First, no woman has to engage in sex if she does not want to, and second, you just wasted your money.

Then the feminists step in and state that this snapshot is diagnostic of the greater picture whereby men are socialized to believe that women are there for the taking and that they are expected to satisfy a man's requests or demands.

Sex is an issue for everyone. Women enjoy sex, just as men do—sometimes more often, sometimes less, sometimes in different ways, and sometimes attaching more emotion to it than men do—but wanting sex is not a man's issue; it is a human issue. I do not intend to support either side of the sexist arguments, chauvinist or feminist, about all the components and dynamics that go into this complex issue. Very simply, sexual violence needs to stop because everyone involved in these situations gets hurt—the victim, the perpetrator, the parents, the coach, the school, the taxpayers. Obviously, the crime does not affect all those parties equally, but the behavior is inherently wrong and needs to be stopped.

At some point in the previous discussion, you may have wondered why we are talking about rape in a book about anger. There are a couple of reasons. First, many experts argue that rape is not a crime about sex but a crime about power and control. In such a model, the sexual act is the weapon, but the motivation can come from several places. A nonexhaustive list could include a man's belief in his entitlement to sex, a man's struggles with inadequacy that he would not be able to engage a partner in sex without the use of force or coercion, and miscommunication about female sexual interest (when a man thinks that he is involved in a consensual interaction, while the woman perceives it as coerced or aggressive). Richard Felson (2002) notes that people engage in aggression for three main reasons:

1. To control the behavior of the target
2. To gain retribution or justice
3. To promote or defend their self-image

At least one author (Katz, 1988) adds a fourth motive:

4. The desire for excitement

Furthermore, when reporting violent crimes, sex offenses and rape are included in the category. As discussed earlier, not all violence is related to anger. Predatory violence is different experientially and physiologically. Nonetheless, when athletes' criminal behavior is reported, sex crimes stand out in preponderance. Some authors use this as evidence that athletes are an out-of-control bunch (Benedict, 1997, 1998, 2004; Benedict & Yaeger, 1998).

Some research identifies athletes as disproportionately represented in sex crimes on campus.

Chris O'Sullivan, a Bucknell University psychologist studied 26 alleged gang rapes that were documented between 1980 and 1990 and found that most involved fraternity brothers and varsity athletes, specifically football and basketball players (as cited in Neimark, 1991). In 1985, Ehrhart and Sandler documented 50 group rape incidents. Of those, 30 percent involved athletes. Furthermore, it was reported that members of sport teams or sport clubs made up 20.2 percent of the men involved in sexual assault or attempted sexual assault, 13.6 percent of the men involved in acts of sexual abuse, and 11 percent of the offenders of reported battery, illegal restraint, or intimidation (Frintner & Rubinson, 1993). This population of students was vastly overrepresented as offenders in these crimes.

A three-year survey by the National Institute of Mental Health found that athletes participated in approximately one-third of 862 sexual attacks on college campuses (Eskenazi, 1990). "Based on an FBI survey, basketball and football players from NCAA colleges were reported to the police for committing sexual assault 38 percent more often than the average males on college campuses" (Bohmer & Parrot, 1993, p. 21).

At the University of Arkansas, a study sampled athletes' rape and relationship violence experiences and attitudes at a university ranked in the NCAA's top 10 in two sports at the time of data selection. The author noted that although campus rape has received increased attention overall, this attention seems magnified for athletes in schools ranked highly by the NCAA. This study found that regarding past perpetration experiences, 11 percent of the athletes had physically assaulted a dating partner, and 4 percent reported that they had physically forced a woman to have sexual intercourse against her will (Jackson, 1991).

A survey of 1,050 athletes and more than 10,000 students by the Towson State University's Center for the Study and Prevention of Campus Violence found that athletes were five and a half times more likely to admit committing date rape than nonathletes were (Wieberg, 1991). Finally, Nicklin (1996) reported that pro football players were four times more likely than the average person to abuse their spouses.

In *Tanja H. v. Regents of the University of California* of 1991, the plaintiff was raped by four members of the University of California football team after a party in a dormitory. The court acknowledged the "outrageous and reprehensible conduct of the perpetrators" but refused to find the university responsible for the athletes' behavior (Bohmer & Parrot, 1993). In 1991 three men on trial from the St. John's University lacrosse team were accused of making a woman perform oral sex on them, after getting her intoxicated with alcohol to the point that she faded in and out of consciousness (Bohmer & Parrot, 1993).

Sounds like pretty convincing evidence, no?

In case it has not already been made clear, I do not intend to paint the picture of athletes being a group of men with halos awaiting sainthood. What I do intend to challenge is the notion that athletes are a violent group. This view is a gross overgeneralization of all athletes (male and female, old and young) as well as an unfair representation of the totality of those competing in more aggressive sports.

I will also argue that the people who are labeling athletes as a violent group, or a group more likely to rape, are simultaneously, and conveniently, minimizing the severity of violence in our culture. Furthermore, the same people have likely spent little time in a correctional facility. Are former athletes in jail? Of course. Do they represent the majority? Not as far as I can tell. The surgeon general of the United States has called violence an epidemic. The

Centers for Disease Control and the National Institute of Mental Health have identified violence as a prime area of study and concern, and nowhere in their available reports is sport identified as a risk factor for violence. I believe that sport has more influence in keeping otherwise delinquent kids out of trouble than it does in causing violence.

I have yet to see research that demonstrates that sport leads to criminal behavior. More specifically, I have seen no evidence that participation in revenue-producing collision sports is predictive of criminal behavior.

Are there some alarming trends that need to be addressed? Yes, and now we will get to the plan about how to deal with the problems.

Through the rest of this chapter, I will outline what I believe to be the crucial components to an effective sexual violence prevention program. Just as important are the nuts and bolts, the how-tos, which I will discuss as well. I will examine a couple of approaches currently being used—what they bring to the table and where they could use improvement.

WHY ARE THESE PROGRAMS NEEDED?

As discussed in the previous section, studies and numerous individual accounts identify athletes as perpetrators in sex offenses. I cannot repeat often enough that focusing on athletes as a population more likely to engage in this behavior greatly minimizes the severity of this problem in our society as a whole.

Statistically, one out of every four women will be sexually assaulted, in some form, during her lifetime, and most often the perpetrator is someone whom the woman knows. The crime transcends racial, monetary, and social lines. We cannot identify a future or past rapist by looking at him. A rapist can be the young man wearing a basketball jersey or the doctor in a white coat. Rape victims display the same patterns: None exist. Whether a woman is wearing revealing clothing is not predictive of her being a victim of a sexual assault. If a woman wears revealing clothing and something does happen, does she deserve it? Of course not! She probably exercised poor judgment, but the punishment for poor judgment should not be rape. To illustrate how ludicrous that thinking is, think about how many times as an adolescent you exercised poor judgment. We want to teach people to think about their behavior, but if they make poor decisions, we still need to support them and take care of them if something bad happens. The last thing we want to do is blame the victim in any way.

The salient point is that sexual violence is not a woman's problem. It is a societal problem that affects all people.

Male Athlete Culture Regarding Sex

Several factors in male athlete culture may contribute to an increase in probability of dating violence. Although research has not supported the conclusion that these factors have directly led to a statistical increase in such offenses (for many reasons this issue is next to impossible to study), they are worth mentioning because negating these factors could prevent incidents. Before we go through these factors, it must be made clear that these factors may contribute to *explanations* for athletes' behavior but should not be misconstrued as *excuses* for sexual violations. When sexual violence does occur, the crime should be prosecuted to the full extent of the law. The athlete's capability of bringing a championship to the team must have no bearing.

An athlete culture in which athletes believe that coaches will remedy any problem that the players may face has developed over a long period. Although this situation is slowly changing, many athletes live in, or once lived in, this world.

Thinking That Others Will Fix a Situation

Many years ago, in a high school far away, a star baseball player with a golden arm was suspended from school for cursing out a teacher. In this town, the high school baseball season was about the biggest thing going. Everyone went to watch—sports fan or not. The players were the heroes of the town, and the coach was more popular than the mayor. To have a player unavailable for a game was unthinkable. Slowly, over time, a culture developed in which a different set of rules governed the behavior of the baseball players. If they did not do their homework or pass their exams, they would get Cs to maintain eligibility. If they got into a fight, they would not be expelled; instead, they would be referred to the coach to handle the discipline. Even when athletes had brushes with the law, the coach would pick them up from the police station, often with no charges pressed.

Eventually, the young men became untouchable. It took on a life of its own. Even the coach could not control it. When he realized that an athlete went too far, the coach could not ban him from playing, even if the player deserved it, because his job was on the line. The winning expectations were firmly hung around his neck, fashioned as a somewhat tragic bull's-eye. Those expectations kept growing, and the coach had to get his athletes on the field and win.

A tragedy then occurred that would change things forever: The principal of the school died unexpectedly. Realizing the pressures associated with the job, none of the assistant principals would step up. Instead, an assistant from a neighboring town signed on as the new principal, and she had new principles. Taking a look at the situation, she boldly decided that the integrity of the school and thus the future of the students hung in the balance. Extricating the young men from trouble would only leave them less prepared to deal with the real world, whenever they got there. She took a stand and met with the coach. She expected a momentous showdown with her colleague and an even greater backlash from the town. It never happened. The coach was relieved not to have to handle all these issues himself. The town had its fair share of angry people, but other parents thought that academics were being undervalued and many students believed that they were marginalized if they were not athletes.

Does any of this sound familiar? In fact, we have heard similar stories from throughout the country. To be truthful, the account is pseudo-fiction—the amalgamation of stories that have checkered our newspapers for the past couple of decades.

Even today, some coaches fix problems that athletes find themselves in. Thus, the athletes come to expect it. They have a sense of entitlement and expect positive things to be handed to them and negative things to be taken away. Although thinking that they can turn to the coach to help them cope with the pressures of life is nice, they should not believe that a coach's help should serve as a substitute for taking personal responsibility.

Because of the scrutiny that athletes face when they are involved in transgressions and because institutions are held financially responsible for what its students do (refer to Title IX in chapter 8), the days of "Coach'll fix it" are dwindling away.

Having a Sense of Entitlement

The preceding theme needs to be extended a bit further. The preferential treatment that student–athletes receive from coaches and teachers is not limited to those benefactors. Although gift giving violates NCAA rules, athletes have been receiving gifts from boosters and potential agents for years. This adds further to their experience that the world is their oyster and that they can select whatever pearls they want. Some develop an inflated ego whereby they believe that everyone wants to cater to them.

Why would we not believe that this sense of entitlement would carry over to sexuality? Some young men already see women as objects rather than people, and they believe that they can have whatever object they choose, so logically they believe that they can have whatever women they choose. Many faults pervade that thinking, but when many factors contribute it, holding athletes singularly accountable is almost unfair. We, as participants in the athletes' world, need to correct this thinking: Women are not objects. Athletes cannot have sex with whatever women they want whenever they want it.

Working to Promote a Manly Image

Ah, summer camp. Not campfires, ghost stories, and marshmallows, but working through two-a-day practices, fighting off heat exhaustion, and hearing the loud snores of exhausted bodies attempting to recuperate before the intense activity of the next day.

Football camp is grueling at all levels. Camp is a time of bonding, a time for young men to prove themselves, and, for some coaches, a time to test their young charges to see how they respond to the rigors of competition. Survival, if you will.

Not surprisingly, coaches have various approaches. Some focus on the positives and shower praise on the successes of their players. Others focus on the negatives, hoping to humiliate their players into improving. Certainly, both approaches can be effective, and focusing on the negatives, in and of itself, is not damaging. If the focus on poor execution is followed up by teaching proper technique, then it may work extremely well in improving performance.

In extreme cases, and it is not specific to football—St. John's head basketball coach Fran Fraschilla, a few years back, was fired shortly after it was reported that he dropped his pants and displayed his testicles to his players to demonstrate what it was that they were lacking—players' toughness and manhood are equated. Not being able to handle the pressures denotes "being a girl."

The association of manhood with being physically dominant can breed problems outside sport. No evidence supports the notion that to induce athletes to play hard, coaches must convince them that if they do not they are weak, and therefore, must be women. This misogyny becomes engrained in the way that athletes see the world and cannot bode well for their treating women with respect. This approach is not necessary to reach athletic goals and is likely to get people hurt. Coaches should get rid of it.

Examples of Sexual Violence in Sport

1. In an Iowa high school in March 2005, it was alleged that older members of the wrestling team, aged 16 to 18, held down a freshman while another pulled down his pants and rubbed his genitals on the face and head of the victim. This incident went beyond taping victims to a goal post or putting mineral ice in their jockstraps, but it was not outside the realm of what has been heard for years about hazing. The difference in this case was that one of the assailants was the coach's son. Not uncommonly, hazing incidents in sports teams have a sexual overtone.

2. Florida State's star linebacker A.J. Nicholson was suspended by the team after being accused of sexual assault by a 19-year-old girl. The woman called police on Thursday, December 29, 2005, at 3 a.m., two hours after the team's curfew, and said that she had been assaulted by a Florida State player, later identified as Nicholson. The alleged assault occurred at the Westin Diplomat Resort and Spa, where the Seminoles were staying. It was reported that Nicholson cooperated with police, who questioned him for two hours. The woman was also interviewed by detectives and taken to a rape treatment center. Nicholson had two previous arrests, one for a DUI and one for resisting arrest.

(continued) ◆

The incident did not end there. Longtime Penn State football coach Joe Paterno found himself in the hot seat following the comments that he made about the incident. In a remark that he made about Nicholson preceding the Orange Bowl, he infuriated the Pennsylvania chapter of the National Organization for Women (NOW), and they demanded an apology and his resignation.

> *There's some tough—there's so many people gravitating to these kids. He may not have even known what he was getting into, Nicholson. They knock on the door; somebody may knock on the door; a cute girl knocks on the door. What do you do? Geez. I hope—thank God they don't knock on my door because I'd refer them to a couple of other rooms. But that's too bad. You hate to see that. I really do. You like to see a kid end up his football career. He's a heck of a football player, by the way; he's a really good football player. And it's just too bad.*

Paterno has won more bowl games than any other coach, but women's rights advocates do not consider his record so stellar. "There is just something he does not get or take seriously about violence against women," said Kathy Miller of the Pennsylvania chapter of NOW (CBS Philadelphia, January 1, 2006).

After his team lost 17-14 to Texas in 1990, Paterno was reported to have said, "I'm going home and beat my wife" (Nack & Munson, 1995). Although this quotation may be taken out of context, given Coach Paterno's reputation as a family man, this type of remark, even if it is sarcastic, reflects a tolerance of such behavior that makes some listeners bristle.

3. And then there was Kobe Bryant. Many details flew around the sexual assault allegations made by a 19-year-old employee of a Vail, Colorado, hotel where Kobe was staying in June 2003. Much of it played out exactly as expected. Allegations come up that a star athlete raped a girl. An African American multimillionaire who any girl would want (or who could have any girl he wanted?) was accused of raping a white adolescent. He denied that he did anything wrong. He hired a high-powered team of attorneys. They proceeded to do what hired guns do. They walked the line perilously close to contempt, bastardizing the rape shield laws developed to protect the identity of the victim and prevent the use of past behavior as evidence in a current charge. They eventually conceded that the sex between the two was consensual and that she, in effect, was a promiscuous, substance-abusing opportunist. Despite judge's orders, her name, which later became more publicly available than the *National Enquirer*, was repeatedly stated in court proceedings. The victim became increasingly intimidated and believed that she would be crucified on the stand.

She did not exactly help matters. It was reported that she used money from the victims' compensation fund that she later had to repay ($20,000) when she decided not to proceed with the trial, although she was willing to proceed with a civil trial that was settled later. The evidence, it was reported, included the victim's having semen from at least one other person in her or on her clothes. The inconsistency in what witnesses reported was troubling. In short, the evidence in this case, even if Kobe was 100 percent guilty, made a conviction practically impossible. There is a huge difference between innocent and not guilty, and many believed that Kobe was guilty but unconvictable.

We can attack the logic on both sides. Kobe is young, rich, and attractive. He would not have to force himself on a woman. And he has a beautiful wife—why would he cheat? He admitted that he cheated. Why? We would have to ask him. The most probable answer is because he could. Furthermore, why would a young, rich, attractive man not want his desires met? The irony is that somehow he was portrayed to be the victim. Considering the money that he lost in investments and the money that he spent on jewelry and other "please forgive me" gifts to his wife, we might say that he lost, but he was no victim. He was in the situation because he put himself in the situation, and if in fact the sex was consensual, he was at the least an adulterer and even more tragically was hustled by a 19-year-old girl.

As for the victim, she lost either way. If she in fact was raped, and the only two people who truly know both have serious credibility issues, it is shameful that the guilty party walked free. Many women never have the courage to even report the crime to the police, let alone stand trial. But she initiated the process and was later scared off, which only cemented the fear, the paranoia, and the realization that no one believed her. I hope that she gets the counseling that she needs and can somehow put her life back together. By the way, legally and in my view, if she said no at any time, even right up to when he penetrated her and proceeded anyway, he is guilty. If, however, she was setting a trap, I am not sad. I am angry—angry because one false report (and they do not happen often) kills the credibility of many legitimate victims, making them more afraid to come forward and more susceptible to the character assassination that they face when they make the allegations. The misogynist masses are more concerned with their beloved hero hitting a game-winning home run or netting the overtime goal than a woman who was violated. Anything that interferes with justice is a problem. No one deserves to have her or his body violated—woman or man, black or white, straight or gay, athlete or nonathlete. We all deserve, at the bare minimum, the sanctity of our bodies.

Being in a Male Group in College

Most research that concludes that athletes are more likely to commit rape and endorse rape-supportive thinking finds the same things about those who belong to fraternities. These two groups stand out for three reasons.

The first reason has more to do with research methodology than anything else. The two groups stand out from any other groups on campus, not to mention that they may overlap. Good research examines issues on multiple levels, but one of the more important components is comparing like groups. Rather than comparing athletes with nonathletes, the research should look at the percentage of athletes who engage in sexually inappropriate behavior or rape-supportive thinking and compare it with the percentage of non-athletes who do the same. The statistical significance of the difference is then determined. Another improvement on standard methods would be to match athletes with their true nonathlete peers, not Psych 101 students who have to participate in a research project as part of their course requirements. Methodological flaws need to be ironed out.

Involvement in a fraternity is not necessarily a bad activity, but it could negatively influence a young man's behaviors. Groupthink, especially paired with alcohol or drugs, can alter an individual's actions, and the results could be devastating.

© David C Ellis/Taxi/Getty Images

The second reason, which is obvious and does not require much more attention than what was afforded it in chapter 6, is the prevalence of drugs and alcohol use in places that both of these groups occupy. Binge drinking and recreational drug use are commonplace at college parties, which creates a domain ripe for sexual exploitation. Inhibitions may dissipate and some drugs, such as ecstasy, may increase a person's libido. Legally, a woman who binge drinks to the point where she cannot say no or defend herself does not forfeit her right to her body. Some women who have drunk to excess have engaged in sex and then regretted it or believed that they were slipped a drug. Legally, they were not able to give consent, so if they had sex then technically they were sexually assaulted. A way to prevent this from happening is to avoid binge drinking, to stay in control. This practice is part of date rape prevention programming.

The third reason that these two groups stand out is group dynamics. When people join a group, being part of the group affects how they think and act. Often, when they are part of a highly cohesive group, people act less like who they are when they are alone. Group norms can have a powerful effect on leading people to engage in behaviors as part of a group that they would never consider alone. Sometimes the behaviors are in direct contrast to the person's morals.

Psychologist Irving Janis coined the term *groupthink* in 1972 to describe the process by which groups make bad decisions when each member conforms to what he or she believes to be the group consensus. This idea was originally postulated to study foreign policy decisions such as those made leading up to the attack on Pearl Harbor or those involving the Vietnam War. The idea can apply to how fraternity or sport team members endorse decisions or behaviors that may ordinarily be discarded.

The power of group dynamics is impressive. For that reason, date rape prevention models that are bystander driven or work on a peer-mentoring basis are not sufficient to solve the problems. One such program is the Mentors in Violence Prevention (MVP program) developed in 1993 by Northeastern University's Center for the Study of Sport in Society, which was founded by Dr. Richard Lapchick. They deserve kudos for developing a mixed-gender, racially diverse team to deliver these services and have been able to deliver more dating violence prevention training to athletes than any other organization. Although they have been tremendously effective in reaching high school and college populations, have moved away from single-session workshops, and offer fairly comprehensive programming, the problem is that the program is based on a bystander model.

Their Web site describes their program this way:

> *Utilizing a unique bystander approach to prevention, the MVP program views student–athletes and student leaders not as potential perpetrators or victims, but as empowered bystanders who can confront abusive peers. This emphasis reduces the defensiveness men often feel and the helplessness women often feel when discussing issues of men's violence against women.*

> *The MVP approach does not involve finger pointing, nor does it blame participants for the widespread problem of gender violence. Instead it sounds a positive call for proactive, preventive behavior and leadership.*

The problem is that some perpetrators respond only to direct confrontation and consequences. The delicate balance required is to avoid stereotyping athletes as rapists but at the same time hold them accountable for their own behavior first and then have them focus on being good role models and leaders to prevent abusive behavior from occurring around them.

I will provide an example to demonstrate the point. A first-year point guard is logging serious minutes and is becoming a leader on the court, but there is no question that he is a rookie. Big for the position, he is 6 feet, 5 inches (196 centimeters) tall, but his height does not give him extra influence with the team; it just keeps him from being singled out as the "little guy." The seniors run the team. They happen to be a group of guys who keep score of the "notches on their belts." The players are out one evening and discussing plans for the night, trying to figure out where the most sexual opportunities will be available and how they might achieve those ends. In the midst of it all, one of the players says that his girlfriend recently broke up with him. One of his teammates suggests that he get back at her by having sex with as many women as he can, even inviting him to participate in an alcohol-assisted orgy. Now do you really believe that this rookie is going to be able to step up and get the older guys to reconsider their ways? It is possible, but the person would have to be extremely strong. He would likely be risking his status as a member of the team. His opposition to the established norms might lead to his being ostracized, singled out as not being "one of them." The bystander approach is a great idea, but unique circumstances are required for it to be consistently effective as the sole intervention strategy.

Lack of Consequences

Ask yourself this question: If you are the coach of a Division I revenue-producing football team and an athlete on your team is arrested on allegations of rape, do you treat him as innocent until proven guilty? Why? Is it because of your faith in the criminal justice system? We are not talking about the player being brought in for questioning. He was arrested and charges were pressed, so some evidence is required. The district attorney's office will later decide whether the evidence to proceed with prosecution is sufficient, whether a deal can be made, or whether any other option is available in the criminal justice system (pretrial intervention, suspended sentence). Do you have your answer?

OK, now imagine that the victim who is pressing charges is your daughter. Would it change your view? Perhaps the safest place the athlete could be would be in jail where you could not act out on your own angry vengeance.

Every victim is someone's daughter, sister, girlfriend, mother, and so on. We need to take these crimes seriously and not be so aloof to right and wrong that we selectively attend to these matters so that athletes can play in the big game for us. Consequences to these behaviors must be swift and fair. If they are not, the problem will continue and likely worsen.

Have you ever wondered why bullies generally do not stop? If I rob you of your lunch money and do not get in trouble, I got reinforced for my behavior by having your money. And the athlete who is able to take sex from someone without consequences is reinforced as well. Why would he stop? After all, police officers are not driving around just looking for people to arrest and charge with rape. And most people who finally make it to state prison have committed several crimes for which they are never convicted.

Personally, I believe that athletes who are arrested and will be arraigned on criminal charges should be suspended from athletic participation until those charges are concluded. One might argue that this approach assumes them to be guilty before they are convicted. It does not. It states that they engaged in behavior that disparages the institution in which they are enrolled—most schools have disciplinary codes that they have violated—and their suspension is pending a criminal decision.

This approach achieves a couple of objectives. First, it says clearly that the organization will not tolerate criminal behavior and that those who engage in it jeopardize their athletic careers. Second, it deters the delaying of criminal proceedings to be convenient for the athlete's participation in the sport schedule. To be fair, an athlete found not guilty should be granted an additional year of NCAA eligibility. If an athlete is found guilty, the criminal justice system can dictate the sentence, but the NCAA, the school, or the organization may mete out further sanctions. An unequivocal message of zero tolerance is needed. When an athlete is falsely accused, all parties have the responsibility to restore the person's reputation to good favor.

To extend this topic further, the consequences for all involved parties should be considered when deciding whether to have a preventative program in place. What are the consequences for the victim?

Anyone who understands the process of achieving a conviction for a rape knows why it is so improbable that a woman would press charges for a rape that did not occur. When a woman wants to report a rape and is taken to an emergency room for an examination, she has to go through what is called a rape kit. This protocol is used to examine the victim, obtain physical evidence to be turned over to the police for prosecution, and determine the need for further treatment. The process is not physically painful, but it is potentially humiliating, and the recently victimized woman will likely experience it as retraumatization. The following is a sample of the protocol used in a local hospital. Slight variations may occur in different jurisdictions.

Rape Kit

1. The attending nurse should individually bag each article of the victim's clothing to be submitted to the investigating police officer or directly to the crime laboratory. Place panties in the bag provided; use larger paper bags or containers for other clothing.

2. Comb the pubic hair region with the comb provided to recover any foreign hair which may have been deposited by the assailant. Place the comb in the envelope provided; seal and initial the envelope.

3. Examine the patient for visible blood or seminal stains; if such stains are observed, moisten one of the gauze pads with water and remove the stain onto the pad. Allow the pad to air dry and place it in one of the plastic bags provided. Document properly, including the area swabbed.

4. Obtain pubic hair control sample (10 to 15) from the victim—preferably pulled, otherwise cut very close to the skin.

5. During the normal vaginal exam please do not lubricate. Use one set of swabs to prepare two vaginal smears on the microscope slides provided. Spray the slides with a cytological fixative (if available) and allow the slides to air dry for three to five minutes. When the slides are dry, label them as vaginal smears and place them into the mailer. Obtain two additional swabs from each of the vaginal and cervical walls and label the swabs as vaginal swabs and cervical swabs, respectively. Please air dry all swabs before placing them in protective envelopes.

6. Examine the fingernails for any blood, hair, or foreign tissue. Scrape under the nails with the wooden splints provided (over a clean white paper; if blood is present, clip the nails).

7. Obtain oral samples by swabbing the mouth with two swabs. Label as oral swabs. Collect a second saliva control on the filter paper disk provided (spittle from the patient onto disk is adequate); this would be used to determine secretor status. If oral genital contact is indicated, please document.

8. If genital anal contact is indicated, prepare anal smears (for spermatozoa) and submit an anal swab.

9. Obtain a blood sample from the victim for later typing. A second tube of blood should be collected and summated to the hospital clinical laboratory for normal serology, pregnancy test, CBC, and so on.

10. Obtain a representative head hair sample (10 to 15)—preferably pulled, otherwise cut very close to the scalp. Place in the envelope provided.

Place all the evidence collected in the original box, seal the box, and place an evidence seal on each side. Provide information requested. Submit this kit in person to the investigating officer or directly to the crime laboratory.

Although an incident is enough to make many victims terrified of leaving home for fear of being revictimized, the rape kit alone can deter women from pressing charges. It is one of the reasons that rape is significantly underreported.

Then the woman has the fear that no one will believe her, that somehow it was her fault. The scrutiny goes like this: "What did you do? Why did you lead him on? You can't get a guy going and then just stop." So if the woman is courageous enough to go to the hospital to get the rape kit and cooperate with the prosecutor's office, then she has her whole life story dragged across the coals during cross-examination.

Throughout the country rape shield laws have been developed (Arizona is the only state that does not have such legislation in place) to prevent a victim's previous sexual history from being used as evidence against her to undermine the credibility of her testimony in any criminal or civil proceeding regarding sexual misconduct. As can be seen in the Kobe Bryant case, however, high-powered attorneys have found their away around rape shield laws in the past.

Remember that in criminal cases the standard of proof is "beyond a reasonable doubt," which means that the case must be proved to the extent that there is no reasonable doubt in the mind of a reasonable person that the defendant is guilty. In contrast, in civil trials the standard is that the "preponderance of evidence" indicates that the proposition is more likely to be true than not. Probabilistically, "preponderance of the evidence," which is the standard of proof used in civil cases, is equated to better than 50% certainty. "Beyond a reasonable doubt," which is used in criminal trials, is a much higher standard of proof. Though it is sometimes estimated as over 90% certainty, in the legal world, caution is used when putting a statistical number on what reasonable doubt means because doing so can create more confusion than clarification Thus O.J. Simpson was found not guilty in a criminal case but responsible in a civil case and ordered to pay damages.

Winning a conviction is difficult, so charges are often dropped and justice is never served.

Table 9.1 outlines just some of the consequences that the relative parties can face.

For athletes, the consequences can be severe. They should be aware that laws have changed. Men can be vulnerable if they are not educated about legal terms and the criteria for ability to give consent.

For institutions and athletics departments, these allegations are public relations nightmares. I have on occasion been retained to offer workshops after an incident has occurred, as if I could somehow undo what happened. Organizations go into damage control because the bad press can spiral out of control. The institution may also face legal culpability, especially if Title IX allows rape victims to sue the deep pockets of the university. In addition,

Table 9.1 Consequences When an Athlete Is Charged With Sexual Assault

Victim	Athlete	Athletics department
Shame, isolation, fear – not knowing who they can talk to, who will believe them and who may make the problem worse, victims are at risk to turn in on themselves.	Suspension from participation. During the time that there is an investigation, an athlete will often (and should be) withdrawn from the opportunity to participate in athletic/team activities.	Bad press—the media swarms on such stories and this is not beneficial for the university.
Anger, depression, anxiety— these are common emotional reactions of survivors of sexual assault.	Expulsion from the school/team for violating conduct policy is a conclusion that can be considered should the allegation be found to be substantiated.	Recruiting problems—often this leads parents to steer their children away from programs that are associated with "bad behavior." This, in turn, can make it difficult to compete.
Post-traumatic stress disorder—this can include flashbacks, nightmares, avoidance of things that remind them of the event, hypersensitivity and paranoia. Treatment by mental health professionals is indicated.	Incarceration—depending upon the severity of the offense, the athlete may await trial in jail. If not, but found guilty, jail and/or prison is likely.	Loss of money—besides difficulty recruiting athletes, parents may steer their non-athlete, prospective students away from universities that tolerate such behavior. This can lead to significant decrease in tuition.

many parents will not want their daughters to enroll in an institution that tolerates such behavior. This failure to attract new students can result in a significant loss of revenue. The school's best approach is to put programs in place prophylactically and proactively.

Some schools bring in speakers in a CYA (cover your ass) move so as to say, "Well, we provided workshops, but that individual is just a bad egg who needed more than we could prudently know to provide." This approach may protect them legally, which is fine as long as the services are really delivered. Institutions should also be educated to identify those people (athletes and otherwise) who should be referred for more services than they can provide. I believe that the perpetrator of any sex crime should be responsible, besides everything else, to pay for the treatment of the victim, both medically and psychologically. If the athlete is in school only through being on a scholarship, then perhaps the school should pay for the victim's treatment.

NECESSARY COMPONENTS OF A DATING VIOLENCE PREVENTION PROGRAM

Providing dating violence prevention programs or workshops is difficult work to begin with. Often, males in the audience hear it as a round of male bashing. Providing such training to athletes is even more difficult. The qualities listed here give such programming the best chance to reach its audience.

Having a Solid Knowledge of Legalese

Those who provide dating violence prevention workshops need to be familiar with the laws that govern their locale and the basic terms and premises used in statutes related to those crimes.

Sexual contact that can lead to criminal prosecution is not limited to vaginal sexual intercourse. It can be touching another person's sexual parts with the hand, mouth, anus, or own genitals. To be criminal, the sexual contact must be without the person's consent.

In most states, lack of consent results from forcible compulsion or incapacity to consent. Forcible compulsion means either by use of physical force or a threat, expressed or implied, that places a person in fear of death or physical harm to her- or himself or another person if she or he does not comply. Not having the capacity to give consent is based on one of four conditions:

1. Mentally defective—suffering from a mental disease or defect that renders the person incapable of appraising the nature of her or his conduct

2. Mentally incapacitated—temporarily incapable of appraising or controlling her or his conduct because of drugs or alcohol administered to the person

3. Physically helpless—unconscious or for any other reason is unable to communicate unwillingness

4. Younger than a statutory-denoted age

In some states, a man cannot be charged for raping his wife. Even if all the criteria listed earlier are met, if the two are married, the act cannot be considered rape in some jurisdictions.

In statutory situations, if both members are underage, the perpetrator can still be charged.

If both male and female are drunk to the point of oblivion and the next day she states that she did not give consent and the act was against her will, she could press charges regardless of the fact that he too may have been unable to give consent. Relevant here is the fact that when inebriated, the man is less likely to read sexual cues appropriately, thus increasing the likelihood of sexual transgressions.

These legal intricacies seem unfair to many men. Laws have swung far back to the conservative side because convicting men who were guilty of these crimes was difficult for a long time. Some have argued that the laws have gone too far. In any case, young athletes should be educated about these issues because their fantasies of being untouchable can quickly grind to a halt. Whether one believes that the laws are unfair does not matter. It is what it is.

Knowing What Jail or Prison Is Like

I may be biased because of my work in prison, but I believe that if we want the worst-case scenario to be a deterrent, we should be able to tell athletes about the prison environment.

It has crossed my mind to take teams to Scared Straight programs. Scared Straight is a lifer's group developed at East Jersey State Prison (one of the prisons in which I oversee mental health), formerly known as Rahway State Prison. Hardened criminals with life sentences confront young men with the realities of prison to deter them from future wrongdoings. In-your-face berating and descriptions of the dangerous details of life in prison can change a person's mind about future criminal behaviors. This approach is particularly needed because in many urban areas doing time in prison is glamorized. Providing real information about what jail and prison are like may deter some athletes from engaging in criminal behavior.

Inmates can expect to be double bunked. Property, visits, phone calls, and privileges are restricted. Although some inmates get better medical and mental health treatment in prison than they would ever get on the streets, they are aware of an undeniable power differential because they are not in charge. There are the threats of rape and murder. People have their property stolen. Inmates can be recruited to join a gang for their own protection, but gang members may threaten to kill a family member if orders are not followed. The fine print in the gang membership agreement has no mention of a retirement program.

Those who have money and can afford good representation may be able to get a plea or a deal and avoid time. "If you cannot afford an attorney," Chris Rock in *Lethal Weapon 4* offered, "we will appoint you the stupidest lawyer we can find." Those convicted generally have to do about seven months on each year sentenced, but they will be different people when they are released.

Being Comfortable Talking About Sex

Anyone who does prevention work on a sexual topic must be comfortable talking about it in explicit detail. Presenters who are likely to be embarrassed by athletes' use of vulgarities or their talk about sex in slang or street terms will lose the audience.

Moreover, when the audience is male, the presenter should probably be a male. Even an excellent, engaging female speaker is likely to be considered a male basher. The best set of circumstances is a male and female team that can play off each other, model appropriate male–female interactions, and deflect attacks from the audience away from one another.

The sex of the speaker is less of an issue if the audience is female. Workshops for dating violence prevention for females tend to focus on staying in control and drinking moderately. These programs resemble a supportive coaching session rather than a finger-wagging lecture.

Hearing from another man that rape is unacceptable is much different than hearing it from a woman. That is not to say that presenting on the topic is easy. Men who do these workshops often have their masculinity questioned (because homophobia is almost a given). Rebounding from these challenges and staying on task can be difficult.

To extend this point, the presenter must be familiar with the many phrases related to sexuality that are not found in textbooks. Restrictions on language lead to restrictions on discussion. By not censoring the athletes' speech, the presenter makes it safer for the audience to process the material discussed. If the presenter is going to challenge myths, familiarity with sexual terms is critical. On pages 233 and 234 are two handouts that are particularly helpful when providing acquaintance rape prevention workshops. The handouts are from Dr. Thomas Jackson's book *Acquaintance Rape: Assessment, Treatment, and Prevention*. This book also has a prevention program specifically designed for athletes.

Their program focuses on seven steps:

- Step 1. The general incidence, prevalence, attitudes, and rape myth components are presented.
- Step 2. The special role of athletes in society is explained. The idea of their being role models and being held to a different set of standards is discussed.
- Step 3. Athletes are told that their status as public figures requires them to use appropriate social skills in public life as part of the general obligation of giving back to the community.
- Step 4. Data demonstrating athletes' incidence rates is shared. They must learn to distinguish the dominating, win-at-all-costs mentality used on the field from appropriate social interactions.
- Step 5. The cost of rape to the perpetrator and his associates is highlighted. Discussion includes the potential for suspension, expulsion, and jail as well as serious negative consequences to the team and school even if criminal charges are not filed.
- Step 6. The possible desensitization of athletes is discussed. Because some coaches stress discipline and a general repression of emotions and feelings, athletes may be vulnerable to either victimization or perpetration because they may miss cues that would warn more sensitive people that they are either about to be taken advantage of or about to cross a boundary with someone else.
- Step 7. Safe dating skills, good sexual communication, and relationship rights are presented.

Do you know that "blue balls" is a fatal condition? *Blue balls* is a term that denotes the discomfort associated with achieving an erection, possibly engaging in some form of stimulation, and then not culminating with ejaculation. Many men have accused a young lady of leading them on and then not being able to stop. Some use the fear of the dreaded blue balls, and some just say that they could not stop.

Imagine this scenario: A hockey player, very popular in school, finds himself alone in his dorm room with a female student. They both have a few beers. They like each other, and she kisses him. Somewhat surprised, he is also happy. This progresses as she unsnaps her bra and takes off her shirt, inviting him to fondle her breasts. Is he getting excited? You bet. They continue to fool around for a bit longer, and he takes his penis out of his pants. She states that she does not want to go any further. She likes kissing him but does not feel comfortable yet. He urges her to masturbate him—after all, that is the least she can do considering she took off her clothes first. Reluctantly, she starts to oblige. He forgets that he had to guilt her into her actions and assumes that her fondling him is a sign that she wants more. He pulls down her pants and attempts to enter her. She says no and asks him to stop, somewhat confused about how things progressed so quickly. He asks her to spread her legs, and she says no. He thinks she is teasing him and becomes frustrated. She starts to feel guilty that she may be giving mixed messages and does not fight for long, eventually succumbing to his advances. Stating that she is not on birth control, she pleads for him at least not to ejaculate in her because she does not want to get pregnant. He ignores her and ejaculates in her, not thinking that he did anything wrong and seemingly oblivious to the sexual assault that he just completed. "Why the fuck did you do that?" she berates. He replies, "You started the whole thing when you took off your top and jerked me off. Besides, I couldn't stop once you got me going."

Suppose the same situation occurred except that her father is walking up the stairs. Do you think he could stop? You bet he could.

The salient point is that those who do these types of prevention programs for athletes need to be aware of sexual issues, be comfortable talking about them, and be knowledgeable enough about athlete culture to gain the athletes' trust to discuss these issues.

Talking About the Involvement of Drugs and Alcohol in Sexual Violence

Although chapter 6 explained the relationship between drugs and alcohol and violence, these topics must be covered in a slightly different way when discussing dating violence prevention. In date rape situations, drugs or alcohol can be used as a weapon to weaken a person's resistance to advances, to increase the likelihood of disorientation, or even to knock the person out cold. Many victims of what have been called date rape drugs have awakened to find one or many men engaging in sexual acts to them.

The weakening of inhibitions can apply to both a potential victim and a potential perpetrator. Furthermore, dwindling inhibitions can enhance group dynamics. I once heard a presenter sum it up this way: "You take a young man who is a follower and really wants to be part of a group, place him in that group in a social setting, and add alcohol? You have instant idiot!"

Grain alcohol or Everclear added to punch or drinks imparts little taste. Recipients will not realize that they are drinking very high-proof alcohol. Date rape drugs such as Rohypnol (roofies), ketamine and gamma-hydroxybutyrate (GHB) all can be slipped to victims who do not realize that they were drugged. Sometimes, they do not remember anything, even after they wake up. The larger the crowd of people is, the easier it is for something to be slipped into a drink if the victim is not careful. Women need to be aware and be cautious. They should always go to parties with a friend and avoid drinking from open containers.

Table 9.2 shows drugs of abuse that have been associated with date rapes as well as some of their common street names.

Athletes must remember that if they or the victim was using drugs or alcohol, circumstances may explain what happened, but they will never excuse it.

Table 9.2 Drugs Commonly Used in Date Rapes

Drug name	Class and origin	Street name
Rohypnol	Benzodiazepine (antianxiety CNS depressant) similar to Ativan and Xanax but much more potent and unavailable in the United States.	Roofies
Ketamine	Dissociative anesthetic similar to nitrous oxide. Still used as anesthetic for humans as well as animals in veterinary medicine.	Special K, K, cat valiums
Methylene dioxymethamphetamine (MDMA)	Mood elevator giving relaxed, euphoric state. Has sometimes been associated with increased sexuality because of enhanced sensations and heightened feelings of empathy, emotional warmth, and self-acceptance.	Ecstasy, XTC, X, Adam
Methamphetamine	Stimulant—produces alertness and confidence, and raises levels of energy and stamina. Also reduces appetite and lessens the desire and ability to sleep.	Speed, ice, chalk, meth, crystal meth, crank, fire
Gamma-hydroxybutyrate (GHB)	Sedative-hypnotic originally developed as a sleep aid. High doses can cause temporary coma or even death.	Grievous bodily harm, G, liquid ecstasy, Georgia home boy
Lysergic acid diethylamide (LSD)	Hallucinogenic or psychedelic drug. Leads to "trips" in which the user may have poor judgment and has the potential for psychotic symptoms.	Acid, boomers, yellow

SUMMARY OF PROGRAM PHILOSOPHIES

Unfortunately, the programs that are least helpful to athletes are the standard university programs geared toward athletes and nonathletes alike. These programs often identify athletes as violent people who must be "changed" to protect potential victims. The approach is predominantly male bashing, it overgeneralizes and implicates nonviolent athletes (who happen to be in the majority), and it is accusatory, often leading to defensiveness that limits any potential success that the approach might have. The actual workshop is often a single hour-long presentation that has variable attendance and generates more resentment among male athletes than changes in thinking.

The second method that programs use to tackle this problem is to have athletes guide their peers toward the idea that dating violence is unacceptable. This approach is consistent with the MVP program from Northeastern University and improves on the first position by increasing the quality and quantity of education. It empowers the athlete to be a bystander who intervenes, and it is nonpejorative. The problems with this approach are that it fails to establish accountability among potential perpetrators in the audience, it implies that the problem is easier to solve than it is, and it underestimates the power of group dynamics, especially on male sports teams.

In my opinion, the best programs are those that arise from the mentor model to include teaching responsibility and skills to allow athletes to reach their goals without hurting anyone else in the process. Such programs make dating violence an athletes' issue. They confront erroneous beliefs when necessary and recognize the athletes' "at-risk" position that results from their popularity. The approach is one of working *with* athletes, not working *on* them. The best programs also include clinical methods to confront anger management issues and trauma-related symptomology.

Examples of such programs are Dr. Tom Jackson's program at the University of Arkansas (discussed earlier in this chapter) and the program developed by Dr. Andrea Parrott and colleagues in conjunction with head football coach Jim Hofher at Cornell University. Parrott described this program in her book *Rape 101: Sexual Assault Prevention for College Athletes*. The appendix contains an outline of the date rape prevention program that I have been using for the past several years with favorable response from my audiences.

Reviewing the characteristics of rapists and rape victims can open the conversation about the myths of rape. The handouts included on the next two pages outline the topic nicely. The reason why these handouts are so useful when doing dating violence prevention work is that athletes, when hearing some of the myths, will often shout out in agreement only to be surprised moments later that they don't understand the issues. This provides excellent material to propagate conversations about difficult topics.

Common Characteristics and Facts

Characteristics of the Rapist

1. The overwhelming majority of rapists are male. In rare cases the rapist is female.
2. Rapists come from every socioeconomic status level and every walk of life. Rapists are not only unemployed blue-collar workers but also professionals.
3. Less than 5 percent of rapists were considered mentally unstable when they were arrested.
4. The majority of rapists know their victim and the victim knows them. They are the victim's neighbor, friend, date, banker, and so forth.
5. Rapists can be any age from 12 to 80 years of age. Statistically, rapists between the ages of 17 and 28 are most prevalent.
6. Rapists can be from any minority or majority group. In general, black men rape black women and white men rape white women.
7. Rapists can be dirty and smelly, but they are just as likely to be clean cut, big-man-on-campus types.
8. Most rapists have at least one consenting sexual partner. They are not raping because they are hard up.
9. Rapists are repeat offenders.

Characteristics of the Victim

1. The victim is almost always female. Male rape is increasing, however, and does occur in settings other than prisons.
2. Victims can be from every walk of life and every socioeconomic class. They are from all races and religions and range in age from a few months to 90 years. Statistically, the age range that is most prone to be raped is 16 to 24.
3. Attractive, unattractive, slender, and overweight women are all raped. The rapist is not looking for an attractive woman to have sex with but for an available, easy target.
4. Victims are never to blame for the rape. A report for the Federal Commission on Crimes of Violence states that only 4 percent of reported rapes involved any precipitative behavior on the part of the victim, including how they dress.

Characteristics of the Rape

1. The majority of rapes occur at night and on weekends, but a high incidence of rape occurs throughout the day and the rest of the week.
2. Rapes do occur in deserted areas such as parking lots and parks, but the majority of rapes occur in the victim's home.
3. Rape is, by definition, a violent crime. Fortunately, however, few victims suffer severe injury or death.
4. Weapons such as guns and knives are used, but rapists more commonly use physical force and threats.

Adapted from K. Caroll and T.L. Jackson, 1996, Rape education prevention training. In *Acquaintance Rape: Assessment, treatment and prevention* (Sarasota, FL: Professional Resource Exchange, Inc.), 190-191.

Common Myths and Facts About Rape

1. **There is no such thing as rape**. This myth goes along with the myth "It's impossible to rape a woman." The statement is incorrect. Rapists are generally stronger and meaner than their victims. They also often have weapons. If a woman is in shock or fears for her life, she is not likely to put up an effective fight and be able to avoid rape.

2. **Women cry rape**. Rape has the same false report rate as other serious violent crimes such as assault and kidnapping.

3. **Rape is easy to prosecute**. Rape is not easy to prosecute. Finding the rapist, let alone convicting him, is difficult. The court proceedings are complex, and the conviction rate is low.

4. **She says no, but she means yes**. When a woman says no, she means no. Statistics point out that 75 percent of men acted on the belief that when a woman said no she meant yes. At the very least this is poor communication, and at the worst it is rape.

5. **After sex starts, men cannot stop**. No physiological reason prevents a man from being able to stop his sexual behavior. A certain degree of discomfort may accompany coitus interruptus, but it is not lethal. Furthermore, if a woman's father walked in while she and her boyfriend were in the act, there is no question that he would be able to stop. Men just need to realize that they can stop as long as they want to.

6. **Women like a "real man."** Some men think that women like a take-charge kind of guy who is persistent and perhaps even rough. But this is a new time. A very few women may like "real men," but most women want to make their own decisions and have those decisions respected, especially their decisions about matters as intimate as sex.

7. **Prior sex? Then a woman cannot say no**. The fact that a man had sex with a woman before, or dated her for three years, or even is married to her does not give him an inalienable right to have sex with her when she does not want to.

8. **If a woman is too drunk to say no, it is not rape**. A sexual act is legally rape if a woman is too drunk to give informed consent.

9. **Pain of rape ends with the assault**. The victim's suffering only begins with the act itself. She has the rest of her life to live with the fact that someone could take away every bit of control that she believed she had over her life.

10. **Women do stupid things and therefore ask to be raped**. A woman may dress suggestively, drink too much, walk in unsafe places, or even flirt with the wrong people, but her punishment for not using good judgment should never be rape.

Data from T.L. Jackson, 1996, *Acquaintance rape: Assessment, treatment & prevention* (Sarasota, FL: Professional Resource Press); R. Warsaw, 1988, *I never called it rape: The Ms. Report on recognizing, fighting and surviving date and acquaintance rape* (New York: Harper & Row).

SUMMARY

In this last chapter of the book we tackled the issue of dating and sexual violence prevention among athletes. This topic was included because studies have pointed to athletes' disproportionate representation among perpetrators of such deviant behavior. Furthermore, these behaviors are related to impulse control problems, which are similar to anger management problems.

Dating violence prevention programs are important for athletes because they often have a sense of entitlement, believe that their coaches will fix problems that they get into, and think that they will face few consequences. Many facets of male athlete culture (which include the need to assert one's "manliness" and the power of groupthink) may contribute to this problem.

We reviewed that all parties involved in an incident of date rape experience negative effects, although not in equal proportions or gravity. The athlete, team, sports program, and university may face negative consequences. A single event may produce several victims. At the same time, we described the experience of being examined as part of a rape kit to generate empathy for victims, to illustrate why rape is not false reported more than other crimes are, and to explain why many victims never come forward.

The chapter concluded with a discussion of the necessary components of effective dating violence prevention programs. The point was made that single-session interventions do not suffice, that ideal programs cover several components of deviant sexual behavior, and that those who provide these workshops need to have a good understanding of the law, be comfortable talking about sensitive sexual issues, and be knowledgeable about how drugs and alcohol contribute to the likelihood of sexual transgressions.

As seen throughout this book, many people associate athletes with various forms of violence. Although little evidence supports this notion, failing to provide athletes with programs that can help prevent their involvement in violent transgressions would be a mistake. The goal of this book was to start that discussion and describe the program elements necessary to meet that need. I encourage you to build from here.

Epilogue

Four years after this book was originally contracted, I found myself reflecting on the content of the book, the dynamics involved in anger and violence in sport, and the progress made in examining this topic in the public's view. I was struck by an image that replayed through my mind several times, one I had seen only hours earlier in the AFC Championship Game between the Pittsburgh Steelers and Baltimore Ravens. With 3 minutes and 29 seconds remaining in the game, Ravens running back Willis McGahee caught a pass from quarterback Joe Flacco and turned upfield in the hope of putting his team back into the game with time running out. Equally determined to prevent this from happening, Steelers safety Ryan Clark unleashed a thunderous hit on McGahee, snapping McGahee's head back and leaving both men immobile on the field. Woozy, Clark made his way to the sideline with the assistance of Pittsburgh staff. McGahee was not so fortunate. He remained on the turf for many minutes before being placed on a stretcher. A collar was placed on his neck to stabilize it, and McGahee was ultimately removed from the field. A look of concern was seen on the faces of both teammates and opponents. A violent sport, with many thrills and cheers, ground to a halt when a big hit unintentionally did more damage than was intended.

What was striking to me was that had the injury been less severe, people's reaction would have been far different. A fine line separates wanting to dominate the opponent and wanting to cause serious injury. Athletes cannot focus on this component of sport lest it distract them from their game plan. Concern for the well-being of an opponent provides an opening for fear and doubt to enter their psyche and diverts them from focusing on the task at hand. Injuries are part of the game. But we need to remember that high-speed collisions in sport can have devastating consequences. For football and hockey, the evolution of the game may be best described by physics: $F = M \times A$, or force equals mass times acceleration. So as the players become bigger and faster, they hit with greater force, increasing the risk of injury.

Why now, at the culmination of this book, am I focusing on this point? The reason is that the issue of violence in sports is complex, and this example captures its complexity. People love to watch football. About 100 million Americans view the Super Bowl each year. We love being amazed by the circus catch, the feats of athleticism, and yes, the bone-crushing hits that communicate unequivocally that one man (representing one team) dominated another. We cheer this, we enjoy this, we encourage this . . . until a serious injury occurs and everyone involved sees that the event boils down to being about people. People are committed to winning, to performing at their best, to running around, over, and through others to achieve their goals. They are trained to be aggressive. They ignore pain and injury to pursue their goals. The willingness to train hard and the courage to persevere are prerequisites to excellence. Whatever the sport, athletes must have determination and hunger to become the best. Having the requisite physical attributes, good technique, and discipline must be at the foundation, but without the necessary drive, the sculpture of success crumbles into dust.

Although these characteristics often separate the wheat from the chaff in athletics, athletes have much in common with their nonathlete peers. All people seem to be increasingly unable to control their impulses, especially their angry impulses, but athletes are held to a different standard. Sports violence may be considered benign in comparison with domestic violence, gang violence, sexual violence, or workplace violence, especially in the context of mass murder like that seen at Columbine High School or Virginia Tech. Nonetheless, when athletes do engage in violent or criminal behavior, greater attention is devoted to it than when nonathletes are involved because sport is so integral to our society.

This book explains why so much attention is paid to violent athletes, but more important, it illustrates the way in which the information is distorted. Research that advances the idea that athletes are more violent than nonathletes was examined and criticized for the skewed hypotheses that drove the studies. Jeffrey Benedict's exhaustive work highlighted his belief that professional athletes are a population that includes a disproportionate number of criminals. Although his data is impressive, it is not difficult to see that his statistics could point to several conclusions. He points to the one that matches his belief. He is not alone in his opinion. The sensationalism surrounding athletes' transgression is ubiquitous. Athletes need to do a better job of avoiding the negative headlines.

Studying anger and violence is a difficult task. Studying it in athletes is even more daunting. Much work needs to be done, and I am sorry to report that inadequate progress has been made in this domain over the past 10 years.

Similarly, little innovation has occurred in anger management and violence prevention programs for athletes. Improvement is needed on both angles of anger management. Further development is needed in programs to help athletes reduce the intense emotions that interfere with peak performance as well as the emotions that can lead to on-field or off-field violence. I have offered my knowledge and programs in this book. I hope that in the coming years we advance at a faster pace and that my work becomes obsolete, that it is seen as a building block for the skyscrapers built by dedicated workers in the field.

I have often wondered aloud how quickly the content of this book would become outdated. I feared that with every startling new story, those used in this text to demonstrate a point would be out of touch. To some degree, this may be true, but the themes will likely remain the same. So as we are bombarded with sensational new headlines, I hope that you ask a few basic questions:

1. Would this story matter to the media if those involved were not famous because of their involvement in sport?
2. Does being an athlete have anything to do with why this athlete did what he or she did?
3. Could we have done something to prevent the occurrence of this incident?
4. If something could have been done, why did we not do it?
5. What more can we do to help athletes control their emotions more effectively so that they can get the most of their potential in life and in sport?
6. Do we really believe that sport is the bane of our society, or does sport bring to the table many more positives than negatives?

After you answer these questions, I hope that you come to the same conclusions I have: Sports are fun! They are remarkable in their ability to build physical health, confidence, teamwork, discipline, a sense of achievement, and appreciation for the value of competition (an undeniable but often slandered component of life in the "real world"). Like many things, sport has a dark side. We need not throw the baby out with the bath water. Instead, we should shine a light on the problems and develop ways to address them.

Athletes are not more violent than nonathletes. Athletes are human. Many people in our society struggle with anger, and some athletes do as well. The goal of this book was to start the journey toward helping athletes and those working with them handle their emotions and live to their fullest potential in life. Won't you join me?

Appendix: Date Rape Prevention

SAMPLE THREE-DAY WORKSHOP

Developed by Mitch Abrams, PsyD

I. Introduction to the three-day workshop

    A. Introduction of the group leaders

    B. Reason for the workshop

    C. Beliefs of the audience

    D. Expectations of the program

    E. Overview of what will be covered over the next three days

        1. Prevalence of athlete violence

        2. Date rape and domestic violence

        3. Anger management

        4. Substance abuse

        5. Consequences

II. Component 1—incidence and dating violence

    A. Are athletes more violent?

        1. Research results

        2. Problems with the research

        3. The reality that violence, specifically domestic violence, is a problem in the United States

        4. Athletes are not insulated from such problems, may be at higher risk

    B. Prevalence of athlete violence

    C. Factors in male athlete culture that may increase the probability of dating violence

        1. Sense of entitlement

        2. Belief that "Coach will fix it"

        3. Group dynamics

        4. Alcohol and drug use

        5. Absence of severe consequences

        6. Maleness and being in an identifiable group—at risk

        7. Sexist mind-set

        8. Hostility bias

D. Date rape, domestic violence, sexual harassment, and assault

1. Definitions: popular and legal

2. Incidence rates

3. Incidence for athletes

4. Programs focused on addressing these problems

   a. Athletes are violent and must be "fixed"

   b. Peer mentoring to reduce violence, focus on the power of bystanders

   c. Comprehensive, multifaceted programs with multiple resources

5. Myths and clarification

   a. Males versus females

      i. Public perception

      ii. Frequency versus severity

      iii. Homosexual violence?

6. Characteristics of the victim or survivor

7. Characteristics of the batterer

   a. Subtypes of batterers

      i. Family only

      ii. Dysphoric or borderline

      iii. Generally violent or antisocial

   b. Cycle of violence

8. Symptomology

   a. PTSD

   b. Depression

   c. Substance abuse

   d. Anxiety disorders

   e. Rape versus domestic violence

9. Treatment issues

   a. Peers

   b. Coaches

   c. Athletics department

   d. Counseling center

   e. Clinical professionals

   f. Hospitalization

E. Sexuality

    1. Masturbation

    2. "Blue balls"

    3. "I couldn't stop"

    4. "Did you get my yes?"

III. Component 2—anger management

  A. What is it and why?

  B. Performance enhancement versus treatment of criminals

    1. Yerkes–Dodson law (inverted U hypothesis)

    2. Zone of optimal functioning

    3. Flow states

      a. Heightened sense of awareness

      b. Feeling of calm

      c. Automatized behaviors

      d. Changes in perception of time

      e. Focus

      f. Filtering out of peripheral stimuli

      g. "Doing everything right, but effortlessly"

    4. Difficulties with cognitive processing

    5. Superstitions, rituals, and slumps

  C. Definitions

    1. Anger

      a. Normal?

    2. Aggression

      a. Instrumental

      b. Reactive

    3. Violence

      a. Sports violence

    4. Hostility

      a. Hostility bias

    5. Assertiveness

  D. Theories about anger

    1. Frustration–aggression hypothesis (1939)

    2. Completion hypothesis (1969)

    3. Catharsis

    4. Modeling

      a. Parents

      b. Coaches

      c. Teammates

      d. Public sports figures

E. "The program"—facilitating athletic success through focused aggression training (FAST FAT)

    1. Emotion labeling

    2. Physiological sequela of anger—fight or flight, adrenalin

      a. Heart rate

      b. Breathing rate

      c. Muscle tension

      d. Feeling flushed

      e. Perspiration or sweating

      f. Urge to urinate

      g. Differences between anxiety and anger

F. Arousal management

    1. Deep diaphragmatic breathing

    2. Progressive muscle relaxation

    3. Imagery and visualization

      a. Relaxing place

      b. Perfect world

      c. Chaotic world—will be revisited with problem solving

    4. Triggers

      a. Verbal

      b. Nonverbal or physical

    5. Assertiveness training and communication skills

      a. Tone of voice

      b. Expectations

      c. How to get your needs met

    6. Problem solving

      a. Identifying the five Ws and H of the problem

      b. Generating the five Ws and H of the solution

      c. Used during imagery and visualization

    7. Prediction of consequences

      a. Antecedents

          b. Behavior

          c. Consequences

          d. The world is not an unpredictable place

          e. Make good decisions

      8. Evaluation and modification

          a. Did I handle the situation well?

          b. Did I get my goals met?

          c. Did my emotions get in the way?

          d. Reward yourself or fix the problem

IV. Component 3—drugs and consequences

    A. Substance abuse

      1. Prevalence

      2. Classes of drugs associated with violence and date rape

          a. Alcohol

          b. Rohypnol—roofies

          c. Ketamine—special K, K, cat valiums

          d. Methylenedioxymethamphetamine (MDMA)—ecstasy, XTC, Adam

          e. Methamphetamine—speed, ice, chalk, meth, crystal, crank, fire, glass

          f. Gamma-hydroxybutyrate (GHB)—grievous bodily harm, G, liquid ecstasy, Georgia home boy

          g. Lysergic acid diethylamide (LSD)—acid, boomers, yellow sunshines

          h. Anabolic steroids and their derivatives

             i. Testosterone

             ii. Nandrolone

             iii. Androstenedione

             iv. Human growth hormone

    B. Consequences

      1. For the athletics department, organization, or professional team

          a. Lawsuits—money

          b. Difficulty with recruiting

          c. Bad press

          d. NCAA, league, or organizational penalties

2. For the athlete
    a. Suspension
    b. Fine
    c. Expulsion from school
    d. Loss in potential revenue (draft status)
    e. Public image
    f. Prison
3. For the survivor
    a. Nightmares
    b. Flashbacks
    c. Depression
    d. Anxiety
    e. Paranoia
    f. Hyperreactivity
    g. Difficulties with social and sexual situations
    h. Trust issues
    i. Difficulties putting words to their emotions
    j. Retraumatization
V. Wrap up of the three-day workshop

References

Abrams, M. (1998, November). Chill out! *Muscle & Fitness*, 138–140, 236–238.

Abrams, M. (1999). *Implications for professional practice in sport psychology*. Participant in discussion titled "Criminality in the NFL—The effects of *Pros and Cons*" presented at the annual convention of the American Psychological Association, Boston.

Abrams, M. (2000). *Anger management as a necessary part of coping*. Lecture presented at the annual conference of the Association for the Advancement of Applied Sport Psychology, Nashville, TN.

Abrams, M. (2001). *Anger management: Successes and failures on an inpatient psychiatric ward*. Presentation given and chaired symposium titled "Violence in our society: Addressing three different populations" at the annual convention of the American Psychological Association, San Francisco.

Abrams, M. (2001). *Clinical pitfalls in sport psychology*. Colloquium presented at the annual conference of the Association for the Advancement of Applied Sport Psychology, Orlando, FL.

Abrams, M. (2002, August). *The myth of violent male athletes*. Paper presented as part of symposium titled "Athletes: Sitting on top of the world . . . right?" sponsored by the annual convention of American Psychological Association, Chicago.

Abrams, M. (2003). *Advanced psychopathology for sport psychologists: What you need to know*. Colloquium presented at the annual conference of the Association for the Advancement of Applied Sport Psychology, Philadelphia.

Abrams, M. (2003). *Anger management for athletes: The nuts and bolts*. Six-hour continuing education workshop presented at the annual conference of the Association for the Advancement of Applied Sport Psychology, Philadelphia.

Abrams, M. (2004). *"Did you get my Yes?"* Workshop presented for the Metro Atlantic Athletic Conference (MAAC) Student Athlete Advisory Committee, Poughkeepsie, NY.

Abrams, M. (2004). *Anger and athletes: A new direction*. Workshop presented at the annual conference of the Association for the Advancement of Applied Sport Psychology, Minneapolis, MN.

Abrams, M. (2004). *Anger management for athletes: The nuts & bolts for academic coach training*. Workshop presented for the academic coaches sponsored by the National Football Foundation and College Football Hall of Fame's Play It Smart program's annual academic coach training, Springfield, MA.

Abrams, M. (2004, October 15). Best to temper our judgment of angry athletes. *Star Ledger*, p. 19.

Abrams, M. (2005). *Sexual violence and athletes*. Lecture given as part of symposium titled "Sex and sexuality issues in training and practice of applied sport psychology" presented at the annual conference of the Association for the Advancement of Applied Sport Psychology, Vancouver, BC.

Abrams, M. (2005). *It's all fun and games until someone gets hurt: Teaching young athletes how to manage their anger*. Invited speaker for the International Youth Sports Congress—Youth Sports: A New World of Possibilities sponsored by the National Alliance for Youth Sports, Denver, CO.

Abrams, M. (2006). *Violence prevention tools for sports*. Lecture presented as part of symposium titled "New directions in anger & sports" presented at the annual conference of the Association for Applied Sport Psychology, Miami, FL.

Abrams, M. (2006). *Initial anger management session with an athlete: An interactive demonstration*. Workshop presented at the 22nd Annual Conference on Counseling Athletes sponsored by the Springfield College Center for Performance Enhancement and Applied Research, Springfield, MA.

Abrams, M. (2006, April 7). *Athletes must be trained as men, too*. Guest op/ed. Newsday. com.

Abrams, M., & Hale, B. (2004). Anger: How to moderate hot buttons. In S. Murphy (Ed.), *The Sport Psych Handbook*. Champaign, IL: Human Kinetics.

Adler, P.A., & Adler, P. (1991). *Backboards & blackboards: College athletes and role engulfment*. New York: Columbia University Press.

All-Pro linebacker Joey Porter shot. (2003, August). Retrieved March 3, 2007, from http://football.about.com/b/a/2003_08.htm

Allen suspended after assault conviction. (2005, August 29). ESPN.com. Retrieved March 3, 2007, from http://sports.espn.go.com/ncf/news/story?id=2146130&CMP=OTC-DT9705204233

Alzado, L. (1991, July 8). I'm sick and I'm scared. *Sports Illustrated*, 21–24.

American Psychiatric Association. (2000). *DSM-IV TR: Diagnostic and statistical manual of mental disorders*. Washington, DC: Author.

American Psychological Association. (1992). Ethical principles of psychologists and code of conduct. *American Psychologist, 47*, 1597–1611.

Andreotti, P.A. (2000). Effects of angry mood on attention and recall (dissertation). *Dissertation Abstracts International: Section B: The Sciences and Engineering, 61*(6-B), 3268.

Anshel, M.H. (1987). Psychological inventories used in sport psychology research. *Sport Psychologist, 1*, 331–349.

Anshel, M.H. (1997). *Sport psychology: From theory to practice* (3rd ed.). Scottsdale, AZ: Gorsuch Scarisbrick.

Armour, N. (2006, January 2). *Paterno tries to keep Penn State sharp*. SportingNews.com. Retrieved March 3, 2007, from www.sportingnews.com/yourturn/viewtopic.php?t=49518

Attner, P. (2005, September 15). No excuse for violence. Message posted to www.sportingnews.com/yourturn/viewtopic.php?t=17169

Averill, J.R. (1982). *Anger and aggression: An essay on emotion*. New York: Springer-Verlag.

Averill, J.R. (1983). Studies on anger and aggression: Implications for theories of emotion. *American Psychologist, 38*, 1145–1160.

Avery-Leaf, S., Cascardi, M., O'Leary, K.D., Smith Slep, A.M. (1996, November). *The prevention of dating violence: The short-term impact of a five-session curriculum on dating aggression and attitudes justifying dating violence*. Poster session presented at the 30th Annual Meeting of the Association for the Advancement of Behavior Therapy, New York.

Ayad, M. (2006, September 15). Jury convicts T-ball coach of beaning: Coach ordered 8 year old to throw ball at autistic teammate. *Pittsburgh Post-Gazette*. Retrieved on March 3, 2007, from www.post-gazette.com/pg/06258/722075-85.stm

Ayd, F.J. (1995). *Lexicon of psychiatry, neurology, and the neurosciences*. Baltimore: Williams & Wilkins.

Azrin, N.H., Hutchinson, R.R., & Hake, D.F. (1966). Extinction-induced aggression. *Journal of Experimental Analysis of Behavior, 9*, 191–204.

Bahrke, M.S., Yesalis, C.E., & Brower, K.J. (1998). Anabolic-androgenic steroid abuse and performance enhancing drugs among adolescents. *Child and Adolescent Psychiatric Clinics of North America, 7*(4), 821–838.

Bandura, A. (1973). *Aggression: A social learning analysis.* Engelwood Cliffs, NJ: Prentice-Hall.

Bandura, A. (1986). *Social foundations of thought and action: A social cognitive theory.* Englewood Cliffs, NJ: Prentice Hall.

Bandura, A., Ross, D., & Ross, S.A. (1963). Imitation of film-mediated aggressive models. *Journal of Abnormal and Social Psychology, 66*, 3–11.

Bandura, A., & Walters, R. (1963). *Social learning and personality development.* New York: Holt, Rinehart & Winston.

Bagatell, C.J., Heiman, J.R., Matsumoto, A.M. (1994). Metabolic and behavioral effects of high-dose, exogenous testosterone in healthy men. *Journal of Clinical Endocrinology & Metabolism, 79*(2), 561–567.

Baseball bat killing after teasing: Witnesses say alleged attacker's team had just lost a game. (2004, April 14). Retrieved March 3, 2007, from www.cbsnews.com/stories/2005/04/13/national/main687936.shtml

Beedie, C.J., Terry, P.C., & Lane, A.M. (2000). The Profile of Mood States and athletic performance: Two meta-analyses. *Journal of Applied Sport Psychology, 12*(1), 49–68.

Berkowitz, L., & Harmon-Jones, E. (2004). Toward an understanding of the determinants of anger. *Emotion, 4*(2), 107–130.

Beck, A.T., Ward, C.H., Mendelson, M., Mock, J., & Erbaugh, J.K. (1961). An inventory for measuring depression. *Archives of General Psychiatry, 4*, 561–571.

Beer online profit guide. Your online guide to beer profitability. Sponsored by Anheuser Busch. www.BeerProfitGuide.com. www.progressivegrocer.com/progressivegrocer/profitguides/beer/v2/market_overview/index.jsp

Beets, M.W., & Pitetti, K.H. (2005). Contribution of physical education and sport to health-related fitness in high school students. *Journal of School Health, 75*, 25–30.

Begel, D., & Burton, R.W. (2000). *Sport psychiatry.* New York: Norton.

Benedict, J. (1997). *Public heroes, private felons: Athletes and crimes against women.* Boston: Northeastern University Press.

Benedict, J.R. (1998). *Athletes and acquaintance rape.* Thousand Oaks, CA: Sage.

Benedict, J. (2004). *Out of bounds: Inside the NBA's culture of rape, violence, & crime.* New York: Harper-Collins.

Benedict, J., & Yaeger, D. (1998). *Pros and cons: The criminals who play in the NFL.* New York: Warner Books.

Bennett, J.C. (1991). The irrationality of the catharsis theory of aggression as justification for educators' support of interscholastic football. *Perceptual and Motor Skills, 72*, 415–418.

Berkowitz, L. (1958). The expression and reduction of hostility. *Psychological Bulletin, 55*, 257–283.

Berkowitz, L. (1964). Aggressive cues in aggressive behavior and hostility catharsis. *Psychological Review, 71*, 104–122.

Berkowitz, L. (1969). The frustration-aggression hypothesis revisited. In L. Berkowitz (Ed.), *Roots of aggression: A re-examination of the frustration-aggression hypothesis* (pp. 1–28). New York: Atherton Press.

Berkowitz, L. (1983). Aversively stimulated aggression: Some parallels and differences in research with animals and humans. *American Psychologist, 38*, 1135–1144.

Berkowitz, L. (1988). Frustrations, appraisals, and aversively stimulated aggression. *Aggressive Behavior, 14*, 3–11.

Berkowitz, L. (1989). Frustration-aggression hypothesis: Examination and reformulation. *Psychological Bulletin, 106*(1), 59–73.

Berman, B., Brigham, C., & Crystal, B. (Executive producers), & Ramis, H. (Director). (1999). *Analyze this* [Motion picture].

Bernardi, B., & Giarraputo, J. (Producers), & Segal, P. (Director). (2003). *Anger management* [Motion picture].

Bernstein, V. (2006, January 7). *Vick's rocky career at Virginia Tech is over.* NYTimes. com. Retrieved March 3, 2007, from www.nytimes.com/2006/01/07/sports/ ncaafootball/07vick.html

Bernstein, V., & Drape, J. (2006, March 29). *Rape allegation against athletes is roiling Duke.* NYtimes.com. Retrieved March 3, 2007, from www.nytimes.com/2006/03/29/ sports/29duke.html?_r=1&oref=slogin

Berrett, D. (2006, April 5). *Sex assault seminar teaches ESU athletes rules to play by.* Pocono Record.com.

Bertuzzi gets probation for hit on Moore. (2004, December 22). USAToday.com. Retrieved March 3, 2007, from www.usatoday.com/sports/hockey/nhl/canucks/2004-12-21- bertuzzi-plea_x.htm

Bettencourt, B.A., & Miller, N. (1996). Gender differences in aggression as a function of provocation: A meta-analysis. *Psychological Bulletin, 119*, 422–447.

Boeringer, S.B. (1999). Associations of rape-supportive attitudes with fraternal and athletic participation. *Violence Against Women, 5*(1), 81–90.

Bohmer, C., & Parrot, A. (1993). *Sexual assault on campus: The problem and the solution.* New York: Lexington Books.

Bowler, R.M., Mergler, D., Schwarzer, R., Bowler, R.P., & Rauch, S. (1991). *Analysis of MMPI-2 and POMS scale scores in solvent exposed and referents.* Manuscript submitted for publication.

Brackenridge, C. (2001). *Spoil sports: Understanding and preventing sexual exploitation in sport.* New York: Taylor and Francis.

Brackenridge, C., Bringer, J.D., & Bishopp, D. (2003). Researching and managing abuse in sport. In CD ROM, *Proceedings of XIth European Congress of Sport Psychology.* Copenhagen, Denmark.

Brawl at youth baseball tourney kills 40 year old man: Dispute in Akron started when someone refused to pay $5 parking fee. (2005, July 4). AOLSports.com. Retrieved March 3, 2007, from http://aolsvc.news.aol.com/sports/article.adp?id=20050704150409990004

Brecklin, L.R., & Ullman, S.E. (2005). Self-defense or assertiveness training and women's responses to sexual attacks. *Journal of Interpersonal Violence, 20*(6), 738–62.

Bredemeier, B. (1975). The assessment of reactive and instrumental athletic aggression. In D.M. Landers (Ed.), *Psychology of sport and motor behavior-II* (pp. 71–83). State College: Penn State HPER series.

Bredemeier, B.J. (1978). The assessment of reactive and instrumental athletic aggression. *Proceedings of the International Symposium on Psychological Assessment.*

Bredemeier, B. (1978). The assessment of reactive and instrumental aggression. In *Proceedings of the International Symposium of Psychological Assessment in Sport* (pp. 136–145). Netanya, Israel: Wingate Institute for Physical Education and Sport.

Bredemeier, B.J. (1985). Moral reasoning and the perceived legitimacy of intentionally injurious sport acts. *Journal of Sport Psychology, 7*(2), 110–124.

Bredemeier, B.J. (1994). Children's moral reasoning and their assertive, aggressive, and submissive tendencies in sport and daily life. *Journal of Sport & Exercise Psychology, 16*, 1–14.

Bredemeier, B., & Shields, D. (1986a). Athletic aggression: An issue of contextual morality. *Sociology of Sport Journal, 3*, 15–28.

Bredemeier, B., & Shields, D. (1986b). Game reasoning and interactional morality. *Journal of Genetic Psychology, 147*, 257–275.

Bredemeier, B.J., Weiss, M.R., Shields, D.L., & Cooper, B. (1986). The relationship of sport involvement with children's moral reasoning and aggression tendencies. *Sport Psychology, 8*, 304–318.

Bredemeier, B.J., Weiss, M.R., Shields, D.L., & Shewchuk, R.M. (1986). Promoting moral growth in a summer sport camp: The implementation of theoretically grounded instructional strategies. *Journal of Moral Education, 15*(3), 212–220.

Breitenbecher, K.H., & Gidycz, C.A. (1998). An empirical evaluation of a program designed to reduce the risk of multiple sexual victimization. *Journal of Interpersonal Violence, 13*, 472–488.

Breitenbecher, K.H. (1999). The association between the perception of threat in a dating situation and sexual victimization. *Violence and Victims, 14*, 135–146.

Brower, K.J. (1992). Clinical assessment and treatment of anabolic steroid users. *Psychiatric Annals, 22*(1), 35–40.

Brower, K.J, Catlin, D.H., Blow, F.C., & Eliopulos, G.A. (1991). Clinical assessment and urine testing for anabolic-androgenic steroid abuse and dependence. *American Journal of Drug and Alcohol Abuse, 17*(2), 161–171.

Brower, K.J., Blow, F.C., Beresford, T.P., & Fuelling, C. (1989). Anabolic-androgenic steroid dependence. *Journal of Clinical Psychiatry, 50*(1), 31–33.

Brower, K.J. (2002). Anabolic steroid abuse and dependence. *Current Psychiatry Reports, 4*(5), 37.

Brown, B.E. (2001). *1001 Motivational messages and quotes: Teaching character through sports.* Monterey, CA: Coaches Choice.

Brown, E.W., Clark, M.A., Ewing, M.E., & Malina, R.M. (Summer 1998). Participation in youth sports: Benefits and risks. *Spotlight on Youth Sports, 21*(2), 1–4.

Brown, S.W., Welsh, M.C., Labbe, E.L., Vitulli, W.F., & Kulkarni, P. (1992). Aerobic exercise in the psychological treatment of adolescents. *Perceptual and Motor Skills, 74*, 555–560.

Brownmiller, S. (1975). *Against our will: Men, women, and rape.* New York: Fawcett Books.

Browns' Dilfer says he endured insult, assault. (2005, June). Retrieved March 3, 2007, from www.daytondailynews.com/sports/content/sports/browns/daily/0113dilfer.html

Brunelle, J.P., Janelle, C.M., & Tennant, L. (1999). Controlling competitive anger among male soccer players. *Journal of Applied Sport Psychology, 11*(2) 283–297.

Bryant defense says $17,000 from victims' fund was incentive for accuser. (2004, July 30). CourtTV.com. Retrieved March 3, 2007, from www.courttv.com/trials/bryant/072904_fund_ap.html

Brzonkala v. Virginia Polytechnic Institute, 935 F.Supp. 779 (W.D. VA. Roanoke Division 1996).

Brzonkala v. Virginia Polytechnic Institute and State U., 132 F.3d 949 (4th Cir. 1997) (three-judge panel).

Brzonkala v. Virginia Polytechnic Institute and State U., 169 F.3d 820 (4th Cir. 1999).

Buckley, S. (1994, February 2). *Gillooly pleads guilty, says Harding approved plot.* Retrieved March 3, 2007, from www.washingtonpost.com/wp-srv/sports/longterm/olympics1998/history/timeline/articles/time_020294.htm

Buckley, W.E., Yesalis, C.E., Friedl, K.E., Anderson, W.A., Streit, A.L., & Wright, J.E. (1988). Estimated prevalence of anabolic-androgenic steroid use among male high school seniors. *Journal of the American Medical Association, 260,* 3441–3445.

Bureau of Justice Statistics (2000, November 29). *Two of three felony defendants represented by publicly financed counsel.*

Bureau of Justice Statistics (2005, December 22). *Criminal sentencing statistics.* Retrieved March 3, 2007, from www.ojp.usdoj.gov/bjs/cample.htm

Burton, D. (1988). Do anxious swimmers swim slower? Reexamining the elusive anxiety-performance relationship. *Journal of Sport & Exercise Psychology, 10,* 45–61.

Burton, R.W. (2000). Mental illness in athletes. In D. Begel & R.W. Burton (Eds.), *Sport psychiatry.* New York: Norton.

Burton, R.W. (2005). Aggression and sport. *Clinics in Sport Medicine, 24,* 845–852.

Bushman, B.J., & Wells, G.L. (1998). Trait aggressiveness and hockey penalties: Predicting hot tempers on the ice. *Journal of Applied Psychology, 83*(6), 969–974.

Buss, A. (1961). *The psychology of aggression.* New York: Wiley.

Buss, A.H. (2004). Anger, frustration, and aversiveness. *Emotion, 4*(2), 131–132.

Buss, A.H., & Durkee, A. (1957). An inventory for assessing different kinds of hostility. *Journal of Counseling Psychology, 21,* 343–349.

Buss, A.H., & Perry, M. (1992). The aggression questionnaire. *Journal of Personality and Social Psychology, 63,* 452–459.

Callahan, G. (1995, July 31). The worst kind of coward: Allegations by Robert Parish's former wife have cast a new light on an old hero. *Sports Illustrated, 83*(5), 76.

Campo, S., Poulos, G., & Sipple, J.W. (2005). Prevalence and profiling: Hazing among college students and points of intervention. *American Journal of Health Behavior, 29*(2), 137–149.

Carey, B. (2004, November 24). *Anger management may not help at all.* NYTimes.com.

Carlin, B., Hamza, J., & Carlin, G. (Producers), & Santos, S. (Director). *Carlin at Carnegie* [Motion picture].

Caron, S.L., Halteman, W.A., & Stacy, C. (1997). Athletes and rape: Is there a connection? *Perceptual & Motor Skills, 85*(3), 1379–1393.

Chaney sent player to foul. (2005, February 28). ESPN.com. Retrieved March 3, 2007, from http://sports.espn.go.com/ncb/news/story?id=1999665

Chang, P.P., Ford, D.E., Meoni, L.A., Wang, N.Y., & Klag, M.J. (2002). Anger in young men and subsequent premature cardiovascular disease: the precursors study. *Archives of Internal Medicine, 162*(8):901–906.

Choi, P.Y., & Pope, H.G. (1994). Violence toward women and illicit androgenic-anabolic steroid use. *Annals of Clinical Psychiatry, 6*(1), 21–25.

Clarkson, M. (1999). *Competitive fire: Insights to developing the warrior mentality of sports champions.* Champaign, IL: Human Kinetics.

Clore, G.L., & Centerbar, D.B. (2004). Analyzing anger: How to make people mad. *Emotion, 4*(2), 139–144.

Coakley, J.J. (1984). Play, games, and sport: Developmental implications for young people. *Journal of Sport Behavior, 24,* 99–118.

Coakley, J. (1996). Socialization through sports. In O. Bar-O (Ed.), *The child and adolescent athlete* (pp. 353–363). Champaign, IL: Human Kinetics.

Coffman, S.G., & Roark, A.E. (1992). A profile of adolescent anger in diverse family configurations and recommendations for intervention. *The School Counselor, 39*, 211–216.

Cohen, W.B. (1977). *Statistical power analysis for the behavioral sciences* (rev. ed.). New York: Academic Press.

Coleman, J.S. (1965). *Adolescents and the schools.* New York: Basic Books.

Coles: I am a survivor of sexual abuse. (2005, September 18). ESPN.com. Retrieved March 3, 2007, from http://sports.espn.go.com/nfl/news/story?id=2165781

Colston, C. (2006, December 19). *NFL fines Cowboys' Owens $35000 for spitting incident.* USAToday.com. Retrieved March 3, 2007, from www.usatoday.com/sports/football/nfl/cowboys/2006-12-18-terrell-owens_x.htm

Cook, W.W., & Medley, D.M. (1954). Proposed hostility and pharisaic-virtue scales for the MMPI. *Journal of Applied Psychology, 38*, 414–418.

Corbett, J. (2007, April 18). *Adrian Peterson runs through anger to the NFL.* USAToday.com. Retrieved April 19, 2007, from www.usatoday.com/sports/football/draft/2007-04-18-sw-adrian-peterson_N.htm

Cosby, W.H., Jr. (Producer & Director). (1983). *Bill Cosby: Himself* [Motion picture].

Cour, J. (2005, July 1). *Rogers suspended 20 games, fined $50,000 for tirade.* Retrieved March 3, 2007, from http:aolsvc.news.aol.com/sports/article.adp?id=20050629191209990004

Cox, D. (2007, March 8). *'Revenge' behind Bertuzzi hit still evident in game.* ESPN.com. Retrieved March 13, 2007, from http://sports.espn.go.com/nhl/columns/story?columnist=cox_damien&id=2790395

Craft, L.L. (2005). Exercise and clinical depression: Examining two psychological mechanisms. *Psychology of Sport and Exercise, 6*(2), 151–171.

Craft, L.L., & Perna, F.M. (2004). The benefits of exercise for the clinically depressed. *The Primary Care Companion to the Journal of Clinical Psychiatry, 6*(3), 104–111.

Craft, L.L., Allor, K.A., & Pivarnik, J.M .(2003). Predictors of physical competence in adolescent females. *Journal of Youth and Adolescence, 32*, 431–438.

Craft, L.L., & Landers, D.M. (1998). The effect of exercise on clinical depression and depression resulting from mental illness: A meta-analysis. *Journal of Sport and Exercise Psychology, 20*, 339–357.

Craft, L.L., Freund, K.M., Culpepper, L., & Perna, F.M. (2007). Intervention study of exercise for depressive symptoms in women. *Journal of Women's Health, 16*(10), 1499–1509.

Craig, K.M. (2000). Defeated athletes, abusive mates? Examining perceptions of professional athletes who batter. *Journal of Interpersonal Violence, 15*(11), 1224–1232.

Crasnick, J. (2006, September 8). *Difficult to assess impact of amphetamines ban.* ESPN.com. Retrieved March 3, 2007, from http://insider.espn.go.com/mlb/insider/columns/story?columnist=crasnick_jerry&id=2578310&univLogin02=stateChanged

Crouse, K. (2002, April 28). *When the strong are sinking.* PalmBeachPost.com. Retrieved March 3, 2007, from www.palmbeachpost.com/sports/content/sports/special/depression/ad1.html

Curry, J. (2005, November 18). *Amphetamines step up to be counted out.* NYTimes.com. Retrieved March 3, 2007, from www.nytimes.com/2005/11/18/sports/baseball/18greenies.html?ex=1289970000&en=7c2aa9c1421510d6&ei=5090&partner=rssuserland&emc=rss

Curry, J. (2006, April 1). *With greenies banned, up for a cup of coffee?* NYTimes. com. Retrieved March 3, 2007, from www.nytimes.com/2006/04/01/sports/ baseball/01greenies.html?ex=1301547600&en=9197f56fdf8d06c6&ei=5088&part ner=rssnyt&emc=rss

Dahlberg, T. (2005, November 10). *Owens not the only athlete to disrupt his team.* Yahoo Sports.com.

Danton pleads guilty in murder plot. (2004, July 16). Retrieved March 3, 2007, from www. tsn.ca/nhl/news_story/?ID=91264&hubname=

Davis V. Monroe County Bd. of Ed. (97-843) 526 U.S. 629 (1999) 120 F.3d 1390, reversed and remanded.

Decety, J. (1996). Neural representations for action. *Reviews in the Neurosciences, 7,* 285–297.

Deffenbacher, J.L. (in press). Cognitive-behavioral treatment of anger. In K.S. Dobson & K. Craig (Eds.), *Progress in cognitive-behavioral therapy.* Newbury Park, CA: Sage.

Deffenbacher, J.L., & Lynch, R.S. (in press). Cognitive/behavioral intervention for anger reduction. In V.E. Caballo & R.M. Turner (Eds.), *International handbook of cognitive/ behavioral treatment of psychiatric disorders.* Madrid, Spain: Siglo XXI.

Deffenbacher, J.L. (1995). Ideal treatment package for adults with anger disorders. In H. Kassinove (Ed.), *Anger disorders: Definition, diagnosis and treatment.* Washington, DC: Taylor & Francis.

Deffenbacher, J.L., & McKay, M. (2000). *Overcoming situational and general anger: A protocol for the treatment of anger based on relaxation, cognitive restructuring, and coping skills training—client manual & therapist protocol.* Oakland, CA: New Harbinger.

Deffenbacher, J.L., Story, D., Brandon, A., Hogg, J., & Hazaleus, S. (1988). Cognitive and cognitive-relaxation treatments of anger. *Cognitive Therapy and Research, 12,* 167–184.

Delco, D. (2006, May 4). *Recent problems are cause for concern at schools.* Retrieved March 3, 2007, from http://www.thisweeknews.com/?edition=common&story=thisweekn ews/050406/CanalWinchester/Sports/050406-Sports-146024.html

Del Vecchio, T., & O'Leary, K.D. (2004). Effectiveness of anger treatments for specific anger problems: A meta-analytic review. *Clinical Psychology Review, 24,* 15–34.

Demasio, N. (1996, April 21). H.S. gridder sex case shakes up quiet upstate Warwick. *New York Daily News,* pp. 98–99.

DeNiro, R. (Producer & Director). (1993). *A Bronx tale* [Motion picture].

Dervin, D. (1985). A psychoanalysis of sports. *Psychoanalytic Review, 72*(2), 277–299.

DeWitt, D. (1980). Cognitive and biofeedback training for stress reduction with university athletes. *Journal of Sport Psychology, 2,* 288–294.

DiGiuseppe, R. (1995). Developing the therapeutic alliance with angry clients. In H. Kassinove (Ed.), *Anger disorders: Definition, diagnosis and treatment.* Washington, DC: Taylor & Francis.

Dixon, O. (2004, October 29). *Holdsclaw suffering from depression.* USAToday.com. Retrieved March 3, 2007, from www.usatoday.com/sports/basketball/wnba/ mystics/2004-10-28-holdsclaw-depression_x.htm

Dodge, K.A. (1985). Attributional bias in aggressive children. In P.C. Kendall (Ed.), *Advances in cognitive-behavioral research and therapy* (Vol. 4). Orlando, FL: Academic Press.

Dodge, K., Price, J., Bachorowski, J., & Newman, J. (1990). Hostile attributional biases severely aggressive adolescents. *Journal of Abnormal Psychology, 99,* 385–392.

Dollard, J., Doob, L., Miller, N., Mowrer, O., & Sears, R. (1939). *Frustration and aggression*. New Haven, CT: Yale University Press.

Domi suspended for the rest of the playoffs. (2001, May 5). ESPN.com. Retrieved March 3, 2007, from http://espn.go.com/nhl/playoffs2001/2001/0503/1191014.html

Donaldson, S.J., & Ronan, K.R. (2006). The effects of sports participation on young adolescents' emotional well-being. *Adolescence, 41*(162), 369–389.

Donner, R. (Producer & Director). (1998). *Lethal weapon 4* [Motion picture].

Dorfman, H.A., & Kuehl, K. (2002). *The mental game of baseball: A guide to peak performance* (3rd ed.). Lanham, MD: Rowman & Littlefield.

Dotson sentenced to 35 years for Dennehy murder. (2005, June 15). USAToday.com. Retrieved March 3, 2007, from www.usatoday.com/sports/college/mensbasketball/2005-06-15-dotson-sentence_x.htm

Doyne, E.J., Ossip-Klein, D.J, Bowman, E.D., Osborn, K.M., McDougall-Wilson, I.B., & Neimeyer, R.A. (1987). Running versus weight lifting in the treatment of depression. *Journal of Consulting and Clinical Psychology, 55*(5), 748–754.

Drake, B., & Pandey, S. (1996) Do child abuse rates increase on those days on which professional sporting events are held? *Journal of Family Violence, 11*(3), 205–218.

Drehs, W. (n.d.). *Tragic turn.* Retrieved on March 3, 2007, from http://sports.espn.go.com/espn/eticket/story?page=ambrogi

Dungy eulogizes son as 'sweet young boy.' (2005, December 27). Retrieved March 7, 2007, from http://www.nfl.com/teams/story/IND/9119135

Dunn, J.G.H., & Dunn, J.C. (1999). Goal orientations, perceptions of aggression, and sportspersonship in elite male youth ice hockey players. *Sport Psychologist, 13*(2), 183–200.

Eckhardt, C., and Deffenbacher, J. (1995) Diagnosis of anger disorders. In H. Kassinove (Ed.), *Anger disorders: Definition, diagnosis, and treatment.* Washington, DC: Taylor & Francis.

Edmondson, C.B., & Conger, J.C. (1996). A review of treatment efficacy for individuals with anger problems: Conceptual, assessment, and methodological issues. *Clinical Psychology Review, 16*(3), 251–275.

Edes, G. (2005, April 15). *Sheffield says he got hit in face.* Retrieved March 3, 2007, from www.boston.com/sports/baseball/redsox/articles/2005/04/15/sheffield_says_he_got_hit_in_face/

Ehrhart, J.K., & Sandler, B. (1985). *Campus gang rape: Party games.* Unpublished manuscript, Association of American Colleges, Project on the Status and Education of Women, Washington, DC.

Elias, P., & Soth, N.B. (1988). The inpatient basketball group as an alternative to group therapy: Helping the "bad boys" feel good about themselves. *Journal of Child Care, 3*(4), 45–54.

Eligon, J. (2005, October 12). Artest returns but says he won't back down. *New York Times.*

Elkins, W.L., Cohen, D.A., Koralewicz, L.M., & Taylor, S.N. (2004). After school activities, overweight, and obesity among inner city youth. *Journal of Adolescence, 72*, 181–189.

Eltman, F. (2005, October 25). *Group calls for action to stem violence by athletes.* Yahoo Sports.com. Retrieved March 3, 2007, from http://sports.yahoo.com/top/news;_ylt=Ai4qeXfC16AKsjt0xAVEY8c5nYcB

Engelhardt, G.M. (1995). Fighting behavior and winning National Hockey League games: A paradox. *Perceptual and Motor Skills, 80*(2), 416–418.

Eron, L.D., Gentry, J.H., & Schlegel, P. (1994). *Reason to hope: A psychosocial perspective on violence & youth.* Washington, DC: American Psychological Association.

Eskenazi, G. (1990, June 3). The male athlete and sexual assault. *New York Times,* section 8, pp. 1,4.

Etzel, E.F., Ferrante, A.P., & Pinkney, J.W. (Eds.) (1996). *Counseling college student-athletes: Issues and interventions* (2nd ed). Morgantown, WV: Fitness Information Technology.

Ex-Red Wings enforcer Bob Probert charged with assault near Windsor. (2005, July 4). USAToday.com. Retrieved March 3, 2007, from www.usatoday.com/sports/hockey/nhl/2005-08-23-probert-arrested_x.htm

Experts: Accuser's civil suit against Bryant could complicate criminal trial. (2004, August 11). CourtTV.com. Retrieved March 3, 2007, from www.courttv.com/trials/bryant/081104_suit_ap.html

Fabian, L., & Ross, M. (1984). The development of the Sports Competition Trait Inventory. *Journal of Sport Behavior, 7*(1), 13–27.

Family reacts to hockey dad sentence. (2002, January 27). TheBostonChannel.com. Retrieved March 3, 2007, from www.thebostonchannel.com/news/1206817/detail.html

Fein, M. (1993). *I.A.M.*: A common sense guide to coping with anger (*Integrated Anger Management.* Westport, CT: Praeger.

Feindler, E.L. (1990). Cognitive strategies in anger control interventions. In P.C. Kendall (Ed.), *Child and adolescent behavior therapy: Cognitive-behavioral procedures.* New York: Guilford.

Feindler, E.L. (1990). Adolescent anger control: Review and critique. In M. Hersen, R.M. Eisler, & P.M. Miller (Eds.) *Progress in behavior modification,* Volume 26, 11–59, Newbury Park, CA: Sage.

Feindler, E.L. (1995). Ideal treatment package for children and adolescents with anger disorders. In H. Kassinove (Ed.), *Anger disorders: Definition, diagnosis and treatment,* Washington, DC: Taylor & Francis.

Feindler, E.L., & Becker, J.V. (1994). Interventions in family violence involving children and adolescents. In L.D. Eron, J.H. Gentry, & P. Schlegel (Eds.) *Reason to hope: A psychosocial perspective on violence & youth.* Washington, DC: American Psychological Association.

Feindler, E.L., & Ecton, R.B. (1994). *Adolescent anger control: Cognitive behavioral techniques.* Needham Heights, MA: Allyn & Bacon.

Feindler, E.L., Ecton, R.B., Kingsley, D., & Dubey, D.R. (1986). Group anger-control training for institutionalized psychiatric male adolescents. *Behavior Therapy, 17,* 109–123.

Feindler, E.L., & Guttman, J. (1993). Cognitive-behavioral anger control training for groups of adolescents: A treatment manual. In C.W. LeCroix (Ed.), *Handbook of child and adolescent treatment manuals.* New York: Lexington Books.

Feindler, E.L., Marriott, S.A., & Iwata, M. (1984). Group anger control training for junior high school delinquents. *Cognitive Therapy and Research, 8*(3), 299–311.

Feindler, E.L., Rathus, J.H., & Silver, L.B. (2003). *Assessment of family violence: A handbook for researchers and practitioners.* Washington, DC: American Psychological Association.

Feinstein, J. (2002). *The punch: One night, two lives, and the fight that changed basketball forever.* New York: Back Bay Books.

Feldman, B. (2002, May 30). Out of control. *ESPN: The Magazine.* Retrieved March 3, 2007, from http://espn.go.com/magazine/vol5no12uab.html

Felson, R.B. (1982). Impression management and the escalation of aggression and violence. *Social Psychology Quarterly, 45,* 245–254.

Felson, R.B. (1984). Patterns of aggressive social interaction. In A. Mummenday (Ed.), *Social psychology of aggression: From individual behavior to social interaction.* New York: Springer-Verlag.

Felson, R.B. (2002). *Violence & gender Reexamined.* Washington, DC: American Psychological Association.

Fernas, R. (2003, July 19). Kobe Bryant charged: Athletes part of a violent trend, victims' advocates say athletes have a better chance of acquittal than other men accused of crimes against women. *Los Angeles Times.*

Feshbach, S. (1964). The function of aggression and the regulation of aggressive drive. *Psychological Review, 71,* 257–272.

Festinger, L., Pepitone, A., & Newcombe, T. (1952). Some consequences of deindividuation in a group. *Journal of Abnormal and Social Psychology, 47,* 283–289.

Findlay, L. C., & Coplan, R. J. (2008, July). Come out and play: Shyness in childhood and the benefits of organized sports participation. *Canadian Journal of Behavioural Science, 40(3),* 153-161.

Fish, J., & Magee, S. (2003). *101 ways to be a terrific sports parent.* New York: Fireside–Simon & Schuster.

Fleisher, A.A. III, Goff, B.L., & Tollison, R.D. (1986). *The National Collegiate Athletic Association: A study in cartel behavior.* Chicago: University of Chicago Press.

Former Iowa star gets two years in prison. (2005, October 29). NYTimes.com. Retrieved March 3, 2007, from www.nytimes.com/aponline/sports/AP-BKC-Pierce-Sentenced.html

Fowler, B. (2005, September 23). *Pacers' Artest, Jackson, O'Neal sentenced for brawl: All three players receive year probation, community service, fine.* AOL Sports.com. Retrieved March 3, 2007, from http://aolsvc.news.aol.com/sports/article.adp?id=20050923095709990028

Frank, M.G., & Gilovich, T. (1988). The dark side of self- and social perception: Black uniforms and aggression in professional sports. *Journal of Personality and Social Psychology, 54(1),* 74–85.

Freeman, M. (2000, May 21). *Lewis murder case putting the NFL's image and discipline on trial.* NYTimes.com. Retrieved March 3, 2007, from http://select.nytimes.com/gst/abstract.html?res=F40C10FB3B5E0C728EDDAC0894D8404482&n=Top%2fReference%2fTimes%20Topics%2fPeople%2fL%2fLollar%2c%20Richard

Freeman, M. (2003). *Bloody Sundays: Inside the dazzling, rough-and-tumble world of the NFL.* New York: Harper-Collins.

Freud, S. (1963). *Beyond the pleasure principle: A study of the death instinct in human behavior.* (J. Strachey, Trans.). New York: Bantam Books (Original work published 1920).

Frintner, M.P., & Rubinson, L. (1993). Acquaintance rape: The influence of alcohol, fraternity membership, and sports team membership. *Journal of Sex Education and Therapy, 19(4),* 272–284.

FSU linebacker A.J. Nicholson accused of sexual assault. (2005, December 29). FOXNews.com. Retrieved March 3, 2007, from www.foxnews.com/story/0,2933,180111,00.html

Funk, G.D. (1991). *Major violation—the unbalanced priorities in athletics and academics.* Champaign, IL: Leisure Press.

Gacano, C.B., & Meloy, J.R. (1994). *The Rorschach assessment of aggressive and psychopathic personalities.* Hillsdale, NJ: Lawrence Erlbaum.

Gacano, C.B. (Ed.) (2000). *The clinical and forensic assessment of psychopathy: A practitioner's guide.* Hillsdale, NJ: Lawrence Erlbaum.

Gardner, F., & Moore, Z. (2006). *Clinical sport psychology.* Champaign, IL: Human Kinetics.

Gidycz, C., & Coble, C., Latham, L., & Layman, M. (1993). Sexual assault experience in adulthood and prior victimization experiences. *Psychology of Women Quarterly, 17,* 151–168.

Gidycz, C., Hanson, K., & Layman, M. (1995). A prospective analysis of the relationships among sexual assault experiences. *Psychology of Women Quarterly, 19,* 5–29.

Gilmore, W., & Pfeffer, R. (Executive Producers) & Reiner, R. (Director). (1992). *A few good men* [Motion picture].

Goldstein, A.P., & Glick, B. (1987). *Aggression replacement training: A comprehensive intervention for aggressive youth.* Champaign, IL: Research Press.

Goldstein, A.P., Huff, C.R. (Eds.). (1993). *The gang intervention handbook.* IL: Research Press.

Goldstein, J. (2005). *A motivational model of "sideline rage" and aggression in parents of youth soccer players.* Lecture presented at the ISSP World Congress of Sports Psychology, Sydney, Australia.

Goldstein, J.H. (Ed.) (1983). *Sports violence.* NY: Springer-Verlag.

Goldwyn, S., Jr. (Producer). (1993). *The program* [Motion picture].

Goodell suspends Pacman, Henry for multiple arrests. (2007, April 11). ESPN.com. Retrieved April 15, 2007, from http://sports.espn.go.com/nfl/news/story?id=2832015

Gottman, J.M., Jacobson, N.S., Rushe, R.H., Shortt, J.W., Babcock, J. La Taillade, J.J., & Waltz, J. (1995). The relationship between heart rate reactivity, emotionally aggressive behavior, and general violence in batterers. *Journal of Family Psychology, 9*(3), 227–248.

Green, T. (1996). *The dark side of the game: My life in the NFL.* New York: Warner Books.

Greene, A.F., Sears, S.F., Jr., & Clark, J.E. (1993). Anger and sports participation. *Psychological Reports, 72,* 523–529.

Gruber, J.J., & Gray, G.R. (1981). Factor patterns of variables influencing cohesiveness at various levels of basketball competition. *Research Quarterly for Exercise and Sport, 52,* 19–30.

Guernsey, L. (1993, February 10). More campuses offer rape-prevention programs for male athletes. *Chronicle of Higher Education, 39*(23), A35, A37.

Guregian, K. (2007, April 26). *Dr. 'T' knows the inside info: Troutwine helps Pats ID right players.* Boston Herald.com. Retrieved April 26, 2007, from http://patriots.bostonherald.com/patriots/view.bg?articleid=196866&format=text

Gustafson, R. (1989). Frustration and successful vs. unsuccessful aggression: A test of Berkowitz' completion hypothesis. *Aggressive Behavior, 15,* 5–12.

Gutierrez, H. (2005, July 6). *Bronco arrested in domestic case: Brandon accused of hitting girlfriend.* Retrieved March 3, 2007, from www.highbeam.com/doc/1P1-110774425.html

Hains, A.A. (1992). Comparison of cognitive-behavioral stress management techniques with adolescent boys. *Journal of Counseling & Development, 70,* 600–605.

Hains, A.A., & Fouad, N.A. (1994). The best laid plans . . . :Assessment in an inner-city high school. *Measurement and Evaluation in Counseling and Development, 27,* 116–124.

Hall, R.C.W., & Chapman, M.J. (2005). Psychiatric complications of anabolic steroid abuse. *Psychosomatics, 46,* 285–290.

Hanin, Y.L. (1989). Interpersonal and intergroup anxiety: Conceptual and methodological issues. In C.D. Speilberger & D. Hackfort (Eds.), *Anxiety in sports: An international perspective* (pp. 19–28). Washington, DC: Hemisphere.

Hanin, Y.L. (Ed.) (2000). *Emotions in sport.* Champaign, IL: Human Kinetics.

Hanson, R.K., & Gidycz, C. (1993). Evaluation of a sexual assault prevention program. *Journal of Consulting and Clinical Psychology, 61,* 1046–1052.

Hare, R.D. (1993). *Without conscience: The disturbing world of the psychopaths among us.* New York: Pocket Books.

Hare, R.D. (1996). Psychopathy and antisocial personality disorder: A case of diagnostic confusion. *Psychiatric Times, 13*(2).

Hare, R.D. (2004). *The Hare Psychopathy Checklist—revised* (2nd ed). Toronto, ON: Multi-Health Systems.

Harrell, W.A. (1980). Aggression by high school basketball players: An observational study of the effects of opponents' aggression and frustration-inducing factors. *International Journal of Sport Psychology, 11,* 290–298.

Heyman, S.R. (1986). Psychological problem patterns found with athletes. *Clinical Psychologist,* Summer, 68–71.

Hickmann, S.A. (2004). Impulsivity as a predictor of athletic success and negative consequences in NFL football players. *Dissertation Abstracts International, 65*(6-B), 3163.

Hilton, N.Z., Harris, G.T., & Rice, M.E. (2000). The functions of aggression by male teenagers. *Journal of Personality and Social Psychology, 79,* 988–994.

Hilyer, J.C., Wilson, D.G., Dillon, C., Caro, L., Jenkins, C., Spencer, W.A, Meadows, M.E., & Booker, W. (1982). Physical fitness training and counseling as treatment for youthful offenders. *Journal of Counseling Psychology, 29*(3), 292–303.

Hines, J. (2004, October 4). *Number of rape victims higher than reports, studies indicate.* (Opinion). Retrieved March 3, 2007, from http://www.statenews.com/op_article.phtml?pk=25893

Hippocrates. (1923). *Epidemics.* Translated by W.H.S. Jones.

'Hockey dad' gets 6 to 10 years for fatal beating. (2002, January 5). Retrieved March 3, 2007, from http://archives.cnn.com/2002/LAW/01/25/hockey.death.verdict/index.html

Hodgkinson, H.L. (1985). *All one system: Demographics of education—kindergarten through graduate school,* Washington, DC: The Institute for Educational Leadership.

Hoffman, J.R., Kang, J., Faigenbaum, A.D., & Ratamess, N.A. (2005). Recreational sports participation is associated with enhanced physical fitness in children. *Research in Sports Medicine, 13,* 149–161.

Holtzworth-Munroe, A., & Meehan, J.C. (2004). Typologies of men who are maritally violent: Scientific and clinical implications. *Journal of Interpersonal Violence, 19*(12), 1369–1389.

Holtzworth-Munroe, A., Meehan, J.C., Herron, K., Rehman, U., & Stuart, G.L. (2000). Testing the Holtzworth-Munroe and Stuart (1994) batterer typology. *Journal of Consulting and Clinical Psychology, 68*(6), 1000–1019.

Holtzworth-Munroe, A., Meehan, J.C., Herron, K., & Stuart, G.L. (1999). A typology of male batterers: An initial examination. In Arriaga, X.B., Oskamp, S. (Ed). *Violence in intimate relationships* (pp. 45–72). Thousand Oaks, CA: Sage.

Holtzworth-Munroe, A., Meehan, J.C., Herron, K., Rehman, U., & Stuart, G.L. (2003). Do subtypes of maritally violent men continue to differ over time? *Journal of Consulting and Clinical Psychology, 71*(4), 728–740.

Holtzworth-Munroe, A., Rehman, U., & Herron, K. (2000). General and spouse-specific anger and hostility in subtypes of martially violent men and nonviolent men. *Behavior Therapy, 31*(4), 603–630.

Holtzworth-Munroe, A., & Stuart, G.L. (1994). Typologies of male batterers: Three subtypes and the differences among them. *Psychological Bulletin, 116*(3), 476–497.

Hooven, C.K., Chabris, C.F., Ellison, P.T., & Kosslyn, S.M. (2004). The relationship of male testosterone to components of mental rotation. *Neuropsychologia, 42*, 782–790.

Hosick, M.B. (2004, November 8). *Treatment* of some disorders poses competitive challenges. NCAA.org. Retrieved March 3, 2007, from www.ncaa.org/wps/portal/!ut/p/kcxml/04_Sj9SPykssy0xPLMnMz0vM0Y_QjzKLN4g3NPUESUGYHvqRaGLGphhCjggRX4_83FR9b_0A_YLc0NCIckdFACrZHxQ!/delta/base64xml/L3dJdyEvUUd3QndNQSEvNElVRS82XzBfMTVL?New_WCM_Context=/wps/wcm/connect/NCAA/NCAA+News/NCAA+News+Online/2004/Association-wide/Treatment+of+some+disorders+poses+competitive+challenges+-+11-8-04+NCAA+News

Hruby, P. (2000, May 1). *Tests of character—psychological testing in National Football League.* Retrieved March 3, 2007, from http://findarticles.com/p/articles/mi_m1571/is_16_16/ai_61934318

Huey, W.C., & Rank, R.C. (1984). Effects of counselor and peer-led group assertive training on black adolescent aggression. *Journal of Counseling Psychology, 31*(1), 95–98.

Huesmann, Guerra, Miller, & Zelli. (1992). The roles of social norms in the development of aggression. In H. Zumkley & A. Fraczek (Eds.) *Socialization and aggression,* New York: Springer.

Hughes, R., & Coakley, J. (1991). Positive deviance among athletes: The implications of overconformity to the sport ethic. *Sociology of Sport Journal, 8*(4), 307–325.

Huizenga, R. (1994). *You're okay, it's just a bruise: A doctor's sideline secrets about pro football's most outrageous team.* New York: St. Martin's Press.

Humphrey, S.E., & Kahn, A.S. (2000). Fraternities, athletic teams, and rape: Importance of identification with a risky group. *Journal of Interpersonal Violence, 15*(12), 1313–1322.

'I was stunned'—Royals first base coach assaulted by father-son duo. (2002, September 21). SI.com. Retrieved March 3, 2007, from http://sportsillustrated.cnn.com/baseball/news/2002/09/19/royals_whitesox_ap/

Isberg, L. (2000). Anger, aggressive behavior, and athletic performance. In Y. Hanin (Ed.), *Emotions in sport.* Champaign, IL: Human Kinetics.

Isidore, C. (2004, March 18). NCAA's bottom line winners—schools in NCAA tourney have 51% profit margin from basketball. Most profitable: Louisville. *Money.*

Jacobs, G.A., Latham, L.E., & Brown, M. (In press). Test-retest reliabilities of the State-Trait Personality Inventory and the Anger Expression Scale. *Journal of Personality Assessment.*

Jacobson, E. (1938). *Progressive relaxation.* Chicago: University of Chicago Press.

Jacobson, E. (1977). The origins and development of progressive relaxation. *Journal of Behavior Therapy & Experimental Psychiatry, 8*, 119–123.

Jacobson, N.S., Gottman, J.M., & Shortt, J.W. (1995). The distinction between Type 1 and Type 2 batterers—Further considerations: Reply to Ornduff et al. (1995), Margolin et al. (1995), and Walker (1995). *Journal of Family Psychology, 9*(3), 272–279.

Jackson, S.A., & Csikszentmihalyi, M. (1999). *Flow in sports: The keys to optimal experiences and performances.* Champaign, IL: Human Kinetics.

Jackson, T.L. (1991). A university athletic department's rape and assault experiences. *Journal of College Student Development, 32,* 77–78.

Jackson, T.L. (1992, October). *Rape education and prevention programs for athletic departments.* Presented at the International Conference on Sexual Assault on Campus, Orlando, FL.

Jackson, T.L. (1994, July). *Sexual responsibility: Assault prevention and safe dating.* NCAA Life Skills Program, Kansas City, MO.

Jackson, T.L. (1996). *Acquaintance rape: Assessment, treatment & prevention.* Sarasota, FL: Professional Resource Press.

Jaffe, A. (1992). Cognitive factors associated with cocaine abuse and its treatment: An analysis of expectancies of use. In T.R. Kosten & H.D. Kleber (Eds.) *Clinician's guide to cocaine addiction: Theory, research, and treatment.* New York: Guilford Press.

Jaffe, J. (1997, December 11–17). In sports, winning isn't everything. *Nassau Herald.*

Jaffe, S.R., & Lansing, S. (Producers), & Lyne, A. (Director). (1987). *Fatal attraction* [Motion picture].

Jags' Darius fined $75K, not suspended, for hit. (2004, December 21). ESPN.com. Retrieved March 3, 2007, from http://sports.espn.go.com/nfl/news/story?id=1951069

Jags' Hanson gashes leg: Pro Bowl punter injured while swinging ax in locker room. Retrieved March 3, 2007, from http://www.jacksonville.com/tu-online/stories/100903/jag_13744128.shtml

Jaschik, S. (2006, March 29). *Anger and consequences.* InsideHigherEd.com.

Jay, T.B. (1980). Sex roles and dirty word usage: A review of the literature and a reply to Haas. *Psychological Bulletin, 88,* 614–621.

Jenson, M., & Parent, R. (2005, October 13). *Penn's Ambrogi still seemed upbeat.* Philly.com. Retrieved March 3, 2007, from www.philly.com/mld/philly/sports/colleges/12886946.htm

Jowdy, D.P., Murphy, S.M., & Durtschi, S. (1989). *An assessment of the use of imagery in elite athletes: Athlete, coach, and psychologist perspectives.* Unpublished report to the United States Olympic Committee. Colorado Springs, CO.

Judge sends former Raider Robbins to jail until trial. (2005, September 23). AOL Sports.com. Retrieved March 3, 2007, from http://aolsvc.news.aol.com/special/1/article.adp?id=20050923114409990005&cid=942

Kaplan, H.I., & Sadock, B.J. (1991). *Synopsis of psychiatry: Behavioral sciences & clinical psychiatry* (6th ed). Baltimore: Williams & Wilkins.

Kassinove, H. (1995). *Anger disorders: Definition, diagnosis, and treatment.* Washington, DC: Taylor & Francis.

Kassinove, H., & Tafrate, R.C. (2002). *Anger management: The complete treatment guidebook for practitioners.* Atascadero, CA: Impact.

Katz, J. (1988). *Seductions of crime: Moral and sensual attractions of doing evil.* New York: Basic Books.

Katz, J. (1995). Reconstructing masculinity in the locker room: The Mentors in Violence Prevention Project. *Harvard Educational Review, 65*(2), 163–174.

Katzmarzyk, P.T., & Malina, R.M. (1998). Contribution of organized sports participation to daily estimated energy expenditure in youth. *Pediatric Exercise Science, 10,* 378–386.

Kazdin, A.E., Bass, D., Siegel, T., & Thomas, C. (1989). Cognitive-behavioral therapy and relationship therapy in the treatment of children referred for antisocial behavior. *Journal of Consulting and Clinical Psychology, 57,* 522–535.

Kearsley, G. (1994c). *Social learning theory (A. Bandura).* [Online]. Available: www.gwu.edu/~tip/bandura.html [December 1, 1999].

Kelly v. Yale University, Civ.A. 3:01-CV-1591, 2003 WL 1563424 (D. Conn. 2003).

Kelly, J.F., & Hake, D.F. (1970). An extinction-induced increase in an aggressive response in humans. *Journal of Experimental Analysis of Behavior, 14*(2), 153–164.

Kendall, P.C., Ronan, K.R., & Epps, J. (1989). Aggression in children/adolescents: Cognitive-behavioral treatment perspectives. In D. Pepler & K. Rubin (Eds.), *Development and Treatment of Childhood Aggression.* The Earlscourt Symposium.

Kerr, J.H. (1999). The role of aggression and violence in sport: A rejoinder to the ISSP position stand. *Sport Psychologist, 13,* 83–88.

Kerr, J.H. (2002). Issues in aggression and violence in sport: The ISSP position stand revisited. *Sport Psychologist, 16,* 68–78.

Kerr, J.H. (2005). *Rethinking aggression and violence in sport.* New York: Routledge, Taylor & Francis.

Kerr, J.H. (2006). Examining the Bertuzzi-Moore NHL ice hockey incident: Crossing the line between sanctioned and unsanctioned violence in sport. *Aggression and Violent Behavior, 11,* 313–322.

Kilmeade, B. (2004). *The games do count: America's best and brightest on the power of sports.* New York: HarperCollins.

Kirby, S., Greaves, L., & Hankivsky, O. (2000). *The dome of silence: Sexual harassment and abuse in sport.* Halifax, NS: Fernwood.

Kohlberg, L. (1968). The child as a moral philosopher. *Psychology Today, 2*(4), 25–30.

Kohlberg, L., & Diessner, R. (1991). A cognitive-developmental approach to moral attachment. In J.L. Gewirtz & W.M. Kurtines (Eds.), *Intersections with attachment.* Hillsdale, NJ: Lawrence Erlbaum.

Kohlberg, L., & Elfenbein, D. (1975). The development of moral judgments concerning capital punishment. *American Journal of Orthopsychiatry, 45*(4), 614–640.

Kohlberg, L., & Puka, B. (Ed.). (1994). *Kohlberg's original study of moral development.* New York: Garland.

Kohler, J. (2004, August 9). *Accuser's attorney blast Bryant judge.* USAToday.com. Retrieved March 3, 2007, from www.usatoday.com/sports/basketball/2004-08-09-judge-attack_x.htm

Kolker, R. (2003, October 27). Out of bounds: When members of a high-school football team on Long Island were accused of sexual attacks, the community was appalled . . . some by the crimes, others by the cancellation of the season. Now the boys may face adult charges, the victims are being ostracized, and the locals are divided. *New York Magazine.* Retrieved March 3, 2007, from http://nymag.com/nymetro/news/features/n_9391/

Koss, M.P., & Gaines, J.A. (1993). The prediction of sexual aggression by alcohol use, athletic participation and fraternity affiliation. *Journal of Interpersonal Violence, 8*(1), 94–108.

Koss, M., & Gidycz, C. (1985). Sexual Experiences Survey: Reliability and validity. *Journal of Consulting and Clinical Psychology, 53,* 422–423.

Koss, M., Gidycz, C., & Wisniewski, N. (1987). The scope of rape: Incidence and prevalence of sexual victimization in a national sample of higher education students. *Journal of Consulting and Clinical Psychology, 55,* 162–170.

Koss, M.P., Goodman, L.A., Browne, A., Fitzgerald, L.F., Keita, G.P., & Russo, N.F. (1994). *No safe haven: Male violence against women at home, at work, and in the community* (1st ed.). Washington, DC: American Psychological Association.

Kosten, T.R., & Kleber, H.D. (Eds.). (1992). *Clinician's guide to cocaine addiction: Theory, research, and treatment.* New York: Guilford Press.

Kram, M. (2003, February 27). The brutal trip down: A tale about Alonzo Spellman, his illness, and a terrifying flight that landed him in jail. *Philadelphia Daily News.*

Kubistant, T. (1988). *Mind pump: The psychology of bodybuilding.* Champaign, IL: Human Kinetics.

Kubler-Ross, E. (1997). *On death and dying.* New York: Touchstone.

Lallanilla, M. (2006, April 10). *Team psychology can contribute to assaults: 'Groupthink' often overrides individual morals.* abcNews.com.

Landers, D.M., & Boutcher, S.H. (1986). Arousal-performance relationships. In J.M. Williams (Ed.), *Applied sport psychology: Personal growth to peak performance* (pp. 163–184). Palo Alto, CA: Mayfield.

Lane's widow pleads guilty to killing him. (2003, August 14). SI.com. Retrieved March 3, 2007, from http://sportsillustrated.cnn.com/football/news/2003/08/14/lane_widow_ap/

Larson, J.D. (1992). Anger and aggression management techniques through the *Think First* curriculum. *Journal of Offender Rehabilitation, 18*(1/2), 101–117.

Lazarus, A. (1975). *Learning to relax* [Tape]. New York: Institute for Rational Living.

Lefkowitz, B. (1997). *Our guys.* New York: Random House.

Leith, L.M. (1989). The effect of various physical activities, outcome, and emotional arousal on subject aggression scores. *International Journal of Sport Psychology, 20,* 57–66.

Leizman, J. (1999). *Let's kill 'em.* Lanham, MD: University Press of America.

Lemieux, P., McKelvie, S.J., & Stout, D. (2002). Self-reported hostile aggression in contact athletes, no contact athletes and non-athletes. *Athletic Insight: The Online Journal of Sport Psychology, 4*(3).

LeUnes, A, & Burger, J. (2000). Profile of Mood States research in sport and exercise psychology: Past, present, and future. *Journal of Applied Sport Psychology, 12*(1), 5–15.

LeUnes, A., & Nation, J.R. (1982). Saturday's heroes: A psychological portrait of college football players. *Journal of Sport Behavior, 5*(3), 139–149.

LeUnes, A., & Nation, J.R. (1996). *Sport psychology* (2nd ed.). Chicago: Nelson-Hall.

Levine, C., Kohlberg, L., & Hewer, A. (1985). The correct formulation of Kohlberg's theory and a response to critics. *Human Development, 28*(2), 94–100.

Lewis, M. (2003). *Moneyball.* New York: Norton.

Lewis murder charges dropped; Ravens' star accepts misdemeanor charge, will testify. (2005, June 5). CNNSI.com. Retrieved March 3, 2007, from http://sportsillustrated.cnn.com/football/nfl/news/2000/06/04/lewis_agreement/

Lipsyte, R. (1995, June 18). Many create the climate for violence. *New York Times*, p. 20.

Llewellyn, J. (2001). *Let 'em play: What parents, coaches & kids need to know about youth baseball.* Marietta, GA: Longstreet Press.

Longman, J. (2006, August 13). *After saying he had changed, Clarett goes down familiar path.* NYTimes.com. Retrieved March 3, 2007, from http://www.nytimes.com/2006/08/13/sports/ncaafootball/13clarett.html

Lorenz, K. (1966). *On aggression.* New York: Harcourt, Brace & World.

Lowe, R. (1971). *Stress, arousal, and task performance of Little League baseball players.* Unpublished doctoral dissertation, University of Illinois, Urbana-Champaign.

Lubrano, A., & Gammage, J. (2004, November 23). *First punches, then questions: Beer, anger and societal changes may have been behind the Friday night fight.* Philly.com. http://www.philly.com/mld/philly/sports/10249930.htm?1c

McCaffrey, G.E., & O'Brien, R.M. (1988, August). *Anger arousal and anger management in high school wrestling.* Paper presented to the American Psychological Association, Atlanta, GA.

McCarthy, J.F., & Kelly, B.R. (1978). Aggression, performance variables, and anger self-report in ice hockey players. *Journal of Psychology, 99,* 97–101.

McCauley, J. (2005, November 5). *From NFL to a mental facility, the rise and fall of a troubled kicker.* CBSSportsline.com. Retrieved March 3, 2007, from www.sportsline.com/nfl/story/9033370/1

McCloskey, J., & Bailes, J. (2005). *When winning costs too much.* Lanham, MD: Rowman & Littlefield.

McGowan, R.W., & Shultz, B.B. (1989). Task complexity and affect in collegiate football. *Perceptual and Motor Skills, 69,* 671–674.

McNair, D.M., Lorr, M., & Droppelman, L.F. (1992). *Profile of Mood States manual* (revised), San Diego, CA: Educational & Industrial Testing Service.

Maganaris, C.N., Collins, D., & Sharp, M. (2000). Expectancy effects and strength training: Do steroids make a difference? *Sport Psychologist, 14*(3), 272–278.

Malone, D.A., Dimeff, R.J., Lombardo, J.A. (1995). Psychiatric effects and psychoactive substance use in androgenic steroid users. *Clinical Journal of Sports Medicine, 5,* 25–31.

Mandak, J. (2005, September 13). *Coroner: Football injuries contributed to death of former Steeler.* SportingNews.com. Retrieved March 3, 2007, from http://www.sportingnews.com/nfl/articles/20050913/647498.html

Mangold, J. (Director). (1999). *Girl, interrupted* [Motion picture].

Margolin, G., Gordis, E.B., Oliver, P.H., & Raine, A. (1995). A physiologically based typology of batterers—promising but preliminary: Comment on Gottman et al. (1995). *Journal of Family Psychology, 9*(3), 253–263.

Margolis, J.A. (1999). *Violence in sports: Victory at what price?* Berkley Heights, NJ: Enslow.

Martens, R. (1975). *Social psychology and physical activity.* New York: Harper & Row.

Martens, R. (1997). *Successful coaching* (2nd ed.). Champaign, IL: Human Kinetics.

Marx, B.P., Calhoun, K.S., Wilson, A.E., & Meyerson, L.A. (2001). Sexual revictimization prevention: An outcome evaluation. *Journal of Consulting and Clinical Psychology, 69*(1), 25–32.

Marx, B.P., & Gross, A.M. (1995). Date rape: An analysis of two contextual variables. *Behavior Modification, 19,* 451–463.

Marx, B.P., Van Wie, V., & Gross, A.M. (1996). Date rape risk factors: A review and methodological critique of the literature. *Aggression and Violent Behavior, 1,* 27–45.

Maxwell, J.P. (2004). Anger rumination: An antecedent of athlete aggression? *Psychology of Sport and Exercise, 5*(3), 279–289.

Maxwell, J.P., & Moores, E. (2007). The development of a short scale measuring aggressiveness and anger in competitive athletes. *Psychology of Sport and Exercise, 8,* 179–193.

Melnick, M. (1992, May–June).Male athletes and sexual assault. *JOPERD, Journal of Physical Education, Recreation & Dance, 63*(5), 32–36.

Meloy, R. (1988). *The psychopathic mind: Origin, dynamics, and treatment.* Northvale, NJ: Aronson.

Meloy, R. (1992). *Violent attachments.* Northvale, NJ: Aronson.

Miller, C.H. (1979). Aggression in everyday life. *American Journal of Psychoanalysis, 39*(2), 99–112.

Miller, K.E., Melnick, M.J., Farrell, M.P., Savo, D.F., & Barnes, G.M. (2006). Jocks, gender, binge drinking, and adolescent violence. *Journal of Interpersonal Violence, 21*(1), 105–120.

Miller, M. (2004, October 2). Player thrown a changeup. *Los Angeles Times.* LATimes.com.

Miller, N.E. (1941). The frustration-aggression hypothesis. *Psychological Review, 48,* 337–342.

Miracle, A.W., Jr., & Rees, C.R. (1994). *Lessons of the locker room: The myth of school sports.* Amherst, NY: Prometheus Books.

"Missouri Facts . . ." (1986). Springfield, MO: Job Council of the Ozarks.

Monahan, J., Steadman, H.J., Silver, E., Appelbaum, P.S., Robbins, P.C., Mulvey, E.P., Roth, L.H., Grisso, T., & Banks, S. (2001). *Rethinking risk assessment: The Macarthur study of mental disorder and violence.* New York: Oxford University Press.

Montaldo, C. (n.d.). *Rae Carruth.* About.com. Retrieved March 3, 2007, from http://crime.about.com/od/murder/p/raecarruth.htm

Morgan, W.P. (1980). Tests of champions: The iceberg profile. *Psychology Today, 14*(4), 92–102, 108.

Morgan, W.P. (1969). A pilot investigation of physical working capacity in depressed and nondepressed males. *Research Quarterly of Exercise and Sport, 40,* 859–861.

Morgan, J., & Shoop, S.A. (2004, January 30). *Terry Bradshaw's winning drive against depression.* USAToday.com. Retrieved on March 3, 2007, from www.usatoday.com/news/health/spotlighthealth/2004-01-30-bradshaw_x.htm

Morrison, M. (n.d.). *To protect and serve: Is vigilante justice necessary in hockey?* Infoplease. Retrieved March 3, 2007, from www.infoplease.com/spot/hockeyfighting1.html

Muehlenhard, C.L., & Linton, M.A. (1987). Date rape and sexual aggression in dating situations: Incidence and risk factors. *Journal of Counseling Psychology, 34,* 186–196.

Mugno, D., & Feltz, D. (1984, July). *The social learning of aggression in youth football.* Paper presented at the 1984 International Olympic Scientific Congress, Eugene, OR.

Murphy, S.M. (Ed.) (1995). *Sport psychology interventions.* Champaign, IL: Human Kinetics.

Murphy, S. (1999). *The cheers and the tears: A healthy alternative to the dark side of youth sports today.* San Francisco: Jossey-Bass.

Murphy, S.M. (Ed.) (2005). *The sport psych handbook: A complete guide to today's best mental training techniques.* Champaign, IL: Human Kinetics.

MVP Program. www.sportinsociety.org/vpd/mvp.php

Nack, W., & Munson, L. (1995, July 31). Sports dirty secret: When scarcely a week passes without an athlete being accused of domestic violence, it is no longer possible to look the other way. *Sports Illustrated, 83*(5), 62–74.

Nack, W., & Munson, L. (2000, July 24). *Out of control: The rising tide of violence and verbal abuse by adults at youth sports events reached its terrible peak this month when one hockey father killed another.* SportsIllustrated.CNN.com. Retrieved March 3, 2007, from http://sportsillustrated.cnn.com/features/cover/news/2000/12/08/yir_courtroom2/

Nation, J.R., & LeUnes, A.D. (1983). Personality characteristics of intercollegiate players as determined by position, classification, and redshirt status. *Journal of Sport Behavior, 6*, 92–102.

NBA suspends Knicks' Davis five games. Forward entered stands to protect wife; fan plans to sue for $1 million-plus. (2006, January 20). MSNBC.com. Retrieved March 3, 2007, from www.msnbc.msn.com/id/10918557/

Neimark, J. (1991, May). Out of bounds: The truth about athletes and rape. *Mademoiselle*, 196-199, 244-246.

Nelson, A.K. (2006, September 8). Health concerns are quite serious. *ESPN: The Magazine.* Retrieved March 3, 2007, from http://sports.espn.go.com/mlb/news/story?id=2578380

Nelson, M.B. (1995, July 30). When athletes abuse, they lose. *New York Times*, p. 21.

Newby, R.W., & Simpson, S. (1991). Personality profile of nonscholarship college football players. *Perceptual and Motor Skills, 73*, 1083–1089.

Nicklin, G. (1996, March 30). Discussant on *Eddie Arcaro's "A View From the Top."* In T. Ferraro (Chair), America at Play: An Interdisciplinary Conference on Psychoanalysis and Culture—A Psychoanalytic Look at the Athlete, the Spectator and the Role of Sports in Cultural and Personal Change. Conference conducted at the Nassau County Medical Center, East Meadow, New York.

Nideffer, R.M. (1981). *The Ethics and practice of applied sport psychology.* Ithaca, NY: Mouvement.

Nideffer, R.M. (1992). *Psyched to win: How to master mental skills to improve your physical performance.* Champaign, IL: Human Kinetics.

Novaco, R.W. (1975) *Anger control: The development and evaluation of an experimental treatment.* Lexington, MA: Heath, Lexington Books.

Novaco, R.W. (1977). A stress inoculation approach to anger management in the training of law enforcement officers. *American Journal of Community Psychology, 5*(3), 327–346.

NOW official says Paterno should resign. (2006, January 9). WashingtonPost.com. Retrieved March 3, 2007, from www.washingtonpost.com/wp-dyn/content/article/2006/01/08/AR2006010800938.html

O'Connor, I. (2002, September 30). *One pitch alone didn't seal Moore's fate.* USAToday.com. Retrieved March 3, 2007, from www.usatoday.com/sports/columnist/oconnor/2002-09-30-oconnor_x.htm

O'Connor, I. (2005, January 9). *Pennington covers his teammate's debt.* USAToday.com. Retrieved March 3, 2007, from www.usatoday.com/sports/columnist/oconnor/2005-01-09-oconnor_x.htm

O'Connor, I. (2005, August 28). Accountability in college athletics a rare occurrence. *Journal News.*

O.J. Simpson murder case. (n.d.). CourtTV.com. Retrieved March 3, 2007, from www.courttv.com/casefiles/simpson/

Olrich, T.W., & Ewing, M.E. (1999). Life on steroids: Bodybuilders describe their perceptions of the anabolic-androgenic steroid use period. *Sport Psychologist, 13*(3), 299–312.

Ornduff, S.R., Kelsey, R.M., & O'Leary, K.D. (1995). What do we know about typologies of batterers? Comment on Gottman et al. (1995). *Journal of Family Psychology, 9*(3), 249–252.

Ostrow, A.C. (Ed.) (1996). *Directory of psychological tests in the sport and exercise sciences.* Morgantown, WV: Fitness Information Technology.

Otto, M.W., Church, T.S., Craft, L.L., Greer, T.L., Smits, J.A.S., & Trivedi, M.H. (2007). Exercise for mood and anxiety disorders. *Journal of Clinical Psychiatry, 68*(5), 669–676.

Owens apologizes to Eagles and fans. (2005, November 9). USAToday.com. Retrieved March 3, 2007, from www.usatoday.com/sports/football/nfl/eagles/2005-11-08-owens-apology_x.htm

Parcells, B., with Coplon, J. (1995). *Finding a way to win: The principles of leadership, teamwork, and motivation.* New York: Doubleday.

Parrot, A., & Bechhofer, L. (Eds.). (1991). *Acquaintance rape: The hidden crime.* John Wiley & Sons: New York.

Parrot, A. (1993). *Coping with date rape and acquaintance rape.* New York: Rosen.

Parrot, A., Cummings, N., & Marchell, T. (1994). *RAPE 101—sexual assault prevention for college athletes.* Holmes Beach, FL: Learning Publications.

Parrot, A., Cummings, N., Marchell, T., & Hofher, J. (1994). A rape awareness and prevention model for male athletes. *Journal of American College Health, 42*(4).

Pasquarelli, L. (2007, April 10). Goodell plays the role of new sheriff in town perfectly. ESPN.com. Retrieved April 15, 2007, from http://sports.espn.go.com/nfl/columns/story?columnist=pasquarelli_len&id=2832237

Penn football player commits suicide. (2005, October 12). USAToday.com. Retrieved March 3, 2007, from www.usatoday.com/sports/college/football/ivy/2005-10-12-penn-rb-suicide_x.htm

Pennington, B. (2005, June 28). As stakes rise, more parents are directing rage at coaches. *New York Times.*

Perez posts bond in rape case. (1995, September 26). *New York Times,* p. B11.

Pirates' Perez breaks toe kicking laundry cart. (2005, June 28). USAToday.com. Retrieved March 3, 2007, from www.usatoday.com/sports/baseball/nl/pirates/2005-06-28-perez-dl_x.htm

Pitcher breaks non-pitching hand in clubhouse. (2004, September 3). ESPN.com. Retrieved March 3, 2007, from http://sports.espn.go.com/mlb/recap?gameId=240903110

Play It Smart: A program of the National Football Foundation and the College Football Hall of Fame. Retrieved March 3, 2007, from http://playitsmart.footballfoundation.com/Play_about.php

Poovey, B. (2005, November 8). *Six Chattanooga football players charged after student reports gang rape.* YahooSports.com. Retrieved March 3, 2007, from http://sports.yahoo.com/ncaaf/news?slug=ap-chatanooga-rapecharge&prov=ap&type=lgns

Pope, H.G. Jr., & Katz, D.L. (1994). Psychiatric and medical effects of anabolic-androgenic steroid abuse. *Archives of General Psychiatry, 51,* 375–382.

Porter, K. (2003). *The mental athlete.* Champaign, IL: Human Kinetics.

Potrykus, J. (2006, May 28). *Stanley incarcerated again.* JSOnline.com. Retrieved March 3, 2007, from www.jsonline.com/story/index.aspx?id=428880

Potter-Efron, R., & Potter-Efron, P. (1991). *Anger, alcoholism and addiction: Treating individuals, couples, and families.* New York: Norton.

Potter-Efron, R., & Potter-Efron, P. (1995). *Letting go of anger.* Oakland, CA: New Harbinger.

Prisco, P. (2002, November 28). *Notebook: Sapp gets away with one.* CBSSportsline.com. Retrieved March 3, 2007, from http://cbs.sportsline.com/nfl/story/5947575

Quotes by and about Ty Cobb. (n.d.). The official website of Ty Cobb. Retrieved March 3, 2007, from www.cmgworldwide.com/baseball/cobb/quotes.html

Ravens' Lewis reaches settlement with victim's daughter. (2004, May 2). CBSSportsline. com. Retrieved March 3, 2007, from http://cbs.sportsline.com/nfl/story/7300688

Ray Lewis pleads guilty to misdemeanor; murder charges dropped. (2005, June 5). CNN.com. Retrieved March 3, 2007, from http://transcripts.cnn.com/TRANSCRIPTS/0006/05/bn.01.html

Reaves, J.A. (2003, November 21). *Authorities putting pieces together in Stenson death.* USAToday.com. Retrieved March 3, 2007, from www.usatoday.com/sports/baseball/nl/reds/2003-11-21-stenson-death-update_x.htm

Reber, A. (1985). *Dictionary of psychology.* New York: Penguin Books.

Recruiting athletes to Wall Street keys to a successful employee hire. (2006, September 11). Business Week online. http://feedroom.businessweek.com/ifr_main.jsp?nsid=a-7cff1bf3:1113d7b3143:2219&fr_story=8361b8c487bb28460858f8bd29a4233d41781 275&st=1173560623687&mp=WMP&cpf=true&fvn=8&fr=031007_040857_w7cff 1bf3x1113d7b3143x221a&rdm=567883.0063012115

Red, C. (2003, September 15). *College sports: Sinking to new lows?* Retrieved March 3, 2007, from www.recruitzone.com/news.asp?ArticleID=177

Rest, J., Turiel, E., & Kohlberg, L. (1994). Level of moral development as a determinant of preference and comprehension of moral judgments made by others. In B. Puka (Ed.), *Fundamental research in moral development.* New York: Garland.

Restoring faith in America's pastime: Evaluating Major League Baseball's efforts to eradicate steroid us: Hearing before the Committee on Government Reform, House of Representatives, 109th Cong., 1st Sess. 109-8 (March 17, 2005) (testimony of Kirk J. Brower, MD).

Rhea, D.J., & Lantz, C.D. (2004). Violent, delinquent, and aggressive behaviors of rural high school athletes and non-athletes. *Physical Educator, 61*(4), 170–176.

Robbins, P., Monahan, J., & Silver, E. (2003). Mental disorder and violence: The moderating role of gender. *Law and Human Behavior, 27,* 561–571.

Robinson, L. (1998). *Crossing the line: Violence and sexual assault in Canada's national sport.* Toronto, ON: McClelland & Stewart.

Rogers shoves cameramen, throws camera to ground in angry tirade. (2005, June 29). ESPN.com. Retrieved March 3, 2007, from http://sports.espn.go.com/espn/wire?section=mlb&id=2097575

Rogers to play while appealing 20-game suspension. (2005, July 1). USAToday.com. Retrieved March 3, 2007, from www.usatoday.com/sports/baseball/al/rangers/2005-07-01-rogers-suspension_x.htm

Romanowski admits he crossed a line. (2005, May 17). ESPN.com. Retrieved March 3, 2007, from http://sports.espn.go.com/espn/news/story?id=2062507

Romanowski, B., with Schefter, A., & Towle, P. (2005). *Romo: My life on the edge: Living dreams and slaying dragons.* New York: HarperCollins.

Rosenberg, J. (n.d.). *Munich massacre.* About.com. Retrieved March 3, 2007, from http://history1900s.about.com/od/famouscrimesscandals/p/munichmassacre.htm

Rotella, B., & Bunker, L.K. (1998). *Parenting your superstar: How to help your child balance achievement and happiness.* Chicago: Triumph Books.

Rotella, R.J. (1985). Strategies for controlling anxiety and arousal. In L. Bunker & R.J. Rotella (Eds.), *Sport psychology* (pp. 185–195). Ann Arbor, MI: McNaughton and Gunn.

Rowley, A.J., Landers, D.M., Kyllo, L.B., & Etnier, J.L. (1995). Does the iceberg profile discriminate between successful and less successful athletes? A meta-analysis. *Journal of Sport & Exercise Psychology, 17,* 185–199.

Rueda, J. (2005, February 19). *Police rescue Urbina's mom from mountain camp.* USA-Today.com. Retrieved March 3, 2007, from www.usatoday.com/sports/baseball/al/tigers/2005-02-18-urbina-mom-found_x.htm

Sachs, C.J., & Chu, L.D. (2000). The association between professional football games and domestic violence in Los Angeles County. *Journal of Interpersonal Violence, 15*(11), 1192–1201.

Sacks, D.N., Petcher, Y., Stanley, C.T., & Tenenbaum, G. (2003). Aggression and violence in sport: Moving beyond the debate. *International Journal of Sport and Exercise Psychology, 1*(2), 167–179.

Sadock, B.J., & Sadock, V.A. (2003). *Kaplan & Sadock's synopsis of psychiatry: Behavioral sciences/clinical psychiatry.* Philadelphia: Lippincott, Williams, & Wilkins.

Sandler, A. (Executive Producer), & Coraci, F. (Director). (1998). *The waterboy* [Motion picture].

Sandler, A. (Executive Producer), & Segal, P. (Director). *The longest yard* [Motion picture].

Saraceno, J. (2005, February 2). *A troubled life on the line.* USAToday.com. Retrieved on March 3, 2007, from www.usatoday.com/sports/football/nfl/2005-02-02-robbins-cover_x.htm

Saraceno, J. (2005, August 24). *Phillips, Osborne still don't get it.* USAToday.com. Retrieved March 3, 2007, from www.usatoday.com/sports/columnist/saraceno/2005-08-23-saraceno-phillips_x.htm

Saunders, P. (2003, March 10). Fearsome opponent: Athletes, who have spent years fine-tuning their bodies, find it difficult to accept mental illness and its stigma. *Denver Post.* Retrieved March 3, 2007, from www.psychologyofsports.com/guest/denverpost.htm

Schafer, W.E. (1969) Participation in interscholastic athletics and delinquency. *Social Problems, 17,* 40–47.

Schiraldi, G.R., & Kerr, M.H. (2002). *The anger management sourcebook.* New York: McGraw Hill.

Schultz, S.D. (1954). A differentiation of several forms of hostility by scales empirically constructed from significant items on the MMPI. *Dissertation Abstracts, 17,* 717–720.

Scranton, P.E. (2001). *Playing hurt: Treating and evaluating the warriors of the NFL.* Washington, DC: Brassey's.

Seahawks' Locklear jailed for investigation of domestic violence. (2006, January 17). ESPN.com. Retrieved March 3, 2007, from http://sports.espn.go.com/nfl/playoffs05/news/story?id=2294536

Seahawks' Locklear jailed after domestic violence complaint. (2006, January 16). CBSSportsline.com. Retrieved March 3, 2007, from http://cbs.sportsline.com/nfl/story/9169090

Seefeldt, V., & Ewing, M.E. (1997). *Youth sports in America: An overview.* Washington, DC: President's Council on Physical Fitness and Sports

Segrave, J.O., & Hastad, D.N. (1982). Delinquent behavior and interscholastic athletic participation. *Journal of Sport Behavior, 5*(2), 96–104.

Segrave, J., Moreau, C., & Hastad, D.N. (1985). An investigation into the relationship between ice hockey participation and delinquency. *Sociology of Sport Journal, 2,* 281–298.

Serok, S. (1975). *Difference in game preference between delinquent and nondelinquent children.* Unpublished doctoral dissertation, Case Western Reserve University, Cleveland, OH.

Shapiro, A. (Producer & Director). (1978). *Scared straight* [Motion picture].

Sharp, M., & Collins, D. (1998). Exploring the "inevitability" of the relationship between anabolic-androgenic steroid use and aggression in human males. *Journal of Sport & Exercise Psychology, 20*(4), 379–394.

Shaw, M. (2004, March 23). *Bryant lawyers continue risky strategy.* USAToday.com. Retrieved March 3, 2007, from www.usatoday.com/sports/basketball/nba/2004-03-23-shaw-analysis_x.htm

Sherrington, C.S. (1906). *Integrative action of the nervous system.* New Haven, CT: Yale University Press.

Shields, D.L.L., & Bredemeier, B.J.L. (1995). *Character development and physical activity.* Champaign, IL: Human Kinetics.

Shields, E.W. (1999). Intimidation and violence by males in high school athletics. *Adolescence, 45*(135).

Siegel, J.M. (1986). The Multidimensional Anger Inventory. *Journal of Personality and Social Psychology, 51*(1), 191–200.

Silver, M. (1998, October 26). Dirty dogs. The NFL's dirtiest players: Who they are, what they do. *Sports Illustrated*, 45–57.

Simonds, R. (Producer), & Dugan, D. (Director). (1996). *Happy Gilmore* [Motion picture].

Simpson, S., & Newby, R.W. (1994). Scores on Profile of Mood States of college football players from nonscholarship and scholarship programs. *Perceptual and Motor Skills, 78*, 635–640.

Simpson v. University of Colorado, 372 F. Supp. 2d 1229 (D. Colo. 2005).

Skeem, J., Monahan, J., & Mulvey. (2002). Psychopathy, treatment involvement, and subsequent violence among civil psychiatric patients. *Law and Human Behavior, 26*, 577–603.

Skeem, J.L., & Mulvey, E. (2001). Psychopathy and community violence among civil psychiatric patients: Results from the MacArthur Violence Risk Assessment Study. *Journal of Consulting & Clinical Psychology, 69*, 358–374.

Skeem, J.L., Mulvey, E.P., & Grisso, T. (2003). Applicability of traditional revised models of psychopathy to the Psychopathy Checklist: Screening Version. *Psychological Assessment, 15*, 41–55.

Smith, R.E., Smoll, F.L., & Smith, N.J. (1989). *Parents' complete guide to youth sports.* Costa Mesa, CA: HDL.

Smith Slep, A.M., Avery-Leaf, S., O'Leary, K.D., & Cascardi, M. (1996, November). *Attitudes accepting of dating aggression: A comparison of three measures.* Paper presented at the 30th Annual Meeting of the Association for the Advancement of Behavior Therapy, New York.

Snyder, E.E., & Spreitzer, E.A. (1989). *Social aspects of sport* (3rd ed.). Englewood Cliffs, NJ: Prentice Hall.

Solso, R.L. (1995). *Cognitive psychology* (4th ed.). Needham Heights, MA: Allyn & Bacon.

Sonstroem, R.J., & Bernardo, P. (1982). Intraindividual pregame state anxiety and basketball performance: A re-examination of the inverted-U curve. *Journal of Sport Psychology, 4*, 235–245.

Sperber, M. (2001). *Beer and circus: How big-time sports is crippling undergraduate education.* Henry Holt.

Spielberger, C.D. (1988). *State-Trait Anger Expression Inventory (STAXI): Professional manual.* FL: Psychological Assessment Resources.

Spielberger, C.D. (1999). *State-Trait Anger Expression Inventory-2 (STAXI-2): Professional manual*. FL: Psychological Assessment Resources.

Spielberger, C.D., Jacobs, G.A., Russell, S., & Crane, R.J. (1983). Assessment of anger: The state-trait anger scale. In J.N. Butcher & C.D. Spielberger (Eds.), *Advances in personality assessment* (Vol. 2, pp. 112–134). Hillsdale, NJ: Erlbaum.

Spielberger, C.D., Johnson, E.H., Russell, S.F., Crane, R.J., Jacobs, G.A., & Worden, T.J. (1985). The experience and expression of anger; Construction and validation of an anger expression scale. In M.A. Chesney & R.H. Rosenman (Eds.), *Anger and hostility in cardiovascular and behavioral disorders*, pp. 5–30. New York: Hemisphere.

Sport parent code of conduct (2000, September 23). Retrieved March 3, 2007, from www.nyssf.org/sportparentcodeofconduct.html

Star implies he won't stop at pretend moon. (2005, January 14). ESPN.com. Retrieved March 3, 2007, from http://sports.espn.go.com/nfl/playoffs04/news/story?id=1966180

Stasi, L. (1996, January 4). Athletes make good sport of assault. *New York Daily News*, p. 18.

Stevens, D., & Bredemeier, B.J.L. (1996). Moral atmosphere and judgments about aggression in girls' soccer: Relationships among moral and motivational variables. *Journal of Sport & Exercise Psychology, 18*(2), 158–173.

Storch, E.A., Werner, N.E., & Storch, J.B. (2003). Relational aggression and psychosocial adjustment in intercollegiate athletes. *Journal of Sport Behavior, 26*(2), 155–167.

Straus, M.A., & Gelles, R.J. (1990). *Physical violence in American families—risk factors and adaptations to violence in 8,145 families*. New Brunswick, NJ: Transaction.

Straus, M.A., Hamby, S.L., Boney-McCoy, S., & Sugarman, D.B. (1996). The Revised Conflict Tactics Scales (CTS2)—Development and preliminary psychometric data. *Journal of Family Issues, 17*(3), 283–316.

Straus, M.B. (1994). *Violence in the lives of adolescents*. New York: Norton.

Surgeon general's report on youth violence. www.surgeongeneral.gov/library/youthviolence/toc.html

Suspension amounts to minimum 17 games. (2004, March 12). ESPN.com. Retrieved March 3, 2007, from http://sports.espn.go.com/nhl/news/story?id=1756628

Swahn, M.H., & Donovan, J.E. (2005). Predictors of fighting attributed to alcohol use among adolescent drinkers. *Addictive Behaviors, 30*, 1317–1334.

Tafrate, R.C. (1995). Evaluation of treatment strategies for adult anger disorders. In H. Kassinove (Ed.), *Anger disorders: definition, diagnosis and treatment*. Washington, DC: Taylor & Francis.

Tarkan, L. (2000, September 26). *Athletes' injuries go beyond the physical*. NYTimes.com. Retrieved March 3, 2007, from http://query.nytimes.com/gst/fullpage.html?sec=health&res=950DE7DD153AF935A1575AC0A9669C8B63

Tatum, J., & Kushner, B. (1979). *They call me Assassin*. New York: Everest House.

Tavris, C. (1982). *Anger: The misunderstood emotion*. New York: Simon & Schuster.

Taylor, J. (1996). Intensity regulation and athletic performance. In J.L. Van Raalte & B.W. Brewer (Eds.), *Exploring sport and exercise psychology*. Washington, DC: American Psychological Association.

Taylor, S.P., & Gammon, C.B. (1975). Effects of type and dose of alcohol on human physical aggression. *Journal of Personality and Social Psychology, 32*, 169–175.

Tedeschi, J.T., & Felson, R.B. (1994). *Violence, aggression, & coercive actions*. Washington, DC, American Psychological Association.

10 hockey violence lowlights: Hunter ends Turgeon's playoff run. Retrieved March 3, 2007, from http://www.cbc.ca/sports/columns/top10/hockey_lowlights.html

Tenenbaum, G., Stewart, E., Singer, R.N., & Duda, J. (1997). Aggression and violence in sport: An ISSP position stand. *Sport Psychologist, 11*, 1–7.

Terry, P.C., & Jackson, J.J. (1985). The determinants and control of violence in sport. *Quest, 37*, 27–37.

The scorpion and the frog. Wikipedia. Retrieved March 3, 2007, from http://en.wikipedia.org/wiki/The_Scorpion_and_the_Frog

Those charged with hazing include one coach's son. (2005, March 23). Retrieved March 3, 2007, from www.ketv.com/news/4313234/detail.html

The technology of prevention. (1986). Tucson, AZ: Associates for Youth Development.

The use of anabolic-androgenic steroids in sports. (1987). *Medicine and Science in Sports and Exercise, 19*, 102.

Title IX, Education Amendments of 1972, Title 20 U.S.C. Sections 1681–1688.

Todd, T. (1987). Anabolic steroids: The gremlins of sport. *Journal of Sport History, 14*(1), 87–101.

Tracey, J. (2003). The emotional response to the injury and rehabilitation process. *Journal of Applied Sport Psychology, 15*(4), 279–293.

Traina, J. (2005, October 20). *Compared to other jerks, Romanowski gets free pass.* SI.com. Retrieved March 3, 2007, from http://sportsillustrated.cnn.com/2005/writers/jimmy_traina/10/20/the.rant/index.html

Troutwine athletic profile. Retrieved March 3, 2007, from http://tapsport.com/

Ulrich, R.E. (1966). Pain as a cause of aggression. *American Zoologist, 6*, 643–662.

U.S. v. Morrison, 529 U.S. 598 (2000).

United States v. Morrison, 2000 U.S. Lexis 3422.

Valade, J. (2006, September 28). *Athletes apprehensive to admit mental illness.* Retrieved March 3, 2007, from www.cleveland.com/sports/plaindealer/index.ssf?/base/sports/1159432247254700.xml&coll=2

Valzelli, L. (1981). *Psychobiology of aggression and violence.* New York: Raven Press.

Van Goozen, S., Frijda, N., & Van de Poll, N. (1994). Anger and aggression in women: Influence of sports choice and testosterone administration. *Aggressive Behavior, 20*(3), 213–222.

Van Raalte, J.L. & Brewer, B.W. (Eds.) (1996). *Exploring sport and exercise psychology.* Washington, DC: American Psychological Association.

Vols receiver off the team. (1995, September 20). *New York Times*, p. B15.

Verducci, T. (2005, January 18). *Speed game: Amphetamines should have been part of new plan.* SI.com. Retrieved March 3, 2007, from http://sportsillustrated.cnn.com/2005/writers/tom_verducci/01/18/steroids.amphetamines/index.html

Very major penalty: McSorley found guilty of assault, avoids jail time. (2000, October 7). SI.com. Retrieved March 3, 2007, from http://sportsillustrated.cnn.com/hockey/nhl/news/2000/10/06/mcsorley_assault_ap/

Vick, dismissed by Hokies, says he will turn pro. (2006, January 7). ESPN.com. Retrieved March 3, 2007, from http://sports.espn.go.com/ncf/bowls05/news/story?id=2282642

Vick reportedly wanted to scare teens after taunts. (20056, January 6). ESPN.com. Retrieved March 3, 2007, from http://sports.espn.go.com/ncf/news/story?id=2285819

Visek, A., & Watson, J. (2005). Ice hockey players' legitimacy of aggression and professionalization of attitudes. *Sport Psychologist, 19*(2), 178–192.

Wadler, G., & Hainline, B. (1989). *Drugs and the athlete.* Davis.

Wald, J. (2003, November 6). *Football coaches fired in alleged hazing aftermath.* Retrieved March 3, 2007, from www.cnn.com/2003/US/Northeast/11/06/coaches.hazing/

Walker, L.E.A. (1995). Current perspectives on men who batter women—implications for intervention and treatment to stop violence against women—comment on Gottman et al. (1995). *Journal of Family Psychology, 9*(3), 264–271.

Walker, T.M. (2005, July 13). *Titans' top draft pick arrested on charges of assault, vandalism.* ESPN.com. Retrieved March 3, 2007, from http://sports.espn.go.com/nfl/news/story?id=2106859

Walton, T. (2001). The Sprewell/Carlesimo episode: Unacceptable violence or unacceptable victim? *Sociology of Sport Journal, 18*(3), 345–357.

Wann, D.L., Culver, Z., Akanda, R., Daglar, M., De Divitiis, & C., Smith, A. (2005). The effects of team identification and game outcome on willingness to consider anonymous acts of hostile aggression. *Journal of Sport Behavior, 28*(3), 282–294.

Wann, D.L. Haynes, G., McLean, B., & Pullen, P. Sport team identification and willingness to consider anonymous acts of hostile aggression. *Aggressive Behavior, 29*(5) 2003, 406–413.

Wann, D.L., Shelton, S., Smith, T., & Walker, R. (2002). Relationship between team identification and trait aggression: A replication. *Perceptual and Motor Skills, 94*(2), 595–598.

Wann, D.L., Hunter, J.L., Ryan, J.A., & Wright, L.A. (2001). The relationship between team identification and willingness of sport fans to consider illegally assisting their team. *Social Behavior and Personality, 29*(6), 531–536.

Wann, D.L., & Wilson, A.M. (1999). Relationship between aesthetic motivation and preferences for aggressive and nonaggressive sports. *Perceptual and Motor Skills, 89*(3, Pt 1), 931–934.

Wann, D.L., Peterson, R.R., Cothran, C., & Dykes, M. (1999). Sport fan aggression and anonymity: The importance of team identification. *Social Behavior and Personality, 27*(6), 597–602.

Wann, D.L., Carlson, J.D., Holland, L.C., Jacob, B.E., Owens, D.A., & Wells, D.D. (1999). Beliefs in symbolic catharsis: The importance of involvement with aggressive sports. *Social Behavior and Personality, 27*(2), 155–164.

Warshaw, R. (1988). *I never called it rape.* New York: Harper & Row.

Webster, C.D., & Jackson, M.A. (Eds.) (1997). *Impulsivity: Theory assessment and treatment.* New York: Guilford.

Weiberg, S. (1991, February 21). Campus crime study not kind to athletes. *USA Today,* p. 2c.

Weinberg, R.S., & Gould, D. (2003). *Foundations of sport & exercise psychology* (3rd ed.). Champaign, IL: Human Kinetics.

Weir, T., & Brady, E. (2003, December 22). *In sexual assault cases, athletes usually walk.* USAToday.com. Retrieved March 3, 2007, from www.usatoday.com/sports/2003-12-21-athletes-sexual-assault_x.htm

Weiss, M.R. (1987). Teaching sportsmanship and values. In V. Seefeldt (Ed.), *Handbook for youth sports coaches.* Reston, VA: AAHPERD.

Weiss, M.R., & Bredemeier, B.J. (1991). Moral development in sport. *Exercise and Sport Sciences Reviews, 18,* 331–378.

Wertheim, L.J. (2003, September 8). Prisoners of depression. *Sports Illustrated Magazine.* Retrieved March 3, 2007, from http://www.smartproinsight.com/SportsIllustrated090803.htm

Widmeyer, W.N., & Birch, J.S. (1979). The relationship between aggression and performance outcome in ice hockey. *Canadian Journal of Applied Sports Sciences, 4*(1), 91–94.

Wilson, A.E., Calhoun, K.S., & Bernat, J. (1999). Recognition of risk in revictimized women: The influence of prior victimization on judgments of sexual aggression in an experimental date rape analogue. *Journal of Consulting and Clinical Psychology, 67,* 705–710.

Wolpe, J. (1954). Reciprocal inhibition as the main basis of psychotherapeutic effects. *AMA Archives of Neurology and Psychiatry, 72,* 205–226.

Wolpe, J. (1958). *Psychotherapy by reciprocal inhibition.* Stanford, CA: Stanford University Press.

Wolpe, J. (1961). The systematic desensitization treatment of neuroses. *Journal of Nervous and Mental Disease, 132,* 189–203.

Wolpe, J. (1981). Reciprocal inhibition and therapeutic change. *Journal of Behavior Therapy and Experimental Psychiatry, 12,* 185–188.

Wolpe, J. (1982). *The practice of behavior therapy* (3rd ed.). Oxford: Pergamon.

Wonderlic. Retrieved March 3, 2007, from www.wonderlic.com

Wooden, J., & Carty, J. (2005). *Coach Wooden's pyramid of success: Building blocks for a better life.* Ventura, CA: Regal Books.

Wooden, J., & Jamison, S. (2005). *Wooden on leadership.* New York: McGraw Hill.

World Anti-Doping Agency. (2006). *The world anti-doping code: The 2006 prohibited list—international standard.* Retrieved March 3, 2007, from www.wada-ama.org

Wulf, S. (2001, June 24). *The spit hits the fan.* Time.com. Retrieved March 3, 2007, from www.time.com/time/magazine/article/0,9171,134797,00.html

Yerkes, R.M., & Dodson, J.D. (1908). The relation of strength of stimulus to rapidity of habit formation. *Journal of Comparative Neurology of Psychology, 18,* 459–482.

Yesalis, C.E. (1990). Winning and performance-enhancing drugs—our dual addiction. *Physician and Sportsmedicine, 18,* 161–163.

Yesalis, C.E., & Cowart, V.S. (1998). *The steroids game: An expert's inside look at anabolic steroid use in sports.* Champaign, IL: Human Kinetics.

Yiannakis, A.(1976). Delinquent tendencies and participation in an organized sports program. *Research Quarterly, 47*(4), 845–849.

Young, K. (1993). Violence, risk, and liability in male sports culture. *Sociology of Sport Journal, 10,* 373–396.

Zaichkowsky, L., & Takenaka, K. (1993). Optimizing arousal level. In R.N. Singer, M. Murphey, & L.K. Tennant (Eds.), *Handbook of research on sport psychology* (pp. 511–527). New York: MacMillan.

Zelin, M.L., Adler, G., & Myerson, P. (1972). The anger self-report: An objective questionnaire for the measurement of expression. *Journal of Consulting Psychology, 39,* 340–352.

Zimmerman, P. (1989, January 30). *Super Bowl XXIII: 49ers-Bengals—Joe Cool—The 49ers' Joe Montana knocked the Bengals cold with a spectacular late rally in the Super Bowl.* SI.com. Retrieved March 3, 2007, from http://sportsillustrated.cnn.com/football/features/superbowl/archives/23/

Zullo, A. (2005). *Wise guys: Brilliant thoughts and big talk from real men.* Naperville, IL: Sourcebooks.

Index

About the Author

Photo courtesy of Emiliano Brooks Photography

Mitch Abrams, PsyD, is a clinician administrator for University Correctional HealthCare/UMDNJ, where he is responsible for the delivery of mental health services for 6 of the state's 13 state prisons. Dr. Abrams co-coordinates the forensic track of UMDNJ's predoctoral psychology internship and has been involved with several aspects of advancing the quality of mental health services in prison systems. He is a clinical assistant professor in the department of psychiatry at UMDNJ/Robert Wood Johnson Medical School and has held adjunct faculty positions at Brooklyn College, C.W. Post, and Fairleigh Dickinson University. Since 2000, he has been in private practice providing sport, clinical, and forensic psychology services.

Dr. Abrams began consulting with athletes in 1997 while developing the only comprehensive anger management program for athletes. He has created a niche in using anger management training to assist athletes in reaching peak performance on the field and in life. He has consulted with thousands of athletes and has developed programs for athletic organizations at the youth sport, high school, and college levels. He is the founder and president of Learned Excellence for Athletes, a sport psychology consulting company located in Fords, New Jersey.

Raised in Brooklyn, New York, Dr. Abrams received a bachelor of science degree from Brooklyn College and earned a master of science degree in applied psychology and a doctorate of psychology (PsyD) in clinical psychology from C.W. Post/Long Island University. He also received specialized training in family violence and anger management. He is a full member of the American Psychological Association as well as its Division 47 (Exercise and Sport Psychology) and Division 41 (American Psychology-Law Society). Further, he holds membership in the Association for Applied Sport Psychology (AASP), where he is also the chair of the Anger and Violence in Sport Special Interest Group (SIG), and the Association for Behavioral and Cognitive Therapies (ABCT).